Britain Votes 2017

Edited by Jonathan Tonge, Cristina Leston-Bandeira and Stuart Wilks-Heeg

University of Liverpool

Withdrawn from stock

OXFORD

UNIVERSITY PRESS

in association with

HANSARD SOCIETY SERIES IN POLITICS
AND GOVERNMENT

OXFORD
UNIVERSITY PRESS

Great Clarendon Street, Oxford OX2 6DP, UK

Oxford University Press is a department of the University of Oxford.
It furthers the University's objective of excellence in research, scholarship,
and education by publishing worldwide in

Oxford New York

Athens Auckland Bangkok Bagotá Buenos Aires
Cape Town Chennai Dar es Salaam Delhi Florence Hong Kong Istanbul
Karachi Kuala Lumpur Madrid Melbourne Mexico City Mumbai
Nairobi Paris São Paulo Shanghai Singapore Taipei Tokyo Toronto Warsaw

and associated companies in
Berlin Ibadan

Oxford is a registered trade mark of Oxford University Press
in the UK and in certain other countries

Published in the United States
by Oxford University Press Inc., New York

A catalogue for this book is available from the British Library

Library of Congress Cataloging in Publication Data

ISBN 978-0-19-882030-7

Typeset by Cenveo publisher services, Bangalore, India
Printed in Great Britain by Bell & Bain Ltd, Glasgow, UK

Acknowledgements

We wish to thank a number of people for their help in assembling this election volume. We are extremely grateful to all contributors for not only producing their work but even adhering to their deadlines. Regardless of their political views, most UK political scientists working on elections were horrified by the calling of the snap election given the addition to our workloads. That everyone recovered from the shock and managed to produce election analyses at short notice was particularly commendable.

In addition to the contributors, we wish to thank Dr Ruth Fox, Director and Head of Research at the Hansard Society, and Vanessa Lacey, Senior Publisher at Oxford University Press. Both have been unstinting in their support and encouragement for the volume and we are very grateful for their assistance. We are also indebted to Katie Kent, Senior Production Editor at Oxford University Press journals, for all her help in steering this volume through the production process with speed and care. Thanks also to Deepu H.R. in the Production team and to Joel Blackwell, Brigid Fowler and Luke Boga Mitchell at the Hansard Society for their assistance. We are also very grateful to Kelly Henwood in Marketing at Oxford University Press for her support.

Finally we wish to thank especially our families for their forbearance as yet more quality time was sacrificed in producing this volume.

Jonathan Tonge, Cristina Leston-Bandeira and Stuart Wilks-Heeg

Contributors and Editors

Tim Bale teaches politics at Queen Mary University of London, where he specializes in party politics and in particular party membership. He is the author of two books on the Tories - *The Conservatives since 1945* and *The Conservatives from Thatcher to Cameron*.

Jonathan Bradbury is Professor of Politics and Director of Research for the College of Arts and Humanities, Swansea University. He researches on territorial politics and constitutional development, party strategies and public policy. He is the Convenor of the PSA Specialist Group on Territorial Politics and his most recent articles have been published in *Regional and Federal Studies* and *Parliamentary Affairs*.

Sir John Curtice is Professor of Politics at the University of Strathclyde and leads the team which analyses the exit poll at UK General Elections. He is also President of the British Polling Council, Senior Research Fellow at NatCen Social Research, and Chief Commentator on the What UK Thinks: EU and What Scotland Thinks websites. His numerous publications include co-editorship of the annual British Social Attitudes report series since 1994 as well as recent journal articles on the Alternative Vote, Scottish independence, and EU membership referendums. Sir John is a regular media commentator on both British and Scottish politics.

David Cutts is Professor in Political Science at the University of Birmingham. His specific areas of interest include political and civic engagement, party and political campaigning, electoral behaviour and party politics, party competition and methods for modelling political behaviour. Professor Cutts has published numerous articles in leading journals including the *American Journal of Political Science, Journal of Politics, European Journal of Political Research* and the *British Journal of Political Science*.

James Dennison is a Research Fellow at the Robert Schuman Centre for Advanced Studies at the European University Institute, where he was awarded a PhD in July 2017. He has published on British, Italian and European politics, as well as writing *The Greens in British Politics: Protest, Anti-Austerity and the Divided Left* (Palgrave, 2016). He was previously a Visiting Fellow at Nuffield College, Oxford and taught quantitative methods at the University of Sheffield. He tweets @JamesRDennison

David Denver is Emeritus Professor of Politics at Lancaster University and the author of numerous publications on British elections and voting behaviour.

Katharine Dommett is Lecturer in the Public Understanding of Politics at the Department for Politics, University of Sheffield. Her research focuses on political parties, political engagement and democratic politics and she has specific expertise on British political parties and governance. Katharine is currently the holder of an ESRC Future Leaders award for a project entitled 'Renewing Party Politics? which is generating new data on public attitudes towards political parties. She has published extensively in leading journals including *Governance, Public Administration, Political Studies* and the *International Public Management Journal.*

Jocelyn Evans is Professor of Politics at the University of Leeds. He has written widely on aspects of voting behaviour and political parties in France, the UK and comparatively. He served as editor of *Parliamentary Affairs* between 2005 and 2011. He is editor, with Kai Arzheimer and Michael Lewis-Beck, of the *Handbook of Electoral Behaviour* (2 vols), Sage, 2017, and the author, with Gilles Ivaldi, of *The 2012 French Presidential Elections: The Inevitable Alternation* and *The 2017 French Presidential Elections: A Political Reformation?* Palgrave, 2018.

Justin Fisher is Professor of Political Science and Head of the Department of Social & Political Sciences at Brunel University London. He has published extensively on party finance and has directed the studies of constituency campaigning at each general election since 2005.

Matthew Flinders is Professor of Politics and Founding Director of the Sir Bernard Crick Centre for the Public Understanding of Politics at the University of Sheffield. He is also President of the Political Studies Association of the UK and served as the Specialist Adviser to the House of Lords Select Committee on Citizenship and Civic Participation (2017-2018). His recent publications include *What Kind of Democracy is This?* Policy Press, 2017 and *Anti-Politics, Depoliticization and* Governance, Oxford University Press, 2017.

Eunice Goes is Professor of Politics at Richmond University. She researches and publishes on political parties, party approaches to the European Union and the role of ideas in politics. Her latest book is *The Labour Party Under Ed Miliband: Trying But Failing To Renew Social Democracy* (Manchester: Manchester University Press, 2016).

Sara Hagemann is Associate Professor in European Politics at London School of Economics and Political Science. In her work, Sara draws on a mix of academic and policy experience as she has held research and policy positions in Brussels, Copenhagen and London. Sara has published extensively on European affairs, in particular on EU government negotiations, transparency and accountability in political systems, EU policy-making processes, the role of national parliaments and the consequences of EU enlargements.

Emily Harmer is Lecturer in Media at the University of Liverpool. Her research analyses the relationship between media and politics, with a specific interest in gendered political communication. Emily is co-convener of the UK Political Studies Association's Media and Politics Specialist Group and Assistant Editor for the *European Journal of Communication.*

Sarah Harrison is an Assistant Professorial Research Fellow in the Department of Government at the London School of Economics and Political Science. Her current research focuses on electoral psychology, elections and youth political behaviour. Recent publications include *Youth Participation in Democratic Life*, 2016, with Cammaerts, Banaji, et al. and co-authored articles in *Nature Human Behaviour* and *Comparative Political Studies.* Her research has been recognised by awards from the ESRC, the political psychology section of APSA and her collaborative projects have been merited by the ERC and the Market Research Society.

Ailsa Henderson is Professor of Political Science at the University of Edinburgh. She was Principal Investigator for the Economic and Social Research Council's 2014 Scottish Referendum Study and 2016 Scottish Parliament Election Study.

Cristina Leston-Bandeira is Professor of Politics at the University of Leeds, where she also co-leads the Centre for Democratic Engagement. She is co-editor of *Parliamentary Affairs* and has published widely on parliament and public engagement. Her publications include *Parliaments and Citizens*, Routledge, 2015, and 'The Institutional Representation of Parliament', *Political Studies*, 2017.

James Mitchell holds a Chair in Public Policy and is Director of the Academy of Government at the University of Edinburgh. His recent works include *The Scottish Question*, Oxford, Oxford University Press, 2014. *Takeover: explaining the extraordinary rise of the SNP*, Biteback, 2016, co-authored with Rob Johns and *Hamilton 1967* (a study of the SNP's breakthrough in the 1960s) Luath, 2017.

Andrew Russell is Professor of Politics and Head of Department at the University of Liverpool. He is best known from writing about political parties, marginalized communities and hard to reach groups. He continues to combine these interests by writing about the British Liberal Democrats! He has a significant media profile including the monthly *Political Ideas Phone-in* on BBC 5Live's *Up All Night* which airs at 2am on a Monday morning.

Rosalynd Southern is a Lecturer in Political Communication at the University of Liverpool. Her research focuses on political communication during election campaigns, particularly online. She has analysed online campaigning by UK parties at the last three UK general elections and during the EU referendum. More recently she has studied how voters use social media to communicate politically via her work on the iBES module of the British Election Study. In addition to this, she has conducted work on female politicians and their use of, and treatment via, various media.

Luke Temple is a Research Assistant in the Department of Politics, University of Sheffield. His research interests focus on citizen conceptualisations of democracy and how they relate to political participation. He has published in journals including *Politics and Policy* and the *Journal of International and Comparative Social Policy*. He also currently teaches Political Geography in the Department of Geography, University of Sheffield, and previously co-edited the *LSE British Politics and Policy blog*.

Jonathan Tonge is Professor of Politics at the University of Liverpool and Principal Investigator of the 2010, 2015 and 2017 Economic and Social Research Council Northern Ireland General Election studies. He has edited studies of the last five general elections in the *Britain Votes* series. Co-authored books include *The Democratic Unionist Party: From Protest to Power*, Oxford University Press, based on a Leverhulme Trust-funded survey of DUP members; *Sinn Fein and the SDLP: From Alienation to Participation* and *Loyal to the Core: Orangeism and Britishness in Northern Ireland*. He co-edits the journal *Parliamentary Affairs*.

Stephen Ward is Reader in Politics, at the Centre for Culture, Communication and Media, School of Arts and Media, University of Salford. He has published widely on Internet politics and, in particular, digital election campaigning and online participation in the UK, Europe and Australia.

Paul Webb is Professor of Politics at the University of Sussex and Editor of the journal *Party Politics*. He is widely published on issues of British and comparative party and electoral politics.

Stuart Wilks-Heeg is Reader in Politics at the University of Liverpool, where he was also Head of Politics from 2014-17. Previously Executive Director of the

Democratic Audit of the UK from 2009-12, he is particularly known for his work on electoral administration and electoral integrity.

Dominic Wring is Professor of Political Communication and a member of the Centre for Communication and Culture at Loughborough University (http://www.lboro.ac.uk/research/crcc/) which has conducted media analyses of every General Election since 1992. He is co-editor (with Roger Mortimore and Simon Atkinson) of a long-running book series the latest of which is *Political Communication in Britain: Polling, Campaigning and Media in the 2015 General Election*, London: Palgrave Macmillan.

CONTENTS

List of tables and figures

Figures

Tables

Britain Votes (2017) 1–7

JONATHAN TONGE, CRISTINA LESTON-BANDEIRA AND STUART WILKS-HEEG*

Introduction: The Mislaying of a Majority

The 2017 General Election added considerably to the rich political drama evident in the UK in recent years. A contest supposed to be one of the most one-sided of all time confounded most predictions in yielding only the third hung parliament of the 20 post-war general elections in the UK. 'May heads for election landslide' trumpeted *The Times* on 19 April, the day after the election was called—and few demurred. Theresa May began her campaign in Bolton North East, where Labour had been in charge since 1997 and enjoyed an 8.4% lead over the Conservatives in 2015. The message from the Prime Minister was clear: this would be a rout in which the governing party would extend its majority and crush a left-wing Labour Party. The Conservatives assumed that many Labour voters would defect and that most of UKIP's vote—which had fallen by 20% in the previous month's council elections—would head their way.

This volume analyses an extraordinary election, one which defied at least four orthodoxies which have conditioned interpretations of outcomes: first, that a campaign does not really matter; second, that the Conservatives are adept at running such campaigns; third, that a left-wing manifesto is inevitably a 'suicide note'; and fourth, that the combined Conservative and Labour share of the vote is in inevitable, long-term decline. Given these apparent truths, and the huge advantage Theresa May was recording in her personal ratings relative to Labour's Jeremy Corbyn, most commentators abandoned any previous caution in their interpretation of opinion polls. Yes, the polls had been wrong in 2015, but that was in the context of a tight race. The margins in 2017 were so wide, anything other than a Conservative majority was unimaginable. Yet, opinion pollsters were

*Jonathan Tonge, Department of Politics, University of Liverpool, j.tonge@liverpool.ac.uk; Cristina Leston-Bandeira, School of Politics and International Studies, University of Leeds, c.leston-bandeira@leeds.ac.uk; Stuart Wilks-Heeg, Department of Politics, University of Liverpool, swilks@liverpool.ac.uk

doi:10.1093/pa/gsx071

keen to learn from the debacle of 2015, and were quietly experimenting with new methods and approaches. The tendency for 'crowding' among polling agencies was less evident in 2017. Accompanied by much derision, Survation polls predicting a hung parliament were dismissed as outliers. A YouGov model using multilevel regression with post-stratification was also widely dismissed for suggesting that the prospect of a hung parliament was more likely than outlandish. In the final event, the YouGov model correctly predicted the outcome in 93% of the 632 constituencies in Great Britain.

Arguably, the certainty of a clear Conservative victory should have been more rigorously challenged at the outset. As John Curtice articulated on BBC News Channel within an hour of the election being announced on 19 April, Theresa May's snap decision was 'not a risk-free enterprise'. With the Conservatives having required a 6.5% lead over Labour merely to obtain their 12-seat majority in 2015, Theresa May's party would need a huge poll lead to be truly confident of annihilating their opponents. Whilst the polls offered encouragement in terms of the raw lead, it was unclear exactly where seat gains were likely for the Conservatives.

As events transpired, many of those gains were made where the Prime Minister was least involved, in Scotland, where Ruth Davidson led the Conservative campaign. Had May been patient, she might have fought the next election on more favourable constituency boundaries. Notwithstanding the considerable flaws in the idea of reducing the number of Commons seats to 600 (an idea best dropped) and thus increasing the workload of already-busy remaining MPs, the principle of equal-sized constituencies was logical and may have assisted her party.

Davidson's verve and enthusiasm served merely to highlight the incompetence of the broader Conservative campaign. May's robotic approach, unconvincing style and unexciting policies ensured that the Conservatives failed to generate enthusiasm, or even to reassure. Saddled with articulating a Brexit policy she had opposed only a year earlier, the Prime Minister's 'strategy' appeared to rely upon her successfully delivering an EU withdrawal she had thought wrong. Beyond that, the belief that Jeremy Corbyn was hopeless and therefore the Conservatives would win big anyway acted as a substitute for ideas or coherence. The assumption that May would always outperform Corbyn in voters' assessments of competency ensured that the Conservative campaign was built around its leader to a remarkable degree. It seemed like the safest of bets. But it turned out to be a mistake.

There was neither a convincing justification for the election offered by the Conservative leader, nor a clear articulation of why voting Conservative was essential. The calling of the contest followed months of denials that it would take place. Voters had been informed regularly that the Prime Minister was 'getting on with the job', a reasonable contention given that it was indisputable that she had the most difficult in-tray of any recent Prime Minister. May's U-turn in opting to trigger an election immediately created a question of trust (as did her subsequent U-turn on a manifesto commitment during the campaign, a scenario without precedent in UK elections). Unlike the electoral logic, the political logic offered for an election appeared spurious. It consisted of the remarkable objection that the opposition were opposing the Conservatives, as if Labour's real role was to operate as an annex of the government. Invited to offer even a modicum of rationale, May's assertion that Labour was attempting to thwart Brexit was extraordinary. In February 2017, only 52 of Labour's 231 MPs voted against the Third Reading of the Bill triggering Article 50 to begin the Brexit process. Most Labour MPs accepted, however reluctantly, that the referendum result had to be respected. For ardent supporters of an EU Remain position, the *lack* of Labour opposition to Brexit was the problem. In offering a risible, implausible basis for the country going to the polls, the Prime Minister neutered her potential assets of reliability and trustworthiness from the outset. Most observers were fully cognisant of the real rationale underpinning the election: Labour's very poor county council results only a few weeks earlier. This appeared the sole motivation.

The UK entered an election that few voters were demanding, aware that no outcome would alter the pre-eminence of Brexit as the dominant item on the agenda. What followed was a campaign punctuated by two terrorist atrocities and otherwise marked by growing Labour momentum and consistent Conservative haplessness. The slide of the Scottish National Party, the failure of Liberal Democrat Europhilia to gain traction and the demise of UKIP, now surplus to requirements, were three other major developments. Despite the ineptitude of the Conservative campaign and growing confidence of Corbyn's Labour, the exit poll on election night still shocked many. This volume analyses how and why parliament was hung.

The plan of the volume

Britain Votes 2017 covers the election results, analyses the campaign that helped bring them about, assesses why each party performed as it did, explores the roles of party finance and new and traditional media, before perusing the implications for the future. It begins with David Denver's outline of the results and the polls from which erroneous predictions of the outcome were frequently made. As his analysis shows, most opinion polls broadly called the Conservative percentage share correctly; by contrast, what was seriously underestimated was Labour's projected share.

John Curtice examines the operation of the electoral system in 2017 and concludes that, as with other recent elections, it is failing to deliver when measured against its own supposed merits. The classic defence of the single member plurality (SMP) system of elections is that it ensures that the largest party secures a healthy working majority and facilitates the easy replacement of one single-party government with another. Yet Theresa May sacrificed her party's slender majority, necessitating a post-election deal with the Democratic Unionist Party (DUP) to remain in power. As Curtice notes, this is the third election in succession that the electoral system has failed to deliver a safe majority for the largest party, a stark contrast to how SMP operated for most of the period from 1945-2005.

The volume then moves to a detailed exploration of the campaigns of each party. Tim Bale and Paul Webb use data from the Economic and Social Research Council party members project to demonstrate that Conservative activism dropped on virtually every indicator in the 2017 campaign compared to 2015. They also indicate how the ancient adage of success having many midwives and failure being orphaned was applicable to the calling of the election. Admissions of responsibility were as frequent as summer snow.

In contrast to the diminished level of Conservative activism outlined by Bale and Webb, Eunice Goes' assessment of Labour's campaign charts the online activism of an army of eager party members. Their enthusiastic backing of Corbyn contrasted with the 'guerilla war', as she describes it, between the parliamentary Labour Party and the Corbyn leadership which preceded the election. With Labour articulating policies designed to interest previous non-voters and new voters, and Corbyn dealing well with the tough questioning about his past (which came at the expense of fuller scrutiny of Labour's economic policies), the party's campaign was a case of Momentum gathering momentum.

In contrast, the Liberal Democrats' campaign failed to develop, despite the election offering seemingly highly propitious circumstances. David Cutts and Andrew Russell show why the party failed to harness more than a fraction of the 48% pro-EU vote on offer from a year earlier, highlighting the lack of positive reasons to endorse the Liberal Democrats. Issues of a lack of identity and absence of clear leadership ensured that only a modicum of the damage wreaked in 2015 was repaired. The party struggled to retain its 2015 vote even among EU 'Remainers'.

James Dennison examines the fate of UKIP and the Greens, the two parties which lost most votes in 2017. Both parties had increased their vote share in 2015, UKIP dramatically so, and had returned one MP each. However, the UKIP vote share plummeted from 12.6% in 2015 to just 1.8% in 2017. Not only did UKIP fail to return a single candidate to the Commons, it also forfeited all 120 of the second places it claimed in 2015. By comparison, the collapse of the Greens was less dramatic. The Greens saw their vote share fall to 1.6%, compared to 3.8% in 2015. The party comfortably retained Caroline Lucas's Brighton Pavilion seat but performed disappointingly everywhere else, claiming only one second place—in the Speaker's seat of Buckingham which, by convention, is not contested by the principal rival parties.

Following the examination of the campaign and performances of the UK-wide parties, *Britain Votes 2017* assesses the distinctive elections in Scotland, Wales and Northern Ireland. Ailsa Henderson and James Mitchell demonstrate how a revived Scottish Conservative Party under Ruth Davidson fused Scottish distinctiveness with uncompromising unionism, on the back of the nationalists' 2014 referendum defeat, to take the Conservatives to their highest Scottish vote share since the advent of Thatcherism in 1979. Nonetheless, their contribution also indicates how Labour, who also benefited from the downward trend of SNP support, might be better positioned to prosper from such a trend. Jonathan Bradbury shows how Wales remained solidly Labour. Despite early polls suggesting as many as ten Conservative gains, May's election, apparently a plan hatched on a North Wales walking break, turned sour as the Conservatives lost three Welsh seats. The significance of Northern Ireland was obvious in the immediate aftermath, the DUP's ten MPs assuming an importance few might have imagined—although the DUP, having unnecessarily prepared for a Conservative minority government in 2015, had a shopping list ready. Nationalist representation disappeared from Westminster for the first time as the SDLP lost its remaining three seats, one to the DUP and the other two to abstentionist Sinn Féin. The DUP's success and the bargain struck by the party are both examined.

In addition to exploring the election context across the constituent parts of the UK, *Britain Votes 2017* assesses the broader European context. Never has an election taken place so overshadowed by an earlier political decision, as Brexit loomed over this contest. Theresa May's election justification was that she was seeking to strengthen her hand in the Brexit negotiations with the EU. As Sara Hagemann notes, the UK was not the only EU member state to go to the polls in 2017. The timing of the French and German elections in 2017 had previously been seen as a critical consideration for Theresa May's government in determining when to trigger Article 50 of the Treaty on European Union to commence formally the process of UK withdrawal from the EU. This wider European electoral context was of clear significance for the Brexit negotiations. The 2017 elections in the Netherlands, France and Germany were all closely watched for signs of surging support for populist parties and politicians and for a possible contagion of anti-EU sentiment emanating from the Brexit vote. Yet whilst a significant force in all three countries, populism was contained. Britain's Brexit was a solo and friendless run for the election victor to manage.

The next section of the volume analyses key aspects of the election campaign: the financing of the battle, digital campaigning strategies, the use of traditional and social media and the degree of political engagement elicited by these efforts. Justin Fisher's chapter on party expenditure before and during the campaign outlines important regulatory changes during the short 2015-2017 Parliament, which affect the way parties are financed. Fisher analyses the trends in party income and expenditure, and how these impacted on the parties' levels of preparation for the unexpected general election. He then outlines the number and extent of donations to parties, to finally analyse parties' expenditure during the electoral campaign, identifying the differing types of activities favoured by the different parties. Labour and the Liberal Democrats found themselves in far stronger financial positions than was the case in 2015 and were well prepared financially for the snap election. Yet by the time of polling day, normal service was resumed, with the Conservatives able to raise significant sums in a relatively short period. However, the snap election influenced the extent to which the parties could exploit their financial position and how campaign expenditure was allocated.

Some of that campaigning was relatively cheap, conducted via Facebook. Katharine Dommett and Luke Temple consider this in their contribution on digital campaigning. They analyse in detail the type of messages used through this platform and the extent to which this reached potential voters. They then outline the way non-party organisations supported the main parties' campaigns, particularly in the case of Labour, developing what the authors label online 'satellite campaigns' conducted by organisations beyond a particular party, but sympathising with one. The authors suggest that Facebook campaigning has been normalised and the potential impact of the expansion of 'satellite campaigns' appears considerable.

Dominic Wring and Stephen Ward assess traditional and newer forms of media coverage of the election. They identify the key elements that failed in the Conservatives' campaign strategy, not least Theresa May's refusal to participate in the leaders' debates—although given the Conservatives' poll lead, the lessons of Cameron's useful aversion to such showpieces in 2015 and May's lack of dexterity, avoidance might possibly have been the best tactic anyway. Wring and Ward show how the digital sphere and mainstream media increasingly overlap and feed off one another. As such, traditional media, television and even the press, are far from dead, but Labour's use of social media helped reach their target audience of young and new voters on perhaps the first occasion that social media was at the heart of a party election campaign. Given that the internet works best for the swift mobilisation of oppositionist movements and social media, its value was apparent for the reinvigorated grassroots networks of Corbyn's Labour Party.

In considering the extent and depth of political engagement generated by these different campaigning techniques, Matthew Flinders focuses on what he sees as the paradoxical anti-politics of the 2017 general election. He argues that its most astonishing feature was the success with which a mainstream party, Jeremy Corbyn's Labour, deployed a form of hybrid populism to channel anti-political sentiment. In effect, Corbyn repositioned the party by adopting techniques more readily associated with contemporary populist movements, thereby recasting Labour as an anti-establishment 'outsider' force. Flinders argues that this strategy was made possible by the reconfiguration of the UK party system following the Brexit vote, particularly the demise of UKIP. He also suggests that this approach was central to the gains Labour made in 2017. For Flinders, Labour's adoption of populism enabled it to cultivate the broad appeal needed to bridge the growing economic, social and cultural divides between the 'cosmopolitan' and 'backwater' constituencies in which its core sets of potential supporters live.

The final two contributions consider the election from the perspective of two categories of voters: women and young people. Emily Harmer and Rosalynd Southern explore the gender dimension of the first election contested by a female Prime Minister since 1987. They argue that women's issues received scant media coverage. Parties offered a range of policies aimed at women in competing for female electoral support, but there were few radical policy proposals. The chapter examines the roles of women both in terms of supply (politicians, media, candidates) and demand (manifestos and women voters). It starts by analysing the extent of women's presence in the campaign, potentially high given several women party leaders.

Finally, Sarah Harrison considers whether the much-vaunted 'youthquake' was a reality at the election, with a slight increase in 18-24 year olds voting and a big swing to Labour among young voters. Harrison outlines the key challenges usually associated with youth participation, acknowledges the combined efforts of a number of organisations to promote voter registration and assesses the specific contextual factors in the 2017 contest, the key to understanding the way young people participated in this election, notably the EU referendum. A detailed analysis of three sample constituencies is offered in identifying the key motivations behind the youth vote in the 2017 election.

The sum of these parts is a comprehensive analysis of a remarkable, dramatic election, whose outcome pleased the second-placed party more than the winners, confounded almost all commentators and did little to resolve the problems confronting the UK.

DAVID DENVER*

The Results: How Britain Voted[1]

In 2011 the then Conservative-Liberal Democrat coalition government under David Cameron passed the Fixed-term Parliaments Act. This piece of constitutional tinkering was introduced for purely political reasons—it was part of the deal to get the Liberal Democrats to enter a coalition with the Conservatives—but the effect was to remove from the Prime Minister the power to call an election at any time of his or her choosing. Election dates were now fixed but could be altered if two-thirds of members of the House of Commons agreed to do so. On Tuesday 18 April 2017, in an announcement headlined by the *Daily Telegraph* next day as 'May's bolt from the blue', the Prime Minister indicated that she would be asking the House of Commons to agree to hold an election on 8 June. The vote in Parliament was held next day and, by 522 to 13, MPs voted to go along with the Prime Minister's wishes. According to taste, this either demonstrates that the Act worked effectively or that it was a piece of unnecessary, even foolish, meddling with the Constitution since no Opposition could ever be seen as being so cowardly as to vote down an electoral challenge proposed by the governing party.

Whatever the case in that respect, Mrs May's decision took almost everyone by surprise—politicians, the media, party activists and, not least, academics in the electoral studies field. Given the short notice involved, the parties were forced to embark on a quick scramble to select candidates in constituencies where they were challengers as well as others where incumbent MPs decided to step down. The decision also meant that the changes to constituency boundaries being worked on by the Boundary Commission—reducing the number of MPs, making constituency electorates more equal and generally believed to favour the Conservatives—were shelved (yet again) for the time being.

Theresa May, having previously said that there was no need for an election, suggested that she changed her mind because of sniping by the opposition parties over the UK's decision to leave the European Union (EU) and the need to

*David Denver, Department of Politics, Philosophy and Religion, Lancaster University, d.denver@lancaster.ac.uk

[1]I am grateful to Mark Garnett and David Cowling for comments on a draft of this chapter.

doi:10.1093/pa/gsx059

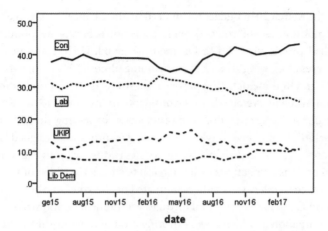

Figure 1.1. Trends in party support, 2015-April 2017
Note: The data shown are the mean monthly voting intentions in published polls reported by Anthony Wells on his *UK Polling Report* website.

strengthen her hand in the forthcoming negotiations over Brexit. The more cynical might suggest that she must also have been influenced by the evident electoral weakness of the Labour party. As the BBC journalist Nick Robinson put it when interviewing the Prime Minister on the *Today* programme: 'What is it about the recent 20% opinion poll [lead] that first attracted you to the idea of a general election?'

1.   The inter-election cycle of party support

In commenting on the results of the 2015 election in the previous volume in this series, I noted that the days have long gone when inter-election cycles followed a fairly simple and familiar pattern—the government would become unpopular and opposition parties more popular until about the middle of the term and then the governing party would gradually recover, while the others faded. There was no sign of this pattern in the period between 2010 and 2015 which was remarkable, rather, for a dramatic slump in support for the Liberal Democrats and an unparalleled level of support for 'others' including, in particular, the SNP in Scotland and UKIP. At the same time, Labour—the official Opposition—peaked in the latter half of 2012 but then drifted gradually downwards for the rest of the Parliament.

The story of the short two-year cycle between 2015 and 2017 is rather different (Figure 1.1). The single most important political event of the period was the referendum on the UK's membership of the EU in June 2016. Before that, there was little change in the popularity of the major parties, although the Conservatives experienced a slight dip and Labour a brief upward movement following the March 2016 budget introduced by the Chancellor, George Osborne, which did not impress the voters (even if it was not as bad as the 'omnishambles' effort he had produced in 2012). On the other hand, UKIP continued to make steady progress following its success in winning almost 13% of the votes in the 2015 election. On these data, the party's peak was achieved in the month of the referendum, when its average share of voting intentions stood at 16.6%.

The result of the referendum vote (a majority for leaving the EU) surprised many—including, notably, David Cameron. He promptly resigned as Prime Minister and was succeeded in July by Theresa May, without party members needing to be consulted, after a rather farcical few weeks in which other (more or less unlikely) contenders were either eliminated by the votes of MPs or withdrew. The effect on Conservative electoral fortunes was immediate and striking. Having inherited a situation in which it was hovering around the mid-thirties in terms of percentage voting intentions, the new Prime Minister's party was well into the forties by October and the upward trend continued thereafter.

Electorally speaking, the second most important event in these two years was the election of Jeremy Corbyn as leader of the Labour party in September 2015. Clearly on the left of the party, Corbyn only just secured enough backing from MPs to enter the leadership contest but, in the event, he then swept to victory. Partly this was because new rules in force enabled anyone to join the party for a few pounds and then have a vote in choosing the leader. Apparently around 200,000 people did so (possibly including mischievous Conservatives and certainly members of assorted left-wing factions). Ominously, however, of the 230 MPs who voted in the ballot only 20 supported Corbyn.

Most new party leaders enjoy a brief honeymoon with the electorate as people take time to get to know about and assess the person concerned. So it proved in this case as Labour support remained steady through late 2015 and early 2016. Nonetheless, the party consistently trailed well behind the Conservatives and the highest point reached was a paltry 33% of voting intentions in March 2016. Thereafter, it was downhill all the way to just over 25% in the first half of April 2017. In these months, assorted front-benchers resigned from the Corbyn team and, by 172 to 40, Labour MPs passed a vote of no confidence in the leader. The MPs, for the most part, were persuaded that Corbyn was not a credible alternative Prime Minister and would prove an electoral disaster. The local and Scottish Parliament elections in the Spring of 2016 seemed to confirm their fears. In the locals in England, despite beating the Conservatives by 33% to 32% in the 'national equivalent vote' calculation, Labour became the first Opposition party in over 30 years to lose ground in local elections held separately from a general election. In Scotland, Labour became the third party in the Parliament with just 24 seats, putting them behind both the SNP (63) and the Conservatives (31). Perhaps unsurprisingly in these circumstances Corbyn was challenged in another leadership election in September 2016. This time, he won even more emphatically than before. The 'Corbynistas' were clearly ascendant in the party if not among its representatives in the House of Commons and the bad electoral news continued.

In five Parliamentary by-elections held from October 2016 to February 2017 (ignoring Batley and Spen which the other major parties did not contest) Labour's vote share declined in all cases. The falls were not large but opposition parties usually make sharp gains in by-elections and the *coup de grâce* was administered in Copeland in Cumbria in February. Labour lost the seat, which it had held since 1935, to the Conservatives. This was the first by-election gain by a governing party from the Opposition since 1982 and must have been a serious blow to Labour morale.

Turning to the other two parties included in Figure 1.1, as noted above UKIP reached a peak around the time of the EU referendum. The success of the Leave campaign immediately raised a problem for the party, however. With its *raison d'être* apparently achieved, voters could legitimately ask whether there was any point in its continued existence. The ever-newsworthy Nigel Farage resigned as party leader soon after the referendum. There followed a period of confused infighting—including, it was reported, physical violence involving Members of the European Parliament—after which Diane James emerged as party leader in September 2016. She resigned after just 18 days in post and confusion reigned anew. Eventually Paul Nuttall was chosen as the new leader in November. These events did little to improve UKIP's standing with the electorate. Performance in by-elections was disappointing, with the failure of Paul Nuttall himself to take Stoke Central from Labour in February 2017, after a notably chaotic campaign, widely interpreted as a severe setback. In the polls, the party sank slowly but steadily and entered the 2017 election on around 11% of voting intentions.

Following the disastrous outcome of the 2015 election, Nick Clegg resigned as leader of the Liberal Democrats and was succeeded in July of that year by Tim Farron, the personable MP for Westmorland and Lonsdale. Nonetheless, the party struggled to regain its former status in the party system. Despite occasional reminders of the old glory days—such as winning the Richmond Park by-election in December 2016—there was not much solid evidence of progress. The 2016 local election results were patchy and in Scotland the Liberal Democrats held on to just five seats in the Parliament—behind even the Green Party on six. Although their poll position improved towards the end of the period it was not a dramatic rise and the Liberal Democrats ended the period only a couple of points ahead of their 2015 score.

There is little doubt that the changing fortunes of the Conservative and Labour parties in the inter-election period reflected the relative popularity of their party leaders. Figure 1.2 shows that in this respect there was not much to

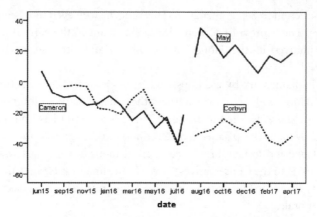

Figure 1.2. Popularity of party leaders 2015-April 2017
Note: The data are net figures from the Ipsos MORI series measuring satisfaction with the performance of party leaders which can be interpreted as a measure of their popularity.

separate David Cameron and Jeremy Corbyn —both fairly quickly became unpopular. With the arrival of Theresa May, however, the situation was transformed. Her ratings were consistently—and strongly—positive while Corbyn continued to languish in negative territory. In September 2016, IpsosMORI reported that May easily outscored her rival on being a capable leader (68% to 24%), being good in a crisis (52% to 18%), being patriotic (75% to 49%), having sound judgement (56% to 30%) and a clear vision for Britain (55% to 38%). In addition, whereas her predecessor, David Cameron, was regularly believed to be 'more style than substance' by 40 to 50 per cent of survey respondents, only 25% thought this of Theresa May.

As suggested above, the surprise announcement of an early election caught the various parties on the hop to varying extents and selections of candidates in many constituencies had to be completed very rapidly. Nomination papers were required to be submitted by Thursday 11 May—just three weeks and a day after the Commons voted for the election. Perhaps unsurprisingly, the number of candidates nominated in Great Britain (the situation in Northern Ireland is discussed in a separate chapter) declined sharply compared with 2015 from 3833 to 3195. The Conservatives and Labour contested all but the Speaker's seat; the Liberal Democrats also maintained this tradition but did not have candidates in two other constituencies. Plaid Cymru and the SNP contested all seats in their respective countries but the smaller parties were more affected by the rush to put candidates in place. The number of Green Party candidates declined from 568 to 460 while UKIP's slumped from 614 to 379. The assorted Independents, eccentrics and inhabitants of the political fringe who constitute the 'Others' were also much less in evidence than usual, their numbers falling from 659 in 2015 to 366 in this election. These declines among smaller parties and others were no doubt caused in part by the difficulty of raising the £500 required for each candidate's deposit in the space of a couple of weeks but the Greens and UKIP also claimed that there was a tactical element to their decisions—trying to help Labour in marginal seats in the first case and not standing against strongly pro-Brexit Conservatives in the second.

2. Trends in party support during the 'short' campaign

Although parties nowadays engage in more or less continuous campaigning, there is clearly an increase in activity when an election is in the offing. Everything reaches a climax in the final few weeks of the 'short' campaign (which in this case was actually unusually 'long'—seven weeks from the election being announced to polling day) since there usually remains much to play for.

In 2010, for example, almost 40% of voters said that they made up their minds about which party to support during the campaign and the (first-ever) televised debates between the party leaders clearly had a dramatic impact on public opinion. In 2015, however, the parties and broadcasters had found it difficult to agree on the timing and format of leaders' debates. In the end, there was only one debate in which David Cameron and Nick Clegg participated and this was something of a farce since it involved the leaders of no fewer than seven parties. In the 2017 election, the Prime Minister made it clear from the outset that she would not participate in a televised debate with the other party leaders and Jeremy Corbyn also initially withdrew. He changed his mind, however, and appeared in a debate broadcast by the BBC in the penultimate week of the campaign, again involving representatives of seven parties, with the Home Secretary, Amber Rudd, standing in for Mrs May. The viewing audience for the programme was not large, however [3.6 million according to Broadcasters' Audience Research Board (BARB) figures], and it appeared to have little impact on the trend in public opinion.

An unusual feature of the 2017 campaign was that almost in the middle of it a major round of local elections took place. These elections, scheduled for 4 May, were for all councils in Scotland and Wales and for county councils, some unitary authorities and some mayors in England. Local parties were already heavily involved in campaigning for them when the general election was called and they went ahead as planned. The only previous occasion that this happened was in 1955. There were June general elections in 1983 and 1987, of course, but in each of these cases the Prime Minister (Margaret Thatcher) cannily waited for a detailed analysis and assessment of the local results before calling the general election.

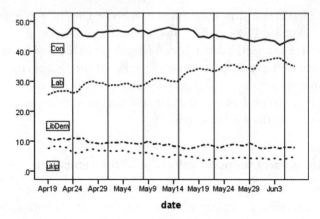

Figure 1.3. Trends in voting intentions during the 'short' campaign
Note: The data are three-day moving averages of polls reported by Anthony Wells on his *UK Polling Report* website. The vertical lines mark each Monday of the campaign.

Had Theresa May followed this practice there seems little doubt that she would have been encouraged to press on with a general election. In England and Wales, the Conservatives gained almost 400 seats while Labour lost almost 250 and UKIP was ousted from every one of the 143 seats that the party defended. In Scotland, the Tories came second in both votes and seats won while Labour support plunged and the SNP—although still clearly the leading party—performed less well than expected.

Figure 1.3 charts the trends in voting intentions for the four leading parties from 19 April (the date of the House of Commons vote agreeing to have an election) on the basis of a three-day moving average of all polls reported by the *UK Polling Report* website. At the outset, the Conservatives enjoyed a huge lead over their rivals and there was much talk of a landslide victory for them and an electoral catastrophe for Labour. Support for the former remained unusually strong until the third week in May, although Labour was clearly already on an upward trend from its very poor starting point. In that week, however, the launch of the Conservative election manifesto took place and it contained controversial proposals relating to paying for social care for the elderly (immediately christened a 'dementia tax' by opponents) which—along with some other items—did not go down well with the electorate. Within a couple of days Mrs May backtracked on the social care proposals. As reporters gleefully noted, far from providing 'strong and stable leadership' (the consistent theme of the Conservative campaign), the Prime Minister now looked 'weak and wobbly'. The gap between her party and Labour in terms of voting intentions subsequently narrowed perceptibly. In the very last week, however, as decision day approached the Conservative ship seemed to steady and the party's lead increased somewhat.

As the Figure makes clear, the 2017 election quickly developed into a two-horse race. When the election was called, UKIP immediately dipped to around eight per cent of voting intentions and, as the campaign progressed, drifted downwards to stabilise at between four and five per cent. The Liberal Democrats also declined a little over the campaign. Having averaged over ten per cent in the first two weeks they had fallen to just under eight per cent by the last two weeks. Clearly, their main message—that there should be a second Brexit referendum—struck few chords with the voters.

In Scotland, meanwhile, there were eleven campaign polls and these suggested that, from a dire position at the outset (less than 20% of voting intentions), Labour had drawn level with the Conservatives by the end, with the average of the last three Scottish polls showing each of them on 26%. These two were vying for second place behind the SNP which averaged 40% in these polls. This gave the party a handsome lead but was significantly lower than the 50% achieved in 2015. In Wales, two early polls surprised observers by showing clear Conservative leads over Labour; later in the campaign, however, three further polls suggested that Labour had resumed its customary position as the dominant party. As in Scotland, these polls suggested that support for the nationalists was somewhat lower than in 2015.

While campaign polls can be fairly characterised as 'snapshots' of opinion at the time, the final polls produced by each company can be treated as predictions of the election outcome. Given a relatively volatile electorate and problems relating to electoral registration and differential turnout among various sections of the electorate, this is not an easy business. Nonetheless, it is surprising to report that among the nine firms polling in the final week estimates of the Conservative lead ranged from one point (Survation) to 13 points (BMG) with the rest averaging eight points. As it turned out, although most were reasonably accurate as far as the Conservatives (and the Liberal Democrats) were concerned, all (including Survation) underestimated the strength of Labour support.

3.   The national result

The shares of votes and the number of seats won by the various parties in 2017 (in Great Britain) and changes from 2015 are shown in Table 1.1. Having started the campaign in the doldrums Labour's steady progress over the seven weeks culminated in the party harvesting 41% of votes, which was well in excess of almost everyone's expectations. Somewhat paradoxically, the Conservative share of 43.4% was the party's best performance since 1983 but this was small comfort in the light of Labour's spectacular improvement in the space of a few weeks. In broad terms, the outcome seems to indicate something of a return to two-party politics (in England and Wales, at least) in that, while support for both the

Table 1.1 Share of votes and number of seats won (Great Britain) and changes from 2015

	Share of votes (%)	Change 2015-17	Number of seats	Change 2015-17
Conservative	43.4	+5.7	317	−13
Labour	41.0	+9.8	262	+30
Liberal Democrat	7.6	−0.5	12	+4
UKIP	1.9	−10.0	0	−1
Green	1.7	−2.1	1	0
SNP/Plaid Cymru	3.6	−1.9	39	−20
Other	0.8	−0.1	1	0

Note: The Speaker, who was not opposed by the Conservatives, Labour or Liberal Democrats, is treated as 'Other'.

Conservatives and Labour increased, every other party lost ground—spectacularly so in the case of UKIP. In terms of 'swing'—which can now be resurrected as the most convenient way of measuring the net movement between the leading parties—the figure was 2.1% from Conservative to Labour. This is not a large swing by historical standards but it was enough to deprive Theresa May of a majority in the House of Commons. Things would have been even worse but for a better than expected result for the Conservatives in Scotland where they took 13 seats as compared with just one in 2015.

I noted above that both UKIP and Greens claimed that there was some tactical element in their decisions about which constituencies to contest—or, perhaps more accurately, from which ones to withdraw. There was certainly discussion about the likely impact of these changes in candidatures during the campaign and doubtless they entered the calculations of party strategists. Table 1.2 attempts to measure the impact of Green and UKIP withdrawals on support for the major parties. The data, relating to constituencies in England and Wales, suggest that voters often do not behave in ways expected by commentators or those at the top of the parties themselves. In constituencies where UKIP stood down but the Greens did not the Conservatives, overall, did worse than elsewhere and Labour slightly better. Where it was the Greens who failed to nominate a candidate, the situation was reversed—Labour, if anything, had poorer results and the Conservatives somewhat better performances.

3.1   Regional variations in party support

Table 1.3 shows the swings between the Conservatives and Labour across English regions and in Scotland and Wales. It is apparent that the movement to Labour was far from uniform across the country. The North East and Scotland moved in

Table 1.2 The impact of UKIP and Green withdrawals of support for major parties (England and Wales)

	Change % Con	Change % Lab	Change % LibDem	N of constits
Neither withdrew	+4.3	+10.5	−0.8	287
Both withdrew	+5.0	+10.2	+1.3	36
UKIP only withdrew	+3.9	+11.3	−0.2	166
Green only withdrew	+7.2	+9.9	−0.2	57

Table 1.3 Conservative-Labour swing in regions

North East	0.3% to Con	London	6.3% to Lab
North West	2.6% to Lab	South East	3.7% to Lab
Yorkshire/Humber	1.1% to Lab	South West	3.3% to Lab
East Midlands	0.8% to Lab		
West Midlands	1.2% to Lab	Wales	2.5% to Lab
Eastern	2.6% to Lab	Scotland	5.5% to Con

favour of the Conservatives relative to their opponents, while in Yorkshire/ Humber and the Midlands the pro-Labour swings were rather smaller than average. In London, by contrast, the 6.3% swing to Labour was considerably larger than anything that occurred elsewhere. In 2015, Labour also had a much larger increase in its vote share in London than anywhere else so that there now appears to be a yawning political rift between the capital and the rest of the country. This was evident, of course, in the EU referendum in 2016 when London was the only 'region' of England and Wales that voted to remain in the EU (and did so by a large margin). There is a suggestion in the election results that, apart from Scotland, there may also have been something of a carryover from the referendum to the election in other regions. Those that were most enthusiastic for leaving the EU (the North East, Yorkshire and the Midlands) were also those where the swing to Labour was smallest (or in the opposite direction).

Nonetheless, regional variations in party support (Table 1.4) show that, with the exception of London, there remains a broad north–south division in England. Labour's strongest areas outside London remain the three northernmost regions. The Midlands had significant Conservative leads but in three southern regions (Eastern, South East and South West) Labour failed to reach a third of votes cast. On the other hand, despite the hopes and fears aroused by early opinion polls, Wales returned to being something of a Labour stronghold. For the second time in a row the election result in

Table 1.4 Party shares of votes and seats won in regions (row per cent)

	Con	Lab	Lib Dem	UKIP	Green	SNP/PC	Other
North East	34.4	55.4	4.6	3.9	1.3		0.5
	3	26					
North West	36.2	54.9	5.4	1.9	1.1		0.5
	20	54	1				
Yorkshire/Humber	40.4	49.0	5.0	2.6	1.3		1.7
Seats	17	37					
East Midlands	50.7	40.5	4.3	2.4	1.5		0.6
Seats	31	15					
West Midlands	49.0	42.5	4.4	1.8	1.7		0.6
Seats	35	24					
Eastern	54.6	32.7	7.9	2.5	1.9		0.3
Seats	50	7	1				
London	33.1	54.5	8.8	1.3	1.8		0.5
Seats	21	49	3				
South East	53.8	28.6	10.5	2.3	3.1		1.7
Seats	72	8	2		1		1
South West	51.4	29.1	14.9	1.1	2.3		1.2
Seats	47	7	1				
Wales	33.6	48.9	4.5	2.0	0.3	10.4	0.2
Seats	8	28	0			4	
Scotland	28.6	27.1	6.8	0.2	0.2	36.9	0.3
Seats	13	7	4			35	

Note: The Speaker is counted as 'Other'.

Scotland was clearly exceptional—but this time for very different reasons. As noted above, campaign opinion polls forecast a decline in support for the SNP as compared with 2015 but the latter's vote share fell by more than even the worst poll report—from 50% to 36.9%—resulting in a loss of 21 seats (and another couple of very narrow squeaks). In the battle for second place, the Conservatives edged out Labour. The Liberal Democrats more or less held their own, enabling them to take three additional Scottish seats.

As far as the other parties in England are concerned there is little to be said. Liberal Democrat support is concentrated in London and the South and the party picked up a few more seats there. However, only one seat was won elsewhere in England and that was held by the party leader, Tim Farron, by only 777 votes (as compared with almost 9000 in the difficult circumstances for Liberal Democrats that prevailed in 2015). It would be fair to say that, after a very strong performance in 2015, the 2017 election reduced UKIP to insignificance across the country and, although the party's leader easily retained her seat in Brighton, the Greens also declined and remain confined to the political fringe. It is perhaps worth noting, however, that UKIP outpolled the Greens in the north of England whereas the latter were the more successful in London and the south.

4.   Constituency variations in changes in party support

Much greater variations in both the direction and extent of changes in party support would be expected at constituency level. General elections are more than simply national contests between party leaders (notwithstanding the impression conveyed by media reporting of the campaign and the relentless focus of the Conservative campaign in this election). Local personalities, issues, events and traditions, as well as demographic changes and constituency campaigning at the grass roots, all have a part to play. As usual, the 2017 contest displayed an impressive level of continuity in the distribution of votes across constituencies. This is verified by the correlation coefficients measuring the strength of the association between the parties' vote shares in 2015 and 2017. Across Britain and including only seats contested on both occasions, these are 0.93 for the Conservatives, 0.97 for Labour ($N = 631$ in both cases) and 0.90 for the Liberal Democrats ($N = 629$). The level of support for UKIP and the Greens was somewhat less predictable on the basis of their performance in 2015, the relevant coefficients being 0.82 ($N = 378$) and 0.77 ($N = 445$) respectively. On the other hand, taking the SNP and Plaid Cymru together, the variation in their vote shares across constituencies in 2017 was very similar to their performance in 2015 (coefficient = 0.97, $N = 99$).

Despite these strong relationships, there remains considerable variation in the extent and direction of change. Across the country, 186 seats swung to the Conservatives (55 of them in Scotland). Even within England, however, there were 17 constituencies which had swings to the Conservatives in excess of 5%. At the other extreme, swings of over 10% to Labour were recorded in 17 constituencies. With only a slight decline overall, the Liberal Democrats improved their position in just over 200 seats, notching up double digit increases in nine, although this was offset by double digit decreases in 13 cases. The story as far as UKIP is concerned is more straightforward: it declined in every constituency that the party fought in both 2015 and 2017. The fall ranged from more than 20 points in 11 seats to fewer than five in 25 but all of the latter were in places where the party had relatively few votes to lose in the first place. Finally, in Scotland the SNP dropped back in every constituency while in Wales Plaid Cymru improved its position in four of the 40 constituencies.

Although specifically local factors explain many constituency variations and thus make it difficult to generalise, it is worth looking for systematic patterns. A first step is to consider how changes in support for the various parties were inter-related and Table 1.5 reports the relevant correlation coefficients (focusing

Table 1.5 Correlations between changes in vote shares (England)

	Change % Con	Change % Lab	Change % LibDem	Change % UKIP
Change % Lab	−0.27	–	–	–
Change % Lib Dem	−0.36	−0.44	–	–
Change % UKIP	−0.81	0.07	0.12	–
Change % Green	0.31	−0.45	−0.05	−0.34

Note: The N for coefficients involving Conservatives, Labour, Liberal Democrats and UKIP only is 532; for the first three and the Green Party it is 501 and for UKIP and Greens 502. All coefficients are statistically significant except for those relating to Labour and UKIP and the Liberal Democrats and the Greens.

on England in order to avoid complications caused by the presence of nationalists in Scotland and Wales). Negative coefficients indicate that where one of the parties concerned did better, the other had poorer results while positive figures mean that the two parties tended to rise and fall together. Notwithstanding the evidence presented earlier relating to the impact of UKIP withdrawals, it is clear that across all constituencies the Conservatives benefited from the decline in UKIP votes. The coefficient (-0.81) indicates a strong relationship. The coefficients for the Greens show that there was a significant, if not very strong, tendency for Labour to do less well where the Greens held up best and for the pattern of ups and downs for the Conservatives and Greens to be similar. Not unexpectedly, changes for both major parties were negatively related to changes in the vote shares of the Liberal Democrats but perhaps the most surprising coefficient is that for the Conservatives and Labour. Although this is in the expected direction it is not large (-0.27), meaning that changes in support for the two were not actually very strongly related. In the good old days of overwhelming two-party dominance an increase in vote share for one would have been matched almost exactly by a decline for the other. Those days have long gone, however, and it is the presence of large numbers of third, fourth and fifth party candidates that makes the relationship between changes in support for the two leading parties less than straightforward.

In Scotland, changes in SNP support were negatively and significantly related to changes in the shares obtained by Labour (-0.28) and the Liberal Democrats (-0.29) but not, strangely, to those for the Conservatives (-0.03). For the latter, variations in their improvement across constituencies were more strongly inversely related to the changes experienced by Labour (-0.37) and the Liberal Democrats (-0.65).

It might reasonably be expected that the nature of party competition in different constituencies would affect changes in party support—as a consequence of

Table 1.6 Changes in overall vote shares in different electoral contexts (England only)

	Top two parties in 2015				
	Con Lab	Con LibDem	Con UKIP	Lab Con	Lab UKIP
Con	+3.7	+4.1	+6.7	+3.8	+10.8
Lab	+10.0	+7.2	+10.6	+11.0	+8.3
Lib Dem	−0.0	+2.6	+0.1	−1.1	−1.4
UKIP	−11.7	−10.4	−15.7	−10.6	−16.1
Green	−1.8	−3.2	−2.0	−2.9	−1.6
(N)	(198)	(44)	(75)	(155)	(38)

tactical voting, for example. Table 1.6, which is again restricted to England, shows changes in vote shares in five different situations. UKIP lost most heavily where it had most votes to lose—in constituencies where it was lying in second place. The Liberal Democrats, on the other hand, did best where they most needed to— in seats where they were second to the Conservatives. There is some evidence that the reported Conservative strategy of trying to attract ex-UKIP voters in working-class areas had an effect in that in Labour-UKIP seats their vote share increased quite sharply while Labour's increased less than elsewhere. Nonetheless, this was an ill-conceived strategy as it was never going to result in very many (if any) seat gains. There is some evidence of tactical voting in Conservative-Liberal Democrat seats since, in addition to seeing the best Liberal Democrat performance these also had the smallest Labour advance.

Changes in support for the two major parties are explored further in Table 1.7 which shows, first, the direction and strength of the relationship between changes in vote shares and a standard set of social and demographic variables for constituencies in England and Wales. The Conservatives had better results and Labour worse ones in seats where there were more manual workers, owner occupiers, people with no educational qualifications and voters aged over 65. On the debit side for the Conservatives, the increase in their vote share was notably less than average in constituencies with a greater middle-class and graduate demographic. They also fared poorly in cities (persons per hectare), areas with more privately rented housing and the larger the ethnic minority electorate. During the campaign and since the election there has been much comment suggesting that Labour (and Jeremy Corbyn in particular) was able to galvanise young people (and especially students) by promising to abolish university tuition fees. The evidence in the table supports this interpretation since it shows that the Conservatives did not

Table 1.7 Bivariate correlations between changes in Conservative and Labour shares of vote 2015-2017 and constituency characteristics (England and Wales)

	Conservative	Labour		Conservative	Labour
% Manual Workers	0.65	−0.11	% Prof./Managerial	−0.64	0.03*
% Owner occupiers	0.34	−0.26	% Private renters	−0.52	0.36
% No qualifications	0.70	−0.16	% With degrees	−0.75	0.12
% Aged 65+	0.42	−0.24	% Aged 18-24	−0.20	0.34
			% Students	−0.35	0.34
			Persons per hectare	−0.45	0.22
			% Ethnic minority	−0.45	0.18
% Leave in EU ref.	0.79	−0.28			

Note: N = 572. All coefficients are statistically significant except the one asterisked.

progress as well in constituencies with larger numbers of young people and students as they did elsewhere. On the other hand, Labour clearly did better in these constituencies.

The kinds of places where the Conservatives did best in comparison to 2015 are strikingly similar to those which had the largest 'Leave' majorities in the EU referendum. The counting areas used in the referendum were local councils but we can use the estimates of how constituencies voted in the referendum, prepared by the House of Commons Library (see https://secondreading.uk/brexit/brexit-votes-by-constituency/), to compare the two votes directly. There was a correlation of 0.79 between the percentage voting 'Leave' in 2016 and the improvement in the Conservatives' position between 2015 and 2017. The more 'Leave' voters there were, the better the Conservatives did. This also means that the more 'Remain' voters the worse was the Conservative performance. With some justification, therefore, the election outcome might be characterised as the 'revenge of the Remainers'.

5.   Patterns of party support in 2017

When we focus on variations in absolute levels of support for the parties rather than change between elections, we would usually be on territory that is much more familiar in that patterns are normally very similar from one election to the next. Table 1.8 shows correlation coefficients measuring the associations between the shares of the vote obtained by the parties in constituencies and the usual range of social and demographic variables. Although the data reveal few surprises, some interesting and important points are worth noting. First, although the Conservatives did better in more solidly middle-class seats and Labour in more working-class seats, the coefficients involved are modest and pale in comparison

Table 1.8 Bivariate correlations between party shares of vote in 2017 and constituency characteristics (England and Wales)

	Conservative	Labour	Liberal Democrat
% Prof./Managerial	0.30	−0.40	0.43
% Manual Workers	−0.27	0.36	−0.40
% Owner occupiers	0.70	−0.65	0.10
% Social renters	−0.67	0.68	−0.23
% Private renters	−0.48	0.38	−0.08*
% Aged 18-24	−0.54	0.46	−0.03*
% Aged 65+	0.60	−0.63	0.18
% In agriculture	0.37	−0.47	0.21
Persons per hectare	−0.58	0.56	−0.05*
% With degrees	0.03*	−0.18	0.41
% No qualifications	−0.23	0.34	−0.43
% Students	−0.53	0.42	0.05*
% With no car	−0.79	0.76	−0.19
% Ethnic minority	−0.52	0.54	−0.12

Note: N = 572 for Conservatives and Labour and 570 for the Liberal Democrats. All coefficients are statistically significant except those asterisked.

with those relating to age. Without going overboard, it could be argued that the pattern of votes across constituencies suggests that the generational divide is more marked than the class divide which once was paramount. Labour's appeal to younger voters appears to be substantiated by these figures as well as those relating to the proportions of students in a constituency. Labour's strength and relative Conservative weakness in the cities (especially London) is reflected not just in the strong correlations with persons per hectare but also in those for % ethnic minority and % with no car. The latter varies with the extent of poverty but is also markedly lower in large cities. Liberal Democrat support in this election was not very clearly structured by social and demographic factors except that the party tended to perform more strongly in more middle-class areas and also (overlapping to some extent) in those where people with degrees were thicker on the ground.

Within Scotland, variations in Conservative and Labour strength were not significantly related to the composition of constituencies in terms of occupational class. Otherwise, the patterns resembled those for England and Wales. In the 2015 edition of this series, I argued that in the election of that year the SNP had clearly moved from being a 'catch all' party without a very distinctive social base and had taken over what were formerly the bases of Labour dominance in Scotland. This remained true in 2017. The SNP vote was correlated positively with % manual workers (0.35), % social renters (0.57), % with no qualifications (0.39) and %

Table 1.9 Regional turnout 2017

	Turnout 2017	Change 2015-17
North East	66.2	+4.2
North West	68.0	+3.6
Yorkshire/Humber	66.5	+3.2
East Midlands	69.3	+2.5
West Midlands	66.9	+2.7
Eastern	70.0	+2.2
London	70.3	+4.7
South East	71.3	+2.5
South West	72.0	+2.3
Wales	68.7	+2.7
Scotland	66.5	−4.6
Great Britain	69.0	+2.4

with no car (0.48). As might be expected there were negative relationships with % professional and managerial (-0.43), % owner occupiers (-0.51) and % with a degree (-0.40). Apart from these class-related variables, it is somewhat surprising to note that there was no significant relationship between the proportion of young people and SNP support although the negative coefficient for those aged over 65 (-0.31) could have been anticipated.

6.   Turnout

Turnout in Britain is measured as the percentage of eligible people on the electoral register who cast a ballot. Properly, therefore, it includes those who voted but whose ballots were rejected for one reason or another (such as 'being unmarked or wholly void for uncertainty'). The numbers of ballot papers rejected are routinely announced at the formal declaration of a constituency result but, unfortunately, are not systematically reported by the media. Many local authorities simply fail to include them in their notifications of results on their websites. Media reports of turnout, therefore, are usually based on valid votes cast rather than all votes. In most cases the difference is small, of course, but in the Buckingham constituency of the Speaker in 2017 there were 1967 rejected ballots and including these clearly makes a difference to the turnout calculation. Across Britain, more than 70,000 ballots were rejected and these are included in the turnout figures in what follows.

Over Britain as a whole, turnout increased from 66.6% in 2015 to 69.0% on this occasion. This was the fourth general election in succession that has seen an increase in turnout; on the other hand, it remains lower than at any election

Table 1.10 Bivariate correlations between turnout in 2017 and constituency characteristics (Great Britain)

% Professional & Managerial	0.71	% Manual Workers	−0.67
% Owner occupiers	0.44	% Social renters	−0.60
		% Private renters	−0.06*
% in agriculture	0.25	Persons per hectare	−0.19
% with degrees	0.62	% No qualifications	−0.71
% Aged 65+	0.30	% Aged 18-24	−0.29
		% Ethnic minority	−0.15
		% with no car	−0.51
Constituency marginality 2015	0.01*		
% Leave in referendum	−0.34		

Note: All coefficients are statistically significant except those asterisked. N = 632.

between 1950 and 1997. Table 1.9 shows that participation by the electorate increased in every region across England and Wales with the largest rise being recorded in London (+4.7). This may be an effect of the relative popularity of Jeremy Corbyn in the capital. In Scotland, however, the situation was reversed with turnout dropping back (-4.6) from what had been an unusually high figure in 2015. In absolute terms, within England the southern regions continued to record higher turnouts than those in the north.

At constituency level, of course, there was much greater variation in turnout. At the bottom end, 32 constituencies failed to reach 60% with Wolverhampton South East taking the wooden spoon with a turnout of 52.0%. At the other extreme, turnout was 75% or greater in 60 constituencies with the highest figure of all (79.7%) recorded in Twickenham where Vince Cable reclaimed the seat for the Liberal Democrats in fine style. Despite the comment above that London turnout may have been influenced by the popularity of the Labour leader, across England and Wales the correlation between the change in constituency turnouts and changes in Labour's vote share is not statistically significant. For the Conservatives, however, the figure is -0.30 so that the more turnout increased, the worse the party did.

As with the distribution of support for the major parties, in examining turnout variations across constituencies we encounter—for the most part—a familiar pattern. Table 1.10 shows correlations between the level of turnout in 2017 and census variables indicating the socio-economic characteristics of constituencies together with two more political variables—their marginality (100—the winning party's percentage majority) in 2015 and the estimated 'Leave' percentage in the 2016 referendum. In general, the coefficients for the social variables indicate that, despite the overall increase in turnout, Britain continues to be divided into relatively low turnout and relatively high turnout constituencies and the two are very different in social terms. The former are mainly urban, working-class and poor; the latter rural and suburban, middle-class and relatively affluent. It is worth stressing that this analysis does not tell us the extent to which people in the various groups listed turned out to vote. Rather, it tells us that the more professionals, owner occupiers, people with degrees, people employed in agriculture and older people there are in a constituency, the higher was its turnout.

Whatever it was that drove turnout in 2017 it was not the marginality—the closeness of the contest—of a constituency in the previous election. For the second election in succession there was no significant relationship between previous marginality and turnout. Worries that the sophisticated targeting of campaign efforts on key seats by parties might lead voters in others (the great majority) to become more apathetic have not been borne out. It is not clear, however, why the formerly strong relationship between marginality and turnout which persisted over many years has now disappeared. On the other hand, the more 'Leave' voters there were in a constituency the poorer was the turnout (coefficient of -0.34). Put the other way, the more 'Remainers' there were, the higher the turnout. 'Remain' support was strongly correlated with some of the other variables in the table (% middle class and % with degrees, for example) so that more complicated statistical analysis than can be presented here would be required to test whether it had an independent effect on turnout. Nonetheless, it is possible that the strongly pro-Brexit stance taken by the Prime Minister increased the determination of 'Remain' voters to go to the polls in the general election.

7. Explaining the outcome

All general elections are interesting; some are surprising; only a few can be described as astonishing. The latter certainly applies to 2017. No election in living memory has seen a party start so far behind and make up so much ground. Never has a party leader who started the campaign so low in the estimation of the electorate (not to mention his party colleagues in Parliament) so clearly confounded critics.

A full evidence-based account of these extraordinary events must await publication of the British Election Study report. In the immediate aftermath of the election, however, attention focused on the failings of the Conservative campaign and the relative performances of the Conservative and Labour leaders.

The Conservative campaign was a disaster. The decision to focus everything on the 'strong and stable leadership' provided by Theresa May is perhaps understandable given what the polls were reporting about the relative standing of the two party leaders at the outset and the Prime Minister's desire for a personal mandate. Even local candidates seem to have been instructed to describe themselves as 'standing with Theresa May'. However, the public's evaluations of

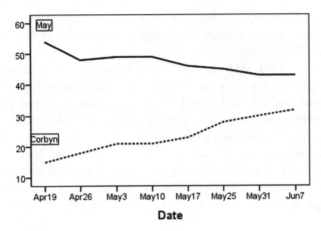

Figure 1.4. Best person for Prime Minister, April-June 2017
Source: YouGov.

individuals are very fickle. Politicians can go from the heights to the depths of popularity very quickly. In addition, the Conservative manifesto was a clear own goal. The proposals relating to social care for the old and winter fuel payments simply provided opposition parties with ammunition to create worry and uncertainty among older voters who normally give strong support to the party. In contrast, Labour's firm manifesto commitment to abolish university tuition fees had immediate appeal to a potentially significant section of the electorate.

It became apparent during the election that Theresa May is not a very good campaigner, with journalists frequently describing her efforts as 'robotic', and the qualities that made people like her over the first months of her time in office receded in importance in the heat of the battle. At the same time, Jeremy Corbyn managed to come across as friendly, and likeable. For many voters, evidently, he was able to resist and reverse the attempts of the Conservatives to portray him as a ruthless hard leftist who was soft on terrorism. The consequence of May's weakness and Corbyn's better than expected performance was that the initial gap in the electorate's evaluation of the two narrowed considerably over the campaign. According to YouGov, in late April May's approval rating (% saying she was doing well minus % saying she was doing badly) was +17. By 1 June it was -5. In the same period Corbyn's rating went from -52 to -2—a truly spectacular improvement in the space of six weeks. On the key question of who would be the best person for Prime Minister, the change in opinion is illustrated in Figure 1.4. Mrs May's lead shrank from 30 points in April to 11 points at the end of the campaign. Even so, to keep things in perspective, the incumbent Prime Minister was the preferred person for the post on the eve of the election and her party did win more votes and more seats than any of the others. Despite the jubilation in Labour circles, the party remains in opposition, far from a majority, and has not won an election since 2005.

The election of 2017 demonstrated very clearly that the 'short' campaign really matters. Just because a party has been leading in opinion polls for some time does not guarantee that the lead will survive the rigours of a campaign. Had the campaign been as short as normal, then the outcome might have been rather different. As it was, however, the seven week slog allowed Labour time to improve the image and standing of both the party and the party leader while the Conservatives stumbled. As a result, rather than being returned with an increased majority as she had initially hoped, Theresa May found herself at the head of a minority government and the country entered a period of serious political uncertainty.

JOHN CURTICE*

How the Electoral System Failed to Deliver–Again

There has long been one principal defence of the use of the single member plurality electoral system in elections to the UK House of Commons. Because it usually gives the largest party a safe overall majority, it is said to facilitate a system of alternating single party majority government under which who governs is determined directly by voters and where responsibility for what government does and does not achieve rests unambiguously with the governing party (Bingham Powell, 2000; Norton 1997; Renwick, 2011). These attributes are claimed to be more important than having a parliament whose composition represents a microcosm of political opinion amongst the electorate at large, such as might be delivered by a system of proportional representation.

Until recently, the system has largely lived up to this billing. In the 17 elections held between 1945 and 2005, only once did it fail to deliver an overall majority at all, and only on three occasions was the government's majority fewer than ten seats. Yet the 2017 election was the third in a row at which the system has failed to deliver a safe overall majority to the winning party. In 2010, no single party enjoyed an overall majority and the outcome led to the formation between the Conservatives and the Liberal Democrats of the first coalition government since 1945. Although in 2015 the Conservatives did secure an overall majority, at just 12 seats it was relatively small and declared insufficient by the Prime Minister, Theresa May, when she decided to precipitate the 2017 election. Meanwhile, instead of providing the Conservatives with a larger and safer overall majority, the 2017 contest saw the party lose its majority entirely, forcing it to form a minority government that is sustained by a 'confidence and supply' arrangement with the largest of the Northern Ireland parties, the Democratic Unionists (DUP).

It would seem that it is time to look afresh at the operation of the single member plurality system. The recent failures to deliver safe overall majorities have not only had an important impact on how governments have been formed, but also would appear to raise questions about the continued validity of the principal argument in favour of the single member plurality system. If single member

*John Curtice, School of Government and Public Policy, University of Strathclyde,
j.curtice@strath.ac.uk

doi:10.1093/pa/gsx060

plurality can no longer be relied upon to produce majoritarian government, per-haps the case for its continued use should be revisited. On the other hand, maybe the outcome of the last three elections has been a sequence of accidents that is unlikely to be repeated, no more than a temporary deviation from a pattern that can soon be expected to return.

1. Background

Why might the single member plurality system be expected usually to produce an overall majority for whichever party wins most seats, even if that party has secured considerably less than 50% of the vote? There are two main reasons. The first is the way that it is likely to discriminate against third parties; the second is how the system can be expected to exaggerate the relative success of the winning party.

Under the plurality system as implemented in elections to the UK House of Commons, the outcome in seats is determined by who comes first in each of 650 wholly separate constituency contests. Inevitably meeting that requirement nor-mally means that a candidate has to win a relatively large proportion of the vote. A party that wins relatively few votes across the country as a whole may conse-quently find it nigh on impossible to win sufficient votes to come first in any par-ticular constituency. As a result, such parties can struggle to secure much, if any representation in the House of Commons. Indeed, aware of the fact that such a party is unlikely to win locally, voters may even be dissuaded from voting for it in the first place (Blais and Carty, 1991). In short, according to what is sometimes known as 'Duverger's Law', small third parties not only struggle to convert votes into seats, but also may well find it difficult to win votes in the first place (Duverger, 1954).

Meanwhile, the party that comes first nationally may well repeat that feat in many an individual constituency. What may be no more than narrow victories locally can be repeated in constituency after constituency, such that the party's success in terms of votes is rapidly exaggerated when it comes to the allocation of seats. Indeed, this tendency has been formulated in the form of a 'cube law' (Butler, 1951; Gudgin and Taylor, 1979; Taagerpera and Shugart, 1989). This states that if under single member plurality the two largest parties win votes in the ratio A:B, the seats that they win will be divided in the ratio $A^3:B^3$. This implies that if a party won, say, 51% of the votes cast for the two largest parties, it would win 53% of the seats—and thus, so long as no more than a handful of seats were won by smaller, third parties, even a narrow electoral success could be expected to deliver the winner a safe overall majority.

However, neither the cube law nor Duverger's Law, are in fact laws that neces-sarily apply whenever the single member plurality system is in use. Both are more accurately described as 'tendencies', that is, patterns whose presence is, above all, contingent upon the electoral geography of party support. The cube law only applies if there are plenty of constituencies that are close contests between the two largest parties, and which thus may well change hands as a result of a relatively small swing of votes from one party to the other. Meanwhile, third parties only find it difficult to secure electoral representation if their votes are evenly spread across the country as opposed to being concentrated in particular constituencies. Neither condition necessarily holds in practice.

2. Marginal Seats

Table 2.1 presents a number of statistics that describe the electoral geography of the division of the votes cast for the Conservatives and Labour (alone) at each election since 1955. Kendall and Stuart (1951) showed that the relationship between seats and votes for those two parties will only reflect the expectations of the cube law if the distribution of the division of the vote for those two parties across constituencies approximates that of a normal distribution with a standard deviation of 13.7. The statistics on the right-hand side of the table enable us to assess how far this condition has been met at each election. The standard deviation is a summary measure of how much the values in question (in this case, the Conservatives' percentage share of the vote cast for the two largest parties, Conservative and Labour) vary from one reading to another (in this case, across constituencies). The larger the figure, the greater the extent of the variation. Meanwhile, the kurtosis is a measure of the extent to which the shape of the distribution matches that of a normal distribution, and in particular whether the values of the distribution are as concentrated in its centre as in the case of a normal distribution. A positive figure indicates that the values are even more concentrated in the centre than would be the case with a normal distribution, while a negative figure means that they are less concentrated in that way.

From these two statistics, we can see that in the 1950s and 1960s the conditions required for the cube law to operate were largely satisfied. The standard deviation was only a little above 13.7, while the kurtosis was only slightly negative. This meant that there were plenty of seats that were marginal between the Conservatives and Labour and thus could change hands of a result of a relatively small swing between them. This is confirmed by the evidence on the left-hand side of the table, which indicates the number of seats that might be regarded as marginal. These are defined as those seats where neither party would have won more than 55% of the votes cast for Conservative and Labour alone (hereafter, the 'two-party vote') in the event that nationally the two parties had won exactly the same share of the vote at that election. In the 1950s and 1960s around 160 seats could be classified as marginal in this way, representing just under the 30% of seats that would be required to satisfy the conditions for the cube law (Curtice and Steed, 1982).

Table 2.1 Distribution of the two-party vote, 1955-2017

	Marginals		Two-Party Vote	
	No.	%	Standard Deviation	Kurtosis
1955	166	27.2	13.5	−0.25
1959	157	25.7	13.8	−0.29
1964	166	27.3	14.1	−0.45
1966	155	25.6	13.8	−0.46
1970	149	24.5	14.3	−0.27
1974 (Feb)	119	19.9	16.1	−0.68
1974 (Oct)	98	16.4	16.8	−0.82
1979	108	17.8	16.9	−0.87
1983	80	13.2	20.0	−1.05
1987	87	14.4	21.4	−1.03
1992	98	16.1	20.2	−1.03
1997	114	19.6	18.1	−0.85
2001	114	19.7	18.3	−0.82
2005	104	18.8	19.7	−0.96
2010	85	15.0	22.2	−1.08
2015	74	13.1	21.7	−1.19
2017	89	15.3	18.6	−0.89

Marginal Seat: Seat where Conservative share of two-party vote - (overall Conservative share of two-party vote -50%) lies within the range 45% -55%
Two-party vote: Votes cast for Conservative and Labour combined.
Table based only on seats won by Conservative or Labour at that election and contested by both parties.
Source: Curtice (2015a) and author's calculations.

However, these conditions have never pertained since. The number of marginal seats fell markedly at the February 1974 election, as the standard deviation of the Conservative and Labour vote increased and the kurtosis became more negative. The decline continued yet further through to 1983, was then reversed somewhat, most notably at the three elections won by Labour under Tony Blair's leadership between 1997 and 2005, but returned again thereafter such that the number of marginal seats has been relatively low once again at each of the last three elections. True, there was actually a modest increase in the number of marginal seats in 2017 (and an accompanying fall in the standard deviation and the kurtosis), but given that the figure was already at an all-time low in 2015, this still meant that the number of marginal seats was relatively low.

These changes in the distribution of Conservative and Labour support have been occasioned by variations in the swing of votes between them. One of the persistent features of elections though to the 1980s was for Labour to advance more (or fall back less) in the northern half of Great Britain and in more urban constituencies, while the Conservatives' vote improved most (or fell back less) in the southern half of the country and in more rural seats (Curtice and Steed, 1982; 1986). This eventually had the effect of making one half of the country increasingly safer for Labour, the other half more of a bulwark for the Conservatives, with the result that there were fewer seats where both parties were relatively strong—and thus marginal between them. This pattern was partially, but in the event only temporarily, reversed by New Labour's attempts to win over the southern half of Britain (Curtice, 2009), but it then set in again thereafter. Both the 2010 and the 2015 elections saw the Conservatives advance more strongly (and Labour suffer less) in constituencies where the party was already strong (Curtice *et al.*, 2010; 2016), a pattern that again was reversed—but only partly— by the tendency in the 2017 election for the Conservative vote to increase most in more working-class seats that had voted strongly in favour of leaving the European Union (see Denver, chapter 1, this volume). Notable though this tendency at the 2017 election was, it was nothing like enough to restore the former ability of the electoral system to exaggerate systematically the lead of the largest party over the second party.

3.   Third Parties

Despite the supposed lack of incentive for voters to support smaller parties, one of the striking features of post-war British politics has been a marked increase in support for parties other than the Conservatives and Labour (see Table 2.2). In the immediate post-war period, Britain's two main parties enjoyed a virtual duopoly of party support, with over 95% of votes cast in the 1951 and 1955 general elections going to one or other of them. But thereafter, that proportion has seemed to have been in long-term decline, such that by 2010 the Conservatives and Labour secured fewer than two out of every three votes cast. So far as dissuading voters from voting for third parties is concerned, the single member plurality system has long not been performing as it is supposedly meant to.

Not even the collapse of the Liberal Democrat vote—hitherto the main variety of third party voting—in the 2015 election occasioned a marked increase in the joint level of support for the Conservatives and Labour. For the Liberal Democrats' decline was counterbalanced by the remarkable success of UKIP in winning one in eight of all votes cast across the UK, and that of the SNP in winning half the vote in Scotland. However, in 2017 Liberal Democrat support remained well below what it had been at any point since 1974, UKIP's vote collapsed and the SNP fell back too. As a result, at just over 82%, the combined level of support for the Conservatives and Labour was higher in 2017 than at any time since 1970, and the joint revival of their fortunes has led some to suggest that the 2017 election marks a return to the two-party politics that the country enjoyed in the immediate post-war period.

Table 2.2 Trends in party support, United Kingdom, 1945-2017

	Con and Lab %	Liberal/Alliance/Liberal Democrat %	Others %
1945	87.6	9.0	3.4
1950	89.5	9.1	1.4
1951	96.8	2.6	0.6
1955	96.1	2.7	1.2
1959	93.2	5.9	0.9
1964	87.5	11.2	1.3
1966	89.9	8.5	1.5
1970	89.5	7.5	3.0
1974(F)	75.1	19.3	5.6
1974(O)	75.1	18.3	6.7
1979	80.8	13.8	5.4
1983	70.0	25.4	4.6
1987	73.1	22.6	4.4
1992	76.3	17.8	5.8
1997	73.9	16.8	9.3
2001	72.4	18.3	9.4
2005	67.6	22.0	10.4
2010	65.1	23.0	11.9
2015	67.3	7.9	24.7
2017	82.4	7.4	10.3

Sources: Rallings and Thrasher (2012); Cowley and Kavanagh (2016); http://www.bbc.co.uk/news/election/2017/results

However, despite this sharp drop in electoral support for third parties, they still constitute a considerable presence in the House of Commons. As is evident in Table 2.3, although the Liberal Democrats' representation remains well below what it was at any time between 1983 and 2010, there are still as many as 70 third-party MPs in the House of Commons, well above the number present at any point before 1997. As far as the composition of the legislature is concerned, the UK is still a long way from having returned to the two-party system of the immediate post-war period.

The single-member plurality system does not necessarily discriminate against smaller parties. It only does so if its vote is much the same from constituency to constituency (Gudgin and Taylor, 1979). That, for example, is the fate that befell UKIP in 2015 when its 12.6% of the UK vote was rewarded with just one seat (or 0.15% of the total). The standard deviation of its share of the vote in the 624 seats it fought at that election was just 6.2, well below, for example, the equivalent figures of 16.9 and 16.5 for the Conservatives and Labour. In contrast, one of the reasons why the Liberal Democrats were able to win more seats between 1997 and 2010 than they did between 1983 and 1992, even though the party's share of the

Table 2.3 Seats won by third parties in UK general elections, 1945-2017

	Liberal/Alliance/Liberal Democrat	Others (GB)	Others (NI)	Total
1945	12 (1)	21 (7)	4	36
1950	9	1	2	12
1951	6	0	3	9
1955	6	0	2	8
1959	6	1	0	7
1964	9	0	0	9
1966	12	0	1	13
1970	6	2	4	12
1974(F)	14	11	12	37
1974(O)	13	14	12	39
1979	11	4	12	27
1983	23	4	17	44
1987	22	6	17	45
1992	20	7	17	44
1997	46	11	18	75
2001	52	10	18	80
2005	62	12	18	92
2010	57	10	18	85
2015	8	61	18	87
2017	12	40	18	70

Figures in brackets in 1945 are seats won on 'university seats' elected by single transferable vote.
Sources: Rallings and Thrasher (2012); Cowley and Kavanagh (2016); http://www.bbc.co.uk/news/election/2017/results

national vote was still much the same, is that the party's vote became somewhat more geographically unevenly spread. Even so, the Liberal Democrats too are at a relative disadvantage on this front. Indeed, at 8.8 the standard deviation of the party's share of the vote was (though slightly above the 8.4 figure that pertained in 2015) somewhat lower in 2017 than the 10.4 figure that was in evidence in 2010, and is no higher than the equivalent figure for 1987. In short, not only has the level of Liberal Democrat support dropped away at the last two elections, but it has also become rather more evenly spread once again.

However, no such difficulties face the Scottish National Party, Plaid Cymru or the parties in Northern Ireland. An entirely separate party system emerged in Northern Ireland in the 1970s, and that continues to be the position (while the number of Northern Irish MPs is now 50% higher than it was before 1983). Plaid Cymru won only 10.4% of the vote in Wales in 2017—and just 0.5% of the UK-wide vote—but its support is heavily concentrated in North and West Wales where the Welsh language is most widely spoken and this proved sufficient for the party to secure four seats, or 0.6% of the total. Indeed, Wales' nationalist party has been able to win either three or four seats at every election since 1987.

But, as in the last parliament, the largest third party in the new House of Commons is by far the SNP. This is despite the fact that the party's share of the vote in Scotland fell by as much as 13 points to 36.9%, and, indeed, even though its support fell more heavily in places where it was previously strongest, leaving its vote very evenly spread within Scotland.[1] For that said, the SNP vote is still wholly concentrated within Scotland, while the party was still the single most popular party north of the border. As a result, it was still able to win as many as 35 seats, or 5.4% of all the seats in the Commons, well above the 3.0% of the UK-wide vote that the party secured. There was little sign here of single member plurality discriminating against smaller parties.

4.   Electoral Bias

One consequence of the Prime Minister's decision to precipitate an early election is that the contest was fought on the same constituency boundaries as the two previous elections (and indeed in Scotland, the last three). In England, these boundaries had been drawn up on the basis of the registered electorate in 2000, and in Scotland and Wales only a year or two (respectively) later, and thus were at risk of being badly out of date. The Conservatives had long sought both to speed up the process of reviewing boundaries and to make the rules under which they were drawn more equitable, reckoning that the current system put the party at a disadvantage as compared with Labour. Predominantly Labour-voting Wales is particularly over-represented in the House of Commons, while a long-term tendency for Britain's population to move out of (mostly Labour voting) inner city constituencies to (more Conservative) rural and suburban ones has meant that over time a gap has tended to emerge between the average electorate in Conservative held seats and that in Labour held ones. However, despite the passage in 2011 of legislation that reset the rules for drawing up parliamentary constituencies, its implementation had been scuppered by Labour and the Liberal Democrats before the 2015 election (Curtice, 2015*b*), while after the 2015 election the Boundary Commissions embarked on a process that did not require them to submit their recommendations to Parliament before 2018.

The argument that the single member plurality electoral system facilitates alternating single party majority government rests not only on the expectation that it systematically exaggerates the lead of the largest party over that of its nearest competitor, but also that it is colour blind in so doing. In other words, the system is expected to benefit the largest party irrespective of whether that party is the Conservatives or Labour. However, inequality in the size of constituencies

---

[1]The standard deviation of the party's share of the vote fell from 8.8 in 2010 and 7.0 in 2015 to just 4.8 in 2017.

can undermine the realisation of this expectation. If Labour held seats typically have fewer registered voters than Conservative ones, this could make it easier for Labour to win a safe overall majority than it is for the Conservatives (Gudgin and Taylor, 1979). Perhaps, then, the main reason why the Conservatives failed to win an overall majority in the 2017 election is because the system was 'biased' against them rather than because of a shortage of marginal seats.

However, inequality in the size of constituency electorates is not the only reason why one of the two largest parties might have an advantage over the other. If the size of the registered electorate is much the same everywhere, but the turnout is typically lower in seats won by party A than it is in those won by party B, this will tend to depress party A's share of the overall national vote without necessarily having any impact on its tally of seats. In other words, the effective size of a constituency depends not just on its registered electorate but also the turnout.

One simple way of assessing whether a party benefits from a difference in the effective size of constituencies is to compare its overall share of the national vote (computed by adding up the votes across all constituencies) with the average (mean) of the shares of the vote won by that party in each constituency. If a party tends to win seats that contain fewer voters, its mean share of the vote will be lower than its overall share (Soper and Rydon, 1958). Focusing on the Conservative share of the two-party vote (as defined above), the first column of Table 2.4 shows the difference between the mean and the overall share of that vote at each election since 1955. A positive figure means that the mean share was higher than the overall share (and thus differences in constituency size were to the advantage of the Conservatives) while a negative one means that the mean share was less than the overall share (and differences in size were to Labour's advantage). The table also shows for those elections that preceded a boundary review an estimate of what this figure would have been if the new boundaries had already been in place, thereby giving us an indication of the extent to which a boundary review reversed any emerging inequality in the size of constituencies.

These figures reveal what up to now has been a very consistent pattern. The longer that has elapsed since the last boundary review, the greater the difference—in a negative direction—between the Conservatives' mean share of the two-party vote and their overall share. Thus, for example, after the boundaries were redrawn after the 1979 election, there was only a −0.1 difference between the two measures, but by 1992 this had grown to −1.2. In other words, there was merit in the Conservatives' claim that delays in the process of redrawing constituency boundaries tend to be to their disadvantage.

However, the 2017 election marks a break with this pattern. Even though the election was fought on the same boundaries as in 2010 and 2015, the difference between the mean and the overall Conservative share of the two-party vote actually fell from -1.6 in 2015 to just -0.4, suggesting that the Conservatives suffered less

Table 2.4 Measures of two-party bias, 1955-2017

		Conservative % two-party vote	
	Mean - Overall	Median - Mean	Median - Overall
1955	+ 0.3	+ 0.6	+ 0.9
1959	+ 0.4	+ 0.8	+ 1.2
1964	+ 0.1	+ 0.4	+ 0.5
1966	− 0.3	+ 0.2	− 0.1
1970	− 0.9	+ 0.8	− 0.1
1970 (NT)	− 0.1	+ 0.5	+ 0.4
1974 (Feb)	− 0.1	− 0.5	− 0.5
1974 (Oct)	− 0.3	+ 1.4	+ 1.1
1979	− 0.7	− 0.5	− 1.2
1979 (NT)	− 0.1	+ 0.9	+ 0.9
1983	− 0.5	+ 1.7	+ 1.2
1987	− 0.8	+ 1.4	+ 0.6
1992	− 1.2	− 0.0	− 1.2
1992 (NT)	− 0.2	− 0.7	− 0.9
1997	− 0.4	− 1.6	− 2.0
2001	− 1.4	− 1.5	− 2.9
2001 (NT)	− 1.1	− 1.4	− 2.5
2005	− 2.1	− 1.1	− 3.2
2005 (NT)	−1.5	−1.0	−2.5
2010	−1.3	−0.8	−2.1
2015	−1.6	+2.1	+0.5
2017	−0.4	+0.6	+0.2

NT: Notional results based on estimates of what the outcome would have been if that election had been fought on the new constituency boundaries that were introduced at the subsequent election. The 2001 redistribution (together with a reduction in the number of seats) was confined to Scotland, while the 2005 one only occurred in England and Wales.
Two-party vote: Votes cast for Conservative and Labour combined.
Figures based on all seats in Great Britain. Northern Ireland excluded.
Source: Author's calculations.

from differences in the effective size of constituencies than at any election since 1997. Evidently a dramatic and unprecedented change occurred in 2017.

One possibility, of course, is that the pattern of population movement has changed, such that people are no longer moving out of Labour-voting inner city constituencies. That process has, indeed, slowed in recent years—but it has not stopped (Champion, 2016). Another possibility is that the introduction of a system of individual electoral registration, the final step towards which was taken shortly after the 2015 election, had a differential impact on the registered electorate in Labour and Conservative constituencies. However, much of the concern about this step focused on its impact on inner city constituencies and those with relatively large student populations (Electoral Commission, 2016; White, 2016). In fact, the gap between the registered electorate in the average Conservative seat and the average Labour one grew somewhat between 2015 and 2017. Amongst those seats won by the Conservatives in 2015, the registered electorate grew on average between 2015 and 2017 by 1240, while in those won by Labour, it grew by just 655. As a result, by the time of the 2017 election there was now a difference of over 4400 between the registered electorate in the average Conservative-held constituency and that in the typical Labour one.

What does explain the decline in the disadvantage that the Conservatives suffer from differences in the size of constituencies are two other developments. The first is a change in the pattern of turnout, the second a decline in the extent to which the Conservative vote is concentrated in larger constituencies. In the 2015 election, turnout stood on average at 68.7% in the average Conservative held constituency, but only at 61.9% in the typical Labour one, a difference of just over seven points. However, while turnout increased in 2017 by 2.3 points in the typical Conservative seat, it rose by 4.2 points in the average Labour one, thereby reducing the difference in turnout to five points (or by some 1300 votes).[2]

The second development arises from the fact that, as we noted above, the Conservatives advanced more strongly in 2017 in relatively working-class, Labour constituencies, which typically have smaller electorates. In general, the smaller the constituency, both in terms of the size of the registered electorate and the level of turnout, the more the Conservative vote increased. For example, in seats where fewer than 72,000 people were registered to vote, the Conservative share of the vote increased on average by just over seven points, whereas in those constituencies where more than 77,000 names appeared on the register the party's vote increased by just over four points. Meanwhile, in constituencies where the turnout was less than 65%, the Conservative share of the vote increased on average by nearly ten points, whereas in seats where the turnout was more than 71% the party's vote increased by just over three points. In short, rather more of the Conservative vote was cast at this election in constituencies with a relatively low effective size, thereby serving to diminish the disadvantage that the party has suffered hitherto from differences in constituency size.

Differences in constituency size are not, however, the only reason why the single member plurality system can reward one of the two largest parties more richly than the other. A party can also be advantaged or disadvantaged by how efficiently its vote is distributed across constituencies. A party's vote can be said to be distributed efficiently if it wins plenty of seats by relatively small margins, and both wins relatively few by a large margin and loses relatively few by a narrow

---

[2]To this we can add the fact that votes for third parties also fell by a couple of points more in seats previously held by Labour. The difference in the size of the two-party vote in seats being defended by the Conservatives and those by Labour fell by just over 700 votes.

margin. Such a pattern means a party is maximising the extent to which its votes translate into seats (Gudgin and Taylor, 1979).

One way of assessing whether one party has a more efficiently distributed vote is to compare its mean share of the vote across all constituencies with its median share (Soper and Rydon, 1958). The median is the value that divides a party's constituency performances into two equal halves, one half comprising seats where it does better (than the median), the other where it does worse. Given that to win any kind of overall majority, the Conservatives and Labour need their median constituency share of the two-party vote to be above 50%, their performance in the median constituency is clearly an important indicator of how they will fare under the single member plurality system.

As the second column of Table 2.4 shows, this potential source of bias has in practice varied over time. In much of the 1950s and 1960s the Conservative vote was more efficiently spread, as indicated by the fact that its median share of the two-party vote was greater than its mean share; the principal explanation lay in the fact that Labour tended to win more seats by very large majorities (Butler, 1963). However, for much of the 1990s and 2000s it was Labour who benefited, after the Conservative vote became more evenly spread (Curtice and Steed, 1997). Then at the 2015 election, the roles were reversed again, following a particularly strong Conservative performance in marginal seats the party was defending (Curtice, 2015a; Curtice *et al.*, 2016).

However, it seems that much of the advantage that the Conservatives gained in 2015 has not been sustained. The party's median share of the two-party vote was only a little higher in 2017 than its mean share. The explanation seems to lie in the relative weakness of the Conservative advance in more middle-class seats. As a result, the party was losing ground relative to Labour most heavily in seats that it already held, thereby reversing some of the distributional advantage it had secured in 2015.[3]

Thus, both of the sources of potential bias addressed by Table 2.4 were less in evidence in 2017 than in 2015, and in so far as they were still present their net effect was largely to cancel each other out (see the final column of Table 2.4). Much the same story is found if we examine another potential source of bias not addressed in Table 2.4, which is the extent to which parties waste votes in seats that are won by third parties. At the 2015 election, following the Conservatives' success in capturing many a Liberal Democrat seat and Labour's heavy losses to

---

[3]On average, the Conservative share of the two-party vote fell by as much as 6.5 points in seats the party won in 2015, while it actually increased, by half a point, in seats that Labour was defending. Of particular note is the fact that in Conservative held seats where the party's lead over Labour was fewer than 15 points, the party's share of the two-party vote fell on average by 3.6 points, well above the average for all seats of 2.1 points.

the SNP, the Conservatives won a lower share of the vote (on average 15.6%) than Labour (23.3%) in such seats, a sharp reversal of what had hitherto been the position. However, a sharp recovery in Conservative support in Scotland (see Mitchell & Henderson, chapter 6, this volume) together with a squeeze on the Labour advance in some Liberal Democrat battlegrounds (Curtice, 2017) ensured that this gap disappeared. On average the Conservatives won 25.7% of the vote in seats won by third parties, almost exactly the same as the 25.9% won by Labour.

In short, there is little sign of the electoral system treating Labour more favourably than the Conservatives in 2017, and the failure of the Conservatives to win an overall majority certainly cannot be said to be the result of any such bias. This becomes quite evident if we simulate what would happen if the two parties were to win the same share of the vote nationally as a result of a 1.25% swing of votes from Conservative to Labour in each and every constituency as compared with what happened in 2017. The outcome (assuming no change in the level of support for third parties) would be Conservatives 298 seats, Labour 286, indicating that, if anything, the system was still treating the Conservatives rather more favourably than Labour.[4] That said, as we might anticipate from our analysis, the net Conservative advantage of 12 seats in this simulation compares with an advantage of 46 seats when the equivalent calculation was made after the 2015 election. The electoral system may not have been as kind to the Conservatives in 2017 as it had been two years previously, but this does not mean that it was treating the party unfairly. Rather, some of the good fortune that it had enjoyed in 2015 failed to repeat itself.

5.　Implications

We have identified three key features of how the single member plurality electoral system operated in the 2017 election. First, as in most previous elections, the ability of the system to exaggerate the lead of the largest party over its principal rival was constrained by a paucity of marginal seats. Second, the system was not particularly effective at denying representation to third parties, many of whose support was geographically concentrated. Third, the system was more (though not perfectly) even handed in its relative treatment of the two largest parties. In short, much of the system's potential to produce a disproportional outcome was not realised. Indeed, the outcome of the 2017 election was the most proportional since 1970. According to the most commonly used measure, the disproportionality score for the 2017 election is 10.1, well down on the near record high of 24.0

---

[4]We might note too that on the same assumptions Labour would have needed nearly a five- point lead, twice that of the Conservatives, to win the 318 seats the Conservatives secured in 2017.

recorded in 2015.[5] Such disproportionality as was in evidence is largely accounted for by an over-representation of the Conservatives (their 42.5% of the UK vote secured them 48.9% of the seats) and an under-representation of the Liberal Democrats (7.4% of the vote, 1.8% of the seats). Most other parties (some very small parties, including UKIP, apart) ended up with something quite close to their proportional share.

Given the relative proportionality of the outcome, it is not surprising that the system should have failed to have produced an overall majority for one party, even though at 2.5 points the lead of the largest party over the second party was bigger than that enjoyed by the winning party (in Great Britain) in four of the seven elections held between 1950 and 1970, none of which resulted in a hung parliament. There were too few marginal seats and too many won by third parties for an overall majority to occur. Yet the use of the single member system did have one important consequence. In treating relatively favourably third parties whose vote is geographically concentrated, its use ensured that it was one of those parties, the DUP, that proved best placed to secure leverage in the new parliament via a confidence and supply arrangement—an arrangement that proved highly controversial within the Conservative party as well as beyond it (*Financial Times*, 2017).

This outcome can be compared with what might have happened if a system of proportional representation had been in place. In Table 2.5 we show what would have happened if a system of regional proportional representation (based on the same regions as used in elections to the European Parliament) had been in place, but with a requirement (as in elections to the London Assembly) that a party needs to win 5% of the vote in a region before it is entitled to win any seats in that region—a stipulation that would ensure that both UKIP and the Greens would fail to secure any representation, as well as deny the Liberal Democrats representation in some regions. Under this scenario, the Liberal Democrats, and not the SNP, would be the third largest party in the House of Commons. Moreover, the only viable administration would have been a Conservative-led one backed (in some way or the other) by the Liberal Democrats. Such an arrangement would doubtless have had its own critics. But the contrast does mean that while single member plurality failed to avoid the need for a post-election deal between two parties, it had a clear effect on between which parties that deal was made (Curtice and Steed, 1982).

---

[5]This figure is the Loosemore-Hanby index, which is the sum of the absolute differences between each party's share of the vote and their share of the seats divided by two (Loosemore-Hanby, 1971). Measuring disproportionality using the Gallagher (6.7) or Sainte-Laguë (12.0) indices (Renwick, 2015) leads to the same conclusion.

Table 2.5 Projected outcome of the 2017 election under regional proportional representation

	Projected Seats	% Share of Seats	% Seats - % Votes
Conservatives	292	44.9	+2.6
Labour	278	42.8	+2.8
Liberal Democrats	39	6.0	−1.4
SNP	21	3.2	+0.2
PC	3	0.5	0.0
UKIP	0	0.0	−1.8
Green	0	0.0	−1.6
Others (NI)	17	2.6	–

Seats allocated by Government Region. Total number of seats in each region proportional to current electorate using Sainte-Laguë divisor. Division of seats within each region determined by D'Hondt divisor, but confined to those parties in a region that won at least 5% of the vote.
Source: Author's Calculations.

6. Conclusion

The Prime Minister called the 2017 election in the confident expectation that it would deliver her a landslide majority of the kind once enjoyed by both Margaret Thatcher and Tony Blair. Instead, the outcome served as a further reminder that nowadays the electoral system cannot necessarily be relied upon to deliver any party an overall majority, let alone a large one. The ability of the system repeatedly to deliver such an outcome requires more marginal seats and a less geographically concentrated pattern of third-party support than was evident in 2017, or indeed has been evident for some time. As a result, the argument that the system facilitates alternating single-party majority government has come to look less convincing than ever before. A new debate about the merits of electoral reform would seem to be timely, yet whether it will occur remains to be seen.

References

Bingham Powell, G. Jr. (2000) *Elections as Instruments of Democracy: majoritarian and proportional visions*, New Haven, CT, Yale University Press.

Blais, A. and Carty, R. (1991) 'The Psychological Impact of Electoral Laws: Measuring Duverger's Elusive Factor', *British Journal of Political Science*, **21**, 79–93.

Butler, D. (1951) 'An Examination of the Results'. In Nicholas, H., *The British General Election of 1950*, Basingstoke, Macmillan, pp. 306–333.

Butler, D. (1963) *The Electoral System in Britain*, 2nd edn, Oxford, Clarendon Press.

Champion, A. (2016) 'Internal Migration and the Spatial Distribution of the Population'. In Champion, A. and Falkingham, J. (eds), *Population Change in the United Kingdom*, London, Rowman and Littlefield, pp. 125–142.

Cowley, P. and Kavanagh, D. (2016) *The British General Election of 2015*, Basingstoke, Palgrave Macmillan.

Curtice, J. (2009) 'Neither Representative Nor Accountable: First Past the Post in Britain'. In Grofman, B., Blais, A., and Bowler, S. (eds), *Duverger's Law of Plurality Voting*, New York, NY, Springer, pp. 27–46.

Curtice, J. (2015*a*) 'A Return to Normality? How the Electoral System Operated', *Parliamentary Affairs*, **68 (suppl. 1)**, 25–40.

Curtice, J. (2015*b*) 'The Coalition, Elections and Referendums'. In Seldon, A. and Finn, M. (eds), *The Coalition Effect, 2010-15*, Cambridge, Cambridge University Press, pp. 577–600.

Curtice, J. (2017) 'The 2017 Election: A Missed Opportunity?', *Journal of Liberal History*, **96**, 10–17.

Curtice, J., Fisher, S. and Ford, R. (2010) 'Appendix 2: An Analysis of the Results'. In Kavanagh, D. and Cowley, P., *The British General Election of 2010*, Basingstoke, Palgrave Macmillan, pp. 385–426.

Curtice, J., Fisher, S. and Ford, R. (2016) 'Appendix 1: The Results Analysed'. In Cowley, P. and Kavanagh, D., *The British General Election of 2015*, London, Palgrave Macmillan, pp. 387–431.

Curtice, J. and Steed M. (1982) 'Electoral Choice and the Production of Government: The Changing Operation of the Electoral System in the UK Since 1955', *British Journal of Political Science*, **12**, 249–298.

Curtice, J. and Steed, M. (1986) 'Proportionality and Exaggeration in the British Electoral System', *Electoral Studies*, **9**, 209–228.

Curtice, J. and Steed, M. (1997) 'Appendix 2: The Results Analysed'. In Butler, D. and Kavanagh, D., *The British General Election of 1997*, Basingstoke, Macmillan, pp. 295–325.

Duverger. M. (1954) *Political Parties: Their Organisation and Activity in the Modern State*, London, Methuen.

Electoral Commission (2016) *The December 2015 Electoral Registers in Great Britain: Accuracy and Completeness of the Registers in Great Britain and the Transition to Individual Electoral Registration*, London, Electoral Commission, accessed at http://www.electoralcommission.org.uk/__data/assets/pdf_file/0005/213377/The-December-2015-electoral-registers-in-Great-Britain-REPORT.pdf on 8 August 2017.

Financial Times (2017) 'A Prime Minister Held to Ransom by the DUP', 26 June, accessed at https://www.ft.com/content/d826df42-5a6e-11e7-b553-e2df1b0c3220 on 8 August 2017.

Gudgin, G. and Taylor, P. (1979), *Seats, Votes and the Spatial Organisation of Elections*, London, Pion.

Kendall, M. and Stuart, A. (1951) 'The Law of Cubic Proportions in Election Results', *British Journal of Sociology*, **1**, 183–197.

Loosemore, J. and Hanby, V. (1971) 'The Theoretical Limits of Maximum Distortion: Some Analytic Expressions for Electoral Systems', *British Journal of Political Science*, **1**, 467–477.

Norton, P. (1997) 'The Case for First Past the Post', *Representation*, **34**, 84–88.

Rawlings, C. and Thrasher, M. (2012) *British Electoral Facts 1832-2012*, London, Biteback.

Renwick, A. (2011) *A Citizens' Guide to Electoral Reform*, London, Biteback.

Renwick, A. (2015) 'Was the 2015 Election the Most Disproportional Ever? It Depends How You Measure It', accessed at https://constitution-unit.com/2015/06/29/was-the-2015-election-the-most-disproportional-ever-it-depends-how-you-measure-it/ on 8 August 2017.

Soper, C. and Rydon, J. (1958) 'Under-representation and Electoral Prediction', *Australian Journal of Politics and History*, **4**, 94–106.

Taagerpera, R. and Shugart, M. (1989) *Seats and Votes: The Effects and Determinants of Electoral Systems*, New Haven, CT, Yale University Press.

White, I. (2016) *Individual Electoral Registration*, Briefing Paper 6764, London, House of Commons Library, accessed at http://researchbriefings.parliament.uk/ResearchBriefing/Summary/SN06764 on 8 August 2017.

TIM BALE AND PAUL WEBB*

'We Didn't See it Coming':[1]
The Conservatives

Theresa May's decision to call an early election was clearly a foolish one—but only in hindsight. After all, opinion polls had been showing the Conservatives way ahead of Labour for months and they had not long before chalked up the first by-election gain from the opposition by a governing party for thirty-five years. Moreover, on almost every leadership measure one cared to mention, Mrs May was beating Labour leader Jeremy Corbyn hands down. And if anyone had counselled her to wait for the results of local election results before deciding, they could easily have been accused of looking unduly cautious: in the event, in England and Wales the Conservatives gained nearly 400 seats, Labour lost nearly 250 and UKIP over 140, while the much-anticipated Liberal Democrat revival came to nothing; north of the border, Labour and the SNP both lost support, allowing the Conservatives to claim second place. Hardly surprising, then, that all the talk was not of whether May would win but by how many seats, and what would that mean both for Brexit and the future of the Labour Party.

1. A personalised campaign with no personality

But behind the scenes at Conservative Central Office (CCHQ), apparently, not everything was tickety-boo. Well-sourced accounts (albeit conflicting ones) of the Conservative campaign suggest that it was, in fact, plagued with problems from the start (Shipman, 2017, McTague *et al.*, 2017). Overseas consultants Lynton Crosby, Mark Textor, and Jim Messina had, along with CCHQ veteran Stephen Gilbert, agreed to get the band back together in order to repeat their 2015 success. But not all of them were convinced that their new lead singer was entirely wise to have called the election in the first place (Walters, 2017).

*Tim Bale, School of Politics and International Relations, Queen Mary University of London, t.bale@qmul.ac.uk; Paul Webb, Department of Politics, University of Sussex, p.webb@sussex.ac.uk

[1]Theresa May, interviewed by Emma Barnett, BBC Radio 5 Live, 13 June 2017.

And none of the band, it seems, were happy with the influence and control afforded to her controversial personal managers, Nick Timothy and Fiona Hill (see Perrior, 2017). For their part (see Timothy, 2017) May's advisors were apparently unhappy at the way their boss was thrust front and centre of what, even in an era of personalized politics, started out as an exceptionally presidential campaign—one which, realising that voters were beginning to worry about the impact of continued austerity on key public services, aimed to capitalize on the fact that the PM was more popular than not only the leader of the opposition but her own party, too.

As a result, the party's direct mail and leaflets played down Tory candidates' Conservative Party affiliation in favour of associating them with the 'strong and stable' prime minister. But, May—by all accounts something of an introvert— was incapable of, or at least uncomfortable with, getting out there and convincingly selling herself. So, rather than being forced to meet ordinary voters, she was instead smuggled into all-ticket events in soulless out-of-town warehouses filled (if that's really the right word) with her own party activists gathered together at short notice for yet another unconvincing photo op. And even those rallies were too often held in constituencies that Labour held on to rather than in those which, in hindsight, the Tories should have been ensuring really were as safe as they, in their hubris, believed. Neither the optics nor the itinerary, in other words, did the PM or her party any favours.

Nor, in all probability, did May's reluctance to take part in the kind of televised debates that had enlivened the elections of 2010 and (to a lesser extent) 2015. That reluctance was understandable—a format that requires a politician to think on their feet and at least pretend to answer questions from 'real people' was unlikely to suit her (see Prince, 2017). And as the incumbent with a record to defend, as well as the apparent front-runner, May probably had more to lose than to gain from appearing. But when Labour suddenly announced that Jeremy Corbyn had decided, after all, to take part in the big, televised leaders' debate on 31 May, the PM's refusal to do the same made her look scared of getting into the ring with him—and she looked even worse, perhaps, when it was revealed that Home Secretary, Amber Rudd, who deputised for her, had agreed to do so just days after the death of her father. May's no-show also re-doubled what by then was already widespread criticism of a Conservative campaign clearly desperate to protect the woman who journalists had cruelly dubbed 'the Maybot' from contact with members of the public—in marked contrast to Labour's Jeremy Corbyn, who was constantly pictured speaking spontaneously and authentically to ecstatic crowds.

Yet when May did come into contact with 'real people', albeit in a television studio, it was immediately apparent why her minders had been so worried about the possibility. It might not have been a complete coincidence that things really began to slip away from the Conservatives after her appearance in front of a live studio audience less than a week from polling day, when, rather patronisingly perhaps, she told a nurse complaining about her pay that 'there isn't a magic money tree that we can shake that suddenly provides for everything that people want.' YouGov's Political Tracker poll showed the Prime Minister's net approval rating dropping from +18 on 11 May to +9 on 25 May and to -5 by 1 June. Wheeling out Boris Johnson, which some at CCHQ were now suggesting in the hope that he could inject a bit of life into the Conservative campaign, could have done nothing to arrest that slide. Indeed, the contrast between his shambling star-quality and her charisma by-pass would only have made things worse.

2.   Underlying organizational and operational shortcomings

Even if Mrs May's own performance hadn't left so much to be desired, the Conservatives would still have had to cope with some long-term structural problems (see Beckett, 2017). The most obvious of these was that the party had (and still has) fewer members (circa 150,000 according to the most recent available estimate) and therefore almost certainly fewer activists, than its Labour rival (517,000 going into the election). Two years previously, the Tories got around this problem by organising *Team 2015* and bussing bunches of activists on 'road trips' to campaign in marginal constituencies. However, they dared not repeat the trick this time around after the resulting row over the allocation of costs between national and constituency campaign expenses got them into considerable trouble (Electoral Commission, 2017). As a result, the Conservatives' 'ground game' almost certainly suffered in comparison to Labour's.

Moreover, the Conservative ground game was further hobbled by CCHQ apparently insisting that the few volunteers local associations were able to muster should focus their voter contact effort on lists of likely supporters conjured from big data compiled at the centre rather than from locally-led canvassing—a decision which, according to many activists, led them to the homes of people who would never have voted Tory in a million years. Things weren't made any better either when, as those activists began to report back that some of the Conservatives' target seats looked less than winnable, there was little or no effort made to divert them back to defending seats that suddenly looked to be in danger.

These issues only served to fuel a degree of distrust between many local associations and Conservative Campaign Headquarters that had already been sparked by the way the latter (perhaps inevitably given the fact that May's sudden announcement of an election left it only a couple of weeks to get things sorted) had short-circuited candidate selection procedures (Wallace, 2017). In constituencies where incumbent Tory MPs were stepping down, and in target seats, CCHQ was permitted to oblige local associations to choose from shortlists (some of them very short indeed) that it had put together without consultation, and in non-target seats it was allowed simply to impose a candidate—indeed, in

Table 3.1 Campaign activities of Conservative and Labour Party members, 2015-2017

% saying they did the following:	Conservative (N=1002)	Labour (N=1024)
Displayed election poster in window	21.6 (-8.0)	55.4 (+4.2)
Delivered leaflets	30.5 (-13.0)	31.6 (-10.9)
Attended public meeting or hustings	19.8 (-11.5)	24.9 (-6.5)
Canvassed face to face or by phone	21.3 (-15.2)	27.1 (-8.6)
'Liked' something by party/candidate on FB	39.3 (-0.3)	63.4 (+12.3)
Tweeted/re-tweeted party/candidate messages	24.2 (-1.8)	38.5 (+1.6)
Helped run party committee	7.0 (-5.0)	4.1 (-4.3)
Drove voters to polling stations	2.3 (-4.1)	4.8 (-2.4)
Other	10.2 (-6.1)	13.6 (-0.6)
None	24.7 (+1.7)	9.3 (-3.6)

Note: All figures are percentages. Figures in parenthesis represent percentage point changes 2015-2017.
Source: Party Members Project surveys, 2015 and 2017. See http://esrcpartymembersproject.org.

Scotland (with one or two exceptions) the latter was the norm. Attempts by associations to push back against such efforts proved fruitless in most cases, serving only to strain relations even further. Moreover, a number of would-be candidates (many of them activists) found themselves left out in the cold by an opaque and sometimes chaotic vetting system that had insufficient time to properly consider applicants' campaign records and, some complained, was designed to allow people favoured by 'the higher-ups' to get the official approval required to be placed on shortlists or imposed on associations. All in all, the process left a bad taste in the mouth of many grassroots members and did nothing to help morale—not good when the party was short of members in the first place and badly needed those it did have to enter the fray with enthusiasm.

The damage done to the morale of the Tory grassroots may go some way to explaining the relative decline in their campaign activity during the election. Table 3.1 reveals that across a range of nine different activities about which the ESRC-funded Party Members Project asked party members during the election campaigns of 2015 and 2017, the percentages of Conservative members claiming to have done them dropped in every case. While this was also true of Labour's members in a number of cases, it was not so for all activities, and never by as much. The Tories suffered particularly notable drops in the proportion of members reporting having delivered leaflets, attended hustings and canvassed—the last of these being of obvious importance for mobilizing electoral support at constituency level. The mean change in the Conservative column of Table 3.1 is -7.2, compared to just -1.7 for Labour—and Labour, of course, had four times as many members in the first place. When it came to grassroots campaign activity, then, the governing party was probably way behind the opposition.

In addition, CCHQ's much vaunted dominance over Labour when it came to digital campaigning in 2015 turned out to be ephemeral, always presuming that it wasn't merely a myth created by Cameron's surprise success last time round. Grassroots Conservatives are not renowned for being up with the latest developments in social media. But even they noticed very early on that they were being outgunned online—not least because CCHQ seemed to think that its paid-for ads on Facebook and YouTube videos would be able to compete with the torrent of rather edgier, savvier and far more share-worthy content and memes being produced by Labour, Momentum, and by their supporters on a do-it-yourself, 'organic' basis. Again, Table 3.1 offers clear evidence that Labour's members were far more politically engaged with social media than their Tory counterparts during the campaign. Moreover, while Labour already enjoyed a head-start over its major party rival at the outset of the campaign, evidence suggests that it further benefited from a 61% increase in the numbers of their 'followers' on social media during the six weeks of the election campaign, compared with a six per cent rise for the Tories (Morgan, 2017). Thus, the digital reach of the Labour Party seems to have been significantly greater than that of the Conservatives.

3.   Self-inflicted wounds

But problems with the operational, organizational and digital aspects of the Conservative campaign cannot disguise, and were not responsible for, its short-term tactical failures. One of the earliest (and least commented on in the so-called 'Mainstream Media', though not on Facebook and Twitter) was a commitment to a free vote in Parliament on the reintroduction of fox-hunting—an activity opposed by over three-quarters of the public. May's support for the idea (according to the many Conservative activists who detected it damaging their cause on the doorstep) badly undermined the attempt made by the party since she took over as Prime Minister in July 2016 to argue that she wasn't one of those 'same old Tories' (Lowe, 2017).

The pledge on fox hunting, however, was just one item among many in a largely uncosted and pessimistic Tory manifesto which might have been expressly designed to re-toxify rather than de-toxify the party (Maltby, 2017) and to put off rather than pull in voters. Special mention, however, should go to those policies impacting on the elderly—a group whose support the Tories could (and perhaps at this election did) take for granted. Believing they would win the election and therefore be back in government, and realising that they needed more room for manoeuvre on the fiscal front, the Conservatives refused to give an open-ended commitment to continuing the so-called 'Triple Lock' on pensions introduced by David Cameron and George Osborne or the winter-fuel payments brought in before 2010.

Even more damaging, however, at least according to both opinion polls and anecdotal evidence, was the proposal that the value of an individual's house (over and above £100,000) should be included in the calculation of assets used to determine their contribution to the bill for their social care—a suggestion swiftly and very effectively branded 'the dementia tax' by opponents and the media. This chorus of criticism precipitated a screeching U-turn by Mrs May, who then managed to make matters even worse for herself by insisting, to the incredulity of everyone watching, that 'nothing has changed'. Turning out to be 'weak and wobbly' rather than 'strong and stable' was bad enough; treating voters like idiots turned out to be calamitous.

4.   Longer-term problems: austerity and insecurity

But it was as much about what was not in the manifesto as about what was in it that got the Tories into trouble. Irritation with May's tin-eared, 'magic money tree' riposte to the nurse who had asked her on live television about pay tapped into wider concern on the part of voters—including some who nevertheless went on to vote Conservative if post-election polling is anything to go by—that key public services (and the people who work in them) were coming under serious financial strain as the result of the austerity policies pursued by the government since 2010. Lived experience remains crucial to the way people vote, and no-one with school-aged children or anyone who had needed to use the NHS could have failed to notice that, however much ministers repeated the mantra that spending on both was at record levels, education and healthcare were running desperately short of resources. At least some of those voters would also have noticed that those same ministers, after years of telling the public that savings must be made in order to balance the books, had not only manifestly failed to achieve that goal but now seemed surprisingly relaxed about extending the timeframe to meet it in order to accommodate any negative economic effects brought about by Brexit—a historic change which, voters had been told during the referendum campaign, would mean an extra £350 million a week for the NHS. Nearly a year later, it was obvious that any such windfall would be a long time coming, if it ever came at all. It was also obvious by then that talk of Mrs May being a new kind of Conservative—talk which seemed to rest on little more than a couple of speeches penned for her by Nick Timothy before she entered Number Ten as Prime Minister—looked wide of the mark. There was certainly precious little sign in the Tory manifesto of much being done either directly or indirectly for the so-called 'Just About Managing', or the public services they relied on, and all this at a time when growth was slow and when even those fortunate enough to get a pay rise were increasingly finding that any gains made were quickly offset by prices driven up by the fall in sterling precipitated by the referendum result (see Corlett *et al.*,

2017). After the election, some Tories wondered why their party hadn't talked more about the economy: they should have realised that there was a reason for that.

Perhaps if the Conservatives had been facing a Labour Party believing that it was on the verge of getting into government and therefore as desperate as it had been in 2015 to (i) prove that it was fiscally responsible and (ii) avoid giving any hostages to fortune, none of this would have proved quite so problematic. Unfortunately, however, Labour under Jeremy Corbyn had few expectations of winning the election and was anyway more ideologically inclined to oppose austerity. As a result, it was prepared to make a positive, optimistic and even idealistic (though some would say unrealistic) offer to the electorate involving an end to pay restraint in the public sector as well as big increases in spending on key services—all paid for by tax rises that would supposedly hit only big business and the rich. Corbyn was also confident enough, after a second terrorist attack during the campaign looked like it might hand an advantage to the Prime Minister, to counter the accusation that, as an apparent supporter of any number of paramilitary organizations around the world, he was 'soft-on-terrorism'. The Labour leader responded with a claim that she, as Home Secretary, had cut police numbers in order to save money and balance the books. The score-draw that resulted from the charge and counter-charge may have been unseemly—Corbyn supporters were particularly irritated by a Tory Facebook advertisement on the issue which achieved 6.6 million views—but the fact that the terrorism issue was not an easy victory for the Conservatives was in effect a win for Labour.

The intense media discussion of both the terrorist attacks and the parties' manifestos also dovetailed with a natural (and some would say entirely proper) desire on the part of journalists during elections, first, to avoid slavishly following the agenda set by politicians and, second, to discuss the policies being presented to the electorate. This proved problematic for a Conservative campaign that had hoped to keep the focus away from policy and instead on who would be best able to negotiate Brexit. As a result—and also as a result of Jeremy Corbyn's better-than-expected media performances and Labour's more-popular-than-expected manifesto—the Conservatives did not enjoy the kind of effortless superiority in broadcast and print coverage that they had anticipated (Deacon and Smith, 2017). Given the fact that they anticipated (quite rightly it turns out) no such superiority when it came to social media, which is clearly becoming an increasingly important part of the mix, this must have come as quite a blow (see Bond, 2017). The media, mainstream or social, doesn't have as big an impact on election outcomes as some imagine (see Newton, 2006) but it's always nice to have it firmly on one's side.

5.   Winners and Losers

We need, however, not to get so carried away by the contrast between what many thought would happen to a Corbyn-led Labour Party and what actually happened (as well as between the smart campaign we expected from the Conservatives and the maladroit one they actually delivered) that we forget the fact that the Tories garnered their biggest share of the vote since 1983. Nor should we ignore their much improved performance in Scotland, where the popularity of Ruth Davidson, the Tory leader there, undoubtedly contributed to the party virtually doubling its share of the vote to 28.6% and boosting its share of Westminster seats from just one to 13. It is also worth noting that, according to a number of large-sample post-election polls (principally those conducted by Lord Ashcroft, YouGov and Ipsos MORI), the Conservatives made big gains in Great Britain as a whole among working-class voters, particularly in the private sector, registering gains of over ten percentage points among not just semi- and unskilled workers but also among the C2 voters fabled for swinging elections one way or another (see Table 3.2). Polling and constituency breakdowns suggest that a large part of that gain derived from Mrs May's much-trumpeted determination to 'take back control' of Britain's borders by ensuring that 'Brexit means Brexit'—hence the six seats gained from Labour in the wake of their recording big majorities for Leave in the 2016 referendum: Copeland, Derbyshire North East, Mansfield, Middlesboro South, Stoke South and Walsall North. More generally, the Conservatives recorded a higher share of the vote in 2017 than they had in 2015 in areas of the country that voted to leave in the referendum.

Those gains were very much of a piece with the strategy followed by Theresa May since becoming Prime Minister, namely to hoover up voters who might otherwise have supported UKIP by offering them not just a hard Brexit and further action on immigration but also signature policies like a return to grammar schools. And, on the surface anyway, the strategy looked like a roaring success. UKIP, now without its iconic leader, Nigel Farage, dropped further and further down in the opinion polls and at the election fell from 12.6% of the vote in 2015 to just 1.8%. Analysis of post-election polling, however, suggests that a significant number of erstwhile UKIP supporters, reassured by a combination of Conservative rhetoric and Corbyn's promise to respect the result of the referendum, felt no obligation to vote Tory, especially when they and those around them probably had more to gain materially from Labour's left-wing pitch than they did from continued austerity under Mrs May and her colleagues. Meanwhile, analysis of constituency voting reveals, possibly rather surprisingly, that in those seats where UKIP decided not to stand a candidate (perhaps in order to give a Brexit-supporting Tory a clear run, perhaps simply to save money), Labour rather than the Conservatives tended to be the main beneficiary. As a

Table 3.2 The demographics of voting, 2017

	Conservative	Labour	Lib Dem	Turnout (registered voters)	Labour to Conservative Swing
All	44 (+6)	41 (+10)	8 (0)	69 (+3)	−2
Gender					
Male	44 (+6)	40 +11	7 (-1)	67 (+2)	−2.5
Female	43 (+6)	42 (+9)	8 (0)	69 (+3)	−1.5
Age					
18-24	27 (-1)	62 (+20)	5 (+1)	64 (+21)	−10.5
25-34	27 (-6)	56 (+20)	9 (+2)	64 (+10)	−13
35-44	33 (-2)	49 (+14)	10 (0)	63 (-1)	−8
45-54	43 (+7)	40 (+8)	7 (-1)	72 (0)	−0.5
55-64	51 (+14)	34 (+3)	7 (-2)	73 (-4)	+5.5
65+	61 (+14)	25 (+3)	7 (-1)	73 (-5)	+5.5
Social Class					
AB	47 (+2)	37 (+11)	10 (-2)	73 (-2)	−4.5
C1	44 (+2)	40 (+12)	7 (-1)	74 (+6)	−5
C2	45 (+13)	41 (+9)	6 (0)	66 (+4)	+2
DE	38 (+12)	47 (+6)	5 (0)	61 (+5)	+3
Housing Tenure					
Owned	55 (+9)	30 (+7)	7 (-2)	73 (-4)	+1
Mortgage	43 (+4)	40 (+8)	9 (0)	72 (+3)	−2
Social renter	26 (+8)	57 (+8)	4 (+1)	60 (+4)	0
Private renter	31 (+3)	54 (+15)	7 (+1)	65 (+14)	−6
Ethnic group					
White	45 (+6)	39 (+11)	8 (0)	69 (+1)	−2.5
All BME	19 (-4)	73 (+8)	6 (+2)	64 (-6)	−6
Education					
No qualifications	52	35	4	64	
Other qualifications	46	39	6	67	
Degree or higher	33	48	12	76	
EU Ref vote					
Remain	33	47	13	78	
Leave	46	39	7	69	
Did not vote	23	66	4	25	

Source: Adapted from 'How Britain Voted 2017', Ipsos MORI estimates , accessed at https://www.ipsos.com/ipsos-mori/en-uk/how-britain-voted-2017-election?language_content_entity=en-uk. All figures are percentages. Figures in brackets indicate change since 2015.

result, and because Labour often had reasonably-sized majorities anyway in many 'Leave' constituencies, the improvement in the Conservatives' vote share in those places was insufficient to deliver them anywhere near the number of seats they had been hoping for.

Moreover, the flip side of the Conservatives' efforts to attract working-class 'authoritarian' and anti-immigration/anti-European voters was the backlash they seem to have suffered in constituencies which voted for Remain, many of them in urban areas containing high concentrations of (often younger) well-heeled, well-educated, AB (or, if they were students, future AB) voters and/or voters from ethnic minorities. As a result, many Labour MPs who thought earlier that they were facing almost certain defeat ended up with much bigger majorities (Rupa Huq in Ealing Central and Acton who won by just 274 votes in 2015 but by 13,807 in 2017 being perhaps the most striking example) while others who thought they had little chance of snatching their seats from Tory incumbents managed to do so—Emma Dent Coad in Kensington springs immediately to mind. Meanwhile, the return to the Commons of the former Liberal Democrat minister Vince Cable, in his old seat in Twickenham, at the expense of the Tory opponent who had defeated him in 2015 was almost certainly down, at least in part, to the Tories' failure to replicate their increased appeal among white working-class voters among their middle-class counterparts.

Every bit as importantly, the Conservatives' nationalistic and narrow-minded thrust did them no favours with younger voters either. And 'young' doesn't mean only those 18-24 year olds (many of them students) who were so taken by Jeremy Corbyn that they contributed to Tory defeats in university towns like previously true-blue Canterbury. It also included (see Table 3.2) 25-44 year olds, a fair proportion of whom were struggling to get on the housing ladder in an era of rising prices, stagnant wages and limited construction, and some of whom were getting letters home from their children's schools asking them to contribute toward basic costs or informing them of cuts to staffing.

The Tories suffered an especially sharp swing to Labour among voters living in the private rental sector, many of whom are increasingly despondent about the prospect of ever owning their own homes given the long-term crisis in housing that has been slowly fomenting across the country. Whether or not the news that, in the wake of the dementia tax, they might not even stand to inherit much from their parents came as the final straw, we may never know; but many of them were clearly unimpressed by a Conservative manifesto and leadership that appeared to offer not much more than Brexit and continuing austerity. Perhaps if Mrs May had been able to offset such losses by boosting turnout among retirees, who continued to vote Tory in much greater numbers, she might have triumphed. But, possibly due to her manifesto, the elderly voted less in 2015 than in 2017 (see Table 3.2)—something that Lynton Crosby, speaking afterward, clearly considered significant (Knaus, 2017).

6. What is to be done?

This was an election at which everything that could go wrong for the Conservatives did go wrong. The manifesto, which May's (now former) Chief of Staff Nick Timothy believed would be an asset, turned into a liability, confirming the belief of her campaign consultant Lynton Crosby that the contest between the parties needed to be framed in terms of leadership. Unfortunately, however, Theresa May simply wasn't the kind of presidential politician who could carry that kind of campaign. Nor did Brexit do her or her party as much of a favour as everyone had expected. For one thing, she seemed to think she could get away with mouthing mantras and platitudes about leaving the EU, opening up a vacuum that other issues rushed in to fill. For another, the number of UKIP, older, poorly-educated and working-class voters that the party gained as a result of the government's tough talk on Europe seems to have been outweighed by the number of younger, better-educated, middle-class, Remain voters who were alienated and infuriated by it—and by May's claim at her party conference that 'If you believe you are a citizen of the world, you are a citizen of nowhere' (Bush, 2017). More generally, the Tories suffered because they were unable or unwilling, ideologically or otherwise, to respond convincingly—or even, to be honest, at all—to increasing voter concern about ongoing cuts to key public services.

Clearly, the Tories need to re-think a number of things in terms of strategy and organisation—something former Party Chairman, Eric Pickles, has since reported back on Conservative Party (2017). How they do voter identification and whether they have over-centralised their operation should clearly be key concerns, as should how they can better exploit truly local intelligence effectively. It will not be easy because any review worth the name is bound to bring into focus the often fraught nature of the relationship between local associations and CCHQ (or Central Office, as it used to be known). Moreover, the Conservatives will have to do all this at the same time as managing a precarious parliamentary situation while charged with the greatest challenge to confront a government in living memory: the successful negotiation of the United Kingdom's exit from the European Union. And the task will be made all the harder by the fact that they are led by a Prime Minister who, in the wake of the election, has manifestly lost the confidence of the British people and many of her own followers and colleagues, despite having garnered an increased share of the vote across the country. The Conservative Party has a history of ruthlessly dispatching leaders once they are perceived to have become electoral liabilities, so Theresa May's time in Downing Street may be limited, even if, in the immediate aftermath of the election, there was little appetite in the party for replacing her, not least because there was no agreement on who might best replace her (Savage, 2017). Whoever eventually does so will be confronted with a huge political task if he or she is to construct a broad and winning electoral coalition better capable of turning votes in the country into seats in parliament.

Acknowledgement

This work was supported by the Economic and Social Research Council (grant number ES/M007537/1). We would also like to thank our colleague on the Project, Dr Monica Poletti.

References

Beckett, A. (2017, 27 June) 'How the Tory Election Machine Fell Apart', *Guardian*, accessed at https://www.theguardian.com/politics/2017/jun/26/tory-election-machine-fell-apart-negative-tactics on 3 September 2017.

Bond, D. (2017, 9 June) 'Labour's Slick Online Campaign Outguns Tory Press', *Financial Times*.

Bush, S. (2017, 27 June) 'How Theresa May Abandoned David Cameron's Playbook—and Paid a Terrible Price', *New Statesman*, accessed at http://www.newsta tesman.com/politics/elections/2017/06/how-theresa-may-abandoned-david-camerons-playbook-and-paid-terrible-price on 3 September 2017.

Corlett, A., Clarke, S. and Tomlinson, D. (2017) *The Living Standards Audit 2017*, London, Resolution Foundation.

Conservative Party (2017) *Eric Pickles' General Election Review*, London, Conservative Party.

Deacon, D. and Smith, D. (2017, 14 June) 'How the Conservatives' media strategy collapsed during the election campaign', *The Conversation*, accessed at https://theconversa tion.com/how-the-conservatives-media-strategy-collapsed-during-the-election-campaign-79291 on 3 September 2017.

Electoral Commission (2017) 'Conservative Party Fined £70,000 Following Investigation into Election Campaign Expenses', accessed at https://www.electoralcommission.org. uk/i-am-a/journalist/electoral-commission-media-centre/news-releases-donations/conservative-party-fined-70,000-following-investigation-into-election-campaign-expenses on 3 September 2017.

Knaus, C. (2017, 11 July) 'Tory Pollster Lynton Crosby Says Theresa May Right to Call Early Election, *Guardian*, accessed at https://www.theguardian.com/politics/2017/jul/ 11/tory-pollster-lynton-crosby-says-theresa-may-right-to-call-early-general-election on 3 September 2017.

Lowe, M. (2017, 13 June) 'Social Care, May Ducking TV Debates, Fox Hunting: What Sank Our Candidacies in the West Midlands', *Conservative Home*, accessed at http:// www.conservativehome.com/platform/2017/06/michelle-lowe-social-care-may-duck ing-tv-debates-fox-hunting-what-sank-my-candidacy-in-the-west-midlands.html on 3 September 2017.

Maltby, K. (2017, 9 June) 'Theresa May Rejected the Tory Detoxification Project. That's What's Behind This Mess', *Guardian*, https://www.theguardian.com/commentisfree/

2017/jun/09/theresa-may-rejected-tory-detoxification-behind-this-mess on 3 September 2017.

McTague, T., Cooper, C. and Dickson, A. (2017, 6 July) 'How Theresa Lost It', *Politico.eu*, accessed at http://www.politico.eu/article/how-theresa-may-lost-it-uk-election-brexit-jeremy-corbyn-jim-messina-lynton-crosby-uk-sarah-palin-campaign/ on 3 September 2017.

Morgan, R. (2017, 14 July) 'CCHQ Must Rebuild its Digital Strategy from the Ground Up', *Conservative Home*, accessed at http://www.conservativehome.com/platform/2017/07/richard-morgan-cchq-must-rebuild-its-digital-strategy-from-the-ground-up.html on 3 September 2017.

Newton, K. (2006) 'May the Weak Force Be With You: The Power of the Mass Media in Modern Politics', *European Journal of Political Research*, **45**, 209–234.

Perrior, K. (2017, 15 July) 'Inside Team Theresa', *Times Magazine*.

Prince, R. (2017) *Theresa May: The Enigmatic Prime Minister* London, Biteback.

Ridge-Newman, A. (2014) *Cameron's Conservatives and the Internet: Change, Culture and Cyber Toryism*, London, Palgrave.

Savage, M. (2017, 23 July) 'Tory Members Turn to David Davis in Battle to Succeed Theresa May', *Observer*.

Shipman, T. (2017, 11 June) 'I Look Stupid, Not Strong and Stable, May Said', *Sunday Times*.

Timothy, N. (2017, 17 June) 'Where We Went Wrong', *Spectator*, accessed at https://www.spectator.co.uk/2017/06/nick-timothy-where-we-went-wrong/ on 3 September 2017.

Wallace, M. (2017, 9 May) 'Centralisation and Chaos—Inside the Rush to Select Conservative Candidates in Time for the Election', *ConservativeHome*, accessed at http://www.conservativehome.com/thetorydiary/2017/05/centralisation-and-chaos-inside-the-rush-to-select-conservative-candidates-in-time-for-the-election.html on 3 September 2017.

Walters, S. (2017, 3 September) 'Bombshell Secret Memo Reveals Theresa May Defied a Warning that Her Snap Election was a "Huge Risk" and could backfire', *Mail on Sunday*, accessed at http://www.dailymail.co.uk/news/article-4847528/May-defied-warning-snap-Election-huge-risk.html on 3 September 2017.

Britain Votes (2017) 59–71

EUNICE GOES*

'Jez, We Can!' Labour's Campaign: Defeat with a Taste of Victory

When on the BBC election-night programme David Dimbleby announced that the exit poll predicted a hung parliament, the Labour leader Jeremy Corbyn just smiled. He had reasons to be cautious. For months, the chatter in Westminster was about Labour's fatal decline. A hung parliament did not feature in this scenario. But voters, a more imaginative bunch than pollsters and pundits, had a surprise in store. Instead of facing a crushing defeat Labour lost the election but by a much smaller margin than anticipated. The party increased its share of the vote from 2015 by almost 10% to 40%, its highest since 2005 and saw 262 MPs elected (30 more than in the previous election). It was the first time since 1997 that Labour increased its representation in the House of Commons. Considering the disastrous results obtained at the 2015 general election and at the local elections of May 2017, winning those extra 30 seats was a considerable achievement. Conservative safe seats like Kensington, Battersea, Canterbury, Portsmouth South and Stroud were not even on the list of the party's top target seats, and yet Labour won them. Similarly, there were signs of a Labour recovery in Scotland. In 2015, the party lost all but one of its 41 seats, but two years later it retained Edinburgh South and won back East Lothian, Midlothian, Glasgow North East, Kirkcaldy and Cowdenbeath, Coatbridge, Chryston and Bellshill, Rutherglen and Hamilton West.

Unsurprisingly Jeremy Corbyn was delighted with this turn of events. But for him the real cherry on the cake was the fact that he was treated as the real winner of the election. The Parliamentary Labour Party (PLP) received him with a standing ovation on the first meeting of the House of Commons following the general election, and even Corbyn's arch-critic Lord Mandelson conceded he had been wrong about the Labour leader. 'Corbynmania' appeared to have an unexpectedly wide reach. For the first time since Corbyn was elected leader, several opinion polls showed that Labour was more popular than the Conservatives. Confirming

*Eunice Goes, CASS, Richmond University, eunice.goes@richmond.ac.uk

doi:10.1093/pa/gsx062

this mood, festivalgoers at Glastonbury chanted 'Oh, Jeremy Corbyn!', while in the corridors of Westminster the idea of a Corbyn-led government was taken seriously for the first time.

This chapter will explain how Labour achieved these surprising results and will argue that the combination of an effective campaign, a popular manifesto, perfect timing, and a healthy portion of luck explain Labour's performance. The chapter will start by contextualising the election of Jeremy Corbyn as Labour leader and his impact on Labour politics.

1. From Miliband to Corbyn

When Jeremy Corbyn was elected Labour leader in September of 2015 the party was staring into the abyss. Just four months earlier, Labour had suffered a disastrous defeat in the general election, winning only 30.4% of the vote. With such humiliating results, the then Labour leader, Ed Miliband resigned immediately triggering a leadership election. But at the time Labour was not ready to plan its next steps.

If it was clear that Miliband's lacklustre manifesto (Goes, 2016), his reputation as leader (Fielding, 2015), as well as the fact that voters still blamed Labour for the 2008 economic recession (Cowley and Kavanagh, 2016, p. 369) partly explain this disastrous defeat, the party was still too bruised to fully understand what went wrong at the election let alone to come up with a blueprint for the future. It did not help that voters sent a confused message to the party. Whilst Labour increased its majorities in London seats and in university towns, the party was under pressure from UKIP in the Midlands and the North East of England and lost all its seats but one in Scotland. In short, developing a programme that would get the approval of these very different voters would not be an easy task.

In this state of intellectual and ideological confusion, it is not surprising that the campaign for the leadership of the Labour Party that took place in the summer of 2015 was mostly uninspiring. Whilst the frontbenchers Andy Burnham, Yvette Cooper and Liz Kendall repeated tired old-mantras about the magic recipe to target aspirational voters, the veteran left-wing backbencher Jeremy Corbyn was given space to shine with his promise of a 'new kind of politics'. Corbyn's unambiguous anti-austerity message attracted thousands of people to the rallies and public hall meetings he held across Britain during that summer (Seymour, 2016, p. 22; Richards, 2017, pp. 76-77). When it became clear that Jeremy Corbyn, who had run for the leadership with the modest goal of opening the debate in the party, was on course to be elected leader alarm bells started to ring across the PLP. A string of former Labour leaders—from Neil Kinnock to Gordon Brown, not forgetting, of course, Tony Blair—tried to reason with Labour members and supporters. But the warnings about Labour's possible annihilation did nothing to dampen the popularity of the veteran left-winger.

Helped by a new method of election that empowered party members and supporters at the expense of the PLP, Corbyn was elected Labour leader with 59.5% of the vote, beating his rivals Andy Burnham (19%), Yvette Cooper (17%) and Liz Kendall (4.5%). For Corbyn, who had spent most of his political career in the backbenches campaigning for human rights, world peace, and social justice, and rebelling against successive Labour leaders, this was a remarkable achievement. Yet Corbyn was given little time to enjoy his victory. As soon as the results were read most members of the PLP mobilised to resist Corbyn and his brand of politics. Many party grandees were sceptical of the idea that mobilising voters who normally did not vote was the road to electoral success. Moreover, they thought that Corbyn's views on everything from the monarchy, to capitalism and nuclear disarmament would condemn Labour to permanent opposition.

Most frontbenchers associated with the Blair, Brown and Miliband eras refused to serve in the shadow cabinet. Those who did agree did not last very long (apart from Andy Burnham who only left last spring to run for the post of Mayor of Greater Manchester). The most militant amongst the Corbyn sceptics—figures like John McTernan and Simon Danczuk—invited the party to organise a coup against the newly elected leader. But not all Corbyn sceptics favoured swift removal. Some preferred slower guerrilla warfare methods and created as much trouble as they could in the vain hope that the new leader would quit in despair. If Labour grandees were horrified with the outcome of the leadership election, the winner was totally unprepared for what followed. It soon became apparent that he was not ready for the daily grind of frontbench opposition politics with all the media exposure that it involves. Corbyn and his team seemed quite unwilling to compromise and to learn from those who had more experience of frontline politics.

2.   Corbyn's Labour: A new type of politics?

The mixing of these ingredients created a permanent civil war between the leader and his team and the PLP. Thus, mass abstentions and rebellions in Parliament, permanent plotting against the leader and a drip feed of damaging leaks to the media about his unsuitability for the job became banal occurrences in Labour politics. If Corbyn claimed to be above this confrontational style and refrained from making personal attacks against his enemies, his team did not. Threats to deselect 'disloyal' MPs and abusive attacks against so-called Blairites on social media were regularly made by zealous 'Corbynistas'.

The grass-roots organisation Momentum, created following Corbyn's election with the purpose of supporting the new Labour leader and transforming the party into a social movement, was deemed responsible for most of the trouble-making. Its innovative campaigning techniques, its willingness to establish alliances with other left-wing forces (including from the far-left) and its social movement culture were resisted and vilified by older party members. More seriously, Momentum was accused, with some justification, of harbouring entryists from the radical left, and of inciting violence and issuing threats of violence against Labour MPs like Stella Creasy, Jess Phillips and Luciana Berger, who were critical of the Labour leader.

Initially, the permanent guerrilla warfare between Corbyn and his team and the rest of the PLP was mostly about ideological and organisational disagreements but as time passed questions about competence became more important. Corbyn's weak performances at the dispatch box, his antagonistic attitude towards the mainstream media, the lack of discipline around policy within the shadow cabinet, the absence of a forensic and systematic opposition to the legislative agenda of the government, not to mention the embarrassing slips like John McDonnell's reference to Mao Zedong's 'little red book', or Corbyn's quotation of the Albanian Communist leader Enver Hoxha to make a banal point, contributed little to improve the party's popularity and credibility. Every month the opinion polls showed that both Labour and Corbyn had reached a new low in the popularity stakes.

The stalemate between Corbyn and the PLP reached a climax in the days following the referendum on EU membership in June 2016. Even some of Corbyn's supporters started to voice their doubts in public. His disappointing efforts to support the Remain campaign led the PLP to press the closest thing it had to an eject button: 172 MPs denounced the Labour leader on a no-confidence motion and hoped that he would resign. But he refused to go. As a last resort, Angela Eagle launched a leadership challenge in early July. Owen Smith followed Eagle and ended up becoming Corbyn's only rival.[1] But the efforts of this broad anti-Corbyn coalition failed. He was re-elected with a bigger majority than in 2015 securing 62% of the vote. At this stage, Corbyn's opponents realised that under the current party rules, the Labour leader was unassailable. This realisation changed the PLP. Instead of plotting to oust Corbyn, most of the PLP succumbed to despair. As the rumours of a snap election in late 2016 did the rounds of Westminster, some Labour MPs and sympathisers talked of defecting to create a new party, but ultimately no one made the first move in that direction.

The majority feeling in the movement seemed to be that Labour was finished as a party. Writing in the pages of *Prospect*, the historian Ross McKibbin argued that 'the only remaining solution—other than to hope that something turns up—was the most drastic: that is, for the bulk of the parliamentary party, those who have made their views on Corbyn very plain, to leave the official party and set themselves up as an independent body—Parliamentary Labour? Sensible

---

[1]Angela Eagle dropped from the race after all anti-Corbynistas coalesced around Owen Smith.

Labour?' (McKibbin, 2017, p 25). In similar gloomy vein, the columnist John Harris (2016) wondered whether 'the Labour Party as we know it may very well soon not exist'. The reality on the ground seemed to confirm this picture. In by-elections held in February 2017, Labour lost the seat of Copeland and only narrowly retained Stoke-on-Trent Central. In May, the party lost 382 seats at the local elections whilst the Conservatives managed the rare feat for a party of government of winning 563 new seats.

As David Denver shows in his contribution to this volume, the opinion polls did not offer any comfort either. When in mid-April the Prime Minister Theresa May called an early election to be held on 8 June, Labour was on average 20 per cent behind the Conservatives. In short, the writing was on the wall. Whilst the Conservatives were predicted to win by a landslide, Labour was expected to suffer substantial losses particularly in the Midlands and the North-East of England. The expectations were so dismal that in private some MPs feared that Labour could only win 140 seats (Hardman, 2017).

3. Old and new campaign techniques delivered for Labour

But the Labour leader was determined to prove his critics wrong. In the first week of the campaign, he visited Birmingham, Croydon, Swindon, Cardiff, Bristol, Manchester, Crewe and Warrington outperforming the Prime Minister Theresa May both in the number of visits and crucially in terms of media visibility. That first week of the campaign set the pattern for Corbyn's electoral strategy. Initially his choice of places to visit raised a few eyebrows. For instance, *Newsnight*'s policy editor, Chris Cook, wondered why the Labour leader was 'holding events in safe seats and in Tory seats which, the polls suggest, are very unlikely to be won', whilst staying away from areas where seats were more likely to change hands At the time, many backbenchers believed that Corbyn was more focused in shoring up support for the anticipated leadership election (that would follow the also expected catastrophic electoral defeat) than in winning the general election.

But the election results showed that there was some method to Corbyn's strategy. In truth, there were good campaign reasons for visiting safe seats. Images of the Labour leader being enthusiastically received by activists at well-attended rallies were shown on television, online and in print media. Those positive and dynamic portrayals of Corbyn contributed to create a buzz around Labour. Arguably, images of the Labour leader reading Michael Rosen's classic 'We're Going on a Bear Hunt' to a group of lively children were more telegenic than those showing the Prime Minister speaking (but not engaging in dialogues) behind a 'Theresa May's Team' backdrop.

The Labour leader campaigned in many other seats, and not all of them safe. It helped that Corbyn was an effective campaigner who enjoyed his time on the campaign trail. In his local branch in Islington North he is known as a 'slow campaigner' because he engages in conversations and even takes time to have cups of tea with voters. In the 2017 electoral campaign this listening style, as well as his informality and ideological clarity were real electoral assets. For the areas where there was potentially a 'Corbyn problem' the party sent to campaigning events popular figures like the London Mayor Sadiq Khan, and frontbenchers like Emily Thornberry, Keir Starmer and others.

The party's media strategy was also key to Labour's results. Team Corbyn decided to ignore mainstream media and to focus instead on a campaign that would combine the old-fashioned method of big rallies with a sophisticated micro-targeting of individual voters on social media. With the help of new software called Promote, the party could target undecided voters in marginal seats by sending advertisements to their Facebook profiles and Snapchat accounts that addressed their specific concerns (Waterson, 2017). Labour's videos promoting Corbyn's policies, which appeared on YouTube and local news sites, as well as the online campaign to promote voter registration, were a key component of the party's online campaign to attract young voters. To reach beyond university students, and to target young disengaged voters in urban areas, the party also engaged a sizable number of grime artists like the Novelist, Akala, Stormzy and JME, who created the campaign #Grime4Corbyn.

The online activism had spillover effects on the ground as hundreds of supporters volunteered to work in the campaign. Here the party was helped by the efforts of organisations like Momentum and Compass and party groups like Progress who recruited hundreds of volunteers. Similarly, the tour of the marginals organised by *Guardian* columnist Owen Jones, which he advertised on Twitter and Facebook, attracted hundreds of supporters from all ages and who were keen to help with Labour's campaign. These volunteers, many of them had never been involved in politics before, spent a great part of the seven-week campaign knocking on doors, delivering leaflets and helping to build Labour's impressive database of voter information. Momentum's advertising on Facebook and other social media platforms reached far and wide. According to data provided by Momentum, 12.7 million people saw the group's election videos (Peggs, 2017). In addition, Momentum's digital map of the marginal seats directed volunteers to campaigning events in the most needed constituencies. On election day, Momentum mobilised 10,000 volunteers who knocked on 1.2 million doors in a last-minute effort to get the vote out.

4. Labour's manifesto: Corbynism or Milibandism on speed?

Labour's enthusiastic and positive campaign had an almost immediate effect. The polling gap between Labour and the Conservatives started to narrow in the first weeks of the campaign, but the real turning point happened when Labour launched its manifesto in mid-May. Here again the party was astute. To ensure maximum publicity and also to test the waters, the party leaked the manifesto a few days before the scheduled date for the official launch.

The manifesto, drafted by Andrew Fisher, was radical but looked credible and deliverable. Most public spending promises were costed and the party claimed to be committed to fiscal probity. The focus on practical policy proposals like banning zero-hours contracts, raising the minimum wage, scrapping tuition fees, introducing free school meals to all children, raising taxes on higher-earners, nationalising the railways and utility companies proved to be popular with most voters, especially with young voters (Ford, 2017). Crucially, each component of the manifesto targeted a specific cross-section of British society that had been affected by the combination of public spending cuts and the pay freeze of the last seven years. If there were questions about how Labour would deliver its promises, they never dominated the campaign for too long.

The manifesto also showed how Jeremy Corbyn had moderated his views on a number of issues. The first sign of his moderation was the title of the manifesto. By choosing 'For the Many Not The Few', Corbyn's nodded to the New Labour era in an almost mischievous manner. 'For the many not the few' were the words that replaced Labour's commitment to public ownership in Tony Blair's reform of Clause Four of the party's constitution. In 2017 these words were chosen to promote, amongst other things, Labour's most ambitious programme of nationalisations since 1983.

But apart from the proposals to nationalise the railways and private utilities and to scrap tuition fees, Corbyn's manifesto was only marginally more radical than the 2015 Labour manifesto. The similarities in approach and tone were immediately noticed by Ed Miliband's former chief adviser Stewart Wood who tweeted that 'Corbyn's manifesto is Milibandism on speed'. Indeed, Corbyn's proposals on macroeconomic policy, industrial policy, welfare, devolution of power to the English cities and towns, immigration and even foreign and defence policies (the 2017 manifesto committed Labour to maintain the Trident programme of nuclear deterrent) mirrored those outlined in the 2015 manifesto.

The differences were mostly about emphasis and language. Whilst Miliband's 'on-the-one-hand-and-on-the-other-manifesto' fudged some issues so that he could address the demands of the different factions of the party, Corbyn was clear about his direction of travel. Wood admitted as much in an interview to the *New Statesman*. As he explained, the 2015 manifesto 'was a mosaic of concessions to different parts of the party, rather than an authentic expression of the radical Ed' (Wood quoted in Eaton, 2017). For example, whilst Miliband's proposals on the Living Wage were aspirational and non-committal (Labour Party, 2015, p. 23), Corbyn proposed to raise the minimum wage to the level of the Living Wage

(Labour Party, 2017, p. 47). Whilst Miliband was ambiguous about nationalisations (Labour Party, 2015, p. 26)[2] Corbyn was clear about his commitment to bring back the railway network, public utilities and the Royal Mail into public ownership (Labour Party, 2017, p. 19). Regarding immigration, Corbyn did not copy Miliband's 'immigration controls' mugs but by accepting that freedom of movement for European citizens would end with Britain's withdrawal from the European Union (Labour Party, 2017, p. 28) it ended up defending a harsher approach.

There were also similarities in the approach to the vexed question of the deficit. Labour's 2017 manifesto was perceived as an anti-austerity manifesto, yet its fiscal rule and commitment to keep the cap on welfare spending were an adaptation of Labour's 2015 promise of a 'triple lock of responsibility' (Miliband, 2015; Labour Party, 2015, p. 2). The party's new fiscal credibility rule would commit a future Labour government to balance 'day-to-day spending' whilst enabling investments in infrastructure, housing and so on (Labour Party, 2017, p. 8). And like Miliband, Corbyn used the welfare budget to demonstrate fiscal responsibility. Indeed, the party announced that a Labour government would not reverse the welfare cuts nor would it remove the benefit cap introduced by the coalition government.[3]

The hard language used to present Labour's fiscal plans suggests that Corbyn and his shadow chancellor John McDonnell understood that Labour could only gain credibility if it were perceived as a prudent manager of the economy. With that goal in mind, McDonnell announced in the first months of the Corbyn leadership, the creation of a New Economic Advisory Committee, composed of academic economists including Joseph Stiglitz, Marianna Mazzucato, Ann Pettifor, Thomas Piketty, Simon Wren-Lewis and Anastasia Nesvetailova, whose role was to help Labour develop an economic programme that jettisoned austerity and promoted sustainable growth.[4]

The 're-packaging' of Jeremy Corbyn was also visible in his image which became smarter during the campaign. Indeed, the Labour leader abandoned his famous ill-fitting blazers and was always seen in the uniform of the professional male Labour politician of navy suit and plain shirt, occasionally adorned by a red

---

[2]The 2015 manifesto did not propose the nationalisation of the railways though Labour's proposals on public procurement left that option open.

[3]This commitment was similar to that one adopted by Ed Miliband while he was leader. This being said, during the 2017 campaign Labour's position on welfare benefits was not entirely clear. Whilst the manifesto pledged to reverse 'the worst excesses' of the benefit cuts, to scrap the 'bedroom tax' and to reintroduce the housing benefit for 18-21 year olds, Emily Thornberry argued that 'I don't think we can reverse it entirely. We shouldn't be promising things we can't afford' (*Independent*, 2017).

[4]Several members of that committee resigned from the advisory committee in June 2016.

tie. He also developed a less confrontational relationship with the media. He did the rounds of the talk-shows on television where he tried to come across as charming as he could (he even offered jars of his homemade jam to BBC presenters) and participated in the last televised debate with great panache.

If Labour's manifesto and Corbyn's moderation contributed to the narrowing of the gap between Labour and the Conservatives, Theresa May's hapless campaign also helped. Her preference for a stage-managed campaign where contact with real voters was kept to a minimum, combined with her refusal to participate in the televised debates, contrasted with Corbyn's easy manner. Her robotic replies to questions became so emblematic of her style that the soubriquet 'Maybot' coined by *Guardian* sketch-writer John Crace became widely used in popular discourse. To make matters worse, the Conservative Party manifesto was deeply unpopular with the party's core voters and with the Tory-supporting media.

It was then not surprising that the momentum for Labour continued until 8 June, even though the campaign was interrupted twice in response to the separate terrorist attacks in Manchester and in London. Indeed, May's attempts to reassure a shocked nation were undermined by the revelations that the number of police officers had been reduced during her tenure as Home Secretary. In short, Corbyn's own shortcomings on security were almost neutralised by those of the Prime Minister.

5. Labour's outcomes

When the seven-week long campaign reached its conclusion, most pollsters predicted a Conservative majority. But clearly something happened in that period that explains both Labour's better than expected results and most pollsters' failure to predict them. A number of ingredients may explain the outcome.

As explained above, Labour's effective campaign and popular manifesto mobilised thousands of voters of most age groups. In addition, Corbyn's reputation as a principled politician with a clear set of values helped to mobilise thousands of young people who voted Labour, some of whom joined and campaigned for the party. Polling analysis shows that Labour's performance was particularly strong in constituencies with large concentrations of young voters (Ford 2017). This in turn highlights how, perhaps contrary to much previous electoral history, the campaign this time had a very substantial impact in the election.

But Labour was also helped by that key ingredient called perfect timing (Lieberman, 2002, p. 709). Without it, Corbyn's agenda would have been rejected like Miliband's was in 2015. Labour's unambiguous anti-austerity message arrived exactly at the time when austerity fatigue had set in. The British Social Attitudes Survey published in June 2017 captured this change in the national mood. The survey, which was carried out in the second half of 2016, showed that for first time since 2008, 48% of people were in favour of higher taxation to fund higher spending in public services and that 42% of people supported redistribution of wealth from the rich to the poor (NatCen, 2017). This change of mood is understandable. After seven years of relentless public spending cuts many voters were aware of the wider impact of austerity. The cuts to school budgets, the closure of public libraries and the longer waiting lists on the NHS affected most voters. And with inflation rising faster than earnings since the beginning of the year voters felt the deterioration of their living standards more acutely. The literature on economic voting that analyses the relationship between notions of subjective well-being and voting behaviour, suggests that voters' egocentric policy evaluations influence their electoral choices (Whiteley *et al.*, 2013, pp. 234-235). In other words, voters whose living standards have deteriorated will tend to punish the party of government at the ballot box; conversely, those whose living standards have improved will tend to vote for the incumbent party.

The results of the 2017 general election indicate that a degree of egocentric evaluations of government policies played a role. Research by the Resolution Foundation shows that whilst the incomes of pensioner households had grown by nine per cent since the mid-2000s, the incomes of households headed by 25-44 year olds were still not back to their pre-crisis peak at the time of the election (Corlett and Clark, 2017, pp. 7-8). Tellingly, the over-60s voted overwhelmingly Conservative, whereas Labour saw its vote share increase in all the other age groups. Other electoral influences were also important. Voters who are more interested or knowledgeable about politics tend to be more ideological or policy oriented whilst less aware voters tend to be influenced by leaders (see e.g. Bartle, 2005, pp. 658-659). Moreover, when political parties offer genuine choice to voters, as they did in this election, it is likely that questions of ideological positioning become more important whereas considerations about the reputation of party leaders and their stances on the valence issues of the day become less important (Green and Hobolt, 2008, p. 473; Evans and Tilley, 2012, p. 974-975; Adams *et al.*, 2005, p. 29). Labour's surge and the noticeable decline in the vote share of the smaller parties seems to suggest that the ideological positioning of the main parties influenced voting behaviour.

Finally, that Brexit featured so little in the electoral campaign also contributed to Labour's better than expected results. Thanks to the lack of media scrutiny the party could get away with its vague and ambiguous stance on Britain's withdrawal from the EU. The electoral results indicate that Corbyn's decision to not to block the triggering of Article 50 and to accept the end of freedom of movement reassured Brexit supporters in safe Labour seats in much of northern England (Whiteley *et al.*, 2017), whilst at the same time his support for immigration and defence of European social legislation guaranteed the support of younger voters in urban and diverse areas, such as London. Indeed, Labour did not suffer the predicted electoral haemorrhage in the areas that voted Leave. In addition, the Labour surge in areas that had voted Remain in the 2016 EU referendum seems to indicate that for many voters—especially in safe Conservative seats like Canterbury, Battersea and Kensington—Brexit was the key factor that influenced their choice.

6. From campaign poetry to the formulaic prose of opposition politics

Labour's better than expected results raised important questions about our understanding of the mechanics of voting behaviour. It has challenged the idea that electoral campaigns and party ideologies do not matter and that most voters base their electoral choices on valence issues and on the personality of leaders. The seven-week long electoral campaign questioned these assumptions. In particular, the electoral results showed that voters react differently when offered genuine ideological choice.

Above all, the results showed that Labour was the beneficiary of the sea change in public attitudes about taxation, public spending and the role of the state in the economy. The British Social Attitudes survey quoted earlier indicates that voters are not only tired of permanent austerity but are starting to be aware of the wider impact in the public realm of public spending cuts and of the small state ideology that has governed Britain since the 1980s. The public reaction to the tragic fire in the Grenfell Tower in London and the ongoing debate in the Conservative Party about austerity are symptomatic of that mood change.

It remains to be seen whether Jeremy Corbyn can take full advantage of this changed environment. At the time of writing, the momentum is with him. Perhaps galvanised by a fragile party unity, Corbyn's performances in the House of Commons have improved and the shadow cabinet seems more focused. But the Labour leader would be foolish to believe that Labour's victory at the next election is a near-certainty. Research by Policy Network shows that in order to win the next election Labour needs to secure 64 seats that are disproportionately populated by lower and lower middle-income voters who thus far have been immune to Corbyn's charm (Diamond and Cadywould, 2017). Moreover, the high volatility observed in this election suggests that electoral politics will remain unstable and unpredictable for the foreseeable future.

More importantly, the ongoing negotiations to leave the EU, which will dominate the political agenda of the next five years, will expose Labour's divisions on Brexit and on immigration. Corbyn will need to summon all his political talent to prevent the resumption of Labour's civil war. If the Labour leader is serious about winning the next election, he needs to demonstrate, in the coming months and years, an ability to focus forensically on the formulaic prose of day-to-day Westminster politics which thus far has been missing from his performance as Labour leader. Only then can Labour show that it is a government in waiting.

References

Adams, J. F., Merrill, S. III and Grofman, B. (2005) *A Unified Theory of Party Competition: A Cross-National Analysis Integrating Spatial and Behavioural Factors*, Cambridge, Cambridge University Press.

Bartle, J. (2005) 'Homogeneous Models and Heterogeneous Voters', *Political Studies*, **53**, 653–675.

Cook, C. (2017, 15 May) 'General Election 2017: A Tale of Two Campaigns', BBC News, accessed at http://www.bbc.co.uk/news/uk-politics-39927866 on 7 June 2016.

Corlett, A. and Clarke, S. (2017) *Living Standards 2017: The Past, Present and Possible Future of UK Incomes*, London, Resolution Foundation.

Cowley, P. and Kavanagh, D. (2016) *The British General Election of 2015*, Basingstoke, Palgrave Macmillan.

Curtis, C. (2017, 13 June) 'How Britain Voted at the 2017 General Election', *YouGov*, accessed at https://yougov.co.uk/news/2017/06/13/how-britain-voted-2017-general-election/ on 27 June 2017.

Diamond, P. and Cadywould, C. (2017) *Don't Forget the Middle: How Labour Can Build a New Centre-Left Majority*, Policy Network Paper, London, Policy Network.

Eaton, G. (2017, 15 June) 'It's Now All About Jeremy: Labour MPs on the Way Forward', *New Statesman.*

Evans, G. and Tilley, J. (2012) 'The Depoliticization of Inequality and Redistribution: Explaining the Decline of Class Voting', *The Journal of Politics*, **74**, 963–976.

Fielding, S. (2015) 'Hell, No!' Labour's Campaign: The Correct Diagnosis But the Wrong Doctor?' In Geddes Andrew and Tonge Jonathan (eds) *Britain Votes 2015*, Oxford, Oxford University Press, pp. 54–69.

Ford, R. (2017, 11 June) 'The New Electoral Map of Britain: From the Revenge of Remainers to the Upending of Class Politics', *Observer*, accessed at https://www.theguardian.com/politics/2017/jun/11/new-electoral-map-for-britain-revenge-of-remainers-to-upending-class-politics on 11 June 2017.

Green, J. and Hobolt, S. B. (2008) 'Owning the Issue Agenda: Party Strategies and Vote Choices in British Elections', *Electoral Studies*, **27**, 460–476.

Hardman, I. (2017, 19 May) 'Labour's Elections Chief Expects Party to Be Cut Down to 140 Seats', *Spectator*, accessed at https://blogs.spectator.co.uk/2017/05/labours-elections-chief-expects-party-cut-140-seats/ on 19 May 2017.

Harris, J. (2016, 22 September) 'New Times: John Harris on Why Labour is Losing Its Heartland', *New Statesman*, accessed at http://www.newstatesman.com/politics/2016/09/new-times-john-harris-why-labour-losing-its-heartland on 16 May 2017.

Independent (2017, 16 May), 'Labour Admits It Will Not End Benefits Freeze After Day of Confusion', accessed at http://www.independent.co.uk/news/uk/politics/general-elec tion-20107-latest-labour-manifesto-benefits-freeze-cap-jeremy-corbyn-a7739471.html on 20 June 2017.

Labour Party (2015) *Britain Can Be Better: The Labour Party Manifesto 2015*, London, Labour Party.

Labour Party (2017) *For the Many Not the Few: The Labour Party Manifesto 2017*, London, Labour Party.

Lieberman, R. C. (2002) 'Ideas, Institutions and Political Order: Explaining Political Change', *American Political Science Review*, **96**, 697–712.

Miliband, E. (2015, 13 May) 'Speech Britain Can Better: Launch of the 2015 Party Manifesto', accessed at http://labourlist.org/2015/04/britain-can-be-better-the-full-text-of-milibands-manifesto-launch-speech/ on 11 December 2015.

McKibbin, R. (2017, April) 'The Red Sag', *Prospect*, 20–25.

NatCen (2017) *British Social Attitudes 34: A Kind-Hearted But Not Soft-Centred Country*, BSA 34 Key Findings, London, NatCen Social Research.

Peggs, A. (2017, 12 June) 'How Momentum Changed British Politics Forever', *Huffington Post*, accessed at http://www.huffingtonpost.co.uk/adam-peggs/momentum-jeremy-cor byn_b_17054254.html on 25 August 2017.

Richards, S. (2017) *The Rise of the Outsiders: How Mainstream Politics Lost Its Way*, London, Atlantic Books.

Smith, M. (2017, 15 June) 'Theresa May is Now Almost as Unpopular as Pre-Campaign Corbyn', *YouGov*, accessed at https://yougov.co.uk/news/2017/06/15/theresa-may-now-almost-unpopular-pre-campaign-corb/ on 15 June 2017.

Seymour, R. (2016) *Corbyn: The Strange Rebirth of Radical Politics*, London, Verso.

Stewart, M. C. and Clarke, H. D. (1992) 'The (Un)Importance of Party Leaders: Leader Images and Party Choice in the 1987 British Election', *Journal of Politics*, **54**, 447–470.

Waterson, B. (2017, 6 June) 'Here's How Labour Run an Under-the-Radar Dark Ads Campaign During the General Election', *Buzzfeed*, accessed at https://www.buzzfeed. com/jimwaterson/heres-how-labour-ran-an-under-the-radar-dark-ads-campaign? utm_term=.iselgX32j#.bn1PKmE23 on 8 July 2017.

Whiteley, P., Clarke, H. and Goodwin, M. (2017) 'Was This a Brexit Election After All? Tracking Party Support Among Leave and Remain Voters', *LSE Brexit*, accessed at http://blogs.lse.ac.uk/brexit/2017/06/15/was-this-a-brexit-election-after-all-tracking-party-support-among-leave-and-remain-voters/ on 25 August 2017.

Britain Votes (2017) 72–90

DAVID CUTTS AND ANDREW RUSSELL*

The Liberal Democrats: Green Shoots of Recovery or Still on Life Support?

Responding to Theresa May's decision to call a snap general election, Liberal Democrat leader Tim Farron was in upbeat mood, proclaiming it 'your chance to change the direction of your country . . . if you want to avoid a disastrous Hard Brexit . . . if you want to keep Britain in the Single Market . . . if you want a Britain that is open, tolerant and united, this is your chance' (quoted in Osborne, 2017). The Liberal Democrats had some good reasons to feel positive. Two years previously the party had been utterly humiliated at the ballot box following five years in coalition government with the Conservatives. Driven out of natural heartlands and only 25,000 votes from total wipe out, the party was left with a rump of eight MPs, most with precarious majorities (Cutts and Russell, 2015).

However, the referendum decision to leave the European Union provided the Liberal Democrats with a potential political lifeline. With Labour in apparent disarray, the Liberal Democrats had an opportunity to be the voice of those who wanted to remain in the European Union. An unequivocal 'Pro-European' message and support for a second EU referendum on the terms of 'Brexit' gave the party political space and a potentially distinctive identity. A return to the 1992 level of parliamentary representation of 20 seats at least seemed a realistic goal. After all, if the Liberal Democrats could not win a healthy number of seats in 2017 and re-impose the party as a third force in British politics when could they? Yet, despite the salience of 'Brexit', the Liberal Democrats failed to gain any electoral traction. Was the party strategy wrong or were other factors to blame for lack of Liberal Democrat progress? We examine what happened and why, and evaluate whether the party has a political future in British politics or remains on life support.

*David Cutts, Department of Political Science and International Studies, University of Birmingham, d.cutts@bham.ac.uk; Andrew Russell, Department of Politics, University of Liverpool, Andrew.russell@liverpool.ac.uk

doi:10.1093/pa/gsx063

1. The 'Brexit' bounce

Before the EU referendum there were few signs that the party had turned the corner. Despite a new leader—Tim Farron—and a record number of people joining the party, the Liberal Democrats continued to record lower poll numbers than their 2015 national vote share. The party performed poorly in by-elections and in the 2016 English local elections the Liberal Democrats managed to take control of one council (Watford) and make only 45 net seats gains despite their historically low local base. The Liberal Democrats retreated further in Wales in the Assembly elections and despite winning two constituency seats in Scotland they did not increase their representative numbers in Holyrood. However, the vote to leave the EU on 23 June 2016 turned British politics upside down and forged an unexpected opportunity for the Liberal Democrats.

In the chaotic immediate aftermath of the 'Brexit' vote, Cameron resigned, prompting a Conservative leadership contest and Labour began to turn on Jeremy Corbyn. A lacklustre performance during the referendum campaign was the final straw for many in the parliamentary Labour party and this became the catalyst for a second leadership election. Amid this turmoil, the Liberal Democrats continued to court the 48% 'Remain' vote, as Farron became the self-styled spokesperson for the progressives. Immediately this paid off as the Liberal Democrats gained almost 16,000 new members in the three weeks following the referendum. At the party's conference in September, party members overwhelmingly backed a resolution demanding a second referendum to ratify Britain's final Brexit deal. As the new Prime Minister May stressed that 'Brexit means Brexit', Farron laid out the Liberal Democrats' position, arguing that 'if we trusted the people to vote for our departure then we must trust the people to vote for our destination' (quoted in Cooper, 2016).

Internally the Liberal Democrats were gearing themselves up for a 'snap' general election. The focal point of their strategy was the reselection of as many defeated 2015 Liberal Democrat MPs as possible. Party strategists felt former MPs retained significant goodwill from local electorates and could tap into a local personal vote, especially as a number of the former MPs seemed to compare favourably to their replacement from other parties. By mid-July 2016, the party had reselected 14 former Liberal Democrat MPs who were defeated in 2015 to stand again. Re-selection of former MPs was only part of a broader strategy. Those not willing to re-stand were replaced quickly to ensure a head-start in campaign preparation. In those 2010-held seats where a new candidate stood in 2015 and subsequently lost, the Liberal Democrats decided to reinstall as many of these candidates as possible to ensure continuity. The party also installed candidates in seats where the Liberal Democrats had fared well in the past, retained a respectable vote in 2015 and had a strong local campaign team to enthuse voters about the cause.

From late October 2016, the Liberal Democrats regularly began to record double digit poll ratings. There was also evidence that Liberal Democrats were starting to pick up at the ballot box with more council by-election gains (31 in total and 28 net gains) in 2016 than ever before. Complementing this upsurge in its local base was a historic by-election win in Richmond Park. The party had always maintained a strong local base and organisation having held the seat from its creation in 1997 until 2010 and controlled the council. It was also a strong 'Remain' constituency with more than 70% of residents voting to stay in the European Union. The incumbent Zac Goldsmith was officially independent in the by-election (having originally been returned as a Conservative MP), and the Liberal Democrats Sarah Olney took the seat by just over 1,800 votes, recording nearly 50% of the overall share, an increase of more than 30% compared to 2015. This represented a swing of more than 21% from Goldsmith.

Following Olney's victory, there was talk of a political realignment in British politics, as Brexit could supersede traditional cleavages to determine party support, although there was scant evidence that the Liberal Democrats were actually 'hoovering' up discontented 'Remain' voters. The Richmond Park by-election did provide a welcome boost for the party's famed campaign machine that misfired in 2015. Whether heavily focused campaigns in target seats would be as successful in the heat of a general election was still a moot point. It was still unclear if lessons had been learnt from the 2015 campaign and whether the culling of experienced activists partly through changes to the internal party structure and latterly because of heavy losses sustained during the coalition era would still come back to haunt them. Nonetheless, there were signs that the Liberal Democrats had not forgotten how to win.

2.   The electoral reality

Liberal Democrat optimism of an electoral 'bounce-back' in the snap June 2017 election was high. A shortened campaign period seemingly favoured the party that had been out resourced by the Conservative 'decapitation strategy' across the south of England in 2015. Then a highly effective 'joined-up' Tory campaign operation, driven by vast amounts of money thrown at key battleground seats not only within but outside the regulated campaign period for nine months or more, outgunned Liberal Democrat opponents. In 2017 a shorter timescale meant that Conservatives had lost some of that advantage.

However, a significant Liberal Democrat resurgence was unlikely despite 'Brexit'. Figure 5.1 shows the % Remain vote from the EU referendum by Liberal Democrat margin—the difference between the constituency Liberal Democrat vote and the winner at the 2015 election—for the 40 most marginal Liberal Democrat targets in 2017.

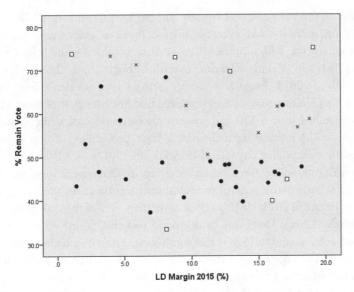

Figure 5.1. % Constituency Remain vote by % 2015 Liberal Democrat margin
*Key: • = Conservative held; □ = Labour held; x = SNP held

There are three visible seat clusters illustrating the difficulties facing the Liberal Democrats. A cluster of nine seats were most vulnerable to the Liberal Democrats if the 'Remain' vote from June 2016 switched to the Liberal Democrats *en masse*, but only four of these seats were held by the Conservatives and two by Labour.[1] The remaining three seats were held by the pro-'Remain' SNP.

A second cluster of ten seats existed where the 'Remain' vote was 50% or more and the Liberal Democrats were up to 20% behind the winning party. Again even a Brexit realignment would limit Liberal Democrat success—only three of these seats were Conservative-held, two were Labour and the other five SNP.[2] The final cluster included a mix of extremely marginal and less marginal seats many of which were around or just under the national average 'Remain' vote but where the Liberal Democrats were between 12-18% behind the winning party in 2015. These were primarily Conservative-held seats where the swing needed by the Liberal Democrats was possible if difficult to achieve. For success across this seat cluster, the Liberal Democrats needed to be the undisputed party of destination for the 'Remain' vote and still rely on some 'Leave' voters either not voting or voting for their chosen party for other reasons than 'Brexit'.

[1] Conservative-held seats: Bath, Twickenham, Kingston and Surbiton, Lewes—and the two held by Labour were Cambridge and Bermondsey and Old Southwark.

[2] Conservative-held seats: Cheadle, Cheltenham and Oxford West and Abingdon—and the two held by Labour were Cardiff Central and Hornsey and Wood Green.

In reality the 2015 electoral context had changed too much. UKIP was hae-morrhaging support—and even candidates. Previous evidence suggested that UKIP's emergence had supressed Conservative support, with those who supported UKIP in recent elections overwhelmingly from those who voted Conservative in 2010 (Evans and Mellon, 2016). Further evidence from wave 10 of the British Election Study panel suggested that just over 70% of those who had already switched from UKIP had gone to the Conservatives, while a quarter of supposed UKIP loyalists actually had a high probability of supporting the Conservatives on polling day (Goodwin and Cutts, 2017*b*). UKIP defections were highest in seats where the Conservatives' main challengers were the Liberal Democrats, particularly across their traditional heartlands in the south-west of England. In fact in 2015, UKIP secured more than 10% of the vote in all but one Conservative-Liberal Democrat battleground seat that polled a lower 'Remain' vote than average, and in 15 of the 16 south-west seats with a higher than average 'Leave' vote. With the Conservatives actively tempting UKIP supporters through a 'hard Brexit' message, there was an effective 'blue wall' of Conservative support that would resist Liberal Democrat challenge and even threaten a number of incumbent Liberal Democrat MPs (Goodwin and Cutts, 2017*a*).

Moreover, pre-election polling data revealed that 'Remainers' were becoming increasingly fractured. A majority believed that the government had a duty to carry out the vote to leave the EU rather than ignoring the result of the referendum. While roughly a quarter supported the Liberal Democrats' position of a second referendum once Brexit negotiations had been completed, fewer than half of 'Remainers' supported it, while more than three quarters of 'Leavers' opposed it (Wells, 2017). Evidence from the British Election Study (wave 10) found few Conservative pro-Europeans or 'Remain' voters willing to abandon the Conservatives in favour of the Liberal Democrats (Fieldhouse *et al.*, 2016). The Liberal Democrats seemingly faced the twin problem of an impenetrable Conservative 'Leave' vote reinforced by ex-UKIP voters who saw the Conservatives as the best vehicle to deliver Brexit, and a soft 'Remain' vote, a majority of whom accepted the outcome of the referendum, but were simply unwilling to leave the Conservative fold.

The May 2017 local elections provided some context for the Liberal Democrat challenge. Despite a four-point increase in their vote compared to 2013, the Liberal Democrats' national share (18%) was still well below their pre-coalition performances in local council elections. There was a small 'Brexit' bonus with the party polling three percentage points higher on average in those wards with the highest 'Remain' vote and there were signs that highly-targeted campaigns in previous strongholds or areas which contained an above average Remain vote could result in the Liberal Democrats' increasing support. However, this did not translate into seats. While their national vote share increased, the party recorded a net

Table 5.1 Liberal Democrat electoral performance 1992–2017

LD	1992	1997	2001	2005	2010	2015	2017
Votes (000)	5,999	5,243	4,814	5,985	6,836	2,416	2,372
% UK Vote	17.8%	16.8%	18.3%	22.0%	23.0%	7.9%	7.4%
Seats Won	20	46	52	62	57	8	12
% Seats Won	3.2%	7.0%	7.9%	9.6%	8.8%	1.2%	1.8%
Votes:Seats*	1.1	2.7	2.8	2.9	2.5	1.0	1.6
Lost Deposits	11/632	13/639	1/639	1/626	0/631	341/631	375/629

*Votes: Seats Ratio derived from dividing LD seats won by LD share of the vote. In 1992, the Liberal Democrats stood in 632 constituencies; and in 2017 they stood in 629.

loss of 40 councillors. The 'Blue wall' of support in Liberal Democrat versus Conservative seats posed a serious threat to Liberal Democrat prospects. The task of a revival in old Liberal strongholds looked particularly bleak with large parts of Cornwall, Devon and Somerset impenetrable.

3.   The electoral outcome

The 2017 general election represented a return to two-party politics in Britain. The combined Conservative and Labour vote share was the highest recorded since 1970. Unsurprisingly, all the other UK parties lost support with UKIP, Greens and SNP losing the most ground. It was no different for the Liberal Democrats. The party obtained 2.37 million votes, 43,952 fewer than in 2015 despite the increase in turnout. Liberal Democrat vote share declined by 0.5% to 7.4%, the lowest level for a 'Liberal' party since 1959. Table 5.1 shows Liberal Democrat performances over the last quarter-of-a-century.

Although Liberal Democrat support in 2017 increased in around one-third of all constituencies, the party fell well short of the 18 seats targeted by Farron. The party's vote share dropped but a net gain of four seats from 2015 was achieved, increasing their numbers in Westminster to 12.

Thanks largely to effective targeting strategies, the Liberal Democrats actually gained five seats—Bath, Eastbourne, Kingston and Surbiton, Oxford West and Abingdon and Twickenham—from the Conservatives and three—Caithness, Sutherland and Easter Ross, East Dunbartonshire, and Edinburgh West—from the SNP. However, Southport, where incumbent John Pugh had stood down, was lost to the Conservatives and by-election victor, Sarah Olney, narrowly fell short in Richmond Park, also against the Conservatives. Meanwhile Greg Mulholland (Leeds North West) and former leader Nick Clegg (Sheffield Hallam) both lost

Table 5.2 Liberal Democrat performance 2015–2017: National and regional breakdown

National & Regional	2017 % LD Vote	2015 % LD Vote	% Change +/-15-17	Seats 2017	Seats 2015	Change 15-17
Country						
UK	7.4	7.9	−0.5	12/632	8/632	+4
England	7.8	8.2	−0.4	8/533	6/533	+2
Scotland	6.8	7.6	−0.8	4/59	1/59	+3
Wales	4.5	6.5	−2.0	0/40	1/40	−1
Region						
East Midlands	4.3	5.6	−1.3	0/46	0/46	0
Eastern	7.9	8.3	−0.4	1/58	1/58	0
London	8.8	7.7	+1.1	3/73	1/73	+2
North East	4.6	6.5	−1.9	0/29	0/29	0
North West	5.4	6.6	−1.2	1/75	2/75	−1
South East	10.5	9.4	+1.1	2/84	0/84	+2
South West	14.9	15.1	−0.2	1/55	0/55	+1
West Midlands	4.4	5.5	−1.1	0/59	0/59	0
Yorkshire & The Humber	5.0	7.1	−2.1	0/54	2/54	−2

their seats to Labour. The Liberal Democrats were also wiped out in Wales where incumbent Mark Williams lost Ceredigion to Plaid Cymru.

Closer inspection of the results suggests that the Liberal Democrats came close to faring significantly better. Four seats—Ceredigion, Fife North East, Richmond Park and St Ives—were missed by wafer thin majorities (although victories in Westmoreland and Lonsdale and Oxford West and Abingdon were also very tight). Despite a low overall share, the party polled more than 30% of the vote in 28 constituencies. Worryingly, Liberal Democrats lost 375 deposits, more than in 2015, and only came second in 38 seats. Of those second places the party is within 10% of the winning party in just nine seats and more than 20% behind in 22 constituencies. There appears to be a low ceiling on the number of winnable seats.

The Liberal Democrats' national vote share still obscures a fair amount of unevenness in their electoral performance. Despite winning four of the 59 constituencies in Scotland, the Liberal Democrats' vote dropped below 7% (see Table 5.2). Three of the five largest declines in the party's share of the vote were in former Scottish strongholds and Scottish Liberal Democrats lost deposits in 46 of the 59 seats. In Wales, the Liberal Democrats fared even worse. Not only is it now without any representation, its vote share declined by 2% to 4.5% and the party only held its deposit in four constituencies.

Across England, there is a north-south divide in the party's vote. In 2017, Liberal Democrat support largely held up in the south of England albeit from a low base. The Liberal Democrats continue to poll relatively strongly in their area of traditional strength: the south west of England. Here there is some evidence that party support has bottomed-out with the Liberal Democrats getting around the same vote share as two years ago. The Liberal Democrats only gained support in two regions: London and the south-east. Liberal Democrat support also largely held up in eastern England and remains above the national average. Elsewhere the picture looks extremely gloomy. Across the midlands, the Liberal Democrat vote has collapsed and is now little above four per cent. There was also a two per cent drop in Liberal Democrat support across the north-east and the Yorkshire and Humber region. In the five regions outside the south of England, Liberal Democrat support is close to three per cent below its national vote share. There is also a geographic divide in Liberal Democrat representation. Westmoreland and Lonsdale is the only northern English Liberal Democrat seat. Of the 38 seats where the Liberal Democrats came second in 2017, only six of these were in the midlands and the north of England. Across the south, the Liberal Democrats lost their deposit in just over a third of the seats. However, in the north, the Liberal Democrats lost their deposit in 201 seats (more than three quarters of those contested).

4. The constituency battle

Table 5.3 examines the Liberal Democrats' 2017 performance by seat type. In 2015, despite the loss of all but eight seats, there was a very modest incumbency effect with the Liberal Democrats doing better in those incumbent seats where candidates were seeking re-election (Cutts and Russell, 2015). Two years later, despite losing five of the nine seats they held at dissolution, Liberal Democrat support rose by 3.3 percentage points in the seats they won in 2015.

Incumbency did not save four Liberal Democrat MPs, but once again those Liberal Democrat incumbents seeking re-election did fare better. Where a Liberal Democrat incumbent stood again, party support increased by 4.2 percentage points. Incumbency matters for the Liberal Democrats but, as in 2015, any expectation that those seeking re-election would be immune from a national surge against them because of their personal standing in the area was simply misguided. More worrying for the Liberal Democrats, the defeats of Nick Clegg and Greg Mulholland suggest that even highly targeted local campaigns backed up by central resources and know-how are insufficient when the tide of support rises against them.

The tactic of re-selecting former Liberal Democrat MPs in key target seats had a modest positive impact on party support but there was unevenness depending on the political context of the seat. There were 12 Liberal Democrat former MPs who lost in 2015 to the Conservatives and who stood again. In these seats, Liberal Democrat support increased by 5.4 percentage points, with three of these MPs re-

Table 5.3 Liberal Democrat performance by incumbency and seat type, 2017

Seats	2017 % LD Vote	2015 % LD Vote	% Change +/- 15-17
Incumbency			
LD 2017 Incumbent Seats (9)	39.3	36.0	+3.3
LD Incumbent Candidates (8)	40.9	36.7	+4.2
LD Non-Held Seats (622)	7.1	7.7	−0.6
2015 Incumbency			
LD 2015 Incumbent Seats (57)	27.3	30.1	−2.8
LD MPs lost 2015 stood again 2017 (20)	31.3	30.6	+0.7
Con-LD MPs lost 15 stood again 2017 (12)	37.2	31.8	+5.4
Lab-LD MPs lost 15 stood again 2017 (6)	19.2	27.5	−8.3
SNP-LD MPs lost 15 stood again 2017 (2)	29.8	32.2	−2.4
Seat Type (LDs Second Place)			
LD All Second Place (62)	26.2	27.2	−1.0
Con-LD Seats (45)	27.9	25.9	+2.0
Lab-LD Seats (9)	17.2	28.7	−11.5
SNP-LD Seats (8)	25.2	32.8	−7.6
Historical Legacy			
LD Legacy February 1974 seats (14)	18.3	20.8	−1.5
LD Heartland 1992 seats (18)	26.3	29.5	−3.2
LD Breakthrough 1997 seats (29)	27.8	25.4	+2.4

Note: Percentages derived from summing LD votes cast/Total Valid Votes Cast*100. 2017 constituencies excludes the Speaker's seat (Buckingham) and Brighton Pavilion both where the LDs did not stand a candidate. Heartland 1992 seats—Liverpool Mossley Hill and Tweeddale, Ettrick & Lauderdale were abolished. Of those LD MPs who stood again, David Ward stood as an Independent in Bradford East and therefore is not counted.

capturing their seats. Other highlights were the strong performances in North Devon and Wells, while in St Ives, Andrew George was just over 300 votes from winning back his seat. It was not all one way traffic. The party went rapidly backwards in Colchester and barely made any ground in Eastleigh and St Austell and Newquay. Selecting previous incumbents proved to be largely ineffective against a resurgent Labour. Only six stood again in the hope of winning their seat from the Labour incumbent. Not only did all fail to get re-elected, but support in these seats tumbled more than eight percentage points as the party's vote share dropped below 20 per cent. There were mixed results against the SNP. Jo Swinson won her seat back in East Dunbartonshire but Alan Reid in Argyll and Bute saw his vote crumble.

One way to illustrate this is to examine the effect of incumbency on Liberal Democrat support in those 14 seats where the previous incumbent stood in 2015 and lost but did not seek re-election in 2017. Eight of these seats were held by the Conservatives while three were held each by Labour and the SNP. In 2017, the Liberal Democrats failed to win any of these seats back. Indeed, in only two

(Lewes +3.8 and Brecon and Radnorshire +0.8 percentage points) did the Liberal Democrats increase their vote share. In the three SNP-held seats, the Liberal Democrat vote fell in 2017 by 15.7 percentage points. Likewise in the three Labour-held seats the Liberal Democrat vote fell by 12.6 percentage points. Even in the eight Conservative-held seats, where the Liberal Democrats enjoyed some success, the party's vote fell by 4.5 percentage points. No doubt the decisions of locally popular former MPs such as Adrian Sanders in Torbay (where the Liberal Democrat vote fell by 8.7%) and Steve Webb in Thornbury and Yate (where the vote fell by 6.5%) not to stand again hampered any chances of a recovery. Moreover, they illustrate just how much of a personal vote these former incumbents generated which was largely masked by the collapse in Liberal Democrat support in 2015.

The Liberal Democrats entered the 2017 general election as the main challenger in 62 seats. Across these constituencies, Liberal Democrat support fell by one percentage point compared to 2015 but again the role of political agency is important. Where the Liberal Democrats were the main challenger to Labour, support crumbled by 11.5%. It was slightly different in Scotland where the Liberal Democrats were caught in the cross-fire of post-independence referendum politics. Only in the four most marginal seats where the party deployed considerable resources did the Liberal Democrat vote hold up. In the 46 seats where the party was second to the Conservatives, the Liberal Democrats fared better, increasing support by two percentage points. Despite reversals in Sutton and Cheam, Thornbury and Yate, and Torbay, closer inspection of the data does suggest marginality mattered. In the ten most marginal (0-10% difference) Conservative-Liberal Democrat battleground seats, there was a 4.2% increase in Liberal Democrat support.

Traditionally the Liberal Democrats' ability to win Conservative seats depends on building and sustaining core support, appealing to wavering Conservatives and persuading centre-left Labour and Green voters to support them tactically to keep out the Tories. Aside from the ruthless and sustained Conservative targeting, a key factor in the Liberal Democrats' 2015 collapse was the tactical unwind of its left of centre vote in these seats. In 2017 the Liberal Democrats enjoyed modest success against the Conservatives. But our evidence suggests that the Liberal Democrats' ability to turn votes into seats was dependent on curbing the Labour vote. In the five seats it took from the Conservatives in 2017, only Eastbourne saw an increase in the Conservative share of the vote. Crucially, though, across these five seats the Labour vote declined by 0.2 percentage points. Moreover, in the three seats where the Greens stood a candidate, their support fell substantially. Despite the Labour surge elsewhere there is plenty of evidence that in these Conservative-Liberal Democrat battlegrounds the Liberal Democrats managed to stop any further centre-left tactical unwind. However, elsewhere it was a different story. In the 20 other Conservative-Liberal Democrat battlegrounds where the Liberal Democrats were 20% or less behind the incumbent, the Labour vote increased by 7.9%. In five of these 20 contests, Labour even relegated the Liberal Democrats to third place. Many Labour voters in these seats, knowing Labour was unlikely to win put voting for their favoured party before lending their support to the second-placed Liberal Democrats. The pattern of the 2015 general election seems to have continued in 2017.

The 2017 general election signified a continuation of the Liberal Democrats' retreat from their traditional heartlands. Of the 14 Liberal constituencies held in February 1974, only one (Orkney and Shetland) is now held by the Liberal Democrats. More worrying for the Liberal Democrats is how it performs in its 1992 seats. This base proved to be a springboard for later gains as the party translated votes into healthy levels of representation at Westminster. Only three of these 1992 seats (Bath, Caithness, Sutherland and Easter Ross and Orkney and Shetland) remain in Liberal Democrat hands 25 years on. The party also continues to lose ground in these seats partly because credibility gained from local success has waned and not recovered since being in coalition. One positive, though, is the improved performance in the 'breakthrough' seats which the Liberal Democrats won in 1997. These were overwhelmingly Conservative and were gained at the height of the anti-Conservative tactical alliance against John Major's government. Given the Liberal Democrats' low base in 2015 there is evidence of a 'bounce-back' in these seats two years on. Five of the 12 seats the Liberal Democrats now hold were first gained in 1997; eight of the 12 also elected Liberal Democrat representatives 20 years ago. Despite the increasing lack of representation from its traditional heartland areas, there is a semblance of historical legacy in Liberal Democrat support and Westminster representation.

One of the key election puzzles is how the Liberal Democrats failed to capitalise on the party's anti-Brexit stance. Of the 12 seats the party currently holds, eight voted 'Remain' in the EU referendum. Two of the Liberal Democrats' gains—Caithness, Sutherland and Easter Ross and Eastbourne—voted 'Leave' while the local personal standing of Tom Brake and Norman Lamb helped ensure their re-election in 'Leave' areas. Four of the five seats lost also voted 'Remain'. Figure 5.2 shows a positive relationship (correlation of 0.15* significant at 99% level) between the change in the Liberal Democrat vote 2015-2017 and the percentage 'Remain' vote for all UK constituencies, although the line is relatively flat, whilst Table 5.4 reveals how the Liberal Democrats performed in 'Leave' and 'Remain' seats in more depth.

In 2017, the Liberal Democrat vote was four percentage points higher in 'Remain' areas than 'Leave' seats and 2.6% higher than their national vote share. When we break down these seats according to support for 'Remain' and 'Leave', it transpires that the Liberal Democrat vote in 'Hard Brexit' areas (with a 60%+

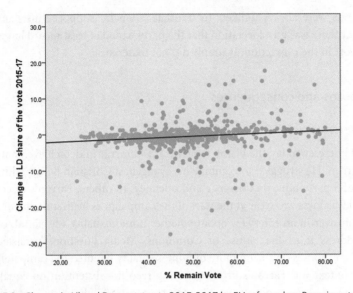

Figure 5.2. Change in Liberal Democrat vote 2015-2017 by EU referendum Remain vote
Correlation—Remain vote & LD 2017 vote share = 0.25*
Correlation—Remain vote & LD 2015 vote share = 0.19*
Correlation—Remain vote & Change LD 2015-17 vote share = 0.15*

Table 5.4 Liberal Democrat performance in Remain and Leave seats, 2017

Seats	2017 % LD Vote	2015 % LD Vote	% Change +/- 15-17
Remain/Leave			
All Leave Seats (393)	6.0	7.0	−1.0
All Remain Seats (237)	10.0	9.8	+0.2
Leave			
'Soft Brexit' Seats 50.1-59.9% (240)	7.3	8.1	−0.8
'Hard Brexit' Seats 60% plus (153)	4.0	5.1	−1.1
Remain			
'Soft Remain' Seats 50.1-59.9% (150)	9.8	9.9	−0.1
'Hard Remain' Seats 60% plus (87)	10.4	9.7	+0.7

Note: 630 seats. We exclude Buckingham and Brighton Pavilion.

'Leave' vote) is 3.3% lower than in 'Soft Brexit' seats. Liberal Democrat support
was marginally higher in 'Hard Remain' (60%+) seats but there was not a great
deal of difference. Table 5.4 also contains party vote share across the 'Leave' and
'Remain' categories in 2015 and notes the change in support. Overall, Liberal
Democrat support in 'Leave' seats dropped by 1% but the real story is the lack of
growth in all 'Remain' constituencies between 2015 and 2017. The Liberal

Democrats were always unlikely to translate 'Remain' support into significant gains but there was an expectation that the party would at least record large shifts of support in their direction. It simply did not materialise.

5. Causes and consequences

5.1 Farron's failure?

It would be easy to lay the blame for Liberal Democrat underachievement upon Tim Farron. He struggled to combine his evangelical Christian beliefs with being leader of a party built on tolerance and openness to others. Farron's discomfort and awkwardness was clear at the start of the campaign as he first declined to give a clear answer in an interview about whether homosexuality was sinful, only to later address it in the House of Commons. Media questions persisted and Farron's responses on the morality of homosexuality haunted the campaign. Part of the context was Farron's previous voting record—abstention on equal marriage bill (third reading); voted against the 2007 Equality Act (Sexual Orientations) regulations—although he had subsequently spoken up for LGBTI rights and supported gay marriage in Commons votes prior to the third reading of the Bill. Ironically Farron had also encouraged internal reform in the party. The manifesto for instance pledged all-LGBTI parliamentary shortlists. Crucially Farron's personal stance was at odds with the very voters that the Liberal Democrats sought to win over: young, cosmopolitan, liberal 'Remainers' who collectively celebrated sexual equality.

Importantly for the party, the issue dominated the first 24 hours and then dogged the latter parts of the campaign just when the Liberal Democrats had an audience for its key election messages. In the past, media exposure during the short campaign period had led to surges in Liberal Democrat support (Russell and Fieldhouse, 2005). Media focus tests the ability of party leaders to deliver messages in a manageable form. For third parties, the leader is arguably even more crucial. They have a limited time during the election campaign to get the right message across but often it is the first time that many in the electorate have paid attention to the leaders of parties other than the main two. Being embroiled in public stand-offs with the media therefore wasted valuable time, drew negative publicity and distracted voters from the party's message.

Farron was unable to build a dialogue with the electorate. His approval ratings actually got worse during the campaign moving from -22 at the start of May to -26 in the week before polling day. Less than two weeks before election-day 52% of those asked in an Opinium poll could not name the Liberal Democrat leader (*Daily Telegraph*, 26 May 2017). By the final week of the campaign, 35% of those asked did not know if he was doing well or badly, compared to 11% for May and

13% for Corbyn (YouGov tracking poll). While a sizeable number of voters were unable to make a judgement on Farron's leadership many others were unconvinced as he simply failed to cut through. Despite his moral anxiety on homosexuality a more fundamental problem was that the party had simply become an irrelevance for many.

Farron had been the overwhelming choice of the Liberal Democrats as the new leader after the 2015 debacle. He had offered a vision of a party reconnecting to its liberal roots, and activist base. Farron was always less comfortable in the Commons than his predecessors as Liberal Democrat leader. Under him the party failed to appreciate the Westminster-heavy knock-on effects of the 2015 result; usurped as the third party in the Commons by the SNP, Farron did not even warrant a weekly slot in Prime Minister's Questions. The profile of the Liberal Democrats sank from the minor coalition partner led by the Deputy Prime Minister to subterranean gang of eight with an anonymous leader.

Whatever discomforts his personal belief system triggered in the party's psyche, it is the inability of Farron's leadership to re-establish liberalism as a viable concern that is his most marked failure. That the party chose 74-year-old retread MP Vince Cable as his replacement in summer 2017 demonstrated a recognition that the party needed to re-establish itself as a parliamentary force again.

Finally even the ability to galvanise his local party deserted Farron. His Westmorland and Lonsdale seat was regarded as the template for Liberal Democrat revival after coalition, yet in 2017 he only held on to a Conservative challenge for the seat by his fingertips. The balance of top-down/bottom-up equilibrium in the party would have to be recalibrated and Farron clearly was not the leader to do this.

5.2   The Campaign

The 2017 Liberal Democrat campaign was a game of two halves. In the first the Liberal Democrats took the 'Brexit' challenge head-on. June 2017 was an opportunity to present the party as the political home for 'Remainers' and give European enthusiasts some hope. A second ballot on the details of Brexit would provide an opportunity for a considered re-think. Yet, for many it smacked of a devious way of re-running the referendum. Indeed one could reasonably make the case that the policy was illiberal and lacked respect for the original referendum result. The policy also lacked political nous since by their own admission, the Liberal Democrats accepted that they would not form the next government and had also ruled out any coalition agreement with Conservatives and Labour—meaning that despite the rhetoric they would not be in a position to implement the policy or have any hope of reversing the Brexit decision through this route. A more focused approach on the economic merits of remaining in the single

Table 5.5 Best party on issues: YouGov tracking poll 5-7 June 2017

Issue	Conservatives (%)	Labour (%)	Lib Dems (%)	Others (%)	None (%)	DK (%)
Health	22	41	4	2	8	22
Immigration	30	25	5	17	8	20
Law & Order	36	26	4	5	6	23
Education	25	36	5	4	7	24
Unemployment	29	30	2	4	8	26
Economy	39	25	4	4	7	24
Housing	21	35	4	4	9	27
EU exit	37	19	7	8	8	21
Security	37	22	3	6	7	25

market and customs union might have proved a much stronger sell and maintained clear water from Labour's ambiguous position.

Beyond Brexit the Liberal Democrats' manifesto contained many headline proposals—1p in the pound on income tax to raise £6bn for NHS and social care services; end the 1% public sector pay cap; reinstate university maintenance grants for the poorest students; extend free childcare to all two year olds.—all tailored to win back those centre-left voters who had deserted the party since 2010. However, this appeal was side-lined by Labour's populist anti-austerity message.

With the Conservatives floundering on social care and the Prime Minister exposed as deficient in the campaign, the Liberal Democrats saw an opportunity to pounce. The second half of the campaign proved to be more successful as the party tapped into concerns about the so called 'Dementia tax' and more generally about Conservative plans for the elderly and social care, as the party sought to capture Conservative waverers, particularly in southern seats who were concerned by the Tory manifesto.

Despite the Liberal Democrats' offensive drive in the second half of the campaign, longstanding problems on political identity and policy appeal remained. In September 2016, a YouGov study found that two-thirds of all voters did not know what the party stands for anymore (Twyman, 2016). The figure was greater for those who voted Liberal Democrat previously, with seven out of ten of former voters stating they were uncertain. Moreover, even 22% of current supporters asked also confessed to not knowing. The 2017 election campaign not only provided an opportunity to put forward a raft of proposals and policy ideas but also to address longstanding concerns by showcasing a distinctive identity. It was also a chance to challenge competitors' longstanding ownership of the most salient issues. Table 5.5 shows YouGov data, collected in the days prior to polling day, on the best party on the key issues in the election.

After six weeks of national campaigning, it made grim reading for the Liberal Democrats. Aside from Europe, on which 7% of respondents named the Liberal Democrats as the best party, the Liberal Democrats simply failed to challenge the main parties' ownership of salient issues. There were also few signs that the policies advocated by the party garnered any meaningful support from the electorate.

5.3　The legacy of coalition

The Liberal Democrats were still toxic for swathes of centre-left and young voters just two years on from the coalition. Labour's pitch to these groups made Liberal Democrat rehabilitation harder. With little prospect of winning back large numbers, the party was left desperately appealing to these voters in target seats to lend them their support to oust the Conservatives. As we have shown, many declined.

The collapse in representation at Westminster also meant that mainstream media exposure became increasingly limited. Despite Farron presenting himself as a dissenter on coalition policies like tuition fees which caused the party so much reputational damage, this simply reminded voters of the coalition and for some what they saw was a betrayal. Whatever way the Liberal Democrats turned after the 2015 general election they were in a bind. In 2017, voters found it difficult to swallow Liberal Democrat assurances that they had learned the lessons from their time in coalition given that many of these words came from people who were heavily involved.

A key legacy of the coalition was the 'hollowing out' of local parties and the loss of experienced political campaigners. As we have noted, in the two years since 2015 the Liberal Democrats have made modest progress locally but remain way below the heights of the past. While the targeting strategy was relatively successful and more realistic than in 2015, the capacity of the Liberal Democrats to run effective campaigns is compromised by the losses endured when in coalition and by the internal reforms made by the party in the early 2010s.

6.　Conclusion

Two years ago there were concerns whether the Liberal Democrats in their current form would survive. The party elected a new leader with the remit of rebuilding from the bottom-up. It was a long-term project. Then David Cameron set a date for a referendum on membership of the European Union. Six months later the public had voted to leave, both major parties faced divisive leadership contests and the Liberal Democrats were thrust into pole position as the spokesperson for the 48% who wanted to remain in the EU. Until Theresa May called a 'snap' general election, the Liberal Democrats were building momentum. Many in the party were convinced by the rather fanciful prospect of a strong performance (and even victory) in the cancelled Manchester Gorton by-election. Just how would the Liberal Democrats have fared in a general election after the Brexit negotiations had taken place? With Europe at the forefront of political debate the battle lines were seemingly drawn. While the rush was on to court the more nativist and authoritarian leanings of the majority, a significant section of the electorate was ostensibly far more sympathetic to a party more cosmopolitan in outlook, a defender of liberal values. In the face of Labour woes the opportunity was there for the Liberal Democrats to fill this void. Yet longstanding issues explain the Liberal Democrats' current electoral predicament. There is little change in the weakness of the party's social and partisan base.

The Liberal Democrats still rely on votes that are lent rather than owned. Beyond their position on Europe, the Liberal Democrats lack a political identity and programme to enthuse support. Part of the problem is that of political distinctiveness and an inability to stake out clear political territory that appeals to voters who ostensibly share liberal values. Of course, the reputational baggage picked up from being in coalition hasn't helped this cause. However, at its heart is not only an ideological and party positioning tension but more importantly it is about the party's strategy of adopting quick-fix solutions at the expense of building a longstanding programme. The party has continuously opted for the former, stressing eye-catching proposals for public consumption. Few parties have produced more policy initiatives, documents and proposals than the Liberal Democrats. The 2017 manifesto continued this trend. Yet, outside the highly politically engaged, most electors would be hard-pushed to know what the Liberal Democrats actually stand for, or recall their policies. The debilitating struggle for media exposure has not helped but this is only a partial explanation. Likewise electoral credibility will always be a problem, but given the Liberal Democrats' current political and electoral predicament, now is the time to play the longer game as the short-term quick-fix solutions seemingly no longer work.

The Liberal Democrats will take some heart from their targeting strategy, which was much more streamlined and focused than in 2015. Campaigning proved effective where the party was on the front foot, but less effective in defensive situations primarily against Labour. Party activism around community-based politics is a vital part of the Liberal Democrats' armoury. It is effective but not a panacea. Comparative advantage offline has gone with other parties copying what works and then tailoring it to suit. Online, Liberal Democrat activity is competitive but has fallen behind the other parties, particularly the organic social media activism undertaken by groups and individuals associated with Labour. How the Liberal Democrats can match and even compete against this is difficult to fathom. Although targeting did help win seats, the strategy may have had unintended consequences. Only nine constituencies are now marginal with a gap of 10% or less between the Liberal Democrat challenger and the incumbent. Barring historic shifts in support, electoral growth looks hamstrung in the short to medium term.

The Liberal Democrats now face a monumental task. The return to two party politics inevitably means that the Liberal Democrats are a spectator on the sidelines rather than taking part in the main game. Nevertheless, British politics is in continuous flux and one would be foolhardy to assume that such clear battle lines will hold. With the Conservatives minority government struggling to see out a full term, Brexit negotiations to dominate political discourse, a Tory party leadership contest seemingly likely at some point, and continued internal party strife in Labour most likely, it is possible that the Liberal Democrats could suddenly benefit from any fall in two party support. However, key decisions about where the party stands, where it goes and how it operates need to be made. After the 2015 general election the Liberal Democrats were on life support and fighting for their political survival. In 2017, the party may have stabilised somewhat but it is still a in a critical condition.

References

Cooper, C. (2016, 20 September), 'Liberal Democrats Back Second Brexit Vote', *Politico Europe*, accessed at http://www.politico.eu/article/tim-farron-liberal-democrats-back-second-brexit-vote-deal-theresa-may-uk/ on 12 August 2017.

Cutts, D. and Russell, A. (2015) 'From Coalition to Catastrophe: The Electoral Meltdown of the Liberal Democrats'. In Geddes, A and Tonge, J. (eds), *Britain Votes 2015*, Oxford, Oxford University Press, pp. 70–87.

Evans, G and Mellon, J. (2016) 'Working-Class Votes and Conservative Losses: Solving the UKIP Puzzle', *Parliamentary Affairs*, **69**, 464-479.

Fieldhouse, E., J. Green., G. Evans., H. Schmitt, C. van der Eijk, J. Mellon and C. Prosser. (2016) British Election Study Internet Panel Waves 1-10. DOI: 10.15127/1.293723.

Goodwin, M. and Cutts, D. (2017a, 24 April) 'Project Comeback: Will the Liberal Democrats Really Give May a Bloody Nose?', *UK in a Changing Europe*, accessed at http://ukandeu.ac.uk/project-comeback-will-the-liberal-democrats-really-give-may-a-bloody-nose/ on 14 August 2017.

Goodwin, M. and Cutts, D. (2017b, 28 April) 'Why UKIP's Collapse Matters', *Politico Europe*, accessed at http://www.politico.eu/article/uk-general-election-ukip-why-collapse-matters-conservative-majority-theresa-may/ on 14 August 2017.

Osborne, S. (2017, 18 April) 'Tim Farron: Lib Dem Leader Says Snap Election is "Chance to Change Direction of Country"', *Independent*, accessed at http://www.independent.co.uk/news/uk/politics/tim-farron-general-election-liberal-democrat-leader-snap-change-country-direction-chance-june-8-a7688486.html on 11 August 2017.

Russell, A. and Fieldhouse, E. (2005) *Neither Left nor Right?*, *Manchester*, Manchester University Press.

Telegraph (2017, 26 May), 'Who's Tim? More Than Half of Voters Do Not Know Who Tim Farron Is', accessed at http://www.telegraph.co.uk/news/2017/05/26/tim-half-vot ers-do-not-know-tim-farron/ on 14 August 2017.

Twyman, J. (2016), 'In Search of the Lost Lib Dems', *YouGov*, accessed at https://yougov. co.uk/news/2016/09/19/tim-who-where-now-liberal-democrats/ on 14 August 2017.

Wells, A. (2017) 'Attitudes to Brexit: Everything We Know So Far', *YouGov*, accessed at https://yougov.co.uk/news/2017/03/29/attitudes-brexit-everything-we-know-so-far/ on 12 August 2017.

Britain Votes (2017) 91–108

JAMES DENNISON*

The Rug Pulled from Under Them: UKIP and the Greens

The two parties that lost the most votes at the 2017 General Election were the United Kingdom Independence Party (UKIP) and the Greens. This contribution considers the causes of the decline of each party. I show that neither was able to find a clear role in the party system following the EU referendum and the election of Jeremy Corbyn, respectively. These two events robbed UKIP and the Greens of their primary appeal to voters, resulting in losses in membership, less media interest and, in the case of UKIP, internal disunity. In response, both parties attempted to strike an awkward balance between three campaigning approaches: advocating or emphasising new policies, retaining their claim as the original and *bona fide* voice of their key policy, and suggesting electoral cooperation with ideologically congruent elements of, respectively, the pro-Brexit Conservatives and Corbyn-led Labour Party. However, once the election was called, neither party was in a position either to campaign effectively against or negotiate with their rivals for votes, leading to a second sudden decline for both, as both the right and left of the British electorate reunified around the Conservatives and Labour respectively.

1. UKIP after the 2015 election

UKIP started the 2015-2017 Parliament having secured a string of historic electoral feats over the preceding few years. After becoming the obvious choice for the soaring numbers of British Eurosceptics at European Parliamentary elections from 1999 onwards, UKIP was able to shift their focus to exploiting Britons' deepening concerns over immigration under the 2010-2015 Coalition government. Meanwhile, UKIP's leader, Nigel Farage, took specific aim at Conservative leader David Cameron, an upper class, self-styled 'heir to Blair', who had aimed to 'modernise' his party through social liberalism and attempting to silence its internal debate over EU membership (Dennison and Goodwin, 2018). Furthermore, the

*James Dennison, Migration Policy Centre, European University Institute, james.dennison@eui.eu

doi:10.1093/pa/qsx064

collapse of the far-right British National Party, the Liberal Democrats' entry into coalition government and the leadership of Labour by the luckless Ed Miliband, all gave UKIP a vast pool of voters from which to draw support.

At the 2013 local elections, UKIP secured 23% of the votes in seats in which they stood candidates, increasing their councillors from four to 147. One year later, UKIP made history by finishing first in the European Elections. At the 2015 general election, UKIP won 12.6% of all votes—the third most—though only one seat. Leader Nigel Farage then upheld his promise to resign should he not win a Westminster seat of his own, only for his resignation to be bizarrely rejected by the party's National Executive Committee amid calls for him to stand down by other, clearly embittered, senior party figures. Despite on-going internal disarray, UKIP not only had electoral momentum but also was still dominating media interest as 'insurgent' outsiders upending the establishment. More tantalising still, UKIP had backed the governing Conservative Party leadership into a corner whereby they were obliged to deliver on a manifesto promise to offer a referendum on EU membership.

2.   UKIP and the EU referendum

Following Farage's reinstallation as leader, UKIP were uncharacteristically quiet over the next year as 'a fragile truce between Farage and a growing number of enemies' within the party emerged in the run-up to the referendum (Grice, 2016). During this period, UKIP's polling performances gradually improved following their post-election chaos, up from an average of around 10% in July 2015 to a peak of around 17% just before the EU referendum. At the May 2016 local elections, UKIP performed well, winning 25 councillors and 12% of the popular vote as both the Corbyn-led Labour and Cameron-led Conservatives lost seats. The party's biggest victory came at the concurrent Welsh Assembly elections, where it won 13% of the vote and seven seats having previously held none. The party also performed well at the London Assembly elections, winning two Assembly members on 6.5% of the London-wide vote.

In the EU referendum campaign, UKIP affiliated itself with the *Leave.EU* campaign group, one of two major pro-'Leave' campaigns alongside the officially recognised *Vote Leave* organisation. Whereas *Vote Leave* tended to offer more economic, moderate and, arguably, cerebral arguments in favour of Britain's exit from the EU, *Leave.EU* tended more towards emotive, populist language with the main policy focus being the threat of greater immigration from the EU. This divide helped to crystalise UKIP's long transition from a Eurosceptic Conservative splinter party to something more akin to the populist radical right found in continental Europe. The twin campaigning approach inadvertently helped the Leave campaign secure a shock victory on 23 June, as 52% voted in favour of ending Britain's 43-year membership of the EU.

3. Internal chaos and polling decline amidst the reunification of the right

In the two months immediately after the referendum, UKIP fell in the opinion polls by around five percentage points, while the Conservatives picked up precisely the same figure. To some Eurosceptics, UKIP's *raison d'être* of withdrawal from the EU seemed complete, a conclusion reaffirmed when new Prime Minister declared that 'Brexit means Brexit'. Moreover, Theresa May echoed much of UKIP's anti-establishment, anti-cosmopolitan rhetoric in her first party conference speech as Prime Minister, stating 'too many people in positions of power behave as though they have more in common with international elites than with the people down the road … if you believe you are a citizen of the world, you're a citizen of nowhere … They find your patriotism distasteful, your concerns about immigration parochial, your views about crime illiberal, your attachment to your job security inconvenient' (May, 2016). May quickly appeared to be in control of both her party and the Brexit process, which, as shown in Figure 6.1, was now the dominant theme in British politics, immediately overtaking immigration and asylum in the aftermath of the referendum.

By contrast, UKIP entered another period of public spats and internal chaos that was acute even by its own high standard. Following Farage's expected resignation after the referendum result, the party's leadership contest quickly became acrimonious as the National Executive Committee declared three of the party's most prominent figures ineligible to run. These included both Stephen Woolfe MEP, one of the 'Faragists' who preferred a strong leader, and Suzanne Evans, who had been suspended by the party and represented its more centrist, collegiate faction. Ultimately, Diane James—MEP for South East England, the party's former immigration spokesperson, an admirer of Vladimir Putin and the chosen candidate of UKIP and *Leave.EU* bankroller Aaron Banks—won the contest with 47% of the vote. At the party conference she promised a more professional type of leadership than Farage and warned Eurosceptics of the dangers of accepting Brexit as a *fait accompli*, stating 'The threats to the referendum outcome are increasing by the day … No to a European associate membership. No to Brexit-lite. No to single market controls. No to unrestricted or uncontrolled freedom of movement into this country' (Cooper, 2016). However, Farage, in attendance, offered his support to the Conservatives on Brexit should they fulfil three criteria: control over fishing territories; remaining outside the single market; and restoring blue passports—essentially giving May tacit, conditional support over UKIP's headline policy.

Q. 'Which of the following do you think are the most important issues facing the country at this time? Please tick up to three.'

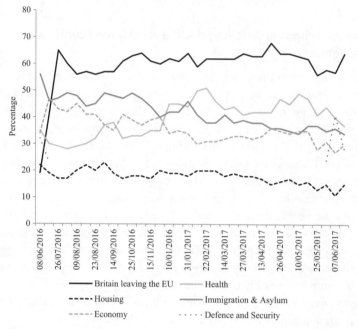

Figure 6.1. The electorate's view on the most important issues facing the country, June 2016-June 2017
Source: YouGov Top Issues Tracker, 2016–2017.

Despite her promise of professionalism, James resigned as leader just 18 days later, stating 'I do not have sufficient authority, nor the full support of all my MEP colleagues and party officers' (Wilkinson, 2016). Incredibly, when registering her leadership of UKIP with the Electoral Commission, she had added the Latin '*vi coactus*', or 'under duress', to her signature. Her resignation prompted a fresh leadership election and even more public accusations and name-calling—as well as a physical altercation in the European Parliament—between the Faragist wing, who this time coalesced around candidate Paul Nuttall, and the centrists, represented again by Suzanne Evans. On 28 November, Nuttall—MEP for the North West of England and previous party deputy leader—came out on top with 63% of the 15,370 votes. In the two months between the two electoral contests alone, UKIP had lost around 6000 members, down to 33,000 from a peak of 47,000 in May 2015.

Rather than aiming to operate merely as a hard-line watchdog on the Brexit negotiations, Nuttall brought with him a broader vision of the party's future and target demographic, stating, 'I want to replace the Labour Party and make UKIP the patriotic voice of working people' (Walker and Mason, 2016). Nuttall advocated 'firm controls' on immigration, British workers 'at the top of the queue', criminal sentences 'that mean what they say' and the reinstating of capital punishment following a referendum, as well as setting an ambition of 'double figures' for the number of UKIP MPs following the next general election (Riley-Smith, 2016). The optimism quickly dissipated following an underwhelming second-place result in the Stoke by-election in the New Year, despite the constituency being dubbed by the media as 'Brexit capital of Britain', leading to criticism from Farage and others that the campaign had been too left-wing economically and lacking in anti-immigration rhetoric (Shute, 2017). During the by-election campaign Nuttall had already come under heavy media scrutiny for a series of claims he had made about his credentials and life experiences, the veracity of which were questioned.

Despite having a plainly less capable leader than Farage and operating in a political context in which the party no longer held a monopoly over the keystone, popular policy of withdrawal from the European Union, UKIP was still polling at around 11%, not much lower than shortly after the 2015 election. However, the fragility of UKIP's position was underscored by the public's shrinking belief—starting from a low base—that it was the best party to handle the Brexit negotiations, as shown in Figure 6.2. Meanwhile belief in the Conservative's competence on the subject rose. Though many British Eurosceptics had seen UKIP as the best vehicle to secure a referendum on EU membership, few believed it would be the best party at handling the actual process of leaving. Furthermore, on other key issues such as housing, health, the economy, tax, unemployment, education and defence, less than 5% of voters believed that UKIP was the best party, little changed from a year earlier.

4. Into the 2017 election

On 18 April, having three weeks earlier triggered Article 50 to begin the Brexit process officially, Theresa May announced a snap general election. She justified the decision stating 'if we do not hold a general election now ... negotiations with the European Union will reach their most difficult stage in the run-up to the next scheduled election. Division in Westminster will risk our ability to make a success of Brexit' (May, 2017). In short, voters who favoured Brexit had a duty to support the Conservatives who, united and with a large majority, could handle the process most effectively. Overnight, a third of UKIP voters switched their vote intention to the Conservatives, pushing Nuttall's party well below the Liberal Democrats to around 7% in polls and Theresa May's party close to 50%.

Nuttall started the campaign by rolling out a series of authoritarian policy proposals designed to marginalise practices widely associated with Islamic

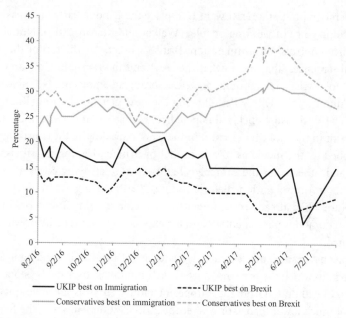

Figure 6.2. Best party to handle Brexit and immigration, June 2016-June 2017
Source: YouGov Tracker Polls, 2016-2017.

communities, such as banning the burqa, sharia law and Islamic schools, as well as a clampdown on female genital mutilation. In response, UKIP's foreign affairs spokesperson hastily stepped down, highlighting divisions in the party, which was no longer able to use EU withdrawal as a lightning rod around which to coalesce its members. Simultaneously, Nuttall announced that UKIP would not stand candidates against strongly Eurosceptic Conservative MPs in marginal seats and refused to even state whether he would stand for Parliament himself. Evidently, neither measure reassured Eurosceptics of the value of voting for UKIP, which lost all of the 145 seats it was defending at the 2017 local elections on 4 May.

Thereafter, the media paid decreasing attention to UKIP as all eyes turned to the surge in support for Labour and its suddenly popular leader Jeremy Corbyn as well as the crumbling Conservative campaign. Internally, UKIP had a far smaller campaigning team to call on, resulting in only 11% of voters being contacted by the party in the four weeks before the election, down from 40% prior to 2015 (Fieldhouse *et al.*, 2017). Despite last-minute attempts by Nuttall to salvage some relevance by announcing new anti-terrorism policies in the wake of attacks in London and Manchester, the public were no longer listening.

5. UKIP's results

Table 6.1 shows the rapid rise and fall of UKIP. The party won 1.8% of the vote across the UK in 2017, a drop of 10.8 percentage points from 2015. A major reason for the fall was the decline in the number of candidates that the party put forward, down by 244. However, Nuttall's party won just 3.2% of the vote on average in the seats in which it stood candidates. Whereas the party saved the vast majority of its deposits in 2015, it saved only 19 two years later, reflecting how thinly-spread the UKIP vote was by 2017. Indeed, far from winning seats in the double-digits as promised, the party won more than 10% of the vote in just two seats in the entire country. As a parliamentary candidate, Paul Nuttall was able to muster just 7.7% of the vote in Boston and Skegness, a seat he specifically chose, having already lost in Stoke, for its pro-Brexit demographic.

6. Who voted UKIP and why

Of UKIP's 2015 voters, only 16% voted UKIP again in 2017. Instead, 51% voted for the Conservatives, 17% voted for Labour and 8% did not vote (Fieldhouse *et al.*, 2017). Conversely, those who did vote for UKIP in 2017 were by and large loyal UKIP voters from two years earlier—a full 71% had voted for Farage's party in 2015. Just 8% came from Labour and less than 7% from the Conservatives. As such, rather than see a complete turnover of voters, it appears that UKIP maintained a core group from two years earlier. Table 6.2 provides details of the type of voter attracted to UKIP at the last two elections.

As we can see in Table 5.2, in socio-demographic terms there were no major differences between the party's 2015 and 2017 voters, except that the latter were older and more likely to own their home. In attitudinal terms, the differences are even less clear. UKIP voters remained broadly the same in their self-placement on the left-right spectrum, averaging just right of centre, though they did become considerably more pro-redistribution and slightly more in favour of the death penalty. Unexpectedly, they also became more in favour of non-EU immigration, though this may be a reflection of their Euroscepticism and the debate around

Table 6.1 UKIP General Election results, 2010-2017

Year	Votes	Vote share (%)	Candidates	Deposits saved	Vote share per candidate (%)
2017	594,068	1.8	377 (58%)	19	3.2
2015	3,881,099	12.6	621 (95%)	545	13.1
2010	919,471	3.1	558 (86%)	99	1.8

Table 6.2 Socio-demographic and attitudinal profile of UKIP voters, 2015-2017

	UKIP 2017	UKIP 2015	Conservative 2017	Sample
Socio-demographics				
Mean Age	54	51	54	47
% Female	48	45	50	51
% white	98	97	96	91
% degree	13	14	20	24
% homeowner	45	40	48	39
Mean household income (£000s)	27	26	32	29
Political attitudes (mean 1-5 unless otherwise stated; 1=disagree; 3=neither; 5=agree)				
Mean left-right position (0-10)	6.2	6.3	6.8	4.9
Govt should redistribute incomes	3.5	3.2	2.6	3.3
Death penalty reintroduced	4.2	4.1	3.8	3.3
Ethnic minority rights too far	3.9	3.9	3.6	3.3
Allow more non-EU workers (0-10)	2.3	1.8	3.1	3.9
% 2016 Remain voters	5	5	27	49
Trust MPs (0-7)	2.5	2.6	4.1	3.3
% contacted by UKIP	38.9	65.1	13.4	11.7
% contacted by Conservatives	69.5	71.3	86.4	76.4

Source: Fieldhouse *et al.*, 2017

Britain's post-Brexit relations with the rest of the world. They were also slightly less likely to have been contacted by the Conservatives prior to the 2017 election. Overall, there is clearly no radical difference between 2015 and 2017 UKIP voters in terms of either socio-demographics or in terms of political attitudes.

In this case, we may be able to better explain the decision of some 2015 UKIP voters to 'stay loyal' and vote UKIP again in 2017 and others to defect to the Conservatives by considering their respective perceptions of each party in both 2015 and 2017. In Table 6.3, we see more significant and consistent differences emerge. Although both defectors and loyalists preferred Farage to Nuttall, loyalists still on average liked Nuttall, unlike defectors. Interestingly, defectors preferred Nuttall in 2017 to Cameron in 2015, despite not particularly liking either, and preferred May to both. In 2015, defectors slightly disliked the Conservative Party as a whole, whereas loyalists very much disliked them, so that though the perception of both groups became more positive to the Tories by 2017, it was only for defectors that the assessment became positive overall.

On specific policy issues, we can see from Table 6.3 that, whereas defectors felt that by 2017 the Conservatives had become an anti-immigration party, UKIP loyalists did not, even though they did accept that the Conservatives had become a Eurosceptic party, albeit significantly less so than UKIP. It would seem then that, given the lack of clear demographic or attitudinal differences between UKIP

Table 6.3 Perceptions of UKIP and the Conservatives of UKIP 'defectors' and UKIP 'loyalists', 2015-2017

	Defectors		Loyalists	
0-10	**April 2015**	**April 2017**	**April 2015**	**April 2017**
Like UKIP leader	7.2	4.1	7.8	5.4
Like Conservatives leader	3.9	6.3	2.8	5.1
Like UKIP	7.9	6.2	8.2	7.7
Like Conservatives	4.1	5.8	2.6	4.5
UKIP immigration position	1.0	0.6	1.5	0.4
Cons. immigration position	5.8	3.9	6.1	5.4
UKIP EU position	0.4	0.8	0.4	0.9
Cons. EU position	5.4	3.0	6.4	4.2

Source: Fieldhouse *et al.*, 2017

defectors and loyalists, it was on the crunch issue of whether the Conservatives would deliver on immigration that kept a small proportion of 2015 UKIP voters from switching to the Conservatives. However, this group remained a small minority, with the vast majority of former 'Kippers keen to rally around May and the Conservatives in order to deliver their long hoped for Brexit.

7.   The Greens after the 2015 election

The Greens had entered the 2015-2017 Parliament with reasons to be confident. Having historically been an afterthought in British politics, the Green Party of England and Wales[1] (GPEW) had shot to national prominence during the 'Green Surge' of late 2014 and early 2015, when an ideologically coherent set of anti-austerity, anti-establishment voters pushed the party's polling into double digits and its membership from 13,000 to 77,000 making the party, temporarily, the third largest by membership in England. It also echoed a similar membership 'surge' for the Scottish Greens in the aftermath of the 2014 Scottish Independence Referendum, when they carved a niche as pro-independence, 'not as an expression of nationalism but as a route to a fairer society' (Dennison, 2016, p. 2).

Both parties had become fixtures, albeit precariously, in the second-tier of their respective party systems. With larger media profiles and membership figures came greater financial and personnel resources, which, in England and Wales,

---

[1]Given that the Scottish Greens and Green Party in Northern Ireland poured significantly more resources into their respective devolved assembly elections earlier in 2017, this chapter will focus on the Green Party of England and Wales.

helped to quadruple their vote share at the 2015 general election to over 1,150,000 votes. Crucially, whereas voters had previously pigeonholed the Greens as single-issue environmentalists, by the 2015 election most voters could identify the Greens as a far-left party (Dennison, 2016, p. 17). Indeed, for left-wing voters, the only thing stopping many voting for the Greens was the electoral logic of first-past-the-post. Unsurprisingly then, with Britain's drift towards multi-party politics seemingly irrevocable, commentators could conclude that 'the Greens now face the potential opportunity of a post-Ed Miliband Labour Party shifting away from the left, giving them more political space' (Walker, 2015). Events would unfold very differently.

8. The Greens and Corbynmania

On 15 June 2015, nominations closed for the Labour Party leadership election. Joining three centrist candidates proclaiming their pro-business credentials was Jeremy Corbyn, a veteran far-left campaigner who secured a place on the ballot paper 'by a whisker' after MPs gave him their nominations solely to ensure 'a wide field of candidates' (Wintour and Mason, 2015). Before securing nomination Corbyn stated that he had already 'put the issues of austerity and nuclear weapons on the agenda.' However, Corbyn's candidacy was to quickly spark a membership surge reminiscent of those of the Greens and SNP in the previous year, only far larger, as over 350,000, overwhelmingly left-wing, new members sought to capitalise on the introduction of a One Member, One Vote electoral system. The immediate electoral threat to the Greens was not only apparent in terms of policy symmetry but also because thousands of registered Green Party members and even over 200 recent national and local Green Party candidates attempted to join Labour to vote for him.

The Greens' official position on the ascendency of Corbyn was supportive. The GPEW immediately congratulated him on securing his nomination, stating 'we welcome your strong anti-austerity voice' (Wilkinson, 2015). Two days later, Caroline Lucas wrote an article in the *Guardian* expressing her relief at Corbyn's participation and called for future electoral cooperation. Similarly, Green MEP Molly Scott Cato, called for a Red-Green coalition and electoral reform. On 24 August, Lucas again sought to directly confront the increasingly apparent election of Corbyn by publishing an open letter arguing that she could 'help you build a progressive majority' via electoral pacts between the parties (Lucas, 2015). More privately, as Green poll ratings slipped, party members were divided. On the one hand were those who wanted the Greens to step aside to give a better-placed anti-austerity champion the best chance possible and, on the other, those who warned 'if we end up hitching our wagon to Corbyn too closely, I think we could go down with that ship' (Dennison, 2016, p. 144). With Corbyn finally elected

Labour leader on 12 September, the Greens rounded out 2015 entirely over-shadowed in the competition for media attention and unsure of their future role in the party system.

9.   2016: Local elections, EU referendum and Green leadership election

By the time of the 2016 local elections, the Greens sensed that their future may not be as bleak as originally feared. Their party political broadcast, which portrayed senior Labour and Conservative politicians as squabbling children, was viewed online over 600,000 times. Moreover, coverage of Labour—which still dominated political media—overwhelmingly focused on the seemingly irrevocable divide between anti-Corbyn centrist MPs and Corbyn's massive membership—a divide which the Greens hoped to exploit. Following a strong policy-focused campaign by Sian Berry in London that explicitly highlighted the centrism of Labour's candidate, the Greens finished third in the mayoral and assembly election, winning 6% and 8% of the vote respectively. Results in the rest of England were more mixed and the party lost three seats, though still won almost 6% of votes. At the Welsh Assembly the party continued its lack of historic success there by winning just 3% of the vote and no seats. Overall, in England and Wales, the local election results were sufficiently ambiguous for the Greens that they could conclude that they were still an electoral force, despite Corbyn.

Ten days after the local elections, Natalie Bennett announced that she would not seek re-election for a third term as GPEW leader. Pleasingly for the Greens, over the next two weeks the media devoted unprecedented attention to speculating on who the next Green leader might be. The key question centred on whether Caroline Lucas would run, a proposition that senior Greens publically advised against in the hope that the party could gain a fresh face. On 31 May, however, Lucas made the surprise move of putting forward a joint leadership bid with Jonathan Bartley, a former advisor to John Major, founder of a Christian think tank and the party's work and pensions spokesman with a notably professional semblance. The nomination immediately drew criticism from a number of Green members who complained that Lucas had transformed the leadership election into a coronation amongst other complaints. The candidacy essentially killed off the leadership election and media interest in it.

However, Lucas saw the tactic as worth it because it overcame her previous dilemma whereby she wanted to lead the national party into any future election but also had to fully dedicate her time during the Parliament to her Westminster seat in Brighton Pavilion. The joint candidacy would also overcome some criticisms that the Greens were a one-woman-show and, by offering an innovative leadership format, had the potential to give the Greens much-needed relevance. Finally,

Bartley's professionalism stood in contrast to the, at times, hapless media performances of outgoing leader Bennett, who had cost the party credibility in the previous election campaign.

In the shadow of Britain's referendum vote to leave the EU, as well as resulting Conservative, Labour and UKIP leadership elections, on 2 September Lucas and Bartley were confirmed the party's new co-leaders. They secured a landslide 86% of the 15,773 votes in the first round of counting against five low-profile competitors. Though the turnout was a record high, it came from just 45,000 members, already down 20,000 from the year before. During their joint victory speech, Lucas and Bartley laid out the five priorities for the party: (i) opposition to Brexit, which was explained as the result of campaign lies, fear of immigrants and economic inequality; (ii) electoral reform towards proportional representation; (iii) 'a progressive alliance' between left-of-centre parties at the next general election; (iv) orthodox left-wing policies of nationalisation, redistribution and greater labour rights, as well as (v) environmentalism. Bartley aimed fire directly at Labour when stating 'we stand here more united as party with two leaders than others are with one' (Sparrow, 2016).

10.   Into the 2017 election

Over the next seven months, the Greens plateaued in the polls at around 4%. They secured intermittent media attention when standing aside for a successful Liberal Democrat in a key by-election—something Lucas said could pave the way for her much desired 'progressive alliance'—and when criticising the ambiguous approach to nuclear power and free movement of persons of the publicly-divided Labour Party.

On the day after Theresa May called the election, the Green co-leaders wrote to Jeremy Corbyn and Tim Farron, leader of the Liberal Democrats, calling for electoral deals between the three parties in a number of seats, in order to halt an impending Conservative majority and hard Brexit, and to subsequently deliver electoral reform. This proposition also allowed the Greens to avoid accusations of dividing the left-wing vote while providing relevance and media attention and an excuse for the Greens to focus their limited resources on a smaller number of seats. Corbyn and Farron both quickly rejected such a proposal. Ultimately, the GPEW put forward candidates in 116 fewer seats than in 2015 and 14 local Green parties explicitly stated they were not standing candidates in order to support Labour, with 13 doing likewise to assist the Liberal Democrats. In return, just two local Liberal Democrat parties stood aside for the Greens and no constituency Labour parties returned the GPEW's favour.

On 4 May, local elections were held in parts of England, where the Greens maintained their 20 seats, across Wales, where they gained one seat, and across

Scotland, where they won five additional seats. Later that month, the GPEW launched their manifesto—the Green Guarantee—focusing on their pledge for a four-hour working week, universal basic income, environmentalism and the promise of a second EU referendum. At the launch, Caroline Lucas was forced to admit there were similarities between her party's proposals and those of Corbyn's but pointed to the approach to Brexit as the defining difference between the two parties. The manifesto was just 23 pages long and described by one commentator as 'small on detail but high on rhetoric', a mistake the party had made two years earlier when, faced with policy confusion, they retreated to their comfort zone of protest politics (Buckwood, 2017).

Also similar to 2015 was the late selection of candidates in many seats as local parties were caught off guard by the election announcement. Similarly, the GPEW was able to raise considerably less funding than two years earlier, with only £400,000 in donations in the first two quarters of 2017, compared to £700,000 over the same period in 2015. Campaign expenditure, which had been over a million pounds in 2015, dropped by over 50% in 2017. Party income and expenditure over time are shown in Figure 6.3.

Partially as a result, whereas 22% of the electorate reported being contacted by the Greens in the four weeks prior to the 2015 General Election, the same figure was 12% 2017, a considerably greater fall than the corresponding decline in Green candidates (Fieldhouse *et al.*, 2017). Moreover, as the campaign went on, Labour's rise in the polls, and their leader's electoral hopes, seemed ever more credible, following a strong manifesto launch, more polished media performances

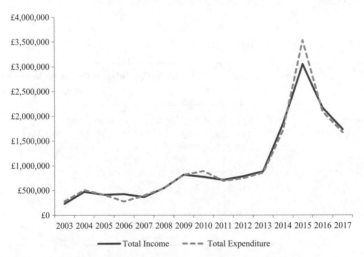

Figure 6.3. Green Party of England and Wales total income and expenditure, 2003-2017
Source: Electoral Commission. 2017 is author's estimate.

and, by contrast, a visibly crumbling Theresa May. In this context, left-wingers of all stripes were willing to put their doubts about Corbyn to one side as the left reunified over the issue of austerity, much like the right had reunified over the issue of Europe nearly a year earlier. Despite some impressive performances in the televised debates by Caroline Lucas, the Greens were left for dust as Britain's two-party system was redeemed.

11. The Greens' results

The GPEW won just 1.8% of the vote in England and Wales, having stood candidates in 457 constituencies, giving the party an average vote share per candidate of 2.2% and saving just eight deposits nationally. Despite this partial crash, the GPEW ended 2017 with the same number of seats that it had had since 2010, Caroline Lucas's constituency of Brighton Pavilion where the party won an increased vote share of 52%. The fact that the GPEW managed to save their electoral deposits in just seven other seats reflects how targeted the party's constituency campaigning was, but also how ill-prepared they were for a general election. Indeed, the party only won more than 10% in the Isle of Wight, in the Speaker's seat of Buckingham, and in Bristol West, where bookmakers had at one point made candidate Molly Scott Cato favourite to win before she eventually finished third. In Scotland, the Greens stood candidates in just three of the 59 seats—reflecting the party's sole and very successful focus on Scottish Parliament elections a month earlier. The Green Party in Northern Ireland was also operating in the shadow of a recent devolved legislature election that had taken place in March in which it retained both of its seats.

Table 6.4 Green Party election results, 2010-2017

Party	Year	Votes	Vote share (%)	Candidates	Deposits saved	Vote share per candidate (%)
Green Party of	2017	512,327	1.8	457 (80%)	8	2.2
England and Wales	2015	1,111,603	4.1	537 (94%)	135	4.4
	2010	265,243	1.0	311 (54%)	5	1.8
Scottish Greens	2017	5,886	0.2	3 (5%)	1	4.1
	2015	39,205	1.3	31 (52%)	3	2.6
	2010	16,827	0.7	20 (34%)	1	2.0
Green Party in	2017	7,452	0.9	7 (37%)	2	2.4
Northern Ireland	2015	6,822	1.0	5 (28%)	2	3.3
	2010	3,542	0.5	4 (22%)	0	2.5

12.   Who voted Green and why?

Of 2015 Green Party voters, only 16% voted Green again at the 2017 General Election, with 57% switching to Labour and 13% voting Liberal Democrat (Fieldhouse *et al.*, 2017). Most of these former Greens had switched soon after Corbyn won the Labour leadership, with 42% of 2015 Greens already declaring their intention to vote Labour in May 2016. Conversely, of 2017 Green Party voters, 25% had voted Green two years earlier, 21% had not voted, 16% had voted for Labour and the Conservatives each and, surprisingly, 9% had voted for UKIP. Not only did the Greens experience a large turnover of voters but, as shown in Table 6.5, the Greens in 2017 were a far more demographically and ideologically diverse group than two years earlier.

Whereas Green 2015 voters were noticeable for their youth, higher education, tendency to be home-renters, and clear far-left, anti-austerity, environmentalist, pro-EU political outlook, their 2017 voters were far more eclectic. Demographically, the Greens' 2017 voters were far more similar to the average voter in the electorate. Most surprising is how sharply the political attitudes of the average Green voter had changed, with Greens now far more right wing than they were two years earlier, less redistributionist, less anti-austerity, and even

Table 6.5 Socio-demographic and attitudinal profile of Green voters, 2015-2017

	Green 2017	Green 2015	Labour 2017	LD 2017	Sample
Socio-demographics					
Mean Age	42	37	42	47	47
% Female	54	54	54	48	51
% white	92	92	87	92	91
% degree	29	42	28	39	24
% homeowner	37	26	31	41	39
Mean household income (£000s)	28	28	28	33	29
Politics (mean 1-5 unless otherwise stated; 1=disagree; 3=neither; 5=agree)					
Mean left-right position (0-10)	4.2	2.8	3.3	4.4	4.9
Govt should redistribute incomes	3.5	4.0	3.9	3.4	3.3
Spending cuts too far	4.0	4.2	4.3	3.9	3.8
Environmental protection too far	2.0	1.6	2.3	2.2	2.5
Allow more non-EU workers (0-10)	4.5	–	4.6	4.7	3.9
% 2016 Remain voters	61.2	80.1	68.3	80.2	49.8
Trust MPs (0-7)	2.9	2.7	3.1	3.3	3.3
% contacted by Greens	58.1	62.6	12.6	13.3	11.7
% contacted by Labour	74.1	80.0	90.7	63.9	76.4
Like Lucas (0-10; Bennett in 2015)	6.3	6.2	5.3	5.5	4.1
Like Corbyn (0-10; Miliband in 2015)	4.4	4.5	6.5	4.1	4.0

Source: Fieldhouse *et al.*, 2017

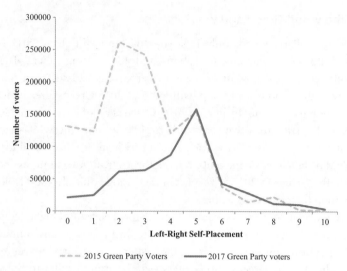

Figure 6.4. Left-right distribution of Green Party voters in 2017 and 2015
Source: Fieldhouse *et al.*, 2017

markedly less environmentalist. Despite the Greens portraying themselves as perhaps the most pro-EU party prior to the election, a significant portion of their voters favoured leaving the EU at 2016 referendum. One of the few attitudes of 2017 Greens that were further from the electorate's average than 2017 Labour voters was their ongoing distrust of MPs, though even this was lower than in 2015. The transformation of the Greens' voter base, however, is perhaps best illustrated by Figure 6.4, which compares the left-right distribution of Green voters in 2017 and 2015. In left-right terms, the Greens started the 2015-2017 Parliament quickly losing their role in the party system and ended it by losing the corresponding ideological voter base.

13. What next for UKIP and the Greens?

Both UKIP and the Greens saw declines in their vote share at the 2017 general election. In each case, a less favourable political context, in which they faced far stiffer competition in the party system, quickly robbed the party of relevance and, subsequently, media interest and resources. Each party then suffered a second sudden decline after the call for a snap election led voters to rally around the Conservatives and Labour. This stood in stark contrast to 2015, when a set election date as well as a recent proportionally elected European Parliament election gave UKIP and the Greens plenty of time and opportunities for media coverage and to reach out to voters.

However, there were also important differences between the two collapses. First, whereas the 2017 UKIP vote was just 15% of its 2015 high, the vote share of the Greens 'merely' halved and they also retained their sole MP. Second, whereas UKIP's collapse came after a major singular policy change of the Conservatives—withdrawal from the EU—the Greens' collapse came after another party took on its ideological outlook *en bloc*, following the GPEW's move to the far left in the 2000s.

Whether each party is able to make a comeback, or even survive, is dependent on the extent to which this situation remains true in the British party system and whether the parties can evolve without disintegrating in the process. Should Britain not end free movement of persons with the European Union, we can expect a resurgence of UKIP, or a similar party. Equally, should Labour move away from the ideological position of 2015 Green Party voters—primarily in terms of orthodox left-wing policies under the banner of anti-austerity—the Greens may also be in a position again to make progress. If these situations do not occur, both parties will be forced to continue the difficult balancing act between the three approaches that both choose between 2015 and 2017—adopting a new ideological outlook, emphasising their claim as the *bona fide* advocate of their previous key policy, and attempting electoral cooperation with their bigger, more established counterpart.

References

Burkwood, L. (2017, 13 June) 'Despite The Poor Election Results, I'm Stick With The Green Party—Here's Why', *The Huffington Post*, accessed at http://www.huffington post.co.uk/lee-burkwood/green-party_b_17069850.html on 12 August 2017.

Cooper, C. (2016, 16 September) 'New UKIP Leader Diane James—I'm Not "Farage-like"', *Politico Europe*, accessed at http://www.politico.eu/article/new-ukip-leader-diane-james-im-not-farage-like/ on 16 August 2017.

Dennison, J. (2016) *The Greens in British Politics: Protest, Anti-Austerity and the Divided Left*, Basingstoke, Palgrave Macmillan.

Dennison, J. and Goodwin, M. (2018, forthcoming) 'The Radical Right in the United Kingdom'. In Rydgren, J. (ed.) *The Oxford Handbook of the Radical Right*, Oxford, Oxford University Press.

Electoral Commission (2003-2017) *Accounts*, accessed at http://search.electoralcommis sion.org.uk/Search/Accounts on 17 August 2017.

Fieldhouse, E., Green, J., Evans, G., Schmitt, H, van der Eijk, C., Mellon, J. and Prosser, C. (2017) 'British Election Study Internet Panel Waves 1-13', DOI: 10.15127/1.293723.

Grice, A. (2016) 'Nigel Farage May Be Over but Ukip is Here to Stay—Whether We Vote to Leave Europe or Not'. *Independent*, accessed at http://www.independent.co.uk/voi ces/nigel-farage-may-be-over-but-ukip-is-here-to-stay-whether-we-vote-to-leave-europe-or-not-a6993081.html on 16 August 2017.

Lucas, C. (2015) 'My message to Jeremy Corbyn: I can help you build a progressive majority'. *Independent*, accessed at http://www.independent.co.uk/voices/comment/my-message-to-jeremy-corbyn-i-can-help-you-build-a-progressive-majority-10469934.html on 12 August 2017.

May, T. (2016, 5 October) 'Theresa May's Conference Speech in Full', *Telegraph*, accessed at http://www.telegraph.co.uk/news/2016/10/05/theresa-mays-conference-speech-in-full/ on 21 December 2016.

May, T. (2017, 18 April) 'Theresa May's General Election Statement in Full', BBC News, accessed at http://www.bbc.co.uk/news/uk-politics-39630009 on 16 August 2017.

Riley-Smith, B. (2016, 26 November) 'Interview: Paul Nuttall, the Scouser Who Wants to Lead Ukip on to Labour's Turf', *Telegraph*, accessed at http://www.telegraph.co.uk/news/2016/11/26/interview-paul-nuttall-scouser-wants-lead-ukip-labours-turf/ on 16 August 2017.

Shute, J. (2017, 24 February). 'Paul Nuttall Drove his Ukip Tank into Stoke-on-Trent—But Was Still Trounced in "Brexit capital of Britain"', *Telegraph*, accessed at http://www.telegraph.co.uk/news/2017/02/24/stoke-on-trent-by-election-narrowing-gap-labour-scant-consolation/ on 16 August 2017.

Sparrow, A. (2016, 2 September) 'Caroline Lucas and Jonathan Bartley Elected Green party Co-leaders—As It Happened', *Guardian*, accessed at https://www.theguardian.com/politics/blog/live/2016/sep/02/green-party-conference-leader-lucas on 12 August 2017.

Walker, P. (2015, 8 May) 'Green Vote Oncreases Four-Fold, But Caroline Lucas Remains Party's Only MP', *Guardian*, accessed at https://www.theguardian.com/politics/2015/may/08/green-party-vote-increases-caroline-lucas on 12 August 2017.

Walker, P. and Mason, R. (2016, 28 November) 'New Ukip Leader Paul Nuttall Plans to Replace Labour', *Guardian*, accessed at https://www.theguardian.com/politics/2016/nov/28/paul-nuttall-elected-as-ukip-leader on 16 August 2017.

Wilkinson, M. (2015, 15 June) 'Jeremy Corbyn is in Labour Leadership Race After Reaching 35 Nominations', *Telegraph*, accessed at http://www.telegraph.co.uk/news/politics/labour/11675256/Jeremy-Corbyn-is-in-Labour-leadership-race-after-reaching-35-nominations.html on 12 August 2017.

Wilkinson, M. (2016, 5 October) 'Nigel Farage Rules Out a Comeback', *Telegraph*, accessed at http://www.telegraph.co.uk/news/2016/10/04/diane-james-quits-as-ukip-leader-after-just-18-days-as-successor/ on 16 August 2017.

Wintour, P, and Mason, R. (2015, 15 June) 'Labour Leftwinger Jeremy Corbyn Wins Place on Ballot for Leadership', *Guardian*, accessed at https://www.theguardian.com/politics/2015/jun/15/labour-leftwinger-jeremy-corbyn-wins-place-on-ballot-for-leadership on 12 August 2017.

YouGov (2016, 2017) *Political Trackers*, accessed at https://yougov.co.uk/publicopinion/archive/?category=political-trackers on 18 August 2017.

AILSA HENDERSON AND JAMES MITCHELL*

Referendums as Critical Junctures? Scottish Voting in British Elections

It has been a turbulent time in Scottish politics. Voters have been to the polls seven times since May 2014, twice in constitutional referendums that offered seismic change. While Scots voted to Remain in the UK in 2014 and voted to stay in Europe in 2016, the prospect of a second independence referendum remains and it appears that Scotland will leave the EU with the rest of the UK. The change a majority rejected in 2014 might yet occur, and the change only a minority wanted in 2016 appears guaranteed. The 2015 Westminster election saw a dramatic increase in Scottish National Party (SNP) support, marking the end of Labour dominance among Scottish MPs, with the SNP finally replicating its status in Scottish electoral politics evident in Holyrood elections since 2007. This chapter explores the impact of the Scottish and Brexit referendum votes upon the 2017 Westminster election in Scotland. It considers the literature on elections in multi-level polities and assesses the respective importance of parties, leaders, and critical junctures to explain the 2017 UK General Election result in Scotland. Using data from the 2014-2015 Scottish Referendum Study and the 2016-2017 Scottish Election Study, we evaluate the claim that the two referendums have served as critical junctures in Scottish electoral politics.

Evidence from Scottish election studies suggest that elections to the Scottish Parliament are first order for a section of the Scottish electorate (Carman *et al.*, 2014, pp. 108-111; Henderson and McEwen, 2010; Henderson and McEwen, 2015). There has been a heightened salience of the Scottish Question due to the 2014 independence referendum, which had an 85 per cent turnout and a very long and intense campaign. This spilled over into the UK general election held in May 2015, where turnout, at 71.1%, was seven points higher than in the previous contest. Even those who might have dismissed devolution as an irrelevance did not dismiss the referendum. Leaders of the parties in Holyrood

*Ailsa Henderson, School of Social and Political Science, University of Edinburgh,
ailsa.henderson@ed.ac.uk; James Mitchell, School of Social and Political Science,
University of Edinburgh, james.mitchell@ed.ac.uk

doi:10.1093/pa/gsx065

were provided with a platform that was likely to enhance their visibility and recognition amongst the electorate. The referendum failed to resolve the Scottish Question and there has remained the possibility of a second independence referendum. The referendum also disrupted what had come to be seen as the norm in Scotland: elections to the House of Commons in Scotland characterised by Labour dominance, with elections to Holyrood home to an intense battle between Labour and the SNP while the Conservatives and Liberal Democrats fought it out for third place. The 2015 UK General Election in Scotland produced an SNP landslide, while the subsequent devolved elections in 2016 saw the rise of the Conservative Party as Scotland's second party, a position it had never previously held in Holyrood contests.

Whether we are witnessing a dealignment, realignment or temporary disruption is as yet unclear. Not only has the Scottish Question gained prominence in Scottish politics, but some Scottish party leaders are now more familiar to voters across the United Kingdom than previously. This notion of referendums as critical junctures influences the relative roles of the core cleavages structuring party competition and voter support, may affect the role of leaders and raises questions about the extent to which elections in a multi-level polity can truly be either first or second order. The extent to which the prominence of the Scottish Question shaped the result of the 2017 UK general election in Scotland should tell us much about the nature of multi-level elections at this point in time and may give an indication of future trends in Scottish and thereby UK politics.

1. 'Indyref' as critical juncture

Critical junctures in electoral politics are rare. Rokkan and Lipset's classic work (1967) identified four key cleavages in European politics that followed the two critical junctures of the national revolutions establishing modern states and the industrial revolution. These included a centre-periphery cleavage that persisted after the establishment of central authorities in the creation of modern states and a class cleavage that emerged from the industrial revolution. The centre-periphery cleavage re-emerged and has competed (or complemented) class in contemporary Scottish politics. The changing fortunes of the different political parties in Scotland certainly suggest that the referendum has served as some sort of critical juncture producing 'distinct legacies' (Collier and Collier, 1991, p. 29). Were we to find that the centre-periphery conflict has supplanted class-based competition we might well point to proof of a critical juncture.

Scottish party competition and voting, however, is more complex. The centre-periphery cleavage existed prior to the rise of the SNP, masked by the appearance of a uniform party system with the two main (class-based) parties dominating politics north and south of the border. Equally, the rise of the SNP, demands for and creation of a Scottish Parliament and continuing debate on Scotland's constitutional status did not so much replace class as a key cleavage as add a territorial dimension to an existing class base. A key explanation for the result of the 1997 devolution referendum focuses on attitudes towards the Conservative Party. Left-inclined voters were more enthusiastic supporters of devolution. Without over-stating it, there was an alignment between left/progressive support and support for some measure of self-government against right support for the *status quo ante* (Denver et al, 2000). In essence, an anti-Tory coalition was created which united behind support for a Scottish Parliament, although it was disunited on Scotland's final constitutional status.

While this was occurring at one territorial level, behaviour in elections to the House of Commons was hardly affected. The creation of a Scottish Parliament therefore saw the creation of two distinct, though overlapping, party systems, one for elections to the Scottish Parliament and the other in elections to the House of Commons. The former diverged from the latter in part because the mixed-member proportional electoral system (commonly known as the Additional Member System in Scotland) created opportunities for smaller parties and in part because debate focused on governing Scotland rather than the UK. Labour's dominance in Scottish elections to the House of Commons was not challenged in the first decade of devolution as the SNP and Liberal Democrats fought for (a distant) second place while the Conservatives struggled to gain and retain a Scottish toehold in the House of Commons after 1997. Elections to Holyrood were entirely different. In 2007, the SNP became the largest party by one seat and extended this lead four years later to an unexpected overall majority. Yet, in winning only six seats, the SNP fared no better in the 2010 Westminster election than the party had in 2005. Indeed in 2010 the SNP vote share exceeded that of the Liberal Democrats by only one per cent and was still 22 percentage points behind Labour. Scotland's constitutional status had not been directly prominent in either the 2007 or 2011 Holyrood elections, though the SNP's support for independence certainly fed into the sense that it prioritised Scottish interests. The 2011 Scottish electorate believed that independence was less important than previously, yet provided the party of independence with its best result. Only nine per cent of the Scottish electorate thought independence was the most important issue in 2011 compared with 19 per cent who thought the constitutional question was the most important issue in 2007 (Carman *et al.*, 2014, p. 112: Johns *et al.*, 2010). The SNP's overall majority was due to the perception that it was the party most competent to govern Scotland, not because it supported independence. But as it included a commitment to an independence referendum in its manifesto, as it had in each election since 1999, the referendum was firmly on the agenda.

The referendum originated as a device in party management. It was designed to allow the SNP to appeal to voters who opposed or might be lukewarm in their view of independence while keeping the party faithful content that independence was still on the agenda. The 2014 referendum campaign saw a major shift in public opinion in favour of independence but not enough to command a majority. What was significant in terms of subsequent political behaviour was the substantial minority of Labour voters who shifted in favour of independence and the relationship between the aforementioned class and centre-periphery cleavages. The message from supporters of independence was based on both centre-periphery and class cleavages. The independence campaign offered a broadly left of centre message. While the unionist camp included the Labour Party, it also included the Conservatives thus inhibiting Labour in its appeal to its working-class core support (though there were efforts, notably by former Prime Minister Gordon Brown, to articulate a left of centre case for the union). Additionally, *Labour for Independence,* a small but vocal group set out to convince Labour voters that supporting independence was not a vote against the Labour Party. Whether Labour voters were repelled by witnessing leading figures aligning themselves with old enemies in the Conservative Party or attracted to the proposition that Labour values were more likely to be enacted under independence, a sizeable minority of Labour supporters voted for independence.

Table 7.1 shows that substantial minorities of Labour and Liberal Democrat voters backed independence in the 2014 referendum. Only for those parties at the poles of the constitutional question, the SNP and Conservatives, did eighty per cent or more of voters support the constitutional view of their party of choice.

This is in part explained by analyses of the referendum vote, which show that owner occupiers were significantly more likely to vote No than those renting accommodation, and those in the lowest income quarter were significantly more likely to vote Yes. These effects survive other socio-economic controls but are perhaps best summarised in Table 7.2, which reports the relationship between social class and referendum vote choice.

Table 7.1 Scottish Parliament vote (constituency 2011) and Scottish independence referendum (2014) vote choice[1]

	Con	Lab	LD	SNP
Voted Yes	12.0	30.4	28.6	79.7
Voted No	88.0	69.6	71.4	19.8
n	191	411	98	661

Source: Scottish Referendum Study 2014-2015 (BESIP post-referendum wave). Results are column percentages.

---

[1] All survey data are weighted. SRS data are weighted by w8_full RJ. SES 2016 (wave1) data are weighted by core_w8. SES 2017 data are weighted by w8.

Table 7.2 Social Class and Scottish independence referendum (2014) vote choice

	ABC1	C2DE
Voted Yes	42.5	54.3
Voted No	57.5	45.3
n	1031	1271

Source: Scottish Referendum Study 2014-2015 (BESIP post-referendum wave). Results are column percentages.

When we explore attitudes to referendum vote choice we can see that those who believed independence would lead to a smaller gap between rich and poor were significantly more likely to vote for change (Henderson and Mitchell, 2015). It would be an exaggeration to suggest that class allegiances aligned behind the two camps in the referendum but it was clear that Labour voters failed to take a cue from the party to the extent that might have been expected from previous studies of referendums (Sniderman, 2000; Lau and Redlawsk, 2001). The referendum's legacy was evident at the 2015 general election. There had been an expectation, or at least hope, amongst opponents of independence that the referendum would see a heavy defeat for independence and seriously damage the SNP. The 2015 general election, coming eight months after the referendum, appeared more like a continuation of the referendum than a return to the normal pattern of UK general elections in Scotland. The SNP appealed to the 45 per cent who had voted for independence. The SNP won half of the vote, becoming the only political party since the extension of the franchise to do so. It succeeded in attracting a combination of Yes voters and previous SNP voters who saw it as the best vehicle for articulating Scottish interests. Labour suffered most and though gaining more votes than any of the three main unionist parties, the electoral system delivered it with a solitary MP putting it on equal footing with the Tories and Liberal Democrats.

The results in Table 7.3 show the transfer in partisan support between 2010 and 2015 and reveal varying abilities of parties to hold on to their previous supporters. The SNP and Conservatives managed to retain a clear majority of voters, more than three quarters of support in the case of the SNP and more than six in ten for the Conservatives. Labour lost approximately half of its support, the bulk of it to the SNP. The Liberal Democrat figures are particularly striking. Not only did the party lose most previous supporters to others, but the portion remaining, roughly equal to the proportion choosing to vote Labour, is less than half the size of the group defecting to the SNP.

To understand the role of the referendum in structuring 2015 vote choice we turn to Table 7.4, which tracks voter movement by referendum vote choice.

In Table 7.4 we see that clear majorities of all supporters moved to the SNP if they were Yes voters, regardless of the party they had supported in 2010. Among

Table 7.3 Transfers of party support, 2010 to 2015 Westminster elections in Scotland

| | **Percentage of 2010 vote retained or transferred in 2015** | | | |
	Con to . . .	**Lab to . . .**	**LD to . . .**	**SNP to. . .**
Con	60.5	5.0	7.3	5.2
Lab	10.7	48.3	19.6	5.2
LD	7.8	3.4	19.9	1.4
SNP	18.2	39.0	45.4	82.4
n	319	656	357	581

Source: Scottish Election Study 2016-2017, wave 1. Results are column percentages. Columns are 2010 vote. Rows are 2015 vote.

Table 7.4 Transfers of partisan support, 2010 to 2015, by referendum vote choice

| | | **No voters** | | | | **Yes voters** | | | |
| | | **2010 voters** | | | | | | | |
		Con	**Lab**	**LD**	**SNP**	**Con**	**Lab**	**LD**	**SNP**
2015	Con	68.1	7.5	12.1	21.4	16.3	0.5	0.0	0.9
	Lab	12.2	66.0	31.1	20.5	2.3	14.0	4.1	1.3
	LD	8.9	4.9	31.1	5.1	2.3	0.5	4.8	0.7
	SNP	7.8	17.2	19.9	42.7	79.1	81.9	82.2	92.9
n		270	429	206	117	43	221	146	448

Source: Scottish Election Study 2016-2017, wave 1. Results are column percentages.

the No voters, however, we see different patterns. Here we see that Labour and the Conservatives were better at retaining 2010 voters if they were No voters, while the SNP retained only one-third of those No supporters who had backed it in 2010. The Liberal Democrats were less likely to retain No supporting voters than were the SNP, a remarkable result for a party that backed the No side in the referendum. The primary beneficiaries of LibDem transfers were the Labour Party. Viewed in this light we can see how the 2014 referendum influenced the 2015 UK General election in Scotland but of interest is whether this disruption would continue, realigning politics more emphatically around the centre-periphery cleavage, whether politics would return to 'normal' or whether a further critical junction might well disrupt partisan preferences.

2. Multi-level elections

The two key events in Scottish politics during the shortest Parliament since that of February-October 1974 were the Holyrood elections in May 2016 and the

Table 7.5 Scottish Parliament elections May 2016

	Constituency		Region		Total
	%	MSPs	%	MSPs	MSPs
Conservatives	22.0	7	22.9	24	31
Greens	0.6	0	6.6	6	6
Labour	22.6	3	19.1	21	24
LibDems	7.8	4	5.2	1	5
SNP	46.5	59	41.7	4	63
Others	0.5	0	4.5	0	0

referendum on European Union membership seven weeks later. Just as the 2015 UK election had been held in Scotland in the shadow of the independence referendum, the 2016 Holyrood elections were held in the shadow of the looming Brexit referendum. The prospect of a second independence referendum also played into the Holyrood elections. The SNP manifesto sought a mandate to hold another independence referendum 'if there is clear and sustained evidence that independence has become the preferred option of a majority of the Scottish people—or if there is a significant and material change in the circumstances that prevailed in 2014, such as Scotland being taken out of the EU against our will' (SNP, 2016, p. 23).

The SNP lost its overall majority in the 2016 devolved elections but retained its position as Scotland's largest party. Labour suffered most, losing its position as Scotland's second party in share of seats won and votes won in the regional list while remaining slightly ahead of the Conservatives in constituency votes. Table 7.5 shows the results.

The referendum on UK membership of the EU was held six weeks after the 2016 devolved elections. The leaders of the three devolved assemblies had written to Prime Minister David Cameron urging him to delay the referendum so that voters in Scotland, Wales and Northern Ireland could focus on the devolved elections, a request that was denied. Party management considerations were uppermost in the commitment to the 2014 and 2016 referendums. As the SNP's overall majority in 2011 ensured an independence referendum was firmly on the agenda, so the Conservatives' overall majority in 2015 meant likewise for a Brexit referendum.

In May 2016, the Scottish Parliament voted by 106 votes to eight (seven Conservatives and one Labour) with three abstentions, to Remain in the EU. This reflected Scottish public opinion at the time, which showed larger support for the EU than in England and Wales. All leaders of the parties represented in Holyrood

Table 7.6 Scottish Parliament 2016 election constituency vote and EU referendum vote choice

	Con	Lab	LD	SNP
Voted Leave	47.3	26.6	29.9	31.7
Voted Remain	49.5	69.4	61.5	57.8
n	319	353	117	742

Source: Scottish Election Study 2016-2017 wave 3. Results are column percentages.

argued in favour of continued EU membership. Ruth Davidson, Scottish Conservative leader, was given a prominent role in the referendum making the case for membership in characteristic adversarial terms. Scotland voted to Remain in the EU by 62% to 38%, with all local authority returning areas recording a vote for Remain.

There were some expectations that support for independence would increase if Scotland voted to Remain while overruled by a vote to Leave by the rest of the UK. In its 2015 UK election manifesto, the SNP had argued for a 'dual majority' requiring a majority of the UK public plus all four components of the UK needed to support Brexit, before it could be triggered (SNP, 2015). In the immediate aftermath of the referendum, First Minister Nicola Sturgeon called for a second independence referendum.

Table 7.6 shows the relationship between voting in the 2016 Scottish Parliament election and the subsequent Brexit referendum. We do this for two reasons. First, the 2016 devolved elections were the most proximate to the referendum, and second, to facilitate comparison to the findings in Table 7.1, which compares Scottish constituency vote and 2014 referendum vote choice. The results show a majority of supporters of each party backed Remain, with the Conservative party most divided in terms of support. The party with the next largest proportion of Leave supporters was the SNP, a finding which is consistent with pre-referendum polling.

3. A tale of two referendums: disruption, turbulence and unsettled electoral politics 2015-2017

Prime Minister Theresa May announced her intention to call a general election just over one month after First Minister Nicola Sturgeon had announced her intention for the Scottish Government to call another referendum on independence. It is perhaps not surprising that political parties in Scotland sought to distinguish themselves by their views on independence and the mandate to hold a second independence referendum in an election that so quickly followed

Holyrood debates on the issue. The consistent message from the Conservatives since the independence referendum has been opposition to another referendum. The Conservatives had previously been undermined by being the unionist party *par excellence* but this stance has recently worked to its advantage. Three elements were evident in the Scottish Conservative strategy. First, it articulated strong opposition to independence and to a second referendum. Polls suggested that there is limited appetite for a second referendum in the near future, even amongst supporters of independence. Second, the Conservatives sought to portray erstwhile partners in *Better Together* as being soft on independence. Presenting themselves as the only party that would stand up to the SNP and unambiguously opposed to independence helped polarise debate to the advantage of the Conservatives. Third, the Scottish Conservatives were remarkably disciplined in keeping on-message. The focus was on the union to the exclusion of almost all else. Indeed, the party marginalised other issues, avoided discussing the record of the Conservative Government in London and sought to focus on Scottish unionism. The party's campaign material gave prominence to its leader Ruth Davidson at the expense of the party name. The Conservative brand remains fairly toxic in Scotland, confirmed by the party's behaviour while in government in London, typified perhaps by its backing of the 'rape clause' for benefits claimants (Bradley, 2017). There is nothing new in 'Conservative' being a toxic brand in Scotland. There are echoes from a century ago when the Scottish Tories abandoned the mantle of Conservatism in favour of Unionism, though the union then referred to was that with Ireland (Mitchell, 1990).

The SNP downplayed the referendum in its campaign, and its candidates found themselves having to defend the record of the SNP administration in Edinburgh, most notably its patchy record on education. This, combined with the attention to an independence referendum, suggested that the 2017 UK general election in Scotland was a second order election. The same could be said of 2015 but the focus on Scottish policy issues in the media added a different dimension.

As Table 7.7 shows, the 2017 General Election saw the SNP emerge again as the largest party, but given the 2015 results the almost 40 percent vote share was portrayed by its opponents as a significant blow. The SNP lost 21 seats, but given the scale of the previous victory this means the party still represents almost 60% of Scottish MPs. The Conservatives saw the biggest increase in vote share and seats, achieving a level of constituency success it has not seen in 25 years (when the party earned 11 Scottish seats in 1992). Labour's significant gain in seats, admittedly from a historic low, masked a more modest increase in vote share, up less than three percentage points on the previous election.

How might we understand the results? On the one hand, we might turn to the notion of critical junctures and determine whether either the 2014 independence referendum or the 2016 Brexit referendum influenced partisan preferences,

Table 7.7 Changes in seat and vote share, UKGE in Scotland, 2015-2017

	Seats (change since 2015)	Share of vote % (change since 2015)	Share of seats %
Conservatives	13 (+12)	28.6 (+13.7)	22.0
Greens	0 (-)	0.2 (-1.1)	0
Labour	7 (+6)	27.1 (2.8)	11.9
LibDems	4 (+3)	6.8 (0.7)	6.8
SNP	35 (-21)	36.9 (-13.1)	59.3
Others	0 (-)	0.5 (**)	0
Total	59	100.1	100.0

through changing cleavages and the perceived influence of territorial scales. The remainder of this analysis examines two such examples: the supplanting of the left-right cleavage with a constitutional (centre-periphery) one, or at the very least the modification of how the class cleavage operates (with its attendant knock-on effect on leaders); and the extent to which devolved issues played a role in electoral vote choice.

How volatile was the 2017 election? The short answer is that it was roughly half as volatile as the previous election. The dissimilarity index for the four main parties in Scotland was 35.1 in 2015 but only 15.2 in 2017.[2] The other thing to note is that while vote share for the SNP fell by around 13 points and we saw a similarly sized rise in Conservative support, this was not a like-for-like transfer of voters. More SNP voters defected to Labour than to the Conservatives. Far larger proportions moved from Labour and the Liberal Democrats to the Conservatives. Put another way, the 2017 Conservative vote comprised half of its supporters from the previous election, one fifth previous Labour supporters, around 15% former SNP supporters and fewer than one in ten were previous supporters of the Liberal Democrats. There was volatility across the political spectrum in Scotland, not a straight transfer of support from the SNP to the Conservatives. Table 7.8 shows transfers of support between the 2015 and 2017 elections.

It is also clear that supporters in 2015 opted in differing degrees not to vote. Our data suggest that 10% of previous SNP supporters stayed at home, while Conservative supporters in 2015 were most likely to return to the polls.[3]

---

[2]The Pedersen index sums the absolute change in vote share for each party and divides by two.

[3]Turnout in 2017 by 2015 vote was 97% Conservative, 92% Labour, 94% Liberal Democrat and 89% SNP.

Table 7.8 Transfers of partisan support, 2015 to 2017 Westminster elections

		2015 vote			
		Con voters	**Labour**	**LD voters**	**SNP voters**
2017 vote	Con	86.2	24.9	30.5	10.2
	Lab	6.2	61.4	16.9	15.9
	LD	1.8	6.2	51.7	1.8
	SNP	4.0	6.2	0.8	70.3
n		225	373	118	679

Source: Scottish Election Study 2016-2017 (wave 3). Results are column percentages.

Diffley (2017*a*) estimates that one quarter of the people who backed the SNP in 2015 stayed at home. Part of the drop in SNP support in 2017 was therefore due not to transfers to other parties, but to its own supporters deciding not to cast a ballot. Such findings also serve to cast doubt over whether the sizeable turnout figures in 2014 and 2015 have had a transformative effect on Scottish political engagement. Turnout in the 2016 devolved elections was up five points on the previous election in 2011, and there was an increase in local election turnout as well (up seven points from the previous election), but turnout in Scotland in 2017 was down almost five points on the previous election (or up three from 2010). The participatory leap some heralded after the referendum is certainly not a foregone conclusion.

The impact of referendums on Scottish political behaviour has been counterintuitive. In one case, referendum losers became general election winners. The SNP was defeated in 2014 but went on to win a landslide in the subsequent UK general election. The Scottish Conservatives, at least their leadership, were on the losing side in the Brexit referendum but went on to increase their support significantly at the 2017 general election. In framing subsequent election debates, these referendums have each disrupted long-standing patterns of political behaviour. Labour was the biggest loser in each case but there has been no consistent winner. The SNP appeared to emerge from the independence referendum as the dominant player in Scottish politics, replacing Labour after that party's half century of dominance. But the 2017 general election results raise questions about the enduring strength of that dominance.

Evidence also suggests that Conservative opposition to a second referendum worked but that it has its limits. Estimates suggest that as much as 35 per cent of the Scottish Tory vote was tactical, in all likelihood expressing opposition to another independence referendum (Diffley, 2017*b*). The Scottish Conservatives may have become Scotland's second party by vigorously opposing independence but the party is now heavily dependent on the threat of independence for this status. Unless it converts these anti-independence voters into Conservative voters then the party could just as easily lose that status especially if they were to succeed in killing off the prospect of independence. The Conservatives were particularly weak when debate strayed off their preferred unionist agenda. Ruth Davidson's communication skills failed her when she was forced to defend Conservative policies. The Conservatives have created an opportunity in building support in Scotland, but their base is fragile and might easily fall away at the next election. The challenge for the Tories will be to consolidate and build on that support. This requires translating unionist votes into Conservative votes. Presently, the Tories are very comfortable fighting elections on the centre-periphery cleavage and are disinclined to move on to an agenda based on class politics. What is significant is that the Ruth Davidson Party managed to create a distinct agenda from that of the party south of the border.

4.   Bifurcated leadership

The two referendums can be interpreted as concerned with centre-periphery politics, albeit that the centre in the independence referendum became the periphery in the Brexit referendum. In the broadest sense, each was concerned with 'taking back control'. Both referendums cut across other cleavages, notably class, though it is too simplistic to portray these referendums as rejections of class politics. Evans and Tilley (2017) have shown that how class politics was manifested in the past may have died but it remains alive. Their key conclusion is important with respect to the role of leadership. They make the case for a 'critical role of top down processes' in accounting for changes in class voting. They distinguish this from 'bottom up' explanations and emphasise the role of agency rather than structure in voting behaviour, with an enhanced role for party leaders. Evans and Tilly (2017, p. 153) single out Tony Blair particularly, citing his declaration (at Labour's 1999 conference) that the class war was over.

It is commonly accepted that the party leader plays an important part in voters' evaluation of political parties and consequently contribute to party support at elections. Elections, including in Parliamentary systems, have become 'presidentialised' (Mughan, 2000; Poguntke and Webb, 2005). There has been some consideration of the leadership *and* multi-level elections but Moon and Bratburg note that debates on multi-level government focus on the 'allocation of power between and within territorial levels' while research on parties focused on 'relations between leaders, activists and voters' (Moon and Bratburg, 2010, p. 53). Mid-term sub-state elections witness candidates either distancing themselves from, or seeking close association with, state-wide leaders depending on the

Table 7.9 Assessments of leader performance in UK General Election

	Con voters	Labour	SNP voters	LD voters
May	.43	.16	.24	.10
Davidson	.76	.54	.60	.45
Corbyn	.50	.78	.60	.68
Dugdale	.44	.49	.43	.29
Sturgeon	.22	.39	.32	.67

Scottish Election Study 2016-2017, wave 3. Results are mean scores (0-1), where 1=had a very good campaign and 0=had a very bad campaign.

popularity of the latter. But in state-wide elections we might not expect that sub-state leaders would perform such a role given the dominance of these first level elections.

This anticipated attention to leaders relates to perceptions about their role according to territorial level at which they operate. Within the Labour party, debate on its improved performance reveal multi-level dynamics. Supporters of Jeremy Corbyn claim credit for the UK campaign and maintain that Scottish Labour's failure to embrace the agenda of the London leadership limited Labour's appeal in Scotland, where the focus was more on opposition to a second Scottish referendum. By this narrative, the failure to prioritise left-right issues at the expense of centre-periphery issues cost the party support. Related to this is the personal popularity of the two Labour leaders. Scottish voters evaluated Jeremy Corbyn's campaign far more favourably than they did Kezia Dugdale (see Table 7.9).

The opposite is true of the Conservative leaders, with Scottish voters assessing Ruth Davidson's performance more favourably than that of the Prime Minister. The improved fortunes of the Conservative party appear to stem from a combination of tepid support in the electorate for a second referendum and the personal popularity of their Scottish leader.

If the 2017 results can be explained by a combination of attention to second order centre-periphery issues and the popularity of leaders, admittedly at different territorial scales, what role if any did the Brexit referendum play? The Brexit referendum was another shock to the system but in a very different way. It appears to have kicked the system in another direction in Scotland. It is not that Brexit replaced the independence referendum any more that centre-periphery replaced class. The combination of the independence and Brexit referendums created greater turbulence in Scotland's party system than anything since the early 1970s. While Brexit was emphatically rejected by the Scottish electorate, there was a sizeable minority who support leaving the EU. Table 7.10 shows where party support in 2015 travelled in 2017, broken down by 2016 Brexit referendum choice.

Table 7.10 Transfers of partisan support, 2015 to 2017, by referendum vote choice

		Leave voters				Remain voters			
		2015 voters							
		Con	Lab	LD	SNP	Con	Lab	LD	SNP
2017	Con	90.8	41.2	51.4	18.9	80.7	16.5	21.8	4.8
	Lab	2.8	45.4	11.4	19.7	10.1	69.4	19.2	13.9
	LD	0.9	4.2	37.1	2.1	2.8	6.9	59.0	1.4
	SNP	2.8	7.6	0.0	57.9	5.5	6.0	0.0	78.4
n		109	119	35	233	109	248	78	416

Source: Scottish Election Study 2016-2017, wave 3. Results are column percentages.

Analysis of the patterns of support shows sizeable volatility in the Labour results among Leave voters, with Leave-supporting Labour voters more likely to desert the party. The party managed to retain 69% of its Remain supporters who had backed them in 2010, but less than half of those Leave supporters who voted Labour in 2010. The same is true of Leave-voting Liberal Democrats. The party managed to retain 59% of its Remain voters but only 37% of its Leave voters. The SNP was able to hang on to a larger proportion of Leave voters in 2017 than No voters in 2015, but it is clear that anti-EU voters decreased support for the SNP. Related to this is the notion of turnout. We know from above that 10% of previous SNP voters opted not to cast a ballot. It appears that Leave-supporting SNP voters were more likely to do so. We can therefore attribute instability of party preferences to party stances to both the 2014 independence referendum as well as the 2016 referendum.

5. Conclusion: turbulent politics

Scottish politics has undergone significant change since devolution but especially since the SNP became Scotland's largest party over a decade ago. The independence referendum had an impact on participation and the party system, with the centre-periphery cleavage manifested in debates on independence taking a prominent role. Critical junctures are defined by leaving a distinct and lasting legacy. Time alone is the test but each election offers evidence. The most obvious conclusion to be drawn from the 2017 general election in Scotland is that the participatory cleavage, common across the UK, that had closed to a large extent in the independence referendum, has returned to Scottish politics.

The election in Scotland highlights the importance of what Evans and Tilly (2017) described as the 'critical role of top down processes'. Party leaders and party strategies are important. There has always been a need for parties seek-ing election in Scotland to create a distinct Scottish role along with the contest for Downing Street. The Scottish Conservatives under Ruth Davidson combined Scottish distinctiveness with staunch unionism to allow it to advance to its high-est vote share since 1979 and biggest seat tally since 1983. In the 1979 election, the Conservatives won seats back from the SNP, including in north east Scotland, on the back of the defeat of devolution in a referendum just over two months before. But the party was unable to translate that anti-SNP vote into support for the Conservative Government at Westminster. The opportunity afforded by the 1979 result was lost. The challenge for the party will be to avoid this happening again and turn the 2017 opportunity into a solid base.

The SNP retained its position as Scotland's largest party. The 2017 election was nothing like 1979 but it is clearly a warning shot. The SNP came to power in Holyrood at the start of a challenging period for the economy and public finan-ces. The next few years will be challenging as a party of government in Scotland. The Conservatives lie in second place in nine seats including five where the SNP majority is in the hundreds rather than thousands. But the main threat to the SNP is likely to come from Labour. The SNP advance came at the expense of Labour (Johns and Mitchell, 2016). It is possible that former Labour voters may use the SNP as a bridge to the Conservatives but it is equally likely that those vot-ers who used the referendum as a bridge from Labour to the SNP will return to Labour. The SNP remains in either first or second place in every seat in Scotland. But Labour lies behind the SNP in 25 seats, seven of which have majorities of under one thousand. Scottish electoral politics will remain hotly contested.

References

Bradley, S. (2017, 25 April) 'Scottish Tories Under Fire at Holyrood for Backing "Rape Clause"', *Scotsman*, 25 April, accessed at https://www.scotsman.com/news/politics/scot tish-tories-under-fire-at-holyrood-for-backing-rape-clause-1-4428711 on 24 July 2017.

Carman, C., Johns, R. and Mitchell, J. (2014) *More Scottish than British*, Basingstoke, Palgrave Macmillan.

Collier, R. B. and Collier, D. (1991) *Shaping the Arena: Critical Junctures, the Labor Movement, and Regime Dynamics in Latin America*, Princeton, Princeton University Press.

Denver, D., Mitchell, P., Pattie C. and Bochel, H. (2000) *Scotland Decides: The Devolution Issue and the 1997 Referendum*, London, Frank Cass.

Diffley, M. (2017a) 'The Lost SNP Voters—What Should the Party Do Next?', *Medium*, accessed at https://medium.com/@markdiff/the-lost-snp-voters-what-should-the-party-do-next-bba4e8123b72 on 24 July 2017.

Diffley, M. (2017b) 'The Tory Revival in Scotland—Where Next?', *Medium*, accessed at https://medium.com/@markdiff/the-tory-revival-in-scotland-where-next-f31fe12daa14 on 24 July 2017.

Evans, G. and Tilly, J. (2017) *The New Politics of Class*, Oxford, Oxford University Press.

Heath, O. (2016) 'Policy Alienation, Social Alienation and Working Class Abstention in Britain, 1964-2010', *British Journal of Political Science*, **45**, 173-193.

Henderson, A. and McEwen, N. (2010) 'A Comparative Analysis of Voter Turnout in Regional Elections', *Electoral Studies*, **29**, 405-416.

Henderson, A. and McEwen M. (2015) 'Regions as Primary Political Communities: A Multi-level Comparative Analysis of Turnout in Regional Elections', *Publius*, **45**, 189-215.

Henderson, A. and Mitchell, J. (2015) *The Scottish Question, Six Months On*, Edinburgh, Transatlantic Seminar Series.

Johns, R., Denver, D., Mitchell, J. and Pattie, C. (2010) *Voting for a Scottish Government*, Manchester, Manchester University Press.

Johns, R. and Mitchell, J. (2016) *Takeover: the Extraordinary Rise of the SNP*, London, Biteback.

Kellas, J. (1971) 'Scottish Nationalism'. In Butler, D. and Pinto-Duschinsky, M. (eds), *The British General Election of 1970*, London, MacMillan, pp. 446-462.

Lau, R. R. and Redlawsk, D. P. (2001) 'Advantages and Disadvantages of Cognitive Heuristics in Political Decision-Making', *American Journal of Political Science*, **45**, 951-971.

Mitchell, J. (1990) *Conservatives and the Union*, Edinburgh, Edinburgh University Press.

Moon, D. and Bratburg, Ø. (2010) 'Conceptualising the Multi-Level Party: Two Complementary Approaches', *Politics*, **30**, 52-60.

Mughan, A. (2000) *Media and the Presidentialization of Parliamentary Elections*, London, Macmillan.

Poguntke, T. and Webb, P. (eds) (2005) *The Presidentialization of Politics: A Comparative Study of Modern Democracies*, Oxford, Oxford University Press.

Scottish Election Study (2010-2017: various years).

Scottish National Party (1974) *General Election Manifesto*, Edinburgh, SNP.

Scottish National Party (2015) *Stronger for Scotland, SNP Manifesto for UK General Election*, Edinburgh, SNP.

Scottish National Party (2016) *Re-Elect, SNP manifesto for 2016 Scottish Parliament General Election*, Edinburgh, SNP.

Sniderman, P. M. (2000) 'Taking Sides: A Fixed Choice Theory of Political Reasoning'. In Lupia, A., McCubbins, M. D. and Popkin, S. L. (eds), *Elements of Reason: Cognition, Choice and the Bounds of Rationality*, Cambridge, Cambridge University Press, pp. 67–84.

JONATHAN BRADBURY*

The Election in Wales: Campaign and Party Performance

Theresa May's decision to call a general election was apparently taken while on a North Wales walking holiday at Easter 2017. The problems of having a small parliamentary majority were mounting and the polls looked strong enough to conclude that winning a larger majority was likely if an election was held. Looking across Wales she would have known that there were prospects for gains even in this Labour stronghold. Labour still held 25 of Wales' 40 seats, but the 2010 and 2015 elections had given them vote shares of 36.2% and 36.9% respectively, their two worst results in Wales since 1918. Meanwhile the Conservative vote share had risen to 27.2% by 2015, and, after taking four seats from Labour in 2010 and a further two in 2015, they held 11 seats (Bradbury, 2015). Given Jeremy Corbyn's apparent unpopularity with many traditional Labour voters it seemed a particularly propitious time for the Conservatives to go for further gains.

However, as the *Western Mail*'s columnist, Caroline Hitt, concluded on the Saturday after the election, the climb towards a larger majority had proved to be 'an ascent as potentially tricky as tackling Crib Goch in flip-flops' (Hitt, 2017). In Wales, as in England, the Conservative Party faced a much stiffer challenge from the Labour Party than it had envisaged. The electoral landscape was redrawn without a Conservative majority and Wales became more firmly entrenched as a Labour country than at any point since the Blair landslide in 1997. How did this phenomenon unfold, and how did political actors view its likely causes and consequences? In answering these questions, we must address the ways in which the UK election campaign interacted with a discernibly Welsh campaign. Consequently, this chapter will review the election campaign and party strategies in Wales, and then examine party performance, and post-election debate. The focus here is on revealing what the parties in Wales did, analysing perceptions of the causes of the result and its implications.

*Jonathan Bradbury, Department of Political and Cultural Studies, Swansea University, j.p.bradbury@swansea.ac.uk

doi:10.1093/pa/gsx066

1. The campaign

When the election campaign began the potential significance of Wales in the election rose even further. An opinion poll in late April showed a Conservative lead of 10% which would have meant them gaining up to ten seats, to take 21 out of Wales' 40 seats (see Table 8.1). The predicted Conservative gains from Labour comprised Bridgend, Cardiff West, Cardiff South & Penarth, Newport East, and Newport West in South Wales; Alyn and Deeside, Delyn, Clwyd West and Wrexham in North-East Wales; and Ynys Mon in the North West. This poll was consistent with large British-wide Conservative poll leads, but in a Welsh context it was a shock. If realised, it would mean that for the first time since 1918 Labour would lose a general election in Wales and for the first time since the 1850s the Conservatives would gain a majority. The Conservatives' projected rise in vote share was largely at the expense of UKIP's collapse; nearly two thirds of former UKIP voters were moving to the Conservatives (*Western Mail,* 2017*a*).

The campaign's early phase in Wales therefore featured the Conservatives seeking to press home their apparent early advantage. Theresa May characterised the pro-Brexit vote in Wales in 2016 as a vote against the Labour establishment in Wales which had taken their votes for granted while delivering poorer public services than in England. The General Election offered the chance to reject this 'politics as usual' and 'to turn their backs on the politicians who have turned their backs on them'. May asked Welsh voters 'to strengthen Britain's hand in the negotiations to come, and to reject the kind of 'politics as usual' that has let people down in Wales for too long' (May 2017). The Conservatives would deliver the kind of Brexit that people wanted and a stronger Britain and Wales that might result. The Prime Minister portrayed Labour and Plaid Cymru as standing in the way of Brexit, whilst also threatening economic instability with profligate spending plans. Visiting Wales on the same day Mrs May made stops in both Newport and Bridgend.

Table 8.1 Welsh political barometer opinion polls: shares of the vote during the campaign

	Cons (%)	Lab (%)	Lib Dems (%)	Plaid Cymru (%)	UKIP (%)	Others (%)
19-21 April (N = 1029)	40	30	8	13	6	3
5-7 May (N = 1018)	41	35	7	11	4	2
18-21 May (N = 1025)	34	44	6	9	5	3
29-31 May (N = 1014	35	46	5	8	5	0
5-7 June (N = 1074)	34	46	5	9	5	1

Source: ITV Cymru Wales and Cardiff University Wales Governance Centre Polls carried out by YouGov.

The framing of the early phase of the election around likely Conservative gains sent shock waves through the Labour Party. Jeremy Corbyn visited Wales early, starting with a rally in Cardiff on 21 April. Welsh Labour First Minister, Carwyn Jones, was careful not to directly criticise Corbyn, and he sustained the idea that Welsh Labour would work in partnership with the Corbyn campaign. Nevertheless, given Corbyn's poor polling, Jones was quoted as saying that Corbyn clearly had 'work to do' and 'a mountain to climb' (*Western Mail*, 2017*b*). He also called on Corbyn to put forward a manifesto with the 'widest possible appeal', and to show it has a 'programme for government' and is not simply a protest group' (*Western Mail*, 2017*c*).

It was also apparent that very early on Jones decided that they could not rely on a Corbyn campaign to win Labour seats in Wales. Welsh Labour promoted the idea that voters should vote for Labour candidates in Wales to stand up for Wales, a campaign approach Jones had first adopted in the 2011 National Assembly election when faced with a Conservative-Liberal Democrat UK Government. In this context, it assumed that the Conservatives were likely to win, but Welsh Labour MPs would help in effective opposition and to protect Welsh interests. This approach suggested that irrespective of how voters felt about Corbyn as a potential prime minister, they could still vote for specifically Welsh Labour candidates.

Understanding the election as a Conservative versus Labour battle potentially ignored the opportunities for Plaid Cymru, but also underlined the difficulties they would have in taking them. The opportunities lay first, as an unambiguously anti-Brexit party, in capturing the large pro-EU minority vote from the 2016 referendum; and second, in pressing home its long campaign to replace Labour when it appeared at its most unelectable under Corbyn. Leanne Wood, the party leader, had the platform of UK-wide leaders' debates to try again to ignite an SNP-like sentiment in voters to switch to Plaid as the only way of making Welsh interests heard at Westminster. However, the key difficulties were that given the early polling it was impossible to present a hung parliament, and therefore the absolute desirability of Plaid Cymru representation, as at all likely, whilst polling indicated that even in its apparently weakened position under Corbyn, Labour was still ahead of Plaid Cymru.

Nevertheless, Plaid Cymru did attempt to replicate the 2015 SNP strategy. In launching the party's campaign in late April under the slogan of 'Plaid Cymru: Defending Wales' Leanne Wood stated that 'in Westminster, we have an increasingly right-wing Tory party in government, hellbent on pursuing reckless social and economic policies. Meanwhile, the Labour Party is too weak and divided to prevent the Conservatives from doing their worst to Wales'. In this context 'a large team of Plaid MPs was needed to defend our nation from further privatisation, more cuts and an ever-weaker economy' (*Western Mail*, 2017*d*). Former party leader, Dafydd Wigley, stressed that any Labour MP elected in Wales was inevitably subject to the UK Labour party whip, leaving Plaid Cymru as the only party representing Welsh interests over Brexit and public services. Even so, Plaid Cymru appeared to limit their targets to Ynys Mon, where former party leader Ieuan Wyn Jones was standing, the Rhondda where Wood had won the Assembly seat in 2016, and Ceredigion, which was a Liberal Democrat-Plaid Cymru marginal.

Party prospects were tested initially in the council elections on 4 May. The results indicated significant movement towards the Conservatives as they gained 80 seats, some movement to Plaid Cymru who gained 33 seats, and problems for Labour as they lost 107 seats. The Liberal Democrats had minor losses and UKIP lost all their seats. In Merthyr Tydfil, the Labour leader, Brendan Toomey, appeared to blame Corbyn for his own defeat, stating that 'It is quite clear that huge numbers of the public aren't entirely happy, to say the least, with the way the Labour Party is going at the moment' (*South Wales Echo*, 2017). This was echoed by Aberavon MP, Stephen Kinnock, who stated that 'The fact of the matter is that Jeremy's leadership does come up on the doorstep on a very regular basis' (*Western Mail*, 2017e).

Nevertheless, Labour still had the largest number of councillors (472) and controlled seven of Wales' 22 councils, including Cardiff, Newport, and Swansea. The results suggested the prospect of Conservative advances in the general election but not quite the political transformation that was augured by the April poll. Subsequently, Carwyn Jones issued a press release suggesting that the Welsh Labour campaign had helped in the local elections and would do so again in the General Election. Making no mention of Jeremy Corbyn he stressed that 'People realise that only Welsh Labour will stand up for Wales'. He then went on to say that the party needed to fight for 'our own Welsh Labour values' to 'stand up for our communities against the Tories' (*South Wales Echo*, 2017). A second general election Welsh poll that came out just after the council elections showed that Labour had cut the gap to 6% behind the Conservatives; even so this still projected the Conservatives to win 20 seats.

The local elections were followed by the build-up to the British-level party manifestoes, with Labour launching on 16 May and the Conservatives on 18 May. The Conservatives committed to leaving the single market and the customs union, and to seeking an EU free trade deal. They would sustain a free market economy, while addressing workers' rights, a modern industrial strategy, aspirations for a new great meritocracy and fairness between the generations. The launch highlighted reform of elderly social care which, whilst presented in terms of supporting inter-generational fairness, was criticised for increasing the costs of the elderly. Labour's manifesto also promised to leave the single market and customs union, but held out ambiguous aims for sustaining partnership on a new basis. In sharper contrast though, the party supported a large increase in public investment, selective nationalisation, and increased spending in public services, including the abolition of student tuition fees. Although the Conservatives stayed ahead in the polls overall, Labour's policies were individually more popular, putting the Conservatives on the back foot for the first time.

The Welsh Conservatives' and Welsh Labour's manifestos were then both launched on 22 May in Wrexham and Delyn respectively, both in North Wales. The choice of locations reflected that North Wales was a major political battleground. The Welsh Conservative manifesto repeated much of the British manifesto, highlighting support for 'our precious Union'. It added that Wales would benefit from the abolition of business rates for all small business with a rateable value of up to £15,000, the introduction of a national productivity investment fund and Future Britain Funds, as well as the scrapping of the Severn Bridge tolls, support for the South Wales metro and sponsorship of Cardiff and Swansea city deals as well as a new North Wales deal. The proposed UK Shared Prosperity fund would support inclusive growth, and apprenticeships would ensure Wales joined in the mission to create a great meritocracy. The UK Government would repatriate all EU powers to the central state initially, but in non-reserved policy areas they expected to devolve significant powers. The manifesto criticised the past practice of 'devolve and forget' and promised a more engaged centre-devolved nation relationship (Welsh Conservatives, 2017).

Overall, the manifesto replicated the themes of the British manifesto, customising it to a Welsh audience. The lack of Welsh party autonomy is perhaps best demonstrated by the apparent imposition of the same proposed elderly social care policy for Wales as for England. This may still have worked as a policy blend to support Welsh campaigning. However, at the Welsh launch Mrs May was forced to address a mainly English media audience to re-frame her social care policy with the promise that there would after all be a cap on costs for the elderly in paying for care. Media commentators met this clarification with great scepticism, and the focus on this controversy meant that the manifesto launch struggled to project any positive messages of what the Conservatives would do for Wales.

Meanwhile, Carwyn Jones in launching the Welsh Labour manifesto described the Conservatives policies of a so-called dementia tax and abolition of the triple lock on pensions as proof that 'the nasty party is back, and how'. In contrast, he stated that a partnership of Labour in government in the UK and Wales would 'make our economy work for everyone, not just a few at the top' (*Western Mail,* 2017g). The Welsh manifesto supported the British Labour Manifesto's ten-year national investment plan, with a national transformation fund of £250 billion. There would be a National Infrastructure Commission and a Development Bank for Wales. Jones expected that the spending plans of a

UK Labour government would also lead to an estimated additional £1.3bn per year of spending in Wales, necessitating a comprehensive spending review to ensure the money was spent well with the priorities of job creation, the NHS and education (Welsh Labour, 2017). Some of the manifesto themes strongly complemented the Corbyn message, including the promise of a fair deal for the economy and education, and the desire for a more equal society. Welsh Labour was opposed to free schools and grammar schools; and it intended to establish a Fair Work Commission, repeal the UK trade Union Act for devolved public services and end the use of zero-hours contracts.

The Welsh manifesto though was specifically titled 'Standing up for Wales' and did offer distinctive messages. It articulated a clearer vision of a soft Brexit, seeking to 'secure unfettered access to the single market' (Welsh Labour, 2017, p. 23), linking future migration to the offer of employment, a copy of the so-called Norwegian option. Welsh Labour also favoured a new public-private partnership funding model to realise £1 billion investment in schools, hospitals, and roads as part of a £5 billion capital infrastructure programme (Welsh Labour, 2017, p. 14). Welsh Labour was also cautious over the British Labour pledge to scrap tuition fees. It could have adopted its ideal that 'education should be free and if funding allowed, there should be no tuition fees' (Welsh Labour, 2017, p. 38), but the manifesto suggested simply that there would be a further review of student funding if Labour won. The Welsh manifesto promised to bring forward the Welsh Government's alternative Wales bill. This would revisit the 2017 Wales Act, granting a separate legal jurisdiction for Wales and the devolution of policing. A constitutional convention would then consider the option of a more federated Britain, and decide where power and sovereignty should lie, including in the justice system. Finally, with the battle against Plaid Cymru for Ynys Mon in mind, Welsh Labour supported a new nuclear power station, Wyfla Newydd, on Anglesey, a policy that ran counter to Corbyn's anti-nuclear instincts.

To gain a march on the two big parties Plaid Cymru launched their manifesto earlier on 16 May (Plaid Cymru, 2017). Its title 'Defending Wales, An Action Plan', reflected a critique both of Conservative policies and of Labour's supposed weakness and division. Plaid Cymru claimed only they truly defended Wales. Its themes were of how Wales had been forgotten, silenced, or neglected in the protection of its interests in Europe, its economic management, the development of public services, the protection of the environment, and the preservation of communities. Within this rhetorical framework, though, policy commitments were similar to Labour's. The manifesto stressed the need to re-invest in public services; to train and employ 1,000 new doctors, and increase funding for schools and hospitals. It also featured a policy of a publicly-owned people's bank with branches to replace the branches closed by existing banks. Its commitments on devolution were strident but more ambiguous, saying 'we will give the National Assembly for Wales the powers it needs to properly represent the people who elect it' (Plaid Cymru, 2017, p. 14).

The campaign also featured televised Welsh leaders' debates, on ITV Wales on 17 May and the BBC on 30 May. Leanne Wood also took part in the Britain-wide five-party leaders' debate on 18 May, and the seven party leaders' debate on 31 May. These debates compounded the problematic reception to Conservative manifesto pledges and the somewhat better reception to Labour ones. In the Wales leaders' debates concerns were raised over the end of EU convergence funding, agricultural subsidies after EU withdrawal, and Conservative commitment to infrastructure projects such as rail electrification and the Swansea Bay tidal lagoon.

The loss of Conservative momentum and the idea that Labour was cutting through was borne out by a reversal of Labour and Conservative fortunes in the third Welsh poll released on 23 May. This reflected the movement of the vote in British-wide polls, but in Wales the movement was more dramatic and resulted in a clear Labour lead. Expectations of Conservative gains from Labour changed to the expectation that Labour would lose no seat and would almost certainly regain Gower, where the Conservatives were defending a majority of just 27. The opinion polls showed a squeezing of the vote for the smaller parties, though it was expected that Plaid Cymru would retain their three seats and the Liberal Democrats their one. Two further polls at the end of May and on the eve of the election showed the same movement back to Labour, though with still a rise in vote share for the Conservatives as the other parties were squeezed. Welsh Labour's final campaign poster bore the slogan 'Don't let the Tories trample over Wales' and featured a picture of the Welsh countryside being flattened by giant black shoes. Carwyn Jones sought to remind voters that 'Tories never cared about Wales', summoning up memories of the Thatcher era and how Labour had been the only party that could fight against cuts and closures (*Western Mail*, 2017j). In response, the Conservatives stuck to their theme of offering a fresh alternative to the Labour establishment. Mrs May made several visits, ending with a stop off in Wrexham on 6 June Meanwhile, Plaid Cymru ran election adverts that proclaimed that 'Wales is being completely ignored in this election ... put our country back on the map and make your voice heard' (*Western Mail*, 2017k).

2. Party performance

Labour not only retained their South Wales and North-East Wales seats, based on concentrations of urbanised population, former industrial communities with strong Labour traditions, and areas of new unionised manufacturing and service sector growth, but also gained three seats, all at the Conservatives' expense:

Table 8.2 Westminster election results in Wales, 1979-2017

	Con	Lab	Lib Dem (formerly Lib and Lib-SDP)	Plaid Cymru	Others (inc. UKIP and Green)
1979					
Vote Share	32.2%	47.0%	10.6%	8.1%	2.2%
Seats	11	21	1	2	1
1983					
Vote Share	31.0%	37.5%	23.2%	7.8%	0.4%
Seats	14	20	2	2	0
1987					
Vote Share	29.5%	45.1%	17.9%	7.3%	0.2%
Seats	8	24	3	3	0
1992					
Vote Share	28.6%	49.5%	12.4%	8.8%	0.7%
Seats	6	27	1	4	0
1997					
Vote Share	19.6%	54.7%	12.4%	9.9%	3.4%
Seats	0	34	2	4	0
2001					
Vote Share	21.0%	48.6%	13.8%	14.3%	2.3%
Seats	0	34	2	4	0
2005					
Vote Share	21.4%	42.7%	18.4%	12.6%	4.9%
Seats	3	29	4	3	1
2010					
Vote Share	26.1 %	36.2%	20.1%	11.3%	6.2%
Seats	8	26	3	3	0
2015					
Vote Share	27.2%	36.9%	6.5%	12.1%	17.3%
Seats	11	25	1	3	0
2017					
Vote Share	33.6%	48.9%	4.5%	10.4%	2.5%
Seats	8	28	0	4	0

Turnout: 1979: 79.4%; 1983:76.1%; 1987: 78.9%; 1992:79.7%; 1997: 73.6%; 2001: 60.6%; 2005: 62.4%; 2010: 64.9%; 2015: 65.6%; 2017: 68.6%.

Cardiff North and Gower in South Wales and the seat of Vale of Clwyd in the North. Labour revelled in turning the two big cities of Cardiff and Swansea entirely red. They also fended off the Conservative challenge in North Wales, which early in the campaign had threatened a swathe of Labour seats. Ian Lucas holding on to Wrexham was a particular success and Chris Ruane's victory in Vale of Clwyd to take back the seat he lost in 2015 represented personal vindication. Labour's share of the vote in Wales of 48.9% was 12 points up on 2015, their highest since 1997. Labour's seat tally of 28 of the 40 seats was the party's best since 2005. Table 8.2 shows the last four decades of general election results in Wales.

For the Conservatives, the three seats lost to Labour represented a loss of footholds in urban/suburban seats in South and North Wales and they were now reduced to 8 seats, all predominantly rural in Monmouth and Vale of Glamorgan in the South East; Carmarthen West & Pembrokeshire South and Prescilli Pembrokeshire in the South West; Brecon & Radnorshire and Montgomeryshire in Mid Wales; and Aberconwy and Clwyd West in the North. They had reduced majorities in these seats, with a mere 314 vote margin in Prescilli Pembrokeshire. Even so, the Conservative vote share of 33.6% still represented a 6.4 point increase from 2015 and their best share of the vote since 1979. Labour may have greatly out-performed them, but the Conservatives still benefited at the expense of UKIP. Four in five voters in the election across Wales voted Labour or Conservative.

This left the other parties to fight over scraps. Plaid Cymru's vote share fell by 1.7 points to 10.4%. Hopes evaporated in Ynys Mon as Labour took the seat with a 5,000 majority and the Conservatives replaced Plaid Cymru in second place. Plaid also lost in the Rhondda. Nevertheless, the party held on to Arfon by 92 votes and then won Ceredigion from the Liberal Democrats by 104 votes, to give them four seats and a net seat gain of one. Fewer than 100 votes going the other way would have created a crisis for the party, but instead Leanne Wood was able to pose for jubilant photo-opportunities in Aberystwyth on the morning after the election with Ben Lake, the victorious candidate in Ceredigion. Their four seats stretched down much of the Western half of Wales—Arfon, Dwyfor Meirionnydd, Ceredigion and Carmarthen East and Dinefwr—all characterised by higher proportions of Welsh speakers and small town, village, and rural populations. It was an advance of sorts but firmly within their own heartlands and under a vote ceiling from which once again they failed to escape.

The Liberal Democrats had a more clearly disappointing result, dropping further by 2 points to 4.5% of the vote and the loss in Ceredigion meant that, for the first time in the history of the Liberals/Liberal Democrats, they had no MP in Wales. The defeat in Ceredigion was accompanied by further embarrassment as Mark Williams, the Liberal Democrat candidate, had to apologise for Facebook adverts and leaflets that suggested that Plaid Cymru was in favour of a hard Brexit when that was clearly not the case. It was hard to say whether this represented terminal decline in Wales or the farthest reaches of bottoming out. Perhaps the most ominous indicator for the future came in Cardiff Central, where having won the seat between 2005 and 2015 the party now came third. Even so, the biggest faller was UKIP, losing 11.6 points to take a vote share of just 2%. The party was all but wiped out as a serious electoral presence, with its former vote shifting to the Conservatives in some constituencies and Labour in others.

In 33 of the 40 seats there was a swing to Labour and most of Labour's 25 sitting MPs saw an increase in their majorities. In Cardiff Central, Labour won a majority of 17,196, the largest in Wales. The Conservative vote rose at UKIP's expense and the six seats where the Conservative vote rose most were all traditional Labour seats where UKIP had polled very well in 2015 and there had been a leave vote in 2016. In Islwyn, Swansea East, and Wrexham there was a small swing from Labour to Conservative. It meant that the Conservative vote share across Wales increased, but Labour too gained voters at UKIP's expense and the distribution of the vote meant that the Conservatives were eclipsed wherever they contested marginals. The results sustained Wales' distinctiveness, with Labour polling 7.9 points more in Wales than across Great Britain as a whole and the Conservatives 9.8 points less. Even so, it still contributed to the strongest return to two-party politics since 1970, with Plaid Cymru marginalised.

Following the election there was speculation as to how much Corbyn's campaign or the Welsh Labour message of standing up for Wales had influenced Welsh voters. Most available evidence suggests both were important. Welsh political barometer polling indicated that while Carwyn Jones had been considerably more popular than Jeremy Corbyn at the start of the campaign, by the time of the election Jones was still more popular but only narrowly so, with both leaders receiving approval ratings of five or just below five out of ten while Mrs May's approval rating had declined from 4.9 to below four out of ten (Scully, 2017). Carwyn Jones also sought to share the credit with Jeremy Corbyn. He emphasised that the Labour party had remained united during the election. Despite the evident strategy of emphasising the Welsh Labour brand, Jones was still able to say 'you will struggle to find any comment I made that was critical of Jeremy. I've worked with him all the time he has been leader. It's important that we work together for Wales and for the UK, and we have done just that' (*Western Mail*, 2017*l*). On the BBC Wales election night programme, Laura McAllister argued both British and Welsh Labour were authors of Labour's relative success in Wales, emphasising the apparent importance of higher turn outs, especially among younger voters, that appeared to be inspired by Jeremy Corbyn. Yet, it was apparent that Labour was doing better in Wales than in the Midlands or parts of the North, suggesting that there was a Welsh Labour effect.

Looking ahead, the Labour party in Wales is still potentially vulnerable to the Conservative challenge but the Conservatives missed a big opportunity in 2017. Labour is also still potentially vulnerable to Plaid Cymru attack, but Plaid Cymru failed again to broaden their appeal and Labour continue to successfully stand on the ground of class and nation. Labour's potential for future resilience after the election was further bolstered by Carwyn Jones' apparent desire to stay on. There had been rumours of him looking to stand down but Brexit and the 2017 election appeared to have given his leadership a new lease of life.

Conservative commentators were of course quick to comment on the fact that the main cause of their problems was the British manifesto. Swansea born Nigel Evans, MP for Ribble Valley, argued that they had made the lazy assumption that all UKIP voters would return to the party and that Jeremy Corbyn would be a no-hoper. They had then derailed their own campaign with disastrous policies on pensions and social care. Yet, the Conservative leader in the National Assembly, Andrew R. T. Davies acknowledged that the Conservatives had not had a clear message tailored to Wales, declaring, 'One of the key flaws is we do not have a designated political leader in Wales under our constitution like Scotland does and so there isn't a single individual who can call the shots here in Wales. I am the leader in the Assembly and that to me has been a deficit that has needed to be addressed for some considerable time, about a single identifiable political leader here in Wales to give that Welsh Conservative edge'. The problems were exemplified by an internal argument over who should represent the party in leaders' debates. The choice appeared to lie between Davies and the Secretary of State Alun Cairns but Darren Millar, an Assembly Member who had been the Party's policy officer, appeared in one debate. Because of a lack of internal grip on organisation the party failed to replicate successful strategies of local campaigning in 2015 around local hospital closures or local school performance issues (*Western Mail*, 2017m).

Looking more broadly, the evidence the election gave of the state of electoral democracy in Wales was something of a curate's egg. On the one hand, it featured higher participation than in 2015, with turnout up 3% to 68.6%, nearly the same as the UK wide turnout. Turnout was up in 39 constituencies with the biggest rise in Merthyr Tydfil and Rhymney from 53% to 61%. The election saw only a 10% turnover of MPs but the number of female MPs still rose slightly from nine in 2015 to 11 in 2017. Ten of these women were Labour MPs, meaning that of Labour's 28 MPs in Wales 35.7% were women. However, there remained no Welsh MPs from an ethnic minority background. The political proportionality of representation also remained poor as Labour won 70% of the seats on less than half the popular vote.

More worryingly, the election was accompanied by significant evidence of intimidation. In Gower Byron Davies, the sitting Conservative MP, was the victim of an online campaign from Labour supporters that included death threats, 'vile abuse' and false accusations that he had been one of the MPs involved in the election expenses fraud' (*Western Mail*, 2017f). In Aberconwy, Labour's female candidate received a series of sexist online comments. Kirsty Williams, the Liberal Democrat Education minister in Wales described an incident that occurred while campaigning in Brecon and Radnorshire when a 'man wound down his window of his vehicle as he was going past. He stuck his hand out of the vehicle in a mock gun, and said, "You Liberals, you all deserve to be shot" and made a gun sound as if he was shooting us and then drove off' *(Western Mail,* 2017*h*). Incidents like this fed into the broader post-election debate about diminished respect for politicians and the role of social media in facilitating public abuse of them, as well as specifically on the Conservative-side allegations against the tactics used by the Corbyn supporting Momentum movement to defeat Conservative candidates.

3. Conclusion

Theresa May had wanted not only to increase her parliamentary majority but also to increase Conservative representation outside England to blunt territorial threats to the Union, as well as challenges to her vision for Brexit that were coming from the devolved administrations. The central story of the 2017 UK General Election was of course that Mrs May lost her parliamentary majority, and in so doing she also lost rather than gained seats in Wales. It was a disaster.

Whether the causes of this outcome included specifically Welsh factors is a matter for debate. Clearly there was a distinct Welsh campaign, marked by party strategies, manifestos, and leaders' debates. In assessing Conservative failure in Wales, party critics highlighted how the British-level manifesto launch was key in undoing the good early work. If it had sought to project a modern-day version of liberal unionism it had ended up looking far from liberal. Even so, more than in previous elections post-election debate acknowledged the lack of a distinct Welsh Conservative voice as a problem. In analysing how Labour ended up doing so well in Wales, many successful candidates who had previously criticised Jeremy Corbyn were quick to thank him for his strong campaign. Yet, many also praised the robustness of the Welsh Labour campaign, giving Labour voters reasons to vote for the party to stand up for Wales even when they didn't support Corbyn for Prime Minister. It represented perhaps the most independent approach yet pursued by Welsh Labour during a UK general election, marking out their own rhetorical message, and distinct emphases in policies over Brexit, public services, and devolution. Plaid Cymru singularly failed to break Labour's dominance in representing the anti-Conservative vote.

The implications of the result in Wales fed into British-wide analyses of political change. The election saw the killing off of the UKIP peripheral revolt, with their support returning to the Conservatives and Labour to restore a two-party system. Plaid Cymru's efficient harvesting of an extra seat aside, the election also saw the clipping of the wings of sub-state nationalism, with declining vote shares for both the SNP and Plaid Cymru. Overall the election saw the centre and unionism re-strengthened. It was simply that Mrs May had to share the political dividend of that re-strengthening with Labour in Wales. Labour's gain of three seats in Wales represented the restoration of only half of the seats lost to the Conservatives in 2010 and 2015 and the Conservatives' vote share had appreciably risen in 2017. There was a potential platform for future success. But it was still Labour's election and compared to the rather gloomy prognoses that followed the 2015 election defeat, the prospects for Welsh Labour to fend off both Plaid Cymru and the Conservatives appeared to have been restored.

During the election, Welsh public life also sadly had to focus on quite a different event. On 17 May former First Minister, Rhodri Morgan, died while out cycling near his home west of Cardiff. At an extended plenary session on 23 May Carwyn Jones said that 'Hywel Rhodri Morgan was named after two kings, and he served this place with distinction as first Minister for nearly ten years'. Jones remarked that 'Wales hasn't just lost a great politician; we've lost a real father figure' *(Western Mail*, 2017*i*). Richard Wyn Jones (2017) reflected on Morgan's contribution also to his party. He described Morgan as a small 'n' nationalist who with great authenticity had differentiated Welsh Labour from British Labour, and had left a legacy for Carwyn Jones to position Labour in post-devolution politics. The effect of such public commentary was not measurable but helped to make sense of Labour's ability to connect to a distinct electorate even in what appeared initially to be a very problematic election. More than a century before, William Gladstone, a frequent visitor to his retreat at Hawarden in North Wales, would have understood this as the successful representation of a strong patriotism that could still be consistent with the Union, something to be grateful for and not taken for granted, and as a result in need of respect by any British-wide party seeking success in Wales.

References

Bradbury, J. (2015) 'Wales: Still a Labour Stronghold but Under Threat?' In Geddes, A. and Tonge, J. (eds) *Britain Votes 2015*, Oxford, Oxford University Press, pp. 101–116.

Hitt, C. (2017, 10 June) 'Bitter Lessons We Can All Learn From May's Election Debacle', *Western Mail*, p. 25.

May, T. (2017, 25 April) 'Reject the Politics as Usual That Has Let People Down in Wales for Too Long', *Western Mail*, p. 19.

Plaid Cymru (2017) *Tarian Cymru/Defending Wales, Action Plan 2017*, Cardiff, Plaid Cymru.

Scully, R. (2017, September) 'Wales: An Unexpected Tale of Labour Resilience', *Political Insight*, pp. 16–17.

South Wales Echo (2017, 6 May), 'Bloody Nose for Labour as it Loses Control of Councils', p. 6.

Welsh Conservatives (2017) *Forward, Together: Our Plan for a Stronger Wales, a Stronger Britain and a Prosperous Future*, Cardiff, Welsh Conservatives.

Welsh Labour (2017) *Standing Up for Wales*, Cardiff, Welsh Labour.

Western Mail (2017*a*, 25 April) 'Welsh Labour Facing a Meltdown with Loss of 10 MPs, Poll Suggests', p. 4.

Western Mail (2017*b*, 25 April) 'Public Have Not Yet Seen Corbyn's Best—Carwyn', p. 5.

Western Mail (2017*c*, 26 April) 'Labour Has a Mountain to Climb says Carwyn as He Calls for Manifesto with Widest Possible Appeal', pp. 4-5.

Western Mail (2017*d*, 26 April) 'Labour Too Weak to Stand Up for Wales—Leanne', p. 5.

Western Mail (2017*e*, 6 May) 'Theresa May Wants to Keep The Focus on Brexit Despite Poll Triumph', p. 4.

Western Mail (2017*f*, 17 May) 'Conservative Candidate Subjected to Abuse and Death Threats', p. 7.

Western Mail (2017*g*, 23 May) '"Nasty Tory Party is Back", Says Carwyn as He Launches Manifesto', pp. 4-5.

Western Mail (2017*h*, 23 May) 'Kirsty: I Was Told I Deserved to be Shot on Campaign Trail', p. 7.

Western Mail (2017*i*, 24 May) 'He Had a Wonderful Life and He Enjoyed Every Minute . . .', p. 12.

Western Mail (2017*j*, 30 May) 'Carwyn: Tories Never Cared about Wales', pp. 6-7.

Western Mail (2017*k*, 7 June), 'Put Our Country Back on the Map and Make Your Voice Heard', p. 11.

Western Mail (2017*l*, 10 June) 'Delighted Carwyn: We Didn't Expect this Success', p. 10.

Western Mail (2017*m*, 10 June) 'Campaign Flaws Scuppered Tories', p. 13.

Wyn Jones, R. (2017, 22 May) 'Rhodri's Lasting Legacy is to Have Acted as Bridge for Both His Party and His Nation', *Western Mail*, p. 23.

Britain Votes (2017) 139–154

JONATHAN TONGE AND JOCELYN EVANS*

Northern Ireland: Double Triumph for the Democratic Unionist Party

The General Election result in Northern Ireland impacted across the UK. The Democratic Unionist Party (DUP) enjoyed a double victory. It extended dominance of the unionist community and collected a bigger prize as its ten MPs (a record tally) held a pivotal position at Westminster. In holding the balance of power in the House of Commons, the DUP was not shy in articulating its price for supporting the otherwise friendless Conservative government in key votes, extracting £1 billion of new funding for Northern Ireland. The DUP's hegemonic position within its unionist constituency was matched by Sinn Féin's obliteration of its Social Democratic and Labour Party (SDLP) rival within the nationalist community, but without any obvious reward for republicans. At a time of considerable instability, with Northern Ireland's political institutions undergoing one of their episodic crises, unionist and nationalist voters overwhelmingly backed the dominant representative forces within their respective ethno-national blocs. This analysis of the election draws upon data from the 2017 Economic and Social Research Council's Northern Ireland General Election study to examine why the DUP and Sinn Féin dominated the contest and looks at the implications of the outcome in Northern Ireland and at Westminster.[1]

1. The results

The onward march of the DUP and Sinn Féin saw the departure from the House of Commons of the two Ulster Unionist Party (UUP) and three SDLP MPs. Table 9.1 shows the results.

*Jonathan Tonge, Department of Politics, University of Liverpool, j.tonge@liverpool.ac.uk; Jocelyn Evans, School of Politics and International Studies, University of Leeds, j.a.j.evans@leeds.ac.uk

[1]The 2017 Northern Ireland general election study is available at https://discover.ukdataservice.ac.uk/catalogue/?sn=8234&type=Data%20catalogue Principal Investigator: J. Tonge; Co-Investigators: J. Evans, B. Hayes, P. Mitchell, P. Shirlow. The authors acknowledge with thanks the support from the Economic and Social Research Council. Data cited are from the survey unless referenced otherwise.

doi:10.1093/pa/gsx067

Table 9.1 Westminster election result in Northern Ireland, 2017 (main parties)

	Seats	Change from 2015	Votes	% Vote share	Change in % vote share from 2015
DUP	10	+2	292,316	36.0	+10.3
Sinn Féin	7	+3	238,915	29.4	+4.9
Independent Unionist	1	–	16,148	N/A	N/A
SDLP	0	−3	95,419	11.7	−2.2
UUP	0	−2	83,280	10.3	−5.8
Alliance	0	0	64,553	7.9	−0.6

Turnout 65.6% (+7.1%)

The DUP and Sinn Féin both enjoyed record highs for their vote shares and seats for a Westminster election and the 'big two' now hold all bar one seat. Two decades earlier, the UUP held ten seats and the SDLP three, with the DUP and Sinn Féin mustering a mere two each. Having regained Westminster representation in 2015, the UUP's Tom Elliott lost Fermanagh and South Tyrone to Sinn Féin despite the DUP again standing aside to aid the chances of a unionist victory, while Danny Kinahan lost South Antrim to the DUP. Sinn Féin captured Foyle and South Down, SDLP seats since 1983 and 1987 respectively, while South Belfast was also lost by the SDLP, to the DUP.

The only seat which did not fall to either of the major parties was North Down, held by the Independent Unionist, Lady Sylvia Hermon (a UUP MP until 2010) with her majority over the DUP reduced from 9202 to 1208 votes. Turnout in nationalist-held constituencies remained higher than those in unionist-held constituencies, at 68.4% to 63.4% respectively. There were swings from the SDLP to Sinn Féin in all constituencies and from the UUP to DUP wherever both those parties contested a seat.

Sinn Féin's electoral successes provoked concerns from political rivals over the use of proxy votes, ballots cast by one person of behalf of an absent other. The SDLP in Foyle, where the seat was lost to Sinn Féin by a mere 169 votes, complained to the Electoral Office for Northern Ireland over the quadrupling of substitute votes, from 330 in 2015 to 1200 in 2017 (*Belfast Telegraph*, 2017b, c). Proxy voting in one Sinn Féin stronghold in Foyle (Brandywell) amounted to 5.57% of all votes cast, 17.5 times the UK average of 0.32% (*Belfast Telegraph*, 2017d). Following considerable tightening of voting procedures in Northern Ireland, including the requirement for photographic identification at a polling station, critics of proxy voting felt it revived old fears of electoral fraud and abuse, once commonplace. Marginal Fermanagh and South Tyrone was the constituency with the highest number of proxy and postal votes issued, 1707 and 2981

Table 9.2 Northern Ireland constituency results, Westminster election 2017

(% vote shares)		DUP	UUP	ALLIANCE	SINN FÉIN	SDLP	OTH	TURNOUT	TURNOUT CHANGE from 2015	% SWING from 2015
Belfast East	DUP HOLD	55.8	3.3	36.0	2.1	0.4	2.4	67.5	+4.7	6.6 Alliance to DUP
Belfast North	DUP HOLD	46.2	N/A	5.4	41.7	4.5	2.2	67.6	+8.4	N/A
Belfast South	DUP GAIN FROM SDLP	30.4	3.5	18.2	16.3	25.9	5.6	66.1	+6.1	N/A
Belfast West	SF HOLD	13.4	N/A	1.9	66.7	7.0	11.0	65.4	+8.8	12.5 OTH to SF
East Antrim	DUP HOLD	57.3	11.9	15.6	9.3	3.4	2.5	60.6	+7.3	14.0 UUP to DUP
East Londonderry	DUP HOLD	48.1	7.6	6.2	26.5	10.8	0.8	61.2	+9.3	6.9 UUP to DUP
Fermanagh & S Tyrone	SF GAIN FROM UUP	N/A	45.5	1.7	47.2	4.8	0.8	75.8	+3.2	1.2 SDLP to SF
Foyle	SF GAIN FROM SDLP	16.1	N/A	1.8	39.7	39.3	3.0	65.4	+12.6	8.0 SDLP to SF
Lagan Valley	DUP HOLD	59.6	16.8	11.1	3.5	7.5	1.5	62.2	+6.3	5.0 UUP to DUP
Mid Ulster	SF HOLD	26.9	6.5	2.3	54.5	9.8	0.0	68.2	+7.9	4.1 SDLP to SF
Newry & Armagh	SF HOLD	24.6	8.3	2.3	47.9	16.9	0.0	68.5	+4.3	7.0 SDLP to SF
North Antrim	DUP HOLD	58.9	7.2	5.6	16.3	5.3	6.8	64.1	+8.9	12.3 OTH (TUV) to DUP
North Down	IND UNIONIST HOLD	38.0	N/A	9.3	1.4	1.0	41.1 IND UNIONIST 9.0 OTH	61.0	+9.2	11.3 IND UNIONIST to DUP
South Antrim	DUP GAIN FROM UUP	38.2	30.8	7.4	18.1	5.5	0.0	63.3	+9.1	5.0 UUP to DUP
South Down	SF GAIN FROM SDLP	17.4	3.9	3.6	39.9	35.1	0.0	67.2	+10.4	9.3 SDLP to SF
Strangford	DUP HOLD	62.0	11.4	14.7	2.8	6.2	2.9	60.4	+7.6	10.3 UUP to DUP
Upper Bann	DUP HOLD	43.5	15.4	4.5	27.9	8.6	0.0	63.9	+4.9	11.7 UUP to DUP
West Tyrone	SF HOLD	26.9	5.2	2.3	50.7	13.0	1.9	68.2	+7.7	5.5 SDLP to SF

respectively. Across Northern Ireland, there was an increase of 18% in the number of proxy votes awarded from the Assembly election held only 98 days earlier and a 20.4% rise in postal votes issued (Devenport, 2017). Table 9.2 provides the Westminster election constituency results.

The thinness of Northern Ireland's centre ground, at least in terms of voters, was again confirmed by the seat-less performance of Alliance, notwithstanding a continuing sizeable vote for the party leader, Naomi Long, in East Belfast. Elections remain contests for ideological true believers. Of electors self-identifying as unionist, 76% voted, whilst 78% of nationalist self-identifiers cast a ballot. Of those declining to identify as unionist or nationalist, only 37% bothered to vote. As always with Northern Ireland elections, the contest was a communal headcount. Table 9.3 shows the unionist, nationalist and non-aligned shares of the vote, in relation to Protestant, Catholic and no-religion proportions of each constituency, while Table 9.4 indicates the continuing extraordinarily strong correlations between Protestant religious community background and the unionist bloc vote and Catholic religious community background and nationalist bloc vote. The strength of those relationships, which almost reach the 'perfect' figure of 1.00, at 0.96 and 0.99 respectively, makes Northern Ireland still very much a place apart, offering by far the strongest link between religious affiliation and party choices anywhere in Europe. In terms of its overarching inter-communal ethno-religious division, Northern Ireland shows little sign of thawing.

The strength of the relationship between Protestant religious community background and unionist bloc voting in each constituency from the 2005 to 2017 general elections is depicted in Figure 9.1, while Figure 9.2 does likewise for the Catholic religious community. There is only one significant outlier, East Belfast, given the very large vote that the non-bloc aligned Alliance Party has achieved there at the last three elections. The very tight constituency clustering across four elections indicates the pervasiveness of religious background as the determinant of unionist or nationalist party choice. A weakening of the relationship would see much greater scattering.

2.   Explaining the result

The DUP's new position of strength represented a dramatic transformation in fortunes from the March 2017 Northern Ireland Assembly election, precipitated when Sinn Féin's Martin McGuinness, in his final political act, resigned as Deputy First Minister, effectively collapsing the devolved Executive and Assembly. At the March contest, the DUP lost ten seats and Sinn Féin closed the gap on the DUP to a solitary seat. For the first time, unionism lost its overall majority at Stormont. The DUP struggled partly because the Assembly was being

Table 9.3 Unionist, Nationalist and Non-Unionist/Non-Nationalist vote shares, 2017 Westminster election

Constituency	Protestant % of constituency	% Unionist vote	Roman Catholic % of constituency	% Nationalist vote	No religion	% Non- Unionist or Nationalist vote
Belfast East	75.4	60.1	12.7	2.5	10.5	37.4
Belfast North	45.7	46.2	46.9	46.2	6.4	7.6
Belfast South	43.7	34.5	44.0	42.2	9.5	23.3
Belfast West	16.7	13.4	80.1	73.7	2.7	13.0
East Antrim	70.1	71.6	20.4	12.7	8.5	15.6
East Londonderry	53.3	56.5	41.7	37.3	4.4	6.2
Fermanagh & S Tyrone	39.1	45.5	57.7	52.0	2.6	2.5
Foyle	22.0	16.1	75.1	79.0	2.1	4.9
Lagan Valley	71.9	77.4	19.0	11.0	8.1	11.6
Mid Ulster	30.8	33.4	66.7	64.3	2.1	2.3
Newry & Armagh	30.6	32.9	66.4	64.8	2.5	2.3
North Antrim	66.0	72.9	28.4	21.6	4.8	5.6
North Down	74.4	81.5	12.6	2.4	11.8	16.1
South Antrim	59.8	69.0	31.9	25.6	7.5	5.4
South Down	26.9	21.3	69.3	75.0	3.4	5.7
Strangford	73.1	74.7	17.3	9.0	8.7	16.3
Upper Bann	50.0	58.9	44.0	36.5	5.1	4.5
West Tyrone	30.2	32.1	68.0	63.7	1.5	4.2

Source for religious composition of constituencies: Russell, R. (2013) *Census 2011: Key Statistics at Assembly Area Level,* Northern Ireland Research and Information Service Information Paper NIAR 161-13, accessed at http://www.niassembly.gov.uk/globalassets/documents/raise/publications/2012/general/7013.pdf on 11 September 2017.

Table 9.4 Correlations between religious community background and Unionist or Nationalist bloc vote, 2005-2017 Westminster elections

	2005	2010	2015	2017
Catholic-Nationalist	0.98	0.99	0.99	0.99
Protestant-Unionist	0.97	0.94	0.92	0.96

*all significant at p < 0.001

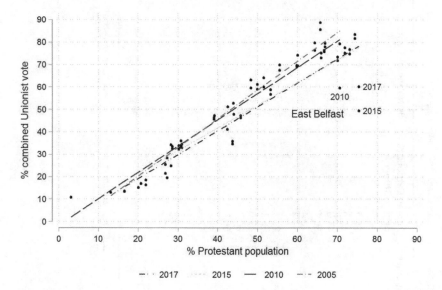

Figure 9.1 Protestant Community Background and Unionist Bloc Constituency Voting 2005-2017[2]

reduced in size from 108 to 90. Representation for each constituency was reduced from six to five Assembly members (MLAs). Most MLAs lost by the DUP were in constituencies where the party was attempting to hold a third seat. DUP losses were inevitable given the diminished Assembly size but, beyond the headline of DUP MLAs losing seats, it was also apparent the DUP remained solidly the dominant party of the unionist bloc. Although heavily criticised for a negative, anti-republican, sectarian headcount campaign, the DUP leader, Arlene Foster, had not misread the mood of unionism in the Assembly election. The UUP's failure to make inroads into the DUP's vote led to its leader, Mike Nesbitt, resigning before all the results were finalised. Three months later, under the first-past-the-

---

[2]Figure 9.1 and 9.2 were generated in Stata using the 'plotplain' scheme from the blindschemes package by Daniel Bischof. See Bischof, D. (2017).

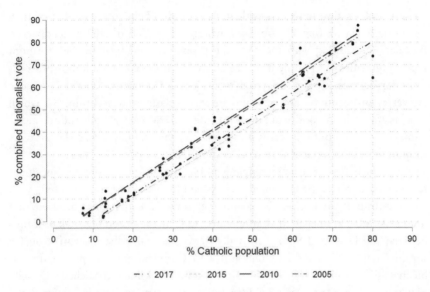

Figure 9.2 Catholic Community Background and Nationalist Bloc Constituency Voting 2005-2017

post, winner-takes-all, voting system used exclusively for Westminster elections, unionists had to choose a solitary constituency representative for their ethnonational bloc. The DUP was clearly seen as the stouter custodian of unionist interests and its vote soared and the UUP vote crumbled.

In the Assembly election, the DUP leader Foster had, however, underestimated the extent of anger among republicans, who she labelled as 'crocodiles', always coming back for more. Sinn Féin fought the March Assembly and June Westminster elections by mobilising nationalists and republicans on a series of grievances against the DUP. These charges included the botched handling of the overly generous Renewable Heating Incentive Scheme by Arlene Foster, which contributed to the collapse of the Assembly, but was less salient as an election feature; Brexit, against which 88% of nationalists voted (Garry, 2017); the continued prohibition of same-sex marriage, blocked by the DUP five times in Assembly votes; the failure to introduce an Irish Language Act and the lack of movement on implementing items supposedly dealing with the past, which were agreed in the 2014 Stormont House Agreement.

By the time of the General Election, a mere three months after the Assembly contest, none of these disputes were any closer to resolution. An inquiry into the heating scheme debacle had been announced but its verdict was a long way off; Brexit continued to polarise; the DUP's defence of 'traditional marriage' was maintained; and there was no Assembly or Executive to bring about an Irish Language Act, not that the unionist parties would have endorsed such a measure anyway. Polarisation remained evident. 84% of Sinn Féin voters wanted an Irish Language Act, with only 4% opposed, whereas only 10% of DUP voters backed the idea. On dealing with the past, the proposals contained in the Stormont House Agreement were only modest and included the continuation of prosecutions for actions during the Troubles, as part of a victim-centred approach. However, prosecutions are rare and invariably contested according to which 'side' is affected. A majority of Sinn Féin voters (57%) back a truth and reconciliation commission but this seems impossible to achieve. Only 12% of DUP voters support amnesties for acts of violence committed during the Troubles.

Amid the belligerence and wrangling, public support for devolved government remained extensive. 70% wanted the Assembly and Executive restored, with cross-community majorities in favour, yet only 27% of voters believed that unionists and nationalists had cooperated well in the Assembly. Relationships between the DUP and Sinn Féin had deteriorated since the halcyon 'Chuckle Brother' days of Ian Paisley and Martin McGuinness and the pragmatic and business-like dealings of Peter Robinson and McGuinness. Michelle O'Neill, McGuinness's successor as Sinn Féin leader in Northern Ireland, declared she would not work alongside Arlene Foster, who was entitled to be First Minster based on the DUP's Assembly mandate. Both Foster and O'Neill benefited from unionist and nationalist intransigence which helped mobilise supporters. On the biggest turnout since 2005, the DUP rallied most pro-Union voters and Sinn Féin proved utterly dominant within nationalism. Foster and O'Neill were popular leaders among their own ranks and regarded with hostility by the other side. Asked to rate the DUP leader on a zero to ten scale, where ten is the highest possible regard, the most common score from DUP voters placed Foster at ten, whilst 62% of Sinn Féin voters placed her at zero. More significantly in terms of the intra-communal battle, Foster was held in reasonably high regard by the remaining supporters of the party she quit to join the DUP in 2003, with three-quarters of UUP voters rating her at five or above. Anathema towards the DUP leader from Sinn Féin's base was heartily reciprocated by DUP backers regarding Sinn Féin's northern leader. Asked to rate Michelle O'Neill, the largest single category awarded by DUP voters was zero, 42% placing her in this negative bracket.

Bereft of Westminster representation (a repeat of 2010-2015) the future of the UUP appears uncertain. The party's very modest revival after the electoral calamities of the post-Good Friday Agreement era (when the DUP prospered by opposing a deal they eventually effectively signed up to) was ended in 2017 and there are no clear indicators as to how the UUP can claw back the support lost to the DUP. It was bitterly ironic for the UUP to witness the DUP reap the rewards of a deal with the Conservatives. From the 1920s until the 1970s, the UUP had taken the Conservative whip at Westminster. The old alliance was revived at the 2010 election by the Conservative leader, David Cameron and the UUP leader, Reg

Empey, under the cumbersome title of Ulster Conservatives and Unionists New Force (UCUNF) but yielded no UUP seats.

On the nationalist side, the 43 years of continuous Westminster representation enjoyed by the Social Democratic and Labour Party (SDLP) were ended, perhaps never to return. Like the UUP, the SDLP had delivered the Good Friday Agreement but since then has appeared a party with its best idea now behind it, offering a less clear manifesto for the future. The years since the Good Friday Agreement have seen a transformation in intra-bloc election fortunes, one difficult to see being reversed. The UUP and SDLP are ageing parties struggling to articulate ideas and visions since the big power-sharing deal of 1998, a consociational deal which reinforced the ethnic identities strongly articulated by the DUP and Sinn Féin. Those ethnic tribune parties (see Mitchell *et al.*, 2009) are seen as the stouter custodians of ethnic interests even though they have moderated their political agendas over the last two decades. A majority of electors—and even 31% of UUP voters—concurred that the DUP had been the more effective party for unionists.

The outcome of the election indicated continuing 'Balkanisation' of Northern Ireland. Its south and west are predominantly Irish nationalist, the British Unionist population confined, in Westminster representation terms, to the north-eastern corner. If partition were occurring today, the contours of the border might be very different. Ironically, however, Brexit may reinvigorate a largely invisible border along its original territorial marking. Although the DUP wants a seamless border along with the British and Irish governments, it also opposes membership of the EU single market and customs union and refuses to countenance special status for Northern Ireland. The election showed little evidence of remorse from the DUP's support base over their stance. At the 2016 Brexit referendum, 70% of DUP voters backed departure from the EU (Garry and Coakley, 2016). At the 2017 General Election, 66% of voters endorsed this stance. Few of Sinn Féin's supporters had altered their views. In 2016, only 14% backed EU withdrawal (Garry and Coakley, 2016); 15% advocated this course in 2017.

Beyond communal grandstanding, the DUP used its election manifesto to emphasise its more left-wing economic agenda, often ignored amid the concentration upon the party's hard-line constitutional approach and moral strictures (Democratic Unionist Party, 2017). The DUP made clear its opposition to the ending of the triple lock on pensions and opposed any means-testing of winter fuel allowances for pensioners. Meanwhile, Sinn Féin campaigned on three core issues: 'No Brexit, No Border, No Tory cuts' and demanded 'designated special status for the North within the EU' and 'continued political representation for the north of Ireland within the EU parliament' (Sinn Féin, 2017, p. 4). Yet neither Sinn Féin's Westminster election manifesto, nor the party's Assembly election manifesto earlier that year, made mention of a border poll, despite the calls for such from the party leadership in the immediate aftermath of the Brexit vote. Unless such a vote was conducted on an all-island basis, in which a close result might ensue, Sinn Féin would surely not achieve a majority for a united Ireland. Within the confines of Northern Ireland, 52% of 2017 Westminster election voters said they would support the constitutional status quo in the event of a poll, with 27% declaring in favour of a united Ireland. Only 18% of the electorate believed Brexit made a united Ireland more likely.

Although generating much passion among some voters, moral or social issues did not feature highly in explanations of party choice. Among DUP voters, more favoured the legalisation of same-sex marriage (44%) than opposed (42%). True, the figure in favour of legalisation were substantially below that found among Sinn Féin voters, of 66%, but it does indicate that the DUP's support base is less vexed over the issue than the DUP's membership, 65% of which believed that 'homosexuality is wrong' a few years earlier (Tonge *et al.*, 2014) and who shared the view of one DUP elected representative, the Assembly member Jim Wells, that 'Peter will not marry Paul in Northern Ireland' (*Belfast Telegraph*, 2017a). Among 2017 election voters, age was a more significant variable than party choice in terms of attitudes to same-sex marriage. Only 7% of 18 to 24 years old voters opposed the legalisation of such unions, whereas only 31% of those aged 65 and over were in favour. Social conservatism was far from the exclusive preserve of DUP voters. Indeed, a higher percentage of DUP voters (41%) supported the legalisation of abortion than did Sinn Féin voters (32%).

The DUP were labelled 'dinosaurs' by critics for their hostility to same-sex marriage and abortion. However, whilst the DUP's social conservatism was thought a possible deterrent to younger voters, 32% of 18- to 24-years-old voters backed the DUP, only five points below the party's overall share, with 26% supporting Sinn Féin. That said, two thirds of electors in that age category did not vote, the majority of those non-voters eschewing unionist or nationalist labels.

The DUP's blocking of same-sex marriage in the Northern Ireland Assembly, using a Petition of Concern which requires cross-community support for a measure, attracted much hostility from those favouring change. It might be recalled, however, that more Conservative MPs voted against the legalisation of same-sex marriage than voted in favour when England and Wales moved to change the law. Moreover, opposition to abortion straddles the unionist and nationalist blocs in Northern Ireland, with the DUP and the SDLP opposed to liberalisation. Most importantly of all though, the DUP's interest lies in preserving prohibitions in Northern Ireland, not imposing its beliefs beyond the region.

3. The consequences of the result

The result was palpably a dream scenario for the DUP. As the monopoly supplier of allies for the Conservatives, Foster's Party could name its price for propping up a government stripped of its overall majority in the House of Commons. A 'confidence-and-supply' deal between the Conservatives and the DUP was confirmed 18 days after the election. The DUP agreed to support the Conservative government in key votes, such as the Queen's Speech, Budget, Brexit and anti-terrorism legislation, in addition to votes of confidence, whilst retaining the right to vote against the government on other issues. In return, the DUP, well-prepared for its pivotal role, extracted a high financial price from the government, to meet its own priorities. Despite some excitable commentary, the DUP had no interest in extending its opposition to same-sex marriage and abortion. The initial demands of the DUP upon the Conservatives also excluded loyalist cultural concerns, such as those around Protestant parades. The 'coalition of crackpots' (*Daily Mirror*, 9 June 2017, p. 1) thus turned out to be a pragmatic parliamentary arrangement, limited in scope, although the areas covered were crucial to the government's survival.

The DUP had long known what it wanted from a minority government. In anticipation of a hung parliament after the 2015 election, the party had produced a detailed 'shopping list'. The Northern Ireland Plan contained 45 items, two thirds of which were financial (Democratic Unionist Party, 2015). In 2017, the focus was again financial. The price for the DUP's parliamentary support was approximately £1 billion in new funding for Northern Ireland for two years, amounting to £550 per head in the region and effectively valuing each DUP MP at £100m. The extra money given to Northern Ireland included £400m for infrastructure projects, £200m to improve health services and £150m for ultra-fast broadband. This additional funding was on top of the £2.5 billion of support offered by the British Government to underwrite the Stormont House and Fresh Start Agreements, reached in 2014 and 2015 respectively to bolster Northern Ireland's devolved government, but which had little beneficial effect in furthering political progress.

The DUP's mildly leftist economic agenda contributed to the dropping of Conservative plans to cut the cost of state benefits. The confidence and supply agreement declared 'that both parties have agreed' to support the maintenance of the status quo on pensions and winter fuel allowances (HM Government, 2017a, p. 2). Precisely how much of this can be attributed to the DUP is uncertain. Fears of Conservative backbench rebellions and adverse electoral impacts may have been as influential as the DUP view. Nonetheless, there was a certain irony in the DUP taking the Conservatives to the left, given much of the initial media commentary on the Tories' new allies, which (unsurprisingly) focused on the party's hard line and controversial views. Three months after the election, the DUP supported Labour's parliamentary motion demanding the ending of the public sector pay cap, further indication that the party would resist the Conservatives in areas beyond where an alliance had been agreed.

In concentrating upon the cash not the (Orange) sash, the DUP played an astute hand. The financial benefits were cross-community and did not appear to challenge the rigorous impartiality between the unionist and nationalist communities required of the UK government under the Good Friday Agreement. The financial award was not explicitly conditional upon the restoration of a devolved executive although it was designed to incentivise its return. The additional finance was justified on the basis that the government 'recognises the unique circumstances of Northern Ireland's history and the effect that this has had on its economy and people from all parts of the community' (HM Government, 2017a), as if the Conservatives had no previous knowledge of the region's difficulties. In 2015-2016, the £10,983 spend per head for Northern Ireland's citizens exceeded that per head in England by more than £2000 (Keep, 2016, p. 5), a differential now increased amid the bypassing of the Barnett Formula.

Confronted by the Conservative-DUP axis at Westminster, Sinn Féin faced a difficult decision whether to return to the Northern Ireland Executive as a counterweight, or at least to spend any money that the DUP managed to obtain from the Conservative Government. A return to direct rule from Westminster would collapse the delicate institutional machinery constructed in the Good Friday Agreement and maintained (with difficulty and episodic hiatuses) ever since. Sinn Féin dismissed any prospect of an end to its policy of abstention from Westminster. Although participation would make the parliamentary arithmetic even more difficult for the Conservatives, the swearing of an oath of allegiance to a British monarch would breach republican principles and divide a party within which a two-thirds majority would be needed for such a major change.

The DUP is likely to prove a solid and reliable voting bloc for the Conservatives on the issues where its support is pledged. Its members do not engage in dissent and rebellion against their party whip. The parliamentary risk comes from the Conservative backbenches not the DUP. The transfer of large sums of money to Northern Ireland is hardly unknown and the sum agreed is a fraction of the cost of the subvention during the Troubles. This notwithstanding, an obvious issue was whether the DUP's ten MPs would act as Oliver Twists, asking for more money at a later date.

The most important role played by the DUP may be in supporting an uncompromising Brexit. In favouring departure from the EU single market and customs union and opposing special status for Northern Ireland, yet wanting a soft border with the Republic of Ireland, DUP positions may be mutually exclusive; tariff and regulatory cross-border checks are the logical consequence. Meanwhile, the text of part of Strand Two of the Good Friday Agreement (the all-island dimension) was rendered redundant because of Brexit, being constructed upon assumptions of joint UK-Irish government EU membership.

In terms of Northern Ireland conflict issues, there was a hint, in the final paragraph ('Legacy') of the deal with the Conservatives, of one of the DUP's concerns. The paragraph insisted that conflict legacy bodies must not 'unfairly focus on former members of the armed forces or police' (HM Government, 2017*b*, p. 4). The DUP perception is that there is a disproportionately high focus upon British state actions during the Northern Ireland Troubles, but this claim is contested by Irish republicans who highlight the very low number of convictions of British forces. The DUP's 2015 Northern Ireland Plan demanded that serving and retired members of the Armed Forces be given protected status and called for a UK-wide definition of a victim which excludes perpetrators of violence.

There are other potential controversies, if the DUP veers from the 'cash to the sash' and attempts to address Loyalist cultural concerns evident amongst the Party's support base. Most notably, it remains DUP policy to replace the Parades Commission, the quasi-judicial body which regulates marches in Northern Ireland and has re-routed or restricted some Protestant Orange Order parades. Most DUP members oppose the Parades Commission and the DUP leader, Arlene Foster, views the Commission as dysfunctional. The DUP may also demand the removal of the allowances paid to Sinn Féin's abstentionist Westminster MPs.

For the DUP, operating in the hermetically sealed dual ethnic bloc voting system of Northern Ireland, there is only a modest electoral risk accruing to a relationship with the Conservatives. The arrangement is readily sellable to the DUP membership, who favour the Conservatives to Labour by seven-to-one (Tonge *et al.*, 2014)—a viewpoint unlikely to change under a Corbyn Labour leadership. It seems, for now at least, a very popular deal among DUP voters, 96% of whom endorsed the arrangement. In contrast, 90% of Sinn Féin voters opposed the DUP-Conservative link-up.

The DUP has come under much greater scrutiny since it attained its pivotal position. The focus upon policy differences between Northern Ireland and the rest of the UK has already led to change which the party, whilst not overly concerned given its focus upon its own region, would not greatly welcome. The first clear example was the adoption of the Labour backbencher Stella Creasy's demand that women travelling from Northern Ireland (where abortion is illegal except where the mother's life is at risk) to elsewhere in the UK to have a termination of pregnancy should have their costs met by the state.

The DUP's near insulation from electoral pressure, even if the alliance with the Conservatives does not yield more fruit, is accompanied by the option to walk away in the unlikely event the deal turns toxic among the unionist electorate. Given the DUP's slender one-seat Assembly lead over Sinn Féin, an unpopular alliance could be costly if there was to be yet another Assembly election. Whilst on current electoral evidence there is little prospect of the UUP stealing a swathe of DUP seats, it would only take minor DUP losses for Sinn Féin to become the largest party in the Northern Ireland Assembly, thus providing the First Minister—if there is an Executive and Assembly in place.

4. Conclusion

The 2017 General Election confirmed the dominance of the DUP and Sinn Féin in Northern Ireland and more broadly gave the DUP unprecedented influence in UK politics. As the unique supplier of additional parliamentary votes, the Party knew a very good financial deal could be extracted from the needy Conservatives. For the Conservatives, the DUP provides a necessary and helpful ally, one with the parliamentary voting discipline crucial given the government's minority status. The Conservatives happily restated loudly their unionist credentials to please their new allies. As the Prime Minister emphasised on the morning after the election, there is a clue in her organisation's title. She leads the Conservative *and Unionist* Party.

To maximise its advantage, the DUP kept its focus economic and did not demand anything exclusively for the unionist community. This partially allayed fears that the Good Friday Agreement's demand for 'rigorous impartiality' was breached by a Conservative-DUP alliance. However, that Agreement (never formally supported by the DUP anyway) was in trouble. The power-sharing institutions created under Strand One were struggling to be reconstituted and parts of Strand Two made little sense in the context of Brexit. Few voters and no parties wanted direct rule from Westminster and only a minority of Northern Ireland's citizens desired Brexit, but the former remained a possibility and latter a probability.

The DUP and Sinn Féin continued to contest the policies a devolved Northern Ireland Executive and Assembly ought to pursue and the Westminster election highlighted the polarity of their views on Brexit, an Irish Language Act, same-sex marriage, how to deal with the past (which appears impossible given the difficulty in handling the present) and of course Northern Ireland's long-term constitutional future. As an exercise in confirming DUP and Sinn Féin communal hegemony, the election served its purpose. It also placed the DUP in a pivotal position at Westminster regardless of what happened next in Belfast. For Sinn Féin, abstention from Westminster remained part of its lingering fundamentalism. The question begged by the election fallout was whether an Irish republican party would return to government in Belfast to help spend the extra money obtained by a unionist party from a Conservative government at Westminster.

References

Belfast Telegraph (2017a, 21 April) 'DUP Faces Split if Party Agrees to Gay Marriage Demand by Sinn Féin', accessed at http://www.belfasttelegraph.co.uk/news/general-election-2017/dup-faces-split-threat-if-party-agrees-to-gay-marriage-demand-by-sinn-fein-35640160.html on 1 July 2017.

Belfast Telegraph (2017b, 8 June) 'Suspected Abuse of Proxy System Could Lead to Results Being Challenged in Court', accessed at http://www.belfasttelegraph.co.uk/news/general-election-2017/suspected-abuse-of-proxy-system-couldlead-to-results-being-challenged-in-court-35801287.html on 5 July 2017.

Belfast Telegraph (2017c, 17 June) 'Voter Fraud Endemic since the Foundation Of Northern Ireland: Study', accessed at http://www.belfasttelegraph.co.uk/news/northern-ireland/voter-fraud-endemic-since-the-foundation-of-northern-ireland-study-35835051.html on 7 July 2017.

Belfast Telegraph (2017d, 24 June) Voting by Proxy in Foyle up to 17 Times UK Level, accessed at http://www.belfasttelegraph.co.uk/news/northern-ireland/voting-by-proxy-in-foyle-up-to-17-times-uk-level-35860053.html on 19 July 2017.

Bischof, D. (2017) 'New Graphic Schemes for Stata: Plotplain and Plottig', *Stata Journal*, **17**, 748–759.

Daily Mirror (2010, 10 June) 'Coalition of Crackpots', p. 1.

Democratic Unionist Party (2015) *The Northern Ireland Plan*, Belfast, DUP, accessed at http://www.mydup.com/publications/view/the-northern-ireland-plan on 19 July 2017.

Democratic Unionist Party (2017) *Standing Strong for Northern Ireland*, Westminster Election manifesto, Belfast, Democratic Unionist Party.

Devenport, M. (2017) 'General Election 2017: Proxy and Postal Votes Up', accessed at http://www.bbc.co.uk/news/uk-northern-ireland-40165035 on 20 August 2017.

Garry, J. (2017) 'The EU Referendum Vote in Northern Ireland: Implications for Our Understanding of Citizens' Views and Behaviour', Northern Ireland Assembly Knowledge Exchange Seminar Series, accessed at http://www.niassembly.gov.uk/globalassets/documents/raise/knowledge_exchange/briefing_papers/series6/garry121016.pdf, p. 2, on 3 August 2017.

Garry, J. and Coakley, J. (2016) 'Brexit: Understanding why people voted as they did in the choice of a lifetime' *News Letter*, 15 October 2016, accessed at http://www.newsletter.co.uk/news/brexit-understanding-why-people-voted-as-they-did-in-the-choice-of-a-lifetime-1-7630272 on 12 September 2017.

Keep, M. (2016, November) 'Public Expenditure by Country and Region', House of Commons Library Briefing Paper, 04033.

HM Government (2017*a*) 'Confidence and Supply Agreement Between the Conservative and Unionist Party and the Democratic Unionist Party', accessed at https://www.gov.uk/government/publications/conservative-and-dup-agreement-and-uk-government-financial-support-for-northern-ireland on 26 June 2017.

HM Government (2017*b*) 'UK Government Financial Support for Northern Ireland', accessed at https://www.gov.uk/government/publications/conservative-and-dup-agree ment-and-uk-government-financial-support-for-northern-ireland/uk-government-financial-support-for-northern-ireland on 26 June 2017.

Mitchell, P., Evans, G. and O'Leary, B. (2009) 'Extremist Outbidding in Ethnic Party Systems is Not Inevitable: Tribune Parties in Northern Ireland', *Political Studies*, **57**, 397–421.

Sinn Féin (2017) *Westminster Election Manifesto 2017*, Belfast, Sinn Féin.

Tonge, J., Braniff, M., Hennessey, T., McAuley, J. and Whiting, S. (2014) *The Democratic Unionist Party: From Protest to Power*, Oxford, Oxford University Press.

SARA HAGEMANN*

The Brexit Context

After the vote for Brexit in the United Kingdom referendum in 2016 and the victory of Donald Trump in the United States, the European Union (EU) faced a make-it-or-break-it moment as it embarked on a year of national elections in key member states: the electorate in the Netherlands voted in March 2017; France went to the ballot box for the presidential and legislative elections in April/May and June; the British also cast their vote in June; Germany held elections in September and the Czech Republic their legislative election in October (Figure 10.1). In each of these elections, the EU was a crucial issue for the candidates and parties. Indeed, in today's Europe, governments and opposition parties are—at least partly—judged by their electorates based on their stance on EU membership and policies. There is some variation in how this is played out across countries (Hobolt, 2016), but after this year's round of elections there is no doubt that national governments' attitudes towards the European Union play an important role at election time.

The EU will not only survive the 2017 round of elections but is now set on a course of further integration between its member states. Such steps will not come without its challenges, as stark divisions between the governments lurk beneath the surface. Nevertheless, in the aftermath of the UK's 2017 general election, the governments of the EU27 (as the remaining member states are popularly referred to) appeared more aligned than for years. Hence, it is within this context, and contrary to Mrs May's plan, that the UK election outcome has left the government between a rock and a hard place: managing difficult domestic challenges—including a hung parliament—while negotiating an all-defining deal with a united and strong European Union.

1. Setting the scene: Europe's reactions to Brexit

In Spring 2016, prior to the Brexit referendum, many analysts warned of a possible contagion effect if the UK was to leave the EU (LSE Commission on Future of Britain in Europe, 2016). Indeed, in several countries, opposition parties and

*Sara Hagemann, European Institute, London School of Economics and Political Science, s.hagemann@lse.ac.uk

doi:10.1093/pa/gsx054

Figure 10.1. National and local elections in the European Union 2017[1]

candidates started to use a similar rhetoric to the British and suggested that their country should follow the UK's lead and allow a referendum on aspects of EU membership or even membership itself. Partly related to the continued rise of populist and nationalist forces (see Figure 10.2), especially in Northern Europe, the European project had become a key target in domestic politics, and the UK referendum campaign served further fuel to these voices.

---

[1]The German presidential election took place on 12 February; the Northern Ireland Assembly election on 2 March; the Hungarian presidential election on 13 March; the Dutch general election on 15 March; the Bulgarian parliamentary election on 26 March; the Finnish municipal elections on 19 April; the French presidential election on 23 April and 7 May; the United Kingdom local elections on 4 May; Croatia local elections on 24 May; the Maltese general election on 3 June; the Latvia municipal elections on 4 June; the United Kingdom general election on 8 June; the Italian mayoral elections on 11-25 June; the French legislative election, on 11 and 18 June; the German federal election on 24 September; the Catalan independence referendum on 1 October; the Portuguese local election on 1 October; the Austrian legislative election on 15 October; the Estonian municipal elections on 15 October; the Czech legislative election on 20-21 October; the Slovenian presidential election on 22 October; the Slovakia municipal elections on 4 November; and Danish local elections on 21 November.

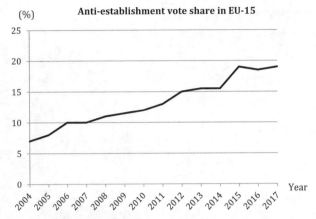

Figure 10.2. Increase in vote share for nationalist and populist parties in EU15, 2004-17
Source: European Policy Information Centre, Authoritarian Populism Index 2017

As the result of the UK referendum became clear in the early hours of 24 June 2016, most governments in Europe reacted with messages that they 'regretted, but respected' the decision by the UK voters.[2] All tried to keep a brave face, but it was clear from the first reactions that many political leaders worried where this would leave the remaining EU members and implicitly also feared for their own domestic situations.[3] If the UK were successful in leaving the EU, and domestic pressures from opposition parties would continue, how could Mrs Merkel, Mr Hollande, Mr Rutte and others fend off demands for their electorates to have a choice as well? It is for this reason that the remaining 27 national governments have a vested interest in how the Brexit negotiation process is handled and in the kind of agreement the UK will be able to get once it has left the Union: their survival depends on it in their own domestic arenas.

At the EU level the immediate reactions to the Brexit result also gave cause for concern as a split started to emerge: an emergency meeting was held between the EU's founding members, without inviting the rest of the governments. In reaction, the Visegrad group facilitated another meeting for other states to discuss their coordinated response to the referendum result. But also here some countries were not invited and the whole situation

---

[2]'We regret this decision but respect it', said European Council President Tusk, European Commission President Juncker, European Parliament President Schulz and Dutch Prime Minister Rutte, as holder of the rotating presidency for the Council of the European Union, in a joint statement the day after the referendum.

[3]For example a visibly shaken Angela Merkel appeared before journalists on 24 June and said she would keep German citizens and German interests in mind during any talks (*Deutsche Welle* (2016, 24 June) 'Merkel calls Brexit a Watershed for Europe').

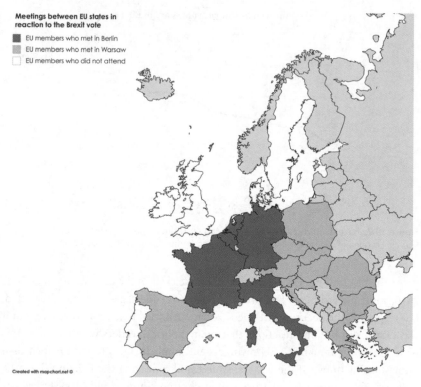

Meetings between EU states in reaction to the Brexit vote

- ■ EU members who met in Berlin
- ▨ EU members who met in Warsaw
- ☐ EU members who did not attend

Created with mapchart.net ©

Figure 10.3. Meetings between heads of governments in Europe immediately following the UK Brexit vote (one month)

suggested the sort of political fragmentation in Europe, which the EU's very existence is intended to overcome. Figure 10.3 above shows the split in terms of meetings in the month after the UK Brexit referendum.

However, before any dividing lines were formed between the EU governments, an effort was made from all sides—in particular the EU institutions—to find common ground. A plan was quickly put in place to arrange for a designated Brexit negotiator in the EU Commission, Michel Barnier, to represent the coordinated position of the EU27, and for European Council President Donald Tusk to lead negotiations at the level of Heads of States and Governments. But more than anything else, in retrospect it is evident that what has united the remaining member states is in fact the UK government's own handling of the Brexit result. The uncertain signals from the British government made it clear from an early stage that it was in the best interest for the EU27 to have a coordinated response.

2.　The EU agenda: Unity above all

As Mrs May became Prime Minister following Mr Cameron's defeat, it was expected that one of the first tasks of the new government would be to lay out a plan for the ensuing Brexit negotiations. Mrs May's decision not to do so at an early stage—even avoiding the confirmation of how and when to trigger Article 50—was first met with a forgiving attitude from the other leaders.[4] However, the tone quickly started to change as Mrs May's government failed to reassure their European partners on the issues that Brussels had immediately sought to get confirmation on: that the UK would guarantee the rights of EU citizens residing in the UK, and that it would honour its existing commitments during the Brexit process. As a consequence, the EU27 governments soon became guarded when it came to discussions about Brexit, and showed remarkable unity as they all stuck to the same reference to the European Council's agreement for the conduct of the negotiations: that talks could only begin with the UK once the British government has provided formal notification of its intention of withdrawing (i.e. 'triggering Article 50').

The unity between the EU leaders became even stronger as events unfolded and the rhetoric by UK government representatives began to indicate a rather uncompromising starting position for the negotiations. In particular, the speeches by Theresa May herself and Home Secretary Amber Rudd at the 2016 Conservative Party conference shocked their European counterparts as they openly threatened the rights of EU citizens in the UK.

It was in this political environment, combined with the new reality of Donald Trump as president in the US, that Europe's leaders began their year of elections in key EU member states. In the first few months of 2017 many worried that the populist wave was now to manifest itself in continental Europe too. The defeat of extreme-right candidate Norbert Hofer in Austria in December 2016 led to an audible sigh of relief on the continent, but as the margins of the victory by Alexander Van der Bellen were extremely narrow, the feeling was nevertheless that nationalism is very much alive and present in today's Europe. However, as political debates developed, as announcements from the new US administration started to worry and appal the Europeans, and as the UK government continued to mismanage its engagements with Brussels, so did the arguments in favour of European cooperation gain in frequency and weight on the continent. A first manifestation became apparent in the Dutch elections—as the first election in 2017—where Mr Rutte's government sidelined Geert Wilders' Party for Freedom, and suggested that the Dutch have finished their 'fling with populism'.

---

[4] For example as reported by CNN: 'Theresa May meets Angela Merkel, says UK seeks "sensible, orderly" Brexit', 20 July, 2016.

But it was in particular the victory of French president Emmanuel Macron which marked a new direction for the EU. His decision to appear in front of the Louvre to the tones of the European anthem after having convincingly beaten Front Nationale's Marine Le Pen was a strong message not only to the French voters but also to France's European partners. The subsequent impressive success of his party 'En Marche!' in the legislative elections gave further merit to his message that the French government is committed and back as a driving force in the EU. Combined with the election of Mrs Merkel for a fourth term in Germany's September elections (albeit tainted and constrained by the strong increase in support for the extreme right AfD party), there is now a sense that Europe will bounce back.

3.   Public opinion in Europe

These results on the continent combined with the disappointing outcome for Mrs May's government in the UK's June election have led many centre-ground pro-Europeans to claim victory over populism in Europe. But as became clear in the German elections, such statements should be met by caution. The electorate remain deeply divided in many countries and large groups of voters express profound dissatisfaction with mainstream politics in Europe, which they feel have left them behind (Hobolt, 2016). Of course, the victory of Macron over Le Pen's right-wing nationalist party in France was of major importance to Europe, as were the defeats of Wilders in the Netherlands and Hofer in Austria. But the 2017 German election results were, in Europe's historical context, rather alarming and a strong manifestation of the populist turn in Europe. It remains a fact that during the past two decades, and especially since the effects of the eurozone crisis have kicked in, populism has been on the increase, gained legislative seats, reached ministerial offices, and shifted the balance of power in many national parliaments. Mainstream parties are not left unaffected by this pressure either, and several have absorbed messages over time which would once have been considered extreme (Norris, 2017).

Keeping these facts in mind, the repeated lauding by pro-Europeans of opinion polls published in the Eurobarometer Spring 2017 survey seemed exaggerated.[5] It is true that there is a notable increase in public support for EU membership in many countries, particularly France, Germany, The Netherlands, Italy, Sweden, Denmark and Austria (Eurobarometer, 2017: 18). Similarly, Figure 10.4 below shows from the same survey the percentage of Europeans who now 'have a total positive image of the EU', 'total negative image', 'neutral' or 'don't know'. The main finding which is stressed in Eurobarometer's report is

---

[5]E.g. Politico (2017, 2 August) 'Europeans are more positive about future of the EU—except the Brits'.

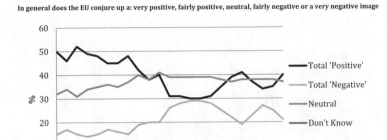

Figure 10.4. Perceptions of the EU's Image across EU Member State Populations
Source: Eurobarometer Spring 2017

that the percentage who find the EU to have total positive image is increasing (40%), while the proportion of voters who feel it has 'a totally negative image' is declining for a second consecutive term. However, in the midst of a prolonged economic and political crisis for the EU, not to mention a very uncertain world political order, it is remarkable that the figures do not, in fact, reflect even greater support for the European project. In particular, the stability of that percentage of the electorate which considers the EU to have a 'neutral' image (37%) stands out during this time. Furthermore, if we consider these attitudes towards the EU in light of the populism figures above, one interpretation may be that, instead of genuine approval of the EU, the increase in support for the EU rather masks a calculated conclusion that—in the political reality of 2017—there is simply no viable alternative (De Vries, 2018). This would mean that voters are not choosing the EU *per se*, but are simply rejecting the alternative of not being members of the Union. If this is the case, then it is clear that pressure has only been temporarily stalled for European leaders when it comes to fending off populism, let alone euroscepticism; the concerns of ordinary voters—who are often opposed to the EU because of concerns about intra-EU immigration, austerity or opaque EU institutions—remain unchanged (De Vries, 2018). Moreover, as Eurosceptic parties across the EU mobilise these concerns effectively, it would only take an unforeseen event or an unpopular move by a government to give these voices a purpose again.

Recent research by Catherine De Vries (2017; 2018) provides further insights and empirical detail regarding this topic. She pointedly shows how euroscepticism takes different forms across member states, and that support for leaving the Union depends on voters' own domestic reality and, measured against this

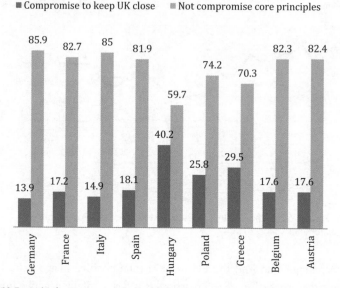

■ Compromise to keep UK close　■ Not compromise core principles

Figure 10.5. Attitudes to compromise in the Brexit negotiations in ten EU member states
Source: Chatham House, March 2017

benchmark, their subjective evaluations regarding costs and benefits of EU membership for their country and their own individual circumstances. The main characteristics are, briefly explained, that voter choices are based on country characteristics (e.g. geography, quality of government) and individual-level factors such as education and income. In today's politics, the dividing lines can be found particularly between high-income earners and people with longer education, who are, generally, more supportive of EU membership than low-skilled/low-income voters. Still, as De Vries convincingly explains, these levels of euroscepticism do not necessarily translate into majorities in favour of leaving the EU: only a small minority of voters want to see their country exit from the system. Therefore, euroscepticism must be considered in its different forms, which spans from critical attitudes towards specific aspects of the EU project to much more radical euroscepticism linked to hard nationalist opinions. Keeping in mind this variation in euroscepticism, Figure 10.5 above shows a striking finding from a recent Chatham House analysis survey in ten EU member states: that voters in key member states do not want to compromise on the EU's core principles in order to keep the UK close post-Brexit. It therefore seems that while the public in EU27 continues to have high levels of scepticism regarding the EU and its institutions, they nevertheless become protective of their EU membership and its core principles when confronted with Brexit.

4.　EU27: Divisions beneath the surface

Despite the recent upturn in support for the EU on the continent as reported by Eurobarometer, the underlying divisions in public opinion pose fundamental problems for the governments. But also between the governments are deep-seeded differences visible beneath the surface. There is no consensus at present regarding how to tackle the EU's most eminent challenges—apart from a common approach to Brexit!

Previous crises in Europe have in several instances been followed by phases of renewed cooperation and integration (Dinan, 2014). This time, however, it took almost a decade and the shake-up referendum in the UK and—more importantly—the election of President Trump in the USA, to get European leaders to become serious about the next steps in the history of European integration. But on each of the most immediate challenges there are deep-running divisions between the member states, and it is difficult to imagine at this point in time how they will all be overcome.

First, the economic and institutional questions around the eurozone continue to threaten the stability of the project and remain the most important for the future of the EU. At the centre of this is the conflict between French and German approaches to the economy and to the single currency. Merkel has indicated a willingness to take further steps to turn the eurozone into a 'fiscal union', as argued for by Macron, in particular with regards to the creation of a new post of eurozone finance minister. But their views on such initiatives vary greatly: to the French this would mean risk sharing in the eurozone; to Germans it means the creation of mechanisms to enforce eurozone fiscal rules. Against the backdrop of the German election outcome, which has left Merkel more constrained than many anticipated, the arrangement is likely to be 'pragmatic'. Second, the migrant/refugee crisis may no longer attract the same headlines as in 2015, but it nevertheless remains highly political and increasingly pervasive in its effects. There has been scant support for the countries most affected by the stream of desperate people fleeing to Europe and thousands still die in the Mediterranean. Whatever steps are taken next will be crucial for the handling of Europe's largest humanitarian and social challenge for years to come. Third, Russian challenges to security are the most difficult they have been at any point in the post-Cold War era. Combined with the uncertainty about the US security guarantee that Trump has created, this makes Europeans suddenly much more vulnerable and it is difficult to see how Europeans can respond to this new situation.

These are just the three foremost challenges the EU are faced with, running in parallel to a whole battery of more 'usual' policy dilemmas. Nevertheless, listing these issues makes it evident that the Brexit negotiations are merely one amongst several for the EU governments, much further down the list than more pressing matters. In fact, different to the other challenges—which are all of existential concern to EU leaders—the Brexit question is one which can be contained and managed in a way that the others cannot (Usherwood, 2017). Of course, negotiations with the UK will prove difficult and require extensive efforts also on the EU side, but these are by no means close to the problems that the EU could be facing if either the eurozone problems, tensions with Russia or the refuge/immigration situation escalate. In the grand scheme of things, Brexit will remain low down the list, and EU member countries will find an intrinsic value in showing that they can stay united and strong throughout the exit process.

This is also the reason that the immediate effect of the UK general election has mainly been domestic, as nothing has changed in the EU's Brexit negotiating position, which was clear before the election. Theresa May would have been met with the same messages if she had secured a landslide victory. Nevertheless, there is no doubt that the environment has changed following the UK results: the continued uncertainty surrounding Mrs May's approach to Brexit combined with the pro-European election outcomes on the continent and the challenging agenda points ahead, mean that the UK will find it hard to secure concessions as negotiations progress. Indeed, the weakened UK government is confronted with a strong and well-prepared EU, set on a course for further collaborations on the continent while the UK disembark. This was evident when Mr Barnier found it politically strategic publicly to stress the EU27's position and firm commitment to its core principles, following the UK general election:

> [S]ome in the UK say you can leave the Customs Union and build
> frictionless trade. That is not possible. Some in the UK say you can leave
> the Single Market and keep all the benefits. That is not possible. All third
> countries must accept our autonomy to set standards. I am not sure this is
> fully understood in the UK. (Barnier, 2017)

This means that from the EU's side there are only two viable options for a Brexit deal. One is high-access, low control arrangement which could be a European Economic Area (EEA) model. The other is a low-access, high-control arrangement which—in its most favourable form—could resemble the EU-Canada agreement (CETA). Of course, whether the EU institutions will be willing or able to maintain this position through to the end of Article 50 remains to be seen; however, given developments to date, it looks much more likely that it will be the UK that has to come to terms with the EU's demands, rather than the other way round.

5.   The EU institutions without the UK

The UK's departure from the European Union will substantially change the internal dynamics of the EU institutions. Those countries who saw the UK as a counter-weight to Germany or France, or who used it to promote liberalising, progressive agendas will now find that they have lost an important partner. This means that states have to think about how to adapt their EU strategies: there is likely to be a realignment of alliances and coalitions, not least with regards to those who are members of the eurozone and those who are not.

In this last section, I briefly discuss how the power balance will shift once the UK representatives have left. Based on the decision records and the composition in the EU's two legislative bodies, the Council of the European Union (the Council) and the European Parliament, it is possible to get an indication of how this will play out, and identify which policy areas may see majorities shift with the absence of the UK representatives.

In the Council, where government ministers meet to negotiate and adopt legislation, Britain has had a number of close allies when negotiating policies and seeking political agreements. We see this in the figures below, which reflect the recorded decisions in the Council and how each member state has voted since the enlargement to Central and Eastern Europe in 2004. First, Figure 10.6 shows the aggregate figures regarding recorded opposition in the Council. Here, it should be noted that the vast majority of legislation is adopted with all countries in favour of the legislation, and that only a small proportion of legislation each year has one or more countries expressing their opposition (Bailer *et al.*, 2015). Still, opposition in Council voting has increased in recent years and becomes particularly notable if one considers not only the formal votes but also the policy statements that member countries can submit following a vote: at times, governments may choose not to vote against a majority when legislation is set to be adopted in any case. Instead they may choose to express their concerns or disapproval of a policy in the Council records as a policy statement (see Hagemann *et al.*, 2017 for more on this). Therefore, it is relevant to look at the level of recorded opposition by each government both in terms of votes and in the statements. Thus, looking at these in Figure 10.6, it becomes clear that the UK has been an outlier in terms of opposing the majority significantly more than any other government.

Apart from voting 'No' more frequently than any other government, it is only the UK which has used the votes more often instead of the policy statements to express their opposition. Other countries, notably France, are much less likely to oppose when voting, but may instead state their concerns in the statements. In research published elsewhere (Hagemann *et al.*, 2017; VoteWatch Europe, 2016) I look more closely into this and also break the figures down into policy areas: since 2004 the data show that British opposition to EU policies occurred especially on

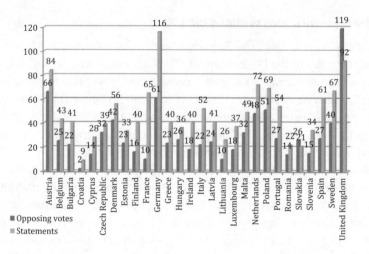

Figure 10.6. Opposing votes and policy statements in the EU Council, 2004-2016
Source: Author's data[6]

budget, foreign policy and foreign aid. Conversely, the UK was not the most oppositional government in several important areas such as the internal market, legal affairs, transport, environment, and fisheries.

Two main conclusions are embedded in these findings: (i) When the UK disagrees with a policy proposal it does not shy away from going on public record to state its opposition; (ii) Over the years, UK representatives have been highly successful in negotiating outcomes favourable to the British position in policy areas of great saliency to them. Indeed, the UK representatives have played a very important role in shaping policy priorities but also had a great influence on *how* legislation is formally agreed. In fact, decision-making in the Council has changed quite markedly during the past ten years. In particular, the 2004 enlargement to Central and Eastern Europe, the introduction of the Lisbon Treaty and changes to the internal rules of procedures in 2009 have led to significant changes. These include, amongst other issues: (i) an increase in the percentage of legislation co-decided with the European Parliament under the Ordinary Legislative Procedure (OLS); (ii) an increase in the formal recording of governments' agreements in the Council; and (iii)) steps towards making the Council's legislative records available to the public. While the UK has not been an avid supporter of the decision to extend legislative powers of the European Parliament, it has been vocal on the

---

[6]As both 'No' votes and 'Abstentions' work against the majority to support a proposal, both of those expressions are considered as 'opposition' in the figures. This is the agreed consensus in the literature as well (Mattila, 2009).

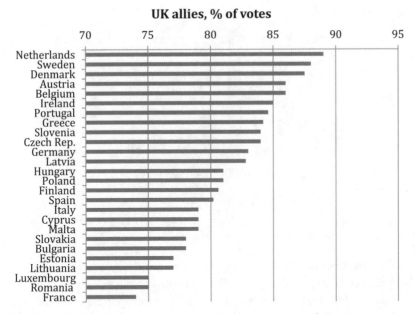

UK allies, % of votes

Figure 10.7. UK's allies in the EU Council, 2004-2016 as a percentage of all votes

need for more formal and transparent decision records (Hagemann, 2014). There is a legitimate concern that with the UK gone, and an emphasis on eurozone priorities, Council politics will revert to greater use of corridor bargaining and non-transparent negotiation outcomes. The effect will be especially hard felt by the UK's closest allies, the Scandinavian countries, Ireland and the Netherlands (see Figure 10.7). These small- and medium-sized countries will lose an important partner in negotiations, and make it more difficult to influence, for example, a majority coalition dominated by German/French priorities.

Turning to the European Parliament, as the EU's other legislative chamber, further details become clear regarding the implications of the UK's departure. Recent research by VoteWatch Europe (2016), a transparency organisation based in Brussels, shows that the UK has been in a weak position in this branch of the EU's legislative system in recent years. Most British MEPs do not sit in the groups that dominate the European Parliament agenda. And even when they do sit in these groups—such as the Conservatives in the European People's Party (EPP) before 2009, and Labour in the Progressive Alliance of Socialists and Democrats (S&D)—British MEPs are more often than their colleagues opposed to the majority positions of these groups. As a result, British MEPs often find themselves on the losing side in key votes. The figure below shows the distribution of UK MEPs across the political party groups in the European Parliament.

Nevertheless, VoteWatch Europe's research—to which I have contributed— also presents the results from running a simulation of what some of the key

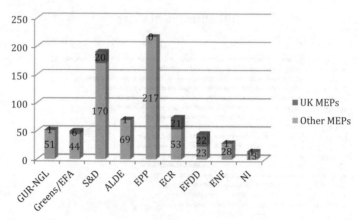

Figure 10.8. British MEPs in the European Parliament's political groups, 2017
Source: European Parliament (www.europarl.europa.eu)

decisions made in the EU institutions in recent years would have looked like if the British politicians had not been there to vote (keeping all else equal). These findings conclude that the UK has played an extremely important role in getting legislation passed: first, British politicians are substantially more favourable to reducing regulation than their continental counterparts. If they no longer take part in the decisions regarding the internal market, the pressure on the EU decision-making apparatus to simplify legislation and reduce regulatory policies will be much weaker. On the contrary, the forces that believe reducing regulation negatively impacts on labour and environmental standards will become stronger and will find it easier to influence the decisions their way. There will also be implications during budget negotiations, where British MEPs have—like their ministers in the Council and in contrast to most other MEPs—continuously argued in favour of a reduced EU budget. Also in the important areas (especially for the UK) of tax harmonisation and higher taxes on financial transactions, UK votes have made a difference in the past, and their absence is likely to be felt in the future. Furthermore, British MEPs have in recent years made a difference in the votes on nuclear energy and alternative energy sources. Here, there will be strong divides between the governments in the EU Council, and the absence of the UK members of the European Parliament may prove crucial for future decisions in these areas.

In sum, these findings make it clear that an EU Council of 27 members and a European Parliament lacking British MEPs will mean a substantial shift in the balance of power in favour of the pro-social/interventionist political forces. On the other hand, the forces that support the free market, less regulation and a more competitive Europe will suffer a substantial blow, as most of the British politicians have been much more favourable to free market-policies than their European counterparts. Of course, an important caveat to the conclusions drawn here is that past data do not take into account our discussion above of how the current political environment in the EU institutions is rapidly changing at the government level, partly due to the political context of Brexit, Trump as US president and the change in government in key member states. Nevertheless, there is no doubt that EU policy-making is taking a new direction—both at the level of Heads of States and Governments as well as in the EU's legislative institutions.

6. Conclusion

The UK's 2017 general election was meant to erase any lingering questions over whether the UK will indeed leave the EU following the referendum in 2016. Prime Minister Theresa May called the election with the intention of securing 'a strong and stable' government mandate in the ensuing Brexit negotiations. In the end the outcome was the opposite: the Conservative government lost their majority, and Brexit continued to be a contentious and divisive issue for the party and for the country.

This chapter has argued that the immediate effect of the UK election has been mainly domestic, as nothing has changed in the EU's Brexit negotiation position. Its negotiating plan was clear already before the election and Theresa May would have been met with the same messages if she had secured a landslide victory. However, there is no doubt that the environment has changed following the UK results: the continued uncertainty surrounding the UK government's approach to Brexit combined with the overwhelming pro-European election outcomes on the continent mean that the UK may find it hard to secure concessions as negotiations progress. The weakened UK government is confronted with a strong and well-prepared EU, set on a course for further integration in key policy areas while the UK disembark.

But the jury is still out when it comes to the ramifications of the UK's decision to leave the EU in the longer run. Some have argued it will keep the project together as voters will see the economic, political and social costs that Brexit imposes on the UK. Others believe that Brexit is the beginning of a process of further political fragmentation in Europe. It is too early to determine which of the two convictions will turn out to be the right one, but it is clear that the UK's negotiation process will take place in a context of great political uncertainty for the remaining member states. The EU27 hence have an incentive to stay firmly united; their survival may depend on it both in the domestic political arenas and on the world stage.

References

Bailer, S., Mattila, M. and Schneider, G. (2015) 'Money Makes the EU Go Round. The Objective Foundations of Conflict in the Council of Ministers', *Journal of Common Market Studies*, **23**, 437–456.

Barnier, M. (2017) Speech to European Economic and Social Committee, 6 July, accessed at http://europa.eu/rapid/press-release_SPEECH-17-1922_en.htm on 13 July 2017.

Dinan, D. (2014) *Europe Recast: A History of European Union*, 2nd edn, Boulder, CO, Lynne Rienner.

De Vries, C. E. (2018) *Euroscepticism and the Future of European Integration*, Oxford, Oxford University Press.

De Vries, C. E. and Hoffmann, I. (2016) 'Fears Not Values: Public Opinion and the Populist Vote in Europe', report for the Bertelsmann Foundation, March 2016, accessed at https://www.bertelsmannstiftung.de/fileadmin/files/user_upload/EZ_eupinions_Fear_Study_ 2016_ENG.pdf on 13 July 2017.

Hagemann, S. (2014) 'A Public Vote on Jean-Claude Juncker in the European Council Could be a Significant Step for Transparency in EU Politics', *LSE European Politics and Policy (EUROPP) Blog (26 Jun 2014)*, accessed at http://eprints.lse.ac.uk/71901/ on 13 July 2017.

Hagemann, S., Bailer, S. and Herzog, A. (2017) 'Signals to Their Parliaments: Governments' Strategic use of Votes and Policy Statements in the Council of the European Union', working paper under review.

Hagemann, S., Hobolt, S.B. and Wratil, C. (2017) 'Government Responsiveness in the European Union: Evidence from Council Voting', *Comparative Political Studies*, **50**, 850–876.

Hobolt, S. B. (2016) 'The Brexit Vote: A Divided Nation, A Divided Continent', *Journal of European Public Policy*, **23**, 1259–1277.

Hobolt, S. B. and de Vries, C. E. (2016) 'Public Support for European Integration', *Annual Review of Political Science*, **19**, 413–432.

LSE Commission on Future of Britain in Europe (2016) 'Overview and Summaries of Reports', accessed at http://www.lse.ac.uk/europeanInstitute/LSE-Commission/LSE-Commission-on-the-Future-of-Britain-in-Europe.aspx on 13 July 2017.

Mattila, M. (2009) 'Roll Call Analysis of Voting in the EU Council of Ministers after the 2004 Enlargement', *European Journal of Political Research*, **48**, 840–857.

Norris, P. (2017). 'Is Western Democracy Backsliding? Diagnosing the Risks', *Harvard Kennedy School Faculty Research Working Paper Series*, 1–26.

Usherwood, S. (2017). '*A Tentative Model of the EU27's approach to Brexit*', blog post 3 August, *Politics@Surrey*, Department of Politics at University of Surrey, accessed at https://blogs.surrey.ac.uk/politics/ on 13 July 2017.

Poole, K. T. and Rosenthal, H. (2011). *Ideology and Congress*, Brunswick and London, Transaction Publishers.

VoteWatch Europe (2016) 'Would Brexit Matter? The UK's Voting Record in the Council and European Parliament', Special Report, April.

JUSTIN FISHER*

Party Finance

With an election having taken place only two years beforehand, there may have been an expectation that little would change in terms of party finance. Yet the period between the 2015 and the 2017 elections demonstrated a surprising amount of change. There were new laws and policies related to party finance and much uncertainty about the legitimacy of some election spending. Moreover, as other chapters also show, the two main opposition parties were fundamentally changed—not only in terms of leading personnel—but also in respect of financial prowess, largely due to an influx of new members and supporters. But despite change, there was also continuity. The national campaign continued to be subsumed into playing a supporting role for the battles in the constituencies, and the growth of digital campaigning continued, though it was still far from the dominant mode of campaigning, especially in terms of expenditure. And, by polling day, 'normal service' was resumed in terms of party income and expenditure, with the Conservatives able to raise significant sums once the election was called. But all of this should also be contextualised by the sudden calling of the election. As this chapter shows, its unexpected nature impacted significantly on parties' spending decisions and their ability to use their money effectively.

1. Developments in party finance rules

While both the 2005 and 2010 Parliaments saw extensive reviews of party finance regulations (Fisher, 2010, 2015), there was no such review during this short Parliament. There were still important developments, however, which had wider implications for funding more generally. Two of these were a result of government policy. The third may result in criminal prosecution. The first was initiated soon after the 2015 election. In July 2015, a Trade Union Bill was presented, which included a clause requiring trade unions with a political fund to operate a 'contracting-in' system rather than a 'contracting-out' one. This went to the heart of the Labour Party's relationship with the trade unions, which—following the *Trade Union Act* 1913—established that for trade unions to engage in political activity, they must create a separate political fund. This covered all political activity—not

*Justin Fisher, Department of Social & Political Sciences, Brunel University London, Justin.fisher@brunel.ac.uk

just that with the Labour Party—and trade union members were actively required to 'contract-out' if they wanted to avoid paying the modest additional fee. The 1913 Act laid the ground rules for an important aspect of Labour funding for much of the next 100 years. Political activity through the Labour Party would be expressed collectively through a union's decision to affiliate to the party.

This had faced challenges in the past. The *Trade Disputes and Trade Unions Act* 1927 determined that trade union members must 'contract-in'—that is, make the decision to pay into the fund rather than opt out. Around a quarter fewer trade unionists opted in to the political levy, though the impact on Labour's finances was mitigated in part by unions raising the affiliation fee for those who continued to pay into the political fund. 'Contracting-out' was restored soon after the Second World War and had remained in place until now. Ed Miliband's changes to Labour Party rules, introduced in the wake of the Falkirk candidate selection controversy (Fisher, 2015) were slightly different. Miliband's reforms initially floated the idea of 'contracting-in' to the political find by union members, together with a positive decision by those paying the levy for a proportion to be paid to the Labour Party (Fisher, 2015). 'Contracting-in' to the levy was ultimately dropped by Labour but the radical step of levy payers opting to contribute to Labour remained.

While this aspect the bill originally passed through the Commons relatively unscathed, it experienced trouble in the House of Lords on its second reading in January 2016. As a result, the Lords established the Select Committee on Trade Union Political Funds and Political Party Funding to examine the relevant clauses. Its report concluded that the re-introduction of 'contracting-in' could have a 'sizeable negative effect' on the number of union members participating in political funds and therefore on the income of the Labour Party. The Lords subsequently voted in favour of a motion to restrict changes to 'contracting-in' to new union members. This change (restricting 'contracting-in' to new members) was accepted by the Government and the Act received Royal Assent in May 2016.

The second reform related to Short Money. Introduced in 1975 and named after the then leader of the House, Edward Short, this is a form of ring-fenced public funding of opposition parties to assist their work in parliament. In the 2015 Autumn Statement, the Chancellor initially proposed reducing Short Money allocations by 19% and freezing them for the remainder of the parliament, the reasoning being that parties must face cuts just as government services have done. However, following discussions with affected parties, a much lower reduction of around 5% in real terms was agreed. These cuts affected the finances of all opposition parties in the Commons as they also applied to the Representative Money Scheme, which applies to parties who do not take up their seats in the House of Commons. No mention, however, was made of Cranborne money—analogous to Short Money, but used to support the work of opposition parties in the House of Lords rather than the Commons.

What unites both these measures are two things. First, the impact on parties is asymmetric. While the measures on 'contracting-in' were not directly related to party funds—they are principally about participation in trade union political funds—it is only Labour's finances that will be affected, though that effect will not be immediate. Similarly, changes to Short Money only affect opposition parties. Secondly, both arguably represented solutions to problems that were not high on the political agenda. Unlike some aspects of the *Trade Union Act*, such as requirements in respect of taking strike action, the issue of 'contracting-out' had not shown itself to be a particular problem. A considerable number of trade union members already exercised the right to contract-out of the political fund, so the case for changing the procedure in isolation and outside a broader examination of party funding was not especially strong. Equally, while recognising that public spending cuts need to be applied across a variety of areas, there had been no clamour to cut the relatively modest sums distributed through Short Money.

Ultimately, however, the impact of these reforms may be longer-term and affect more parties. In the case of Labour, changes to 'contracting-in' may impact significantly upon the party's income base in the longer term—especially if its reliance on trade union income continues. But for party finance reform more generally, the asymmetric effects of these changes are such that a future Labour or Labour-led government may exact some form of 'revenge', either through excessively partisan measures or through a root and branch reform of party finance regardless of any opposition from the Conservative Party. This will leave the vexed question of party finance reform open for a lot longer and with reduced prospects for consensus as a result.

The third issue related to the appropriate allocation of campaign expenditure to candidates or parties. There has been growing issue in British politics in respect of the blurring between what counts as national party level and what counts as candidate expenditure at the constituency level (Fisher, 2015, p. 153). Ostensibly, the distinction is clear—that which promotes a party is counted as national (party) expenditure, while that which promotes the candidate is counted as constituency-level. However, the distinction in reality is not so neat. Nor is the blurring a new concern. In the general elections of 1950 and 1951, there was controversy over a poster campaign opposing Labour's policies (1950) and an advert in *The Times* doing likewise (1951). In both cases, it was argued that these were political propaganda and contravened the legislation that no expenditure should be incurred to procure the election of a candidate unless authorised by the candidate's electoral agent (who is responsible for approving all campaign expenditure in support of the candidate). The 1951 case came to court in 1952 and *The Times* was acquitted on the grounds the advertisement was general propaganda and did not assist a particular candidate (Butler, 1952, p.33). The implication of this ruling was that posters and newspaper advertisements (and indeed any other form of advertisements) where a candidate was not named, did not contravene the rules on candidate spending. As far back as 1952, Butler (1952, pp. 33-34) argued that the ruling had far reaching implications. He was right.

Certainly, what has become clear over the last twenty-five years is that developments in technology and campaign techniques have become such that the boundaries between national and constituency-level spending have become even less distinct. We can observe this in at least five ways. First, all parties have developed facilities for telephone voter identification (Fisher *et al.*, 2007; Fisher *et al.*, 2011). The calls generally focus in parties' key seats, but critically, the purpose is not to promote a particular candidate. Rather, it seeks to assess the level of commitment in respect of the vote intention and enquire as to the voter's principal policy concerns. This feeds into the second key development: nationally sent direct mail. Voters' policy concerns as expressed through telephone voter identification and other means of voter contact are followed up by bespoke direct mail. Importantly, the direct mail is tailored both to voters' concerns and their demographic profile (Fisher *et al.* 2007; Fisher et al., 2011). This tends to be focussed on voters in target seats, but again candidates' names are not mentioned, thus deeming this activity as national (party) expenditure. The third area is the use of targeted advertisements in social media, undertaken by national parties—in effect, a digital evolution of the approached adopted by direct mail. And as with direct mail, it does not promote a particular candidate, but will typically be targeted on key voters in target seats.

In addition to these technology-driven developments, two further approaches, rooted in more traditional modes of campaigning, illustrate this trend. National party figures tend to focus their election tours on particular seats. Of course, tours by key party figures have long been a highly visible component of campaigning, going as far back as the nineteenth century (Hanham, 1978, pp. 202-204). But from the 1970s, there has been a far greater emphasis on focusing leadership tours on marginal seats (Butler and Kavanagh, 1974, p. 224; Fisher and Denver, 2008, p. 816), with expenditure being ascribed principally to the national party, rather than the candidate.

The fifth development ironically relates to the most traditional campaign approach: face-to-face campaigning. Party volunteers often descend on target seats to assist with campaigns. Again, this practice is not entirely new. Activists have often campaigned in nearby constituencies if that seat was more marginal and their own was safe. However, some parties have struggled more than others to get large numbers to campaign outside their own constituency. As a consequence, parties have assisted with transport. The effects of this have been comparable with the other blurred distinctions. Such expenditure (typically travel) has counted as national (party) expenditure rather than constituency (candidate) expenditure.

These developments have been important for three reasons. First, the national campaign has been effectively subsumed into supporting constituency-level activities (Fisher, 2010, 2015). Second, and as a consequence, the distinctions between expenditure on national and constituency-level campaigns have become increasingly blurred, and the ability to ascribe expenditure meaningfully as being national or constituency-level has become increasingly challenging. Third, the increasing blurring has led some to claim that the candidate spending limits in districts are now effectively meaningless, since so much national spending is devoted to supporting campaigns in particular constituencies. Developments during this Parliament, however, meant that what was principally a discussion about campaign developments became a potentially criminal affair.

Beginning in January 2016, *Channel 4 News* broadcast a series of reports suggesting (amongst other things) that expenditure ascribed to the national Conservative Party campaign in the 2015 General Election should have been ascribed to those campaigns of particular Conservative candidates. The key areas of importance were hotel expenses paid in respect of activists in one seat, and the use of the election 'Battle Bus' to transport activists to key seats. The Electoral Commission began investigating the matter in February 2016 and published its conclusion in March 2016, which resulted in the Conservative Party being fined £70,000 in respect of these matters and apparent breaches in respect of by-elections in 2014 (Electoral Commission, 2017, p. 4). This alone was damaging (and it should be noted that Labour and the Liberal Democrats were also fined by the Commission in respect of inaccuracies in their election expenses). However, more potentially damaging was that the Commission drew the attention of the Crown Prosecution Service (CPS) to the Conservatives' misreporting. The matter was investigated by 15 separate police forces and potentially affected up to 20 Conservative MPs. If the CPS had decided to proceed, those MPs could have faced criminal charges and would have been disqualified if found guilty. Obviously, disqualifications on this scale would have denied the Conservatives its majority. But potentially more seriously, there would have been significant political damage from such a large number appearing before the courts.

When Theresa May called the election, she was still unaware of whether the CPS would proceed with charges. After dissolution, the MPs in question could no longer be disqualified, but the potential for serious political damage remained. On 10 May, however, it was announced that no charges would be brought against all but one candidate under investigation, the CPS concluding that there was insufficient evidence in respect of the 'Battle Bus' expenses to prove to a criminal standard that any candidate or agent had acted in a dishonest matter (Crown Prosecution Service, 2017a). However, a decision on a case being investigated by the Kent police would only be made later and published on 2 June: the case of the Thanet South Constituency (Crown Prosecution Service, 2017*b*). The CPS concluded there was sufficient evidence to authorise charges against three people: the candidate, his election agent, and a Conservative Party official. One might have expected this to be hugely damaging electorally for the candidate and the Conservative Party. It may well have been for the party in an abstract sense, but just six days later, the candidate was re-elected with a 12.6 percentage point increase in his vote share (and over 6000 additional votes), achieving more than 50% of the vote. Ultimately, the impact of these investigations, however, may be less visible than any public rejection of a party or candidate. Rather, all parties will seek to make sure that they are not vulnerable to accusations of mis-apportioning funds through effective self-policing.

2.   Trends in party income and expenditure

The normal pattern of party income is that it cycles with general elections—rising sharply in the year before an election and falling away again in the year after. With an election so soon after the last one, one might have expected little change in this regard. In fact, the reverse was true for Labour and the Liberal Democrats. The Labour leadership election of 2015 produced many new members, topped up by those who wished to participate in the election, adding up to significant financial contributions. And the repeat election in 2016, as a result of the challenge to Jeremy Corbyn's leadership, boosted income further in what would normally be a year where income fell. As Labour noted in its accounts for 2016, this enabled the party to establish a general election trust fund, something that in previous post-election periods, would have been 'unthinkable'. The Liberal Democrats also enjoyed a growth in income—up over £1 million mainly through growth in party membership and donations.

By way of contrast, Conservative income in 2016 fell as would be expected. This meant that at the turn of the election year, Labour enjoyed the kind of financial advantage over the Conservatives not seen since the Blair years. This is illustrated both in Figure 11.1 (Central Party Income) and in Figure 11.2, which shows Labour central income as a percentage of Conservative central income.[1] These differentials between Labour and the Conservatives were also reflected in central expenditure up to the end of 2016. While both parties' expenditure declined relative to 2015 (as we would expect), Labour was outspending the Conservatives six months before polling day (Figure 11.3). Overall, by the end of 2016, all three parties were displaying the kind of financial prudence that has

---

[1]As with all figures in the chapter, the source of the data is the Electoral Commission's Party and Election Finance Database and the parties' own accounts.

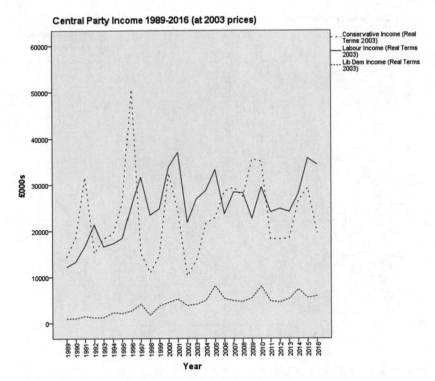

Figure 11.1. Central Party Income 1989-2016 (at 2003 prices)

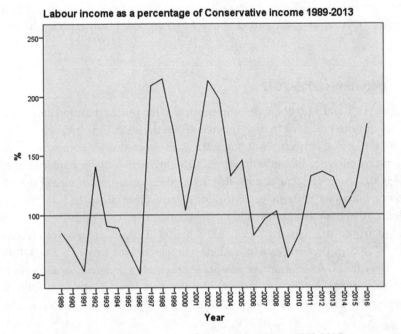

Figure 11.2. Labour income as a percentage of Conservative income 1989-2016

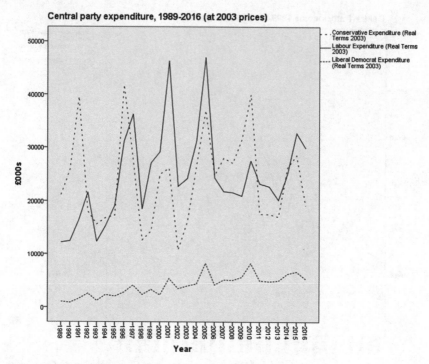

Central party expenditure, 1989-2016 (at 2003 prices)

Figure 11.3. Central Party Expenditure 1989-2016 (at 2003 prices)

characterised the last ten years with expenditure rarely exceeding income (Figure 11.4). In sum, the parties entered 2017 in better than expected financial health.

3. Donations 2015-2017

Figures 11.5 and 11.6 show the number and value of declared donations (over £7500 in value) received in each quarter. Given the short time between the elections, the period between 2010 and 2015 is also included for comparison, with the x-axis reference line in both set at 2015 Quarter 3—the first quarter of the 2015-2017 cycle. The figures show that declared donations in advance of the 2017 election mirrored patterns prior to 2015—the Conservatives had a significant advantage in both the number and the value of declared cash donations. Over the period from 2015 Quarter 3 to 2017 Quarter 2, the Conservatives received £48,867,408 in declared cash donations, compared with Labour's £24,981,055. Yet, the Conservative advantage was heavily skewed to declared donations in the last six months before the election. In the first two quarters of 2017, the Conservatives received 492 donations totalling over £27 million; Labour received

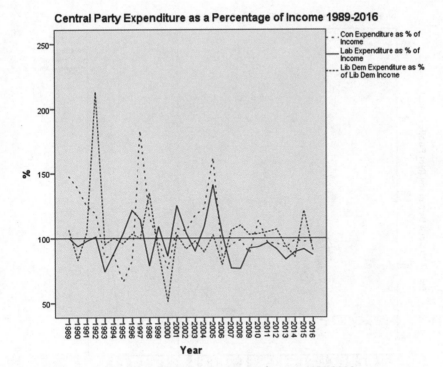

Figure 11.4. Central Party Expenditure as a Percentage of Income 1989-2016

183 totalling just under £10 million, while the Liberal Democrats received 99 totalling just under £3 million.

Of course, declared donations do not tell the whole story. As we have seen, Labour was very successful in 2015 and 2016 in generating a large number of small donations as a result of the leadership contests that took place. In 2015, for example, the party generated £3 million in low-value donations in addition to a surge in membership, meaning that the party was finally able to clear its unsecured loans. Nevertheless, the 'normal situation', whereby the Conservatives were able to attract more income, was confirmed in the six months prior to the election.

The Conservative income advantage was further illustrated by donations in the six weeks before polling day (see Tables 11.1 and 11.2). The *Political Parties, Elections and Referendums Act* 2000 requires donation declarations to be made weekly during the period between dissolution and polling day. Although delivering more in the way of transparency than the regular quarterly donations, they have previously told us comparatively little about the impact of party finance on the election as the money would have arrived too late to have a substantial effect. Traditionally, most income has been generated in the year before an election, in

Number of Declared Donations to Central Party 2010 Q3 - 2017 Q2

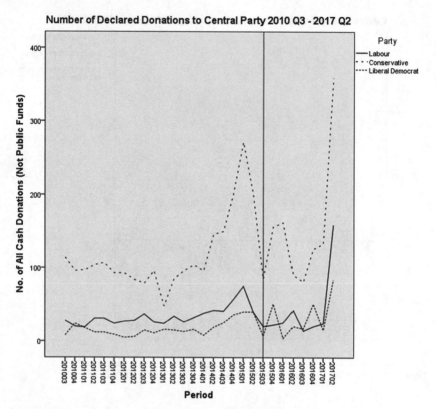

Figure 11.5. Number of Declared Donations to Central Party 2010 Q3-2017 Q2

part because many campaigning activities such as direct mail require a long lead time for the activities to yield payoffs. However, the growth of digital campaigning, which often has a shorter lead time than other campaign methods, means that these data are increasingly helpful in understanding parties' finances at elections.

During this period, the Conservatives received over £12.5 million from 221 declared cash donations, compared with Labour's £4.5 million from 40. This represented more than double the level of Conservative donations that the party received in the same period prior to the 2015 election (Fisher, 2015). By way of contrast, Labour generated only 69% of the declared cash donations it received in the 2015 campaign period and in real terms, the proportion is even lower at 66%. The Liberal Democrats generated twice the level of declared donations in 2017 in the last six weeks before the election compared with the same period in 2015. The most lucrative period for the two largest parties was in the first week, where the Conservatives generated £4.3 million, and Labour £2.7 million. But, as

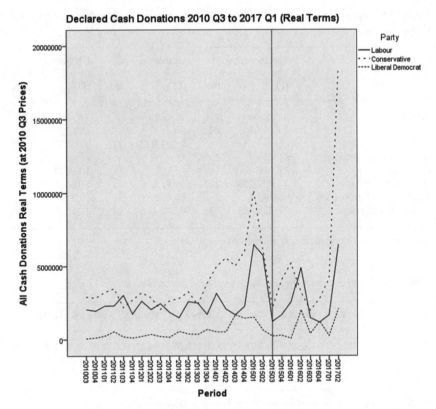

Declared Cash Donations 2010 Q3 to 2017 Q1 (Real Terms)

Party
— Labour
- - Conservative
---- Liberal Democrat

Figure 11.6. Declared Cash Donations 2010 Q3-2017 Q1 (Real Terms)

Table 11.2 shows, money flowed into Conservative coffers in fairly sizeable amounts throughout the campaign.

Of course, the snap election will have prompted some of this late fundraising, but a further reason for the large sums raised may also be political. One of the explanations for the shift in Conservative funding from individual donors to institutional ones in the 1920s was a fear amongst some companies of the Labour Party (Fisher, 2000, p. 20). That motivation had declined over the last 30 years as fewer companies saw the prospect of a Labour government as a threat (Fisher, 1994). Certainly, corporate donations to the Conservatives in the 2001 and 2005 campaigns were modest (Fisher, 2001, 2005). They were larger in 2010 and 2015, but the sum raised from companies in 2017 was 37% higher in real terms than the prior high level of company giving in 2010. Although this can only be properly verified through donor surveys (Fisher, 1994), it does suggest at least that companies are more likely to support the Conservative party financially when Labour is seen as being more threatening.

Table 11.1 Source of Election Period Declared Cash Donations and Levels of Declared Non-Cash Donations

	Conservative		Labour		Lib Dems	
	(£)	No.	(£)	No.	(£)	No.
Individual	9,672,049	170	189,699	8	776,950	27
Company	2,885,000	48	–	–	299,750	6
Trade Union	–	–	4,302,917	32	–	–
Unincorporated Associations	61,000	2	–	–	–	–
Public Funds	21,247	1	–	–	108,024	1
Total Cash Donations	12,639,296	221	4,492,616	40	1,184,724	34
Total Non-Cash Donations	85,742	2	54,800	3	30,870	2
Total All Donations	12,725,038	223	4,547,416	43	1,215,594	36

Source: The Electoral Commission Party and Election Finance Database.

Table 11.2 Timing of Weekly Declared Cash and Non-Cash Donations

£s	Week 1	Week 2	Week 3	Week 4	Week 5	Week 6	Total
Conservative	4,343,000	1,639,108	3,785,050	1,115,833	1,605,800	236,247	12,725,038
Labour	2,683,300	382,925	359,499	1,046,692	75,000	0	4,547,416
Lib Dems	180,000	160,750	310,500	210,394	353,950	0	1,215,594

Source: The Electoral Commission Party and Election Finance Database.

It is also worth noting Labour's reliance on declared donations from trade unions during the campaign period. Trade unions accounted for 96% of Labour's declared donations in the six weeks leading up to polling day, up from 72% in the comparable period in 2015, 64% in 2010 and 41% in 2005. Over the same period, there has been a decline in declared individual donations. In 2005, 41% of Labour's election period declared donations were from individuals. The figures for 2010, 2015 and 2017 were 24%, 12% and 4% respectively.

4. Election Period Expenditure

4.1 *Conservatives*

An important area of expenditure was digital campaigning. A feature of the 2015 campaign had been a very successful campaign on Facebook, with the micro-targeting opportunities that this presented. 2017 was no different.

The party's strong financial position and prior success meant that the digital operation was very well resourced. But, there were some issues that hindered the full potential of this approach. First, there were data weaknesses. According to Mark Wallace (2017*a*), centrally held data used for the purposes of targeting voters were out of date compared with 2015, and critically, were focused on the type of contests fought in 2015 rather than 2017. For example, while the Conservatives had very successfully targeted Liberal Democrat seats in 2015, the circumstances in 2017 were very different as a function of the EU Referendum. In the aftermath of that, the kinds of voters the party sought to target were former UKIP voters and Labour Leave voters. The party recognised this disparity and spent time early in the campaign on new polling and consumer data (Wallace, 2017*a*). A second issue, according to Wallace (2017*a*), was that the party assumed that young voters were not a priority. This informed the choice of digital platforms, where Labour proved to be much more innovative (see below).

As in previous elections, however, it was print that continued to be a significant source of expenditure. This manifested itself in two prominent ways. First, the party engaged significantly in 'wraparound' adverts in local and regional newspapers. These are adverts that wrap around the newspaper, meaning that the front and back pages of the paper constitute a party advertisement. Not surprisingly, these were focused on areas with target seats. The second major area was direct mail, although the problems with central data described above did apparently cause some delays in distribution. But according to Wallace (2017*b*), there was one unforeseen problem beyond the control of the party—namely a difficulty in getting huge amounts printed at short notice, in part because of an apparent shortage of paper! The party's financial advantage did mean however, that it was able to have more professional staff on the ground. A survey of party agents indicates that some 21% of agents were employed by the national party or local associations (compared with 3% for Labour) (Fisher, Cutts and Fieldhouse, 2017)

At party headquarters, however, the snap election meant that it was difficult to fully exploit the party's financial advantage. For example, as Figures 11.1 and 11.3 show, party income and expenditure cycles closely around the timing of general elections. The key here, is Conservative expenditure—this fell sharply in 2016 as per previous elections. In one sense, this is to be expected, since income falls noticeably in the same period. However, the outcome for the Conservatives in 2017 was that when the election was called, the level of staffing at all levels of party headquarters compared with the run-up to the 2015 election was far lower. Thus, while the party was ultimately able to engage staff, the sudden calling of the election meant that it was at a potential disadvantage having lost many staff who helped fight the election two years previously. Critically, this included senior figures such as Lynton Crosby who were hired as consultants, but who were based abroad when the election was called (Wallace, 2017*a*).

Overall, the Conservative national expenditure revealed the continuation of particular trends. First, based on the success of its use in 2015 and the shorter lead time compared with print, digital campaigning continued to grow in importance. Second, however, print campaigning was far from obsolete and continued to be an important campaigning tool. Third, the national campaigning continued to be effectively subsumed into one that supported the campaigns in the key constituencies. Fourth, the Conservative Party's strong financial position meant that it was able to spend sufficient funds on a range of activities. Yet, for all the financial advantages in the short term, the party's campaigns were not without difficulties on account of the snap election. It took time to re-establish the staff complement and the data underpinning the print and digital campaigns presented some problems—at least initially. In sum, the Conservatives' considerable short-term financial advantage was offset to a degree by the sudden calling of the election.

4.2   Labour

A number of financial aspects influenced Labour's campaign. First, the snap election meant the bulk of the spending was compressed at the backend of the campaign. Second, and perhaps most critically, there was no agreed list of target seats. A combination of the party's poor opinion poll position and the need to select candidates at short notice in a number of seats meant that in many ways, this was a less coordinated campaign compared with previous elections. But it was still, in effect, a national campaign that was subordinate to the constituency efforts.

However, one particular financial windfall benefited Labour quite significantly, despite the snap election. The leadership election in 2016 generated significant income and as a result, Labour was able to spend £2 million almost as soon as the election was called. This opportunity was particularly welcome as the main donations from trade unions did not appear until the second half of May and, as in 2015, some unions were keen that their contributions should be focused on particular candidates who shared their own ideological preferences (Fisher, 2015, p. 150).

Overall, the party spent around £11 million. As in previous elections, printed matter continued to represent a significant item of expenditure, but developments in digital campaigning continued and were a key feature of the party's campaign, if not its expenditure. Overall, Labour spent £1.2 million on digital campaigning. The bulk of this was on Facebook, but a feature of this campaign was the way Labour diversified its digital activity. In addition, the party also utilized YouTube, Twitter and for the first time, Snapchat. Labour was of the view that to mobilize younger voters it needed to engage with a platform used overwhelmingly by them, especially as its digital team reported that young people were now less likely to use Facebook. The party spent £100,000 on Snapchat adverts, which generated 7.8 million views (interview with party official). On polling day, Labour also spent £90,000 on a promoted post on Twitter, while on YouTube the party invested in non-skippable adverts of around fifteen seconds (interview with party official).

In addition, as Chapter 12 explains, the party had developed a new digital tool called Promote, which allowed the party's existing databases and the electoral roll to link with Facebook IDs, meaning that voters could receive messages both through the direct mail medium and through Facebook. This meant that the digital targeting was much more precise than in previous elections, but equally represented an evolution from targeted direct mail rather than something that was fundamentally different. And critically, the party still focused more attention on print advertising for the simple reason that only an estimated 60% of the population uses Facebook. Elsewhere, the party invested in other digital tools to assist in internal campaign organisation. Chatter was a text message based system whereby potential campaign volunteers could be contacted, while Dialogue allowed volunteers to contact voters by telephone from home without their number being revealed. Beyond these initiatives, the absence of some older campaign approaches was again apparent. Labour did not invest in any fixed billboards or national newspaper advertising. Where there was non-constituency-focused advertising, it was in local newspapers covering a few seats, where the party took out around 40-50 advertisements.

Overall, Labour's campaign and spending confirmed previous trends: the supporting role of the national campaign to constituency efforts, the growing importance of digital approaches, but also the continued importance of direct mail. However, what marked it out was the relative lack of coordination at national level. In effect, there were two campaigns: one run by the central party and one run by the leader's office. All in all, while this election continued the decline of the national campaign, the sudden nature of the election, together with the lack of coordination meant this was a more haphazard affair.

4.3 Liberal Democrats

The Liberal Democrats were the best prepared of the three principal parties, having started to prepare in the summer of 2016, following the referendum and the change of Conservative leader. This meant that unlike the other parties, their candidates were already in place. Coupled with that, the party's financial situation had improved, in part because of a surge in membership.

A variety of campaign activities were funded. Despite the lack of lead time, a significant sum was spent on direct mail, which was heavily targeted on key voters in key seats. Equally, the leader's tour was also a crucial component of the target seat strategy, as was telephone voter identification, which took place both at the party's headquarters and through 'virtual' phone banks. Like Labour, there were no national newspaper advertisements or fixed billboards—only mobile digital billboards on vans, just as in 2015 (Fisher, 2015, p. 151).

In addition to this campaign spending on established approaches, the Liberal Democrats also spent heavily on digital techniques. The party has embraced digital campaigning for some years now, even claiming it 'won the digital war' at the 2010 general election (Fisher *et al.*, 2011, p. 205) and indeed, claimed it ran its biggest ever digital campaign in 2017. Facebook was the principal platform, the party viewing it as having the most volume, the level of resource behind Facebook meaning that response rates would be likely to be better. The party used it in a number of ways, including individual and geo-targeting of advertisements as well as videos. The party also made use of Facebook Live. In sum, despite the party's perilous electoral position following the 2015 election, it went into the 2017 campaign with healthier finances, significantly more members and, under the circumstances, with good levels of preparation. Coupled with the growing emphasis on digital campaigning, the party was able to take advantage of the significant level of fundraising it achieved during the campaign, which was nearly double that which was collected in 2015.

5. Conclusion

The sudden calling of the general election in April 2017 had significant implications in terms of party finance. At the start of the year, Labour was in the relatively unusual position of being at a financial advantage relative to the Conservatives—ironically, in part due to the instability surrounding the party's leadership between 2015 and 2016. But by the time of the election, the Conservatives had re-asserted their financial dominance, raising very significant sums in a short period of time. In the longer term this initial advantage for Labour may be more difficult to achieve, since there will not be the one-off events of leadership elections generating new income, and the effects of 'contracting-in' for new trade union members may be unpredictable.

The snap election also impacted upon spending decisions and critically, the ability of parties to exploit their financial position. Yet it also affected how parties spent money on campaigning. More established methods like direct mail require long lead times to be truly effective. But as digital campaigning continued to grow, the short lead time meant that it made more sense to accelerate the use of these methods. The key benefit of digital campaigning in 2017 was that it presented more opportunities for 'late spend'—campaign expenditure right up to polling day. There was variation by party in the extent and diversity of digital campaigning, but overall, it continues to grow, with its use increased by the snap election. But that does not mean that everything has changed. Print campaigning was still the dominant form of campaign expenditure, not least because of its wider reach. Digital approaches remain second best in terms of reaching large numbers of voters and the much-trumpeted micro-targeting represents an evolution of that which has gone on for many years with direct mail, rather than a revolution in voter contact. The balance between campaigning tools will no doubt continue to shift towards digital, but for now, it continues to play second fiddle in terms of campaign expenditure.

References

Butler, D.E. (1952) *The British General Election of 1951*, London, Macmillan.

Butler, D.E. & Kavanagh, D. (1974) *The British General Election of February 1974*, London, Macmillan.

Crown Prosecution Service (2017a, 10 May), 'CPS Statement on Election Expenses', accessed at http://www.cps.gov.uk/news/latest_news/cps-statement-on-election-expenses/ on 2 August 2017.

Crown Prosecution Service (2017b, 2 June) 'CPS Statement on Election Expenses', accessed at: http://www.cps.gov.uk/news/latest_news/cps-statement-election-expenses/ on 3 August 2017.

Electoral Commission, *Party and Election Finance Database*, accessed at http://search.electoral commission.org.uk/?currentPage=0&rows=10&sort=AcceptedDate&order=desc&tab=1&et=pp&et=ppm&et=tp&et=perpar&et=rd&prePoll=false&postPoll=true&optCols=CampaigningName&optCols=AccountingUnitsAsCentralParty&optCols=IsSponsorship&optCols=RegulatedDoneeType&optCols=CompanyRegistrationNumber&optCols=Postcode&optCols=NatureOfDonation&optCols=PurposeOfVisit&optCols=Donation Action&optCols=ReportedDate&optCols=IsReportedPrePoll&optCols=ReportingPeriod Name&optCols=IsBequest&optCols=IsAggregation.

Electoral Commission (2017, 16 March) *Investigation in Respect of the Conservative and Unionist Party Campaign Spending Returns for the 2014 European Parliamentary Election, and 2015 Parliamentary Election, and in Respect of Parliamentary By-Elections in Clacton, Newark and Rochester and Strood*, accessed at https://www.electoralcommis sion.org.uk/__data/assets/pdf_file/0005/222935/Report-in-respect-of-the-Conservative-and-Unionist-Party.pdf on 2 August 2017.

Fisher, J. (1994) 'Why Do Companies Make Donations to Political Parties?', *Political Studies*, **42**, 690–699.

Fisher, J. (2000) 'Party Finance and Corruption: Britain'. In Williams (ed.), *Party Finance and Corruption*, London, Macmillan, pp. 15–36.

Fisher, J. (2001) 'Campaign Finance: Elections Under New Rules', *Parliamentary Affairs: Britain Votes 2001*, **54**, 689–700.

Fisher, J. (2005) 'Campaign Finance'. In Geddes and Tonge (eds) *Britain Decides: The General Election of 2005*, Basingstoke, Palgrave Macmillan, pp. 170–186.

Fisher, J. (2010) 'Party Finance—Normal Service Resumed?', *Parliamentary Affairs*, **63**, 778–801.

Fisher, J. (2015) 'Party Finance: The Death of the National Campaign?' *Parliamentary Affairs*, **68** (Suppl 1), 133–153.

Fisher, J., Denver, D. Fieldhouse, E., Cutts, D. and Russell, A. (2007) 'Constituency Campaigning in 2005: Ever More Centralization?' In Wring D., Green J., Mortimore R. and Atkinson, S. (eds) *Political Communications: The British General Election of 2005*, Basingstoke, Palgrave Macmillan, pp. 79–92.

Fisher, J. and Denver, D. (2008) 'From Foot-Slogging to Call Centres and Direct Mail: A Framework for Analysing the Development of District-Level Campaigning', *European Journal of Political Research*, **47**, 794–826.

Fisher, J., Cutts, D. and Fieldhouse, E. (2011) 'Constituency Campaigning in 2010'. In Wring D., Mortimore R. and Atkinson S. (eds) *Political Communication in Britain: The Leader Debates, the Campaign and Media in the 2010 General Election*, Basingstoke, Palgrave Macmillan, pp. 198–217.

Fisher, J., Cutts, D. and Fieldhouse, E. (2017) *Survey of Election Agents—Constituency Campaigning in the 2017 General Election* (Unpublished dataset).

Hanham, H. J. (1978) *Elections and Party Management*, Sussex, The Harvester Press.

Wallace, M (2017a) 'Our CCHQ Election Audit: The Rusty Machine, Part One. Why the Operation that Succeeded in 2015 Failed in 2017', *ConservativeHome*, accessed at https://www.conservativehome.com/majority_conservatism/2017/09/our-cchq-election-audit-the-rusty-machine-part-one-why-the-operation-that-succeeded-in-2015-failed-in-2017.html on 11 September 2017.

Wallace, M. (2017b) 'Our CCHQ Election Audit: The Rusty Machine, Part Two. How and Why the Ground Campaign Failed', *ConservativeHome*, accessed at https://www.conservativehome.com/majority_conservatism/2017/09/our-cchq-election-audit-the-rusty-machine-part-two-how-and-why-the-ground-campaign-failed.html on 11 September 2017.

Britain Votes (2017) 189–202

KATHARINE DOMMETT AND LUKE TEMPLE*

Digital Campaigning: The Rise of Facebook and Satellite Campaigns

Studies of digital campaigning have revealed substantial change in the nature of political campaigns. Tracing the rise of email, party websites, social media, online videos and gamification, scholars have shown how, since the 1990s, parties have become heavily dependent on digital technology (Gibson, 2015). In this chapter we focus on two elements of the 2017 digital campaign: Facebook advertising and what we term 'satellite campaigns'. Whilst resisting claims of revolution and transformational change (Kreiss, 2010, Williamson, Miller and Fallon, 2010) we nevertheless argue that these digital practices have important implications for parties' organisational structures, practices and behaviour, as well as for public expectations of campaigning. Through this analysis we contend that the 2017 general election provides further evidence that 'digital media are reconfiguring party-related engagement' (Vaccari and Valeriani, 2016, p. 295), and agree with Gibson (2015, p. 191) that by 'chaf[ing] against embedded organisational routines and norms' these developments challenge established understandings of parties' campaign strategies.

In examining digital, we adopt an expansive definition of the term. Alongside an interest in social media and party websites, we also examine the organisational digital infrastructure on which parties rely. Including digital databases, canvassing systems, online phone banks, and email lists, digital infrastructure is pivotal to parties' diverse campaign activities by enabling participation through the reduction of resource costs. In the analysis that follows, we employ this expansive conception of digital to consider developments within the Labour and Conservative parties, using these examples to illustrate wider emerging trends.

By April 2017, few were predicting an early general election, but in the days that elapsed between Theresa May's surprise announcement on 18 May and the vote on 8 June, parties across the spectrum exhibited formidable online and offline campaigns. In the digital realm, Twitter, Facebook, YouTube, Snapchat, and

*Katharine Dommett, Department of Politics, University of Sheffield, k.dommett@sheffield.ac.uk; Luke Temple, Department of Geography, University of Sheffield, l.temple@sheffield.ac.uk

doi:10.1093/pa/gsx056

Instagram all played a part in the campaigns (Dutceac Segesten and Bossetta, 2017) with numerous graphics, videos and messages shared online. While all parties were active on these platforms, emerging analysis has demonstrated the degree to which Labour, and particularly Jeremy Corbyn, dominated support on these platforms (Cram *et al.*, 2017; Dean, 2017; Shephard, 2017). Organisationally, digital proved key to volunteer mobilisation, voter identification activities, and message targeting. Particularly prominent within the wider picture of social and digital media use were two elements of the digital campaign: parties' use of Facebook advertising and the role of what we term 'satellite campaigns' facilitated by non-party intermediary organisations such as Campaign Together and CrowdPac. Considering these two developments in detail, we argue that such changes represent important new evolutions in political campaigning, and raise interesting questions for parties, the public and our expectations of political campaigning.

1. Facebook advertising—the new normal?

Parties' use of Facebook advertising was heralded as a key component of the 2017 campaign (Bakir and McStay, 2017; Walsh, 2017; see also Bond, 2017; Ward, 2017; Waterson, 2017). Using this tool, parties across the spectrum targeted content at specific groups of voters. Drawing on demographic data such as age, postcode, religion, and gender, combined with indicators of users' interests, parties were able to identify those with, say, a passion for cycling, international travel, or beer, and use these interests to filter messages about the environment, foreign affairs or taxation. Parties were therefore able to identify electorally significant voter groups, such as women over 65 in marginal constituencies, and tailor messages to their interests and ideas in attempts to win appeal. The uptake of this tool was especially notable in the two main parties. Labour, in particular, embraced Facebook advertising (Waterson, 2017), investing heavily at a national level in adverts designed to promote electoral registration, but also creating a new organisational tool, Promote, which allowed local parties to target their own Facebook adverts. Similarly, the Conservatives invested in adverts promoting Theresa May and questioning the leadership credentials of Jeremy Corbyn. Reportedly, these campaigns saw Labour and the Conservatives spend over £1 million each on the platform, although formal electoral commission figures have yet to be released (Bond, 2017). Due to their targeted nature, capturing the range of adverts is exceedingly challenging. Initiatives such as *Who Targets Me* allow users to track the adverts targeted at them (via web-browser extension) to offer some insight into the number, form, and focus, of party adverts; however, these data are yet to be analysed in full.

Given the evidence that seeing a political message on a friend's page can affect voting behaviour (Bond *et al.*, 2012), Facebook provides parties with a range of new capacities that can enhance their campaigns. As a social media platform, Facebook allows parties to connect with voters where they are, building on existing networks through sharing, comments, and reactions. In this way, an advert targeted to one voter may be liked and shared, signalling to friends and acquaintances that voter's views and affiliation. This kind of sharing enables messages to be organically disseminated (Dutceac Segesten and Bossetta, 2017) and, as previous studies have shown, voters are increasingly comfortable sharing election related information online (Aldrich *et al.*, 2016, p. 174).

Whilst the prominence of Facebook in 2017 may suggest the emergence of a new campaign tool, it is important to recognise that the use of targeted social media advertising in the UK is part of a developing trend. This technique was prevalent during the EU referendum the previous year (Cookson and Gordon, 2016) and at the 2015 general election the Conservatives embraced Facebook advertising, declaring a spend of £1.2 million to the Electoral Commission on this platform alone (Electoral Commission, 2016, p. 29). Reflecting on the success of the 2015 digital campaign, interviews with Conservative Party strategists have demonstrated that Facebook in particular was viewed as 'the best place to advertise' (Interview with Conservative Party official, February 2017),[1] an idea that has infused the strategies of other parties in 2017. Moreover, despite the increased prominence of Facebook as a campaigning space, the targeting it enables is by no means new. Parties have long focused on identifying and targeting their vote with the aim of refining communication strategies and identifying where the vote needs to be mobilised on election day (Whiteley and Seyd, 2003). However, historically, parties have been restricted by data protection laws to using the electoral roll (a list of everyone registered to vote), the marked register (a list of each elector's voting history), commercially available data (from private companies) and their own canvassing databases to target voters. Facebook is distinctive in offering a new source of voter information to parties that reflects voters' interests and social preferences, whilst also providing the platform for communication.

From this perspective, we argue that rather than signalling radical change, the use of Facebook in 2017 represented a 'normalized revolution' (Wright, 2012), as it has adapted and extended party activities, whilst not radically changing what it is that parties do. In reaching this conclusion, we nevertheless argue that parties' use of Facebook has important implications for public perceptions, control, and resource, that warrant further discussion.

---

[1] This interview was conducted as part of a wider ESRC funded research project and focused on parties use of digital in the 2015 General Election.

First, in regard to public perceptions, Facebook allows parties to target content at highly localised audiences with greater precision than was previously possible (Aldrich *et al.*, 2016; O'Brien, 2015; Council of Europe, 2017, p. 11). This ensures that voters hear about topics they are likely to be interested in/receptive to, which, given that social media is an increasingly important source of news and information for many voters (Miller, 2016), has the potential to yield significant effects (Marengo, 2013). Whilst companies such as Amazon and Google have been utilising targeting techniques to filter desirable content to users for years, parties' use of this data is less familiar,[2] and the consequences of such targeting are unknown. Some scholars have already theorised that 'unsolicited messages are likely to be regarded as more intrusive than a "cold call" to a landline or flyer posted through the mailbox' (Aldrich *et al.*, 2016, p. 166). Whilst the use of Facebook data is often not as sophisticated as may be presumed, the degree to which parties *should* be able to access and, indeed, purchase additional information about voters raises potential concerns. Asides from issues of resource inequality (discussed further below), the idea that private information is being used by actors in the public realm to further their own electoral success raises issues of transparency and appropriate democratic behaviour. The norms here are not absolute, but research indicates that politicians are held to higher standards than other people (Allen and Birch, 2015, p. 71), suggesting that commercially-accepted practices may not be tolerated to the same degree in the political realm. In this context, questions emerge around how parties can and should use data to connect with voters, questions that the Electoral Commission need to consider when re-examining existing regulations.

Second, we argue that whilst the unique attributes of Facebook offer parties advantages in terms of connectivity and reach, this platform also raises issues of control. While Facebook can be used to target official party adverts, it is also a forum in which unofficial campaign interventions can be made in an untargeted manner. While the Conservatives developed videos comparing their position on taxation to Labour, and Labour made videos citing 10 reasons to vote Labour, many other videos from 'unofficial' sources could also be found. From Cassetteboy's remixes of political speeches, to memes mocking parties' manifesto positions (see for example *The Metro*, 28 July 2017), Facebook provides a platform for a range of different political interventions. This raises a series of questions about the degree to which parties can exercise control and maintain campaign coherence, but also about how targeted campaigns intersect with other content. To take one example, during the 2017 election, Momentum generated high-profile Tory attack advertisements, one of which, set in 2030, depicts a

---

[2]This is not to say that use of these data is new, but rather that such usage has been less publicly overt before.

young girl asking her Conservative-voting father if he hates her, to which he replies, 'Obviously!' Shared entirely on digital platforms including Facebook, Momentum activists claim the video was watched over 5.4 million times in two days (Peggs, 2017).[3] This content had huge reach, but the stylistic approach is unlikely to have ever been sanctioned as part of an official Labour campaign, and it may be that many voters being targeted by official Labour advertisements were put off by the tone. The relationship between official and unofficial material, and the interactions between targeted and untargeted social media material are therefore far from clear, but they suggest a tension between parties' desire to execute targeted campaigns and their capacity to do so on an open platform such as Facebook.

Third, Facebook raises issues of resource. On one level, the implications are organisational. Facebook demonstrates that digital has the potential to greatly reduce resource costs in terms of the efficiency of disseminating political campaign material, but also shows that there is a trade-off with the organisational capacity required to utilise digital tools effectively. As Labour's experience in 2017 shows, parties' use of digital requires investment not only in the cost of adverts, but also in the skills base of activists and organisational software. The tool Promote, developed by Labour's Digital Transformation Team, allows local parties to identify their own target voters and deploy appropriate adverts, yet parties' ability to design text and graphics likely to win attention and be shared is by no means guaranteed. As one digital consultancy company indicated, social media 'has to give people something they cannot get elsewhere, and it needs to be designed for the environment it is appearing in. Otherwise, you've just made another trivial but terrible contribution to Sharemageddon' (DigitalsLBi, 2015, p. 4). Ensuring that party activists have the capacity to generate attractive media poses a significant challenge to parties and may lead to a divide between 'digitally native' activists (Nielsen, 2013) and those lacking digital skills. As this divide is closely linked to generational profile, the Conservatives could be at a natural disadvantage when it comes to both their activist pool and their wider support base (Bale, 2017). This suggests that while parties face common challenges, these will be manifested in different ways depending on party context and culture.

At another level, Facebook also reveals issues of resource inequality. Whilst parties' financial capacities have often been unequal—restricting their capacity to produce leaflets or commission campaign billboards—on Facebook, parties'

---

[3] It is worth noting that the video does not at any point say, 'Vote Labour'. Rather it draws on Labour-like slogans in Labour-like brand colours and font to finish by saying 'Let's Build a Different Future—Get out the Vote on Thursday June 8th' before providing a link to a website that does explicitly promote voting for Labour. Furthermore, a new video released after the campaign—'They Just Don't Get It''—mentions Corbyn and Momentum, but again not Labour.

differing ability to buy advertising space raises important concerns about fairness, equality and transparency (see Norris, 2012). Whilst Labour and the Conservative Party used Facebook adverts extensively, other parties such as the Greens did not have the financial capacity to devote extensive resource. Moreover, it appears that, in certain marginal constituencies, only those parties willing to pay inflated prices for advertising space were able to promote their messages to voters (Cadwalladr, 2017). The importance of money for success in this realm, and the lack of transparency around how and why content appears in people's Facebook feeds, raises issues about the fairness of elections.

These issues have begun to be noted by campaign regulators but, as yet, regulations have not been fully adapted to reflect the realities of digital campaigns. The Council of Europe therefore recently noted that 'The Internet and new communications technologies undermine the ability of existing regulation to maintain a level playing field in electoral communication between new and established, rich and poor, corporate and civil society campaigns' (2017, p. 2), and yet the Electoral Commission in the UK has only partially adapted for online campaigns. Hence, while recommending that organisations include an imprint on their online materials (Electoral Commission, 2017, p. 11) formal regulations have not been fully adapted in the UK to take account of issues such as campaign funding and political transparency.[4]

Parties' use of Facebook therefore raises a series of questions about the acceptable use of personal data, parties' control of election campaigns and the role of money and resource in elections. These questions have important consequences for the perceived fairness of elections, regulation and public tolerance of different kinds of campaigning intervention. As Facebook becomes a permanent part of the electoral landscape, these issues will only grow in pertinence.

2.   Satellite campaigns

A second development in the digital sphere concerns the increased visibility of digital infrastructure offered by non-party organisations to encourage voting and campaigning. Though evident to different degrees, with greater activity around the Labour Party as opposed to the Conservatives, these organisations were seen to mobilise new activists and campaigners to parties' causes. Innovations such as Momentum's 'My Nearest Marginal' App, fundraising sites such as CrowdPac and campaigning hubs like the Progressive Alliance or Campaign Together were seen to empower and connect individuals to contribute to electoral campaigns via non-traditional routes. Organisations beyond parties were identifying,

---

[4]It should be noted that in Scotland there was a legal requirement to include a digital imprint on online materials at the Independence Referendum in 2015.

mobilising and organising citizens to deliver leaflets, canvass voters, and organise on- and offline. This development represents a distinctive and important shift in campaigning. It suggests that, in addition to Whiteley and Seyd's categories of the central party campaign, centrally coordinated local campaigns, and purely locally directed campaigns (2003, p. 638), we can also identify campaigns originating beyond party structures and control—those termed here 'satellite' campaigns.

Satellite campaigns can be supported by a range of different organisations, making it useful to refer to Edwards' (2006, pp. 8-9) notion of 'democratic intermediaries'. Edwards outlines three types of intermediary that we apply to describe non-party organisations operating during the 2017 election. First, there are preference intermediaries, organizations that articulate and aggregate political demands and in 2017 were evident in the form of Momentum and Grime4Corbyn. Second, information intermediaries are seen to provide users with political information and details on voter registration; at the latest general election platforms like GE2017, Rize Up, and Turn Up fitted these criteria. Third, interactional intermediaries facilitate political participation, capturing tactical voting platforms such as Swap My Vote, tactical canvassing networks such as Campaign Together, and the crowdfunding and campaign-match tool CrowdPac. Whilst some organisations exhibit functions in multiple categories—Momentum, for example, could also be classified as informational and interactional—this framework demonstrates the different ways in which campaigning initiated beyond the official party campaign can occur.

Whilst affiliate organisations such as trade unions, business organisations, and community groups, have long provided an additional resource for parties' electoral campaigns, the capacities of digital appear to have altered previous practice. Rachel Gibson has highlighted the capacity of digital technology, and specifically social media, to alter the power relations between citizens and central party headquarters. Tracing the rise of 'citizen-initiated campaigning', she describes the emergence of a 'more devolved or "citizen-initiated" approach to campaign organization' (Gibson, 2015, p. 183). The creation of tools by party candidates and teams that enable citizens to canvass voters on remote phone bank applications, raise money online, organise campaign events or disseminate party materials on social media are seen to enable 'autonomous action and tactical control of campaign operations at the local level on a scale that was not possible in the pre-digital era' (Gibson, 2015, p. 187). Numerous other scholars have picked up on this theme: Vaccari and Valeriani (2016, p. 306) have argued that social media are helping 'new digital foot soldiers to emerge and allow existing members to expand their repertoires', whilst Lilleker and Jackson (2010, pp. 74-75) have discussed the internet's ability to encourage 'individual production and user-generated content', creating supportive material, endorsing campaigns, and sharing campaigns through online networks (see also Chadwick and Stromer-Galley, 2016).

The idea of satellite campaigns mirrors these themes, but extends them by recognising the increasing importance of intermediary, unofficial, organisations beyond parties that facilitate and promote campaigning activities. A campaign can be classed as satellite when vote-seeking activism is primarily driven by intermediary organisations without the control of a party. The rise of digital media platforms does not determine that satellite campaigning will take place; however, it does greatly facilitate it. Satellite campaigns have the capacity to challenge 'the professionalized top-down approach that has dominated post-war elections, particularly over the past three decades' (Gibson, 2015, p. 183). However, these organisations should not be seen as a threat to parties as institutions because, primarily, they are not vote-seeking themselves, but also because they remain reliant on party infrastructure and activity. For instance, Campaign Together lacks its own canvassing system and instead organises by directing new activists towards existing *party-led* campaigns they identify in key marginal seats—the organisation brands itself as a part of a progressive alliance united by an aim to 'stop the Tories'. Utilising digital media, intermediary organisations help to bring together, train, mobilise, and inspire individuals who may not engage through traditional (and often staid) party structures and have the potential to provide a considerable additional resource for parties. As a regional organiser of Campaign Together reflected:

> I think why people got involved with campaign tools like Campaign Together and what Momentum were offering is because a lot of people, and I heard this from talking to people, were similar to me in that they were intimidated to go to [party] meetings or they didn't enjoy them and they found it hard to get involved and they wanted to—this felt like something autonomous or indirect. (Interview with regional organiser, July 2017)

These bodies innovatively utilise important resources in the form of email lists, digital media presence, and organisational tools (such as Slack, WhatsApp and Facebook) that help to get people involved. This potential is significant when considering the principle-agent problem parties usually face when using members (who often lie at the ideological extremes) to communicate with voters. As Enos and Hersh's work (2015) has shown, parties' reliance on members that are unrepresentative of the general public can prove counterproductive in attempts to campaign. By drawing on the energies of citizens who may not feel sufficiently enthused to join a party, but who may nevertheless share party values, satellite campaigns can provide parties with a wider set of advocates, who may be better placed to articulate their appeal. Digital therefore helps to enable the transition back and forth between being a party-sympathizer to carrying out the role of a party-activist, further blurring the lines between models of party membership and affiliation (Chadwick, 2007, 2017; Scarrow, 2015; Guaja, 2015). This can occur in the confines of one party or across party boundaries, as organisations like Campaign Together directed citizens to campaign for a range of different parties in order to minimise the Conservative Party's electoral success. Intermediary bodies can therefore enhance party campaigns by providing new activists and resource.

An additional benefit of satellite campaigns is the potential for innovation. As organisations less restricted by legal requirements and responsibilities, these bodies have the space to innovate and trial new tools that parties may be wary of promoting. In this way, Momentum developed the 'My Nearest Marginal' tool which allowed campaigners to identify marginal seats and offer lifts or car shares with others from their area who wanted to travel to campaign. This tool helped to target the campaigning activities of hundreds of volunteers into the areas where campaigning was deemed to have the most significant effect. The capacity of a central party to develop and regulate such software is far more complex due to legal duties (especially when encouraging car sharing), hence innovation might emerge more easily when originating from beyond parties (Williamson, Miller and Fallon, 2010).

Despite these advantages, satellite campaigns also raise multiple questions regarding party control, specifically in terms of how parties should link to and work alongside these campaigns. Although some intermediary organisations have permanent infrastructure, others emerge purely around elections. Whilst, as Marengo (2013) argued, electoral campaigns are an opportunity to reach out to and empower non-party members, there is a challenge in capitalising on such links throughout the electoral cycle. It is not yet clear how embedded these organisations are in the campaign landscape, and so, even for strongly partisan organisations, parties cannot necessarily rely on—or even predict—their support. Furthermore, it is unclear whether the support offered by satellite campaigns is always welcomed. In the high-profile seat of Sheffield Hallam, where Labour defeated the former Liberal Democrat leader Nick Clegg, the contribution of satellite campaigns was unclear. On the one hand the winning Labour candidate Jared O'Mara was quoted as saying, 'The contribution of Momentum members in South Yorkshire and beyond was exemplary . . . It was a blessing to have them on board campaigning to get me elected.' (*The Week*, 2017). However, an interview piece in *The Guardian* provides a different take:

> Momentum has, incidentally, tried to claim Hallam for one of its victories. But O'Mara isn't having this. 'No, no. I reject that entirely. I was

grateful for their help, but it was a victory for every shade of red in the party. There are some really good eggs in there, but there are also a few people that ... well, I maybe want to put a bit of distance between them and myself.' (Cooke, 2017)

Parties will therefore need to consider whether and how they relate to intermediary organisations and satellite campaigns, and whether there may be institutional advantages to creating links that help to sustain and harness this enthusiasm. This is particularly important because organisations such as Campaign Together and Momentum maintain their own activist lists and communication channels that parties do not control. This lack of direct access to a reserve army of additional volunteers renders parties reliant either on building productive links with intermediary bodies, or developing their own systems by which to capture contact information and attempt to involve such individuals in party activities. Yet such activities may undermine what is attractive about satellite campaigns: that they are flexible and orbiting, not integrated into official party campaigns. They appeal to activists who consider themselves as 'doers' and not 'joiners' (Scarrow, 2015). If these organisations become more embedded in the campaign landscape in the long term, negotiating this boundary will be key.

3.   Conclusion

The 2017 digital election campaigns may well be remembered for the normalisation of Facebook advertising and for the developing significance of satellite campaigns, but we should remember that digital remains one of many tools used by political parties. Like the printing press, typewriter or computer before it, digital technology enables parties to carry out existing functions more efficiently and within more expansive parameters, but its capacity to transform current practice is not deterministic. Rather, political activists, and especially those within parties, must consciously decide to engage with digital tools to promote a different kind of practice if lasting change is to occur (Lilleker and Jackson, 2010, p. 92).

Clearly, parties' use of Facebook advertising relocates activities that have previously been conducted using internal party databases on to a digital social media platform. Traditional electoral campaigning has not been revolutionised in this sense— it has just gained a new dimension alongside face-to-face canvassing, leafleting, and phone banking. But the normalisation of this type of campaigning does raise important questions about public acceptance of such tools, as well as the complexities of regulating the digital sphere and the subsequent power of finance to buy electoral advantage.

Digital media in the general election of 2017 has also facilitated the growing visibility of satellite campaigns. However, the success of these campaigns and the intermediary organisations that drive them rests on contingent factors that make it difficult to assess at this stage both their influence and permanence as a feature of electioneering. Much of this infrastructure appears left-leaning or more specifically driven by support for the current Labour leader, and hence may be far more unfamiliar to the Conservative Party or UKIP. Given the unpredictability of the 2017 results, and our understanding of the difference that grassroots campaigns can make (Fisher, Cutts and Fieldhouse, 2011), this suggests that more traditionally right-wing parties could benefit from promoting and encouraging such bodies to emerge. However, if there is no organic support for such developments, parties could be accused of 'astroturfing' such campaigns, which is unlikely to get them the support and resources they need to target marginal seats in an effective way.

Cumulatively, these insights reveal that there is considerable ambiguity about the implications of these trends, specifically in terms of what we expect from campaigns. Whether driven by ethical concerns over the conduct and regulation of parties' Facebook advertising, or reflecting ambiguity over the boundaries and scope of parties' 'official' campaigns, our understanding of what constitutes electoral campaigning is evolving in line with developments in the digital realm. For parties it appears that there are considerable benefits to be gained from experimenting with new technology, learning from others, and perhaps most controversially, being willing to relinquish some control over their election campaigns. And yet the longer-term implications of these trends are by no means clear. The public's tolerance of new practices, and their willingness to embrace different organisational forms and ideas, requires further investigation to examine what is wanted and expected of parties' campaigns today.

References

Aldrich, J., Gibson, R., Cantijoch, M and Konitzer, T. (2016) 'Getting Out the Vote in the Social Media Era: Are Digital Tools Changing the Extent, Nature And Impact of Party Contacting in Elections?', *Party Politics*, **22**, 165–178.

Allen, N. and Birch, S. (2015) *Ethics and Integrity in British Politics: How Citizens Judge their Politicians' Conduct and Why It Matters*, Cambridge, Cambridge University Press·

Bakir, V. and McStay, A. (2017) 'Was it AI wot won it'? Hyper-Targeting and Profiling Emotions Online', accessed at http://www.electionanalysis.uk/uk-election-analysis-2017/section-5-the-digital-campaign/was-it-ai-wot-won-it-hyper-targeting-and-profiling-emotions-online/ on 26 July 2017.

Bale, T. (2017) 'Was It the Labour Doorstep or the Labour Smartphone that Swung It for Jeremy?', accessed at http://www.electionanalysis.uk/uk-election-analysis-2017/section-4-parties-and-the-campaign/was-it-the-labour-doorstep-or-the-labour-smartphone-that-swung-it-for-jeremy/ on 26 July 2017.

Bond, D. (2017, 14 May) 'Facebook Key to Winning UK General Election, Political Parties Say', *Financial Times*, accessed at https://www.ft.com/content/c78c3bd0-36f8-11e7-99bd-13beb0903fa3?mhq5j=e2 on 12 July 2017.

Bond, R., Fariss, C., Jones, J., Kramer, A., Marlow, C., and Settle, J. (2012) 'A 61-Million-person Experiment in Social Influence and Political Mobilization', *Nature*, **489**, 295–298.

Cadwalladr, C. (2017, 27 May) 'Revealed: Tory "Dark" Ads Targeted Voters' Facebook Feeds in Welsh Marginal Seat', *Guardian*, accessed at https://www.theguardian.com/politics/2017/may/27/conservatives-facebook-dark-ads-data-protection-election on 31 July 2017.

Chadwick, A. (2017) 'Corbyn, Labour, Digital Media, and the 2017 UK Election', accessed at http://www.electionanalysis.uk/uk-election-analysis-2017/section-5-the-digital-campaign/corbyn-labour-digital-media-and-the-2017-uk-election/ on 28 July 2017.

Chadwick, A. (2007) 'Digital Network Repertoires and Organizational Hybridity', *Political Communication*, **24**, 283–301.

Chadwick, A. and Stromer-Galley, J. (2016) 'Digital Media, Power, and Democracy in Parties and Election Campaigns: Party Decline or Party Renewal?', *The International Journal of Press/Politics*, **21**, 283–293.

Cooke, R. (2017, 18 June) 'Jared O'Mara, the Pub-owning First-time MP Who Won Nick Clegg's Seat', *Guardian*, accessed at https://www.theguardian.com/politics/2017/jun/18/jared-omara-labour-mp-sheffield-hallam-defeated-nick-clegg on 1 August 2017.

Cookson, R. and Gordon, S. (2016, 25 April) ' EU Referendum Campaigns Make Facebook Their Friend', *Financial Times*, accessed at https://www.ft.com/content/82be41ce-088c-11e6-a623-b84d06a39ec2 on 26 July 2017.

Council of Europe (2017, 9 March) 'Feasibility Study on the Use of Internet in Elections', *Committee of experts on Media Pluralism and Transparency of Media Ownership (MSI-MED)* accessed at https://rm.coe.int/16806fd666, on 12 September 2017.

Cram, L., Llewellyn, C., Hill, R. and Magdy, W. (2017) 'UK General Election 2017: a Twitter Analysis', Neuropolitics Research Lab, University of Edinburgh, UK in Changing Europe, accessed at http://ukandeu.ac.uk/research-papers/general-elections-2017-a-twitter-analysis/ on 28 July 2017.

Dean, J. (2017) 'Politicising Fandom', *The British Journal of Politics and International Relations*, **19**, 408–424.

DigitalsLBi (2015) 'The General Election 2015: Insights on Digital Activity', *DigitalsLBi*, accessed at https://www.iabuk.net/system/tdf/white-paper-docs/General%20Election%202015%20-%20Whitepaper%20by%20DigitasLBi%5B1%5D.pdf?file=1&type=node&id=23331 on 12 July 2017.

Dutceac Segesten, A. and Bossetta, M. (2017) 'Sharing is Caring: Labour Supporters Use of Social Media #GE2017', accessed at http://www.electionanalysis.uk/uk-election-analysis-2017/section-5-the-digital-campaign/sharing-is-caring-labour-supporters-use-of-social-media-ge2017/ on 26 July 2017.

Edwards, A. (2006) 'ICT Strategies of Democratic Intermediaries: A View on the Political System in the Digital Age', *Information Polity*, **11**, 163–176.

Enos, R. and Hersh, E. (2015) 'Party Activists as Campaign Advertisers: The Ground Campaign as a Principal-Agent Problem', *American Political Science Review*, **109**, 252–278.

Fisher, J., Cutts, D., and Fieldhouse, E. (2011) 'The Electoral Effectiveness of Constituency Campaigning in the 2010 British General Election: The "Triumph" of Labour?', *Electoral Studies*, **30**, 816–828.

Gibson, R. (2015) 'Party Change, Social Media and the Rise of "Citizen-initiated" Campaigning', *Party Politics*, **21**, 183–197.

Guaja, A. (2015) 'The Construction of Party Membership', *European Journal of Political Research*, **54**, 232–248.

Kreiss, D. (2010) 'Digital Campaigning'. In Coleman, S., and Freelon, D (eds) *Handbook of Digital Politics*, Cheltenham, Edwards Elgar, pp. 118–135.

Lilleker, D. and Jackson, N. (2010) 'Towards a More Participatory Style of Election Campaigning: The Impact of Web 2.0 on the UK 2010 General Election', *Policy and Internet*, **2**, 69–98.

Marengo, U. (2013, 23 May) 'Real Time Political Engagement', *Policy Network*, accessed at http://www.policy-network.net/pno_detail.aspx?ID=4406&title=Real+time+political+engagement on 28 July 2017.

Metro (2017) 'The Memes that Decided the Outcome of the General Election', accessed at http://metro.co.uk/2017/06/11/the-memes-that-decided-the-outcome-of-the-general-election-6701277/#ixzz4oPOgL8ky on 28 July 2017.

Miller, C. (2016) *The Rise of Digital Politics*, London, Demos.

Nielsen, R. (2013) 'Mundane Internet Tools, the Risk of Exclusion, and Reflexive Movements—Occupy Wall Street and Political Uses of Digital Networked Technologies', *The Sociological Quarterly*, **54**, 173–177.

Norris, P. (2012) *The Digital Divide: Citizen Engagement, Information Poverty, and the Internet Worldwide*, Oxford, Oxford University Press.

O'Brien, S. (2015, 13 March) 'Chalk + Talk—Digital Campaigning: Where is it happening?' *Social Market Foundation*, accessed at http://www.smf.co.uk/chalk-talk-digital-campaigning-where-is-it-happening-who-does-it-reach-and-does-it-work/ on 3 November 2016.

Peggs, A. (2017, 12 June) 'How Momentum Changed British Politics Forever', *The Huffington Post*, accessed at http://www.huffingtonpost.co.uk/adam-peggs/momentum-jeremy-corbyn_b_17054254.html on 26 July 2017.

Scarrow, S. (2015) *Beyond Party Members*, Oxford, Oxford University Press.

Shephard, M. (2017) 'Corbyn and the Social Media Breakthough', accessed at http://www.electionanalysis.uk/uk-election-analysis-2017/section-5-the-digital-campaign/social-media-and-the-corbyn-breakthrough/ on 27 July 2017.

The Electoral Commission (2016) *UK Parliamentary General Election 2015: Campaign Spending Report*, London, The Electoral Commission.

The Electoral Commission (2017) *The 2016 EU referendum*, London, The Electoral Commission.

The Week (2017, 12 June) 'How Momentum Helped Sway the General Election', *The Week*, accessed at http://www.theweek.co.uk/general-election-2017/85501/how-momentum-helped-sway-the-general-election on 1 August 2017.

Vaccari, C. and Valeriani, A. (2016) 'Party Campaigners or Citizen Campaigners? How Social Media Deepen and Broaden Party-Related Engagement', *International Journal of Press/Politics*, **21**, 294–312.

Walsh, M. (2017) 'The Alternate and Influential World of the Political Parties' Facebook Feeds', accessed at http://www.electionanalysis.uk/uk-election-analysis-2017/section-5-the-digital-campaign/the-alternate-and-influential-world-of-the-political-parties-facebook-feeds/ on 28 July 2017.

Ward, M. (2017, 2 June) 'Facebook Becomes Key Tool in Parties' Political Message', BBC, accessed at http://www.bbc.co.uk/news/election-2017-40119962 on 12 July 2017.

Waterson, J. (2017, 6 July) 'Here's How Labour Ran An Under-The-Radar Dark Ads Campaign During The General Election', *Buzzfeed Politics*, accessed at https://www.buzzfeed.com/jimwaterson/heres-how-labour-ran-an-under-the-radar-dark-ads-campaign?utm_term=.beqae9KNj#.jm7p1m8vV on 1 August 2017.

Whiteley, P. and Seyd, P. (2003) 'Party Election Campaigning in Britain: The Labour Party', *Party Politics*, **9**, 637–652.

Williamson, A., Miller, L., and Fallon, F. (2010) *Behind the Digital Campaign: An Exploration of the Use, Impact and Regulation of Digital Campaigning*, London, Hansard Society.

Britain Votes (2017) 203–221

STEPHEN WARD AND DOMINIC WRING*

Out with the Old, In with the New? The Media Campaign

The 2017 General Election will likely be remembered as the campaign where the once dominant forms of TV and print journalism were challenged by digital platforms. This chapter analyses this development while also acknowledging that social media networks do not operate in isolation from their more traditional counterparts and content is often shared between them. That said, digital networks did provide Labour Party supporters with significant opportunities to challenge and rebut claims made by the Conservative-dominated press during this campaign. A significant amount of this material focused on the merits (or not) of the two major rival parties and most especially their leaders. In comparison, other politicians received considerably less attention than in 2015.

The 2017 media campaign was not expected to showcase the kinds of innovation or generate the many surprises it subsequently provided. Its unexpected calling meant there was minimal time for campaign planning. In media terms, the rival platforms were often portrayed as though they were operating in parallel universes. So-called traditional media, especially newspapers, were seeking to appeal to older core voters and seen as relentlessly negative, anti-Jeremy Corbyn and pro-Conservative. By contrast, social media was viewed as a vibrant sphere dominated by young, left-leaning voices with a heavily pro-Corbyn agenda. In the aftermath, it could be argued that 2017 marked a watershed moment, one where social media finally proved its electoral worth and the power of the press was significantly challenged. Intriguingly, the media election was not, however, solely characterized by innovation given it too would hark back to an era of two-party politics. Thus the campaign proved to be a highly presidential affair dominated by both of the main parties and their leaders. These factors will be in turn considered in assessments of the role and nature of traditional, as well as social, media in this election.

*Stephen Ward, Department of Politics, University of Salford, s.j.ward@salford.ac.uk; Dominic Wring, Department of Social Sciences, Loughborough University, d.j.wring@lboro.ac.uk

doi:10.1093/pa/gsx057

1.   'Strong or stable'? The Tories' communication malfunction

It came as a shock when, shortly after the UK had agreed to invoke Article 50 to leave to the EU, Theresa May reneged on her earlier promise and called the General Election for 8 June. Although a surprise, the *Daily Mail* welcomed this as an opportunity to 'CRUSH THE SABOTEURS', a reference to parliamentarians opposed to Brexit (*Daily Mail*, 2017a, p. 1). Unfortunately for May, the supportive media coverage and consistent polling leads she had enjoyed since entering Downing Street were about to come to a dramatic end. May's limitations as a communicator were exposed during the election. Her apparent discomfort and even robotic style became self-evident in the way she repeatedly recited the party's initial advertising strap-line 'Strong (and) Stable Leadership in the National Interest' during her opening campaign appearances. Later, forced to deny she had performed a 'U-turn' over her manifesto's so-called 'dementia tax', the 'Maybot' was increasingly criticised by media commentators and satirists who recycled the 'strong and stable' phrase to mock her (Crace, 2017). The Prime Minister remained the overwhelmingly dominant face of her party in news coverage terms (Scammell, 2017).

The two rivals for the premiership dominated reporting of this campaign (Table 13.1). Significantly, in percentage terms the Tory leader featured twice as much in reporting of the election as her predecessor David Cameron had in 2015 (Deacon *et al.*, 2015). That Cameron had, like May this time, been the single most prominent politician two years before underlined the even more highly personalised, presidential nature of the 2017 campaign.

Despite her media prominence Theresa May refused to appear on live television alongside her rivals. Her strategists likely calculated that the Conservatives'

Table 13.1 Most prominent politicians (TV and print news appearances)

Rank	Politician	% items
1	Theresa May (Con)	30.1%
2	Jeremy Corbyn (Lab)	26.7%
3	Tim Farron (Lib Dem)	6.8%
4	Nicola Sturgeon (SNP)	3.7%
5	Boris Johnson (Con)	3.6%
6	John McDonnell (Lab)	3.4%
7	Paul Nuttall (UKIP)	3.4%
8	Amber Rudd (Con)	2.8%
8	Diane Abbott (Lab)	2.8%
10	Emily Thornberry (Lab)	1.8%

Source: Deacon *et al.*, 2017a, p. 7.

substantial lead in the polls meant the Prime Minister had little to gain from participating in face-to-face debates (Coleman, 2017). Although initially uncontroversial with most colleagues, May's risk-averse decision might not have been so harmful to her reputation had other aspects of the ensuing Conservative campaign not proven so problematic. The Prime Minister explained her refusal to appear in leader debates was because she preferred to 'get out and about and meet voters' (BBC, 2017). But this claim was visibly undermined when May was subsequently filmed knocking on a door and failing to elicit any response from the occupant. When the Prime Minister did spontaneously converse with a voter in Oxfordshire it proved an uncomfortable experience in which she listened to complaints about government funding cuts to disability care (Shaw, 2017). Both embarrassments highlighted the obvious limitations of interpersonal campaigning, not to mention May's stated reason for not participating in a media opportunity that would have reached the largest possible audience of voters.

May's refusal to participate in face-to-face leader debates rendered her open to the charge she was seeking to avoid proper democratic scrutiny. This perception was reinforced by carefully controlled 'public' appearances in which she spoke in front of supporters holding Conservative placards. This now familiar, but somewhat staid format, was increasingly criticised by journalists keen to cross-examine politicians about live stories rather than passively listen to their pre-scripted messages (for an earlier critique of this see Oborne, 2005). This tension was palpable in the questioning of a seemingly panicked May about her so-called 'dementia tax' in what was intended to be another routine controlled appearance soon after the party's manifesto launch. Elsewhere even straightforward queries from a local reporter in Plymouth were met with stock responses from the Prime Minister during an awkward interview where the journalist likened their encounter to 'a postmodern version' of popular BBC radio comedy programme *Just A Minute* (Blackledge, 2017).

Once the Prime Minister's credibility had been questioned, particularly over the Conservatives' apparent manifesto U-turn, every aspect of her self-promotion was more readily challenged. Her appearance on supposedly 'softer' interview programmes did not necessarily convey the impression she might have hoped. On primetime BBC1 magazine-style *The One Show* May and her husband Philip digressed into talking about who did the 'boy jobs' and 'girl jobs' at home. Similarly, when ITV journalist Julie Etchingham asked the Conservative leader what was the 'naughtiest' thing she had done in her life, her surreal response was to admit to once running through a field of wheat when she was younger. The light-hearted questioning elicited responses that were further gifts for satirists and also offered a demonstration of how even the most seemingly innocuous queries could help undermine a politician's image as a credible figure.

2. For many audiences not a few journalists: Labour's media strategy

There was a marked consensus among the expert 'commentariat' that Labour was on course for a major defeat in this election. The *Financial Times'* political correspondent summed this up when he suggested that 'One thing is certain: this is going to be a very bad election for a divided Labour Party and a weak Mr Corbyn' (Payne, 2017). The reasons for the impending landslide defeat were the supposedly ineffectual Jeremy Corbyn, the party's 'lurch to the left' and its alleged lack of credibility on key issues. Corbyn's leadership abilities had been constantly questioned since his elevation to the post and were once again challenged on ITV's *Good Morning Britain* only hours before the election was announced. Interviewer Piers Morgan compared his guest to Arsène Wenger, the beleaguered manager of their favourite football team Arsenal, in suggesting he too might want to consider his position so that the team could recover and progress. The ensuing General Election would prove to both a liberating period, as well as a turning point for the Labour leader.

The campaign Jeremy Corbyn led confounded expectations, particularly among his many critics in the media, which had even included Labour-leaning newspapers such as the *Guardian* and the *Mirror*. As the election progressed they were the only dailies that supported the party, as Table 13.2 shows. The overwhelming majority of national newspaper coverage remained trenchantly hostile towards Labour, rather than favourable towards the Conservatives.

This, however, temporarily changed during the hiatus over the 'dementia tax' when the focus of criticism briefly switched to the Tories, as Figure 13.1 demonstrates (see 'Week 3'). Nonetheless the overwhelming bulk of commentary in the

Table 13.2 Political allegiance and circulation of daily national Newspapers, May 2017

Title	Declaration	Print Circulation (m)	Unique online browsers (m)
Daily Mirror	Labour	0.65	5.41
Daily Express	Conservative	0.38	2.05
Daily Star	No declaration	0.43	1.02
Sun	Conservative	1.58	4.96
Daily Mail	Conservative	1.44	15.37
Daily Telegraph	Conservative	0.48	4.78
The Guardian	Labour	0.15	8.47*
The Times	Conservative	0.46	Paywall
I	No declaration	0.27	6.58 (NB independent.co.uk)
Financial Times	Conservative	0.20	Paywall

Sources: Mayhew, 2017*a*, *b*; Ponsford, 2017.
Note: *denotes figure for April

press was negative rather than positive, and most of the negative was overwhelmingly directed at Labour.

Lurid headlines in right-wing newspapers depicted Corbyn and some of his colleagues as extremists with unacceptable views on terrorism, an issue that became highly salient during the campaign because of the heinous attacks on London and Manchester. The *Sun* (2017, p. 10) used the testimony of a former Irish Republican paramilitary to accuse the Labour leader and Shadow Chancellor John McDonnell of being 'IRA fanboys' in the past. The *Daily Mail* similarly condemned Corbyn, McDonnell and Shadow Home Secretary Diane Abbott as 'this troika' of 'APOLOGISTS FOR TERROR' on account of them allegedly 'befriending Britain's enemies' (*Daily Mail*, 2017b, p. 1). On polling day, the *Sun* rehearsed many of the now familiar attacks with a front-page mock-up of the party leader and a plea to readers 'DON'T CHUCK BRITAIN IN THE . . . COR-BIN' alongside a ten point charge list that denounced him as a 'TERRORIST FRIEND', 'ENEMY OF BUSINESS' and 'MARXIST EXTREMIST' among other things. Perhaps unsurprisingly Labour strategists shunned most mainstream print journalism, with the exception of friendlier publications such as those belonging to the Mirror Group (Waterson, 2017).

Some of the negative stories in the print media about Corbyn also featured in broadcast coverage of the election. For instance, Sky News' interviewer Sophy Ridge cross-examined Corbyn over his past involvement in Northern Irish politics prior to the peace process. This led to some tense exchanges during a campaign in which he appeared to gain confidence. Rather than passively accept journalists' preconceived agendas, Labour also sought to shape the news and this

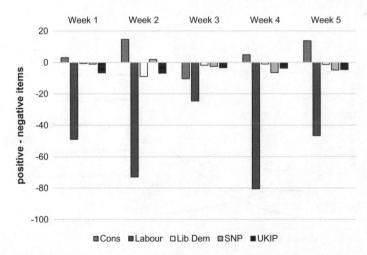

Figure 13.1. Weekly campaign press evaluations of parties (weighted by circulation)
Source: Deacon *et al.*, 2017b.

was most amply demonstrated in the days following the two atrocities that temporarily suspended campaigning.

Speaking after the Manchester bombing, Corbyn linked the outrage to foreign policy decisions he had previously opposed and now contended were destabilising the world. Similarly, following the London attack, Labour argued the government cuts would further hamper the ability of the police and public services to prevent and respond to similar incidents in the future. Far from being potentially damaging to a party depicted as being 'soft' on the issue, an increased prominence afforded to defence and security related news coverage (Figure 13.2) was met with a clear response from Corbyn. More predictably, Brexit was also an issue during the campaign, particularly at the beginning, but not the all-consuming one some had predicted.

The leaking of the Labour manifesto before its launch proved fortuitous given journalists spent more time discussing its contents than they might otherwise. This is not to say the party's presentation of its policies was without incident. Corbyn's record and plans were closely interrogated by a vocal group of voters, some highly critical, on the BBC1 *Question Time Leaders' Special*, as well as Channel 4's equivalent programme. Although he appeared resilient during these occasionally uncomfortable experiences, the party leader was not always able to readily respond. When asked on BBC Five Live about the cost implications of his ambitious plans for childcare on the day the policy was being promoted, Corbyn struggled to answer. Similarly, Diane Abbott was embarrassed during an interview with LBC radio in which she was unable to explain the amount of funding that would be needed to support an expansion in police numbers.

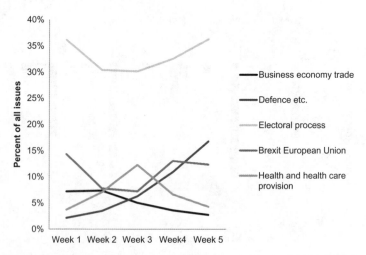

Figure 13.2. Proportional prominence of campaign issues, week by week (TV and Press)
Source: Deacon *et al.*, 2017a, p. 16.

High-profile gaffes like those of Corbyn and Abbott contributed to a greater emphasis being placed on policy, at the expense of 'process' that typically dominated election news; in 2017 this figure was at a third of all coverage, markedly down on its 2015 equivalent (Deacon *et al.*, 2017*b*). And although Labour appeared keen to campaign on substantive issues, Corbyn did emulate his Conservative opponent by appearing on *The One Show* where he seemed comfortable talking about his upbringing and hobbies. Unlike May, the Labour leader's partner was not a fellow guest and nor did he talk much about his current family life. The popular appeal of Corbyn was perhaps most memorably captured in television footage of his tour of the country where he was met by enthusiasm (Parry, 2017). Facing a concert crowd in Wirral he was greeted by an apparently spontaneous chant of his name that would continue to be heard throughout the rest of the campaign and beyond.

3. Finding their voices? Coverage of the minor parties

The growing confidence of the Labour campaign led Corbyn to make a surprise appearance in the final major face-to-face televised leaders' debate. Previously he had said he would not participate without the Prime Minister also being involved. Although these kinds of live encounters are scrutinised for any perceived gaffes by those speaking, it was perhaps Theresa May's decision to stay away that was more important than anything that happened on the night itself. The controversy over May's no-show also gave Liberal Democrat leader Tim Farron one of his few opportunities to make an impression on the campaign. Using his closing remarks as the penultimate speaker, Farron rounded on May and the Home Secretary who was representing her: 'Amber Rudd is up next. She is not Prime Minister. The Prime Minister is not here so she can't be bothered, so why should you. In fact *Bake Off* is on BBC2 next, why not make yourself a brew? You are not worth Theresa May's time, don't give her yours' (Mortimer, 2017). Moreover, he urged viewers to change channels before the Prime Minister's stand-in Amber Rudd made her final remarks.

The Liberal Democrat leader's bonhomie was in evidence when he showed himself to be open to scrutiny by engaging in conversation during a televised encounter with an irate Leave supporter. But Farron was less patient when the issue of whether his Christianity conflicted with party policy advocating gay equality was repeatedly brought up in media interviews. Similarly, when challenged over his support for a second EU referendum by the BBC's lead interrogator Andrew Neil, their interview descended into a row. The Farron interview was one of a number Neil conducted with party leaders on behalf of the BBC. In his programme with Neil, UKIP's Paul Nuttall was similarly discomforted when asked about inflammatory comments attacking Islam made by one of his fellow

MEPs. Nuttall had been keen for positive public exposure due to the marked decline of news interest in his party that mirrored its collapse in the polls. UKIP also lost the support of the *Express*, the fiercely Eurosceptic newspaper that had been the only daily national newspaper to endorse it during the previous election.

Having assumed a high profile in 2015, national news coverage of the SNP also substantially declined in this campaign, the reporting of which was now dominated by the two major parties as shown by Figure 13.3. Despite enjoying representation in the leaders' debate, the Greens and Plaid Cymru were largely ignored by the media. But at least they, unlike the similarly marginalised DUP, had a place in the live UK-wide televised leaders' programming. The Northern Irish party had protested its exclusion from this by broadcasters. Following the result and election of a hung parliament that gave them the balance of power, there was far greater coverage of the DUP than the tiny amount it had received in the preceding campaign (Deacon *et al.*, 2017*a*).

4. Parties and social media competition: The unexpected election?

At the outset of the election, there was arguably less media interest in online campaigning than the previous four campaigns. The ubiquitous nature of Internet technologies meant their novelty value for journalists had worn off. Moreover, the seemingly pre-determined nature of the result did little to stimulate interest in the campaign. Rather than the usual hype around whether the Internet would swing it for one particular party, there were fears, following the US presidential election, of social media promoting fake news, abuse and a polarization of the electorate. Yet, as the campaign progressed, social media was highlighted as a

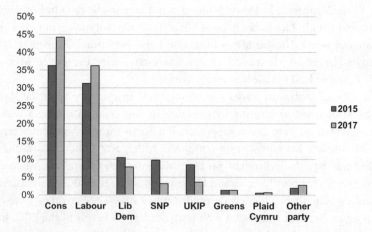

Figure 13.3. Party prominence in the 2017 versus 2015 general elections (TV and press)
Source: Deacon *et al.*, 2017*b*, p. 370.

significant factor in the unexpected rise in support for Labour. It was generally accepted, even by some Conservatives, that Labour won the 2017 social media battle and had been particularly successful at mobilizing young voter support.

Social media has sometimes been viewed as a more open and less skewed communication playing field producing different patterns of competition and more accessibility for minority parties than mainstream media channels (Ward *et al.*, 2018). At the previous 2015 election, there were mixed messages in terms of online campaign competition. Labour was seen as dominating the Twittersphere, whilst the Conservatives utilised negative advertising on Facebook (Wring and Ward, 2015).

The 2017 campaign was somewhat different with Labour and Jeremy Corbyn seen as a dominant force across a range of platforms. Moreover, in line with Labour's rise in the opinion polls, Labour's advantage appeared to increase over the course of the campaign. Labour maintained their dominant position on Twitter in terms of a range of basic measures such as followers, likes and shares (Bauchowitz and Hanska, 2017). Labour supporting hashtags and accounts outperformed the Conservatives. Similarly, when examining the most popular election hashtags, the Labour advantage was again underlined with groupings of both Labour and Corbyn hashtags appearing in the top six election terms. While the Conservatives and May hashtags appear in eighth/ninth position, they were a long way distant in terms of numbers. By the last two weeks of the campaign, one study indicated that Labour's dominance was increasing—Labour accounted for 61.9% of party related tweets during one week compared to just 17% for the Conservatives (Kaminska *et al.*, 2017).

Twitter also seemed to magnify the importance of party leaders and their personal accounts. Here again, Labour dominated with Corbyn's account gaining by far the most mentions and retweets—twice as many as May and four times as much as official Labour and Conservative party accounts. Corbyn began with the campaign with over twice as many followers as May and extended this advantage during the campaign with a 45% increase (Cecil, 2017).

Whilst Labour may have maintained and extended its advantage on Twitter, Facebook was seen as the key social media battleground for three main reasons: first, it reaches a greater potential share of the electorate with well over half UK population now having Facebook accounts; second, its demographic profile, although still skewed, is more diverse than other social media; third, Facebook offers the greatest potential in terms of data mining, profiling and then advertising and targeting. As with Twitter, Labour's Facebook following grew substantially to close to a million over the course of the campaign; the number of likes grew by 75% compared to just 10% for Conservatives; Labour also had three-times as many Facebook shares.

Use of other social media platforms appeared more-patchy. However, the Conservatives reportedly used paid advertising on a range of other outlets particularly YouTube. According to BBC reports though, these were more randomly distributed compared to the micro-targeting on Facebook. Snapchat, one of the most popular social media outlets amongst teenagers, was used fairly cautiously. The main party leaders and the co-leaders of the Green Party took part in a rather awkward Snapchat Q&A session. Labour latterly appealed to Snapchat users to turn out to vote, while the Conservatives experimented with paid content (BBC, 2017).

Despite its reputation as being a more open media space for minority parties, few minor parties made much of an impact online in 2017. The eventual dominance of the two main parties in vote-share terms was reflected in many of the social media metrics. The increasing complexities and resource demands of data-driven marketing strategies clearly limit smaller parties' ability to compete. But even in basic terms, the Liberal Democrats, for example, didn't even appear in the top 20 election-hashtag groupings. Amongst the smaller parties, only the SNP and Nicola Sturgeon managed to register much of a presence across Twitter and Facebook in terms of following, discussion and sharing (Cram *et al.*, 2017; Kaminska *et al.*, 2017).

Patterns of major party dominance were also seen in terms of candidate presence on the two main social media platforms. Overall, 68% of candidates ran Twitter accounts with a similar number maintaining a Facebook presence. This masks slightly different underlying patterns. Labour had most candidates on Twitter with 88%, well ahead of the Conservatives, SNP and Liberal Democrats. On Facebook, SNP candidates had the largest presence followed by Labour. Other minor parties, however, lagged well behind with a 62% Facebook presence and only just over half their candidates being found on Twitter. Indeed, the UKIP Party Chairman was reported to have instructed candidates to close their own social media sites as he 'hated social media' because it simply caused 'more grief for the party' (www.order-order.com, 2017).

Whilst basic social media metrics such as followers, retweets and links are fairly crude measures of the importance or success of campaigns, this time most pointed in one direction. As one media report put it, 'Labour tweeted more, posted more and shared more than all its rivals' (Turner and Kahn, 2017).

5. Online campaign organisation: Networks, movements and sharing

Over the past decade, two broad models of social media campaigning have attracted attention. First, a more decentralized, networked, citizen-led style of campaign (Gibson, 2013), tending to focus on social media's participatory possibilities and where the actions of campaign activists/supporters determine the direction or focus of a campaign. Participatory acts and engagement are often at the heart of this approach. The second emergent model is that of data-driven or big-data campaigns (Anstead, 2017). Here the concentration is on the exploitation of data gathering/mining possibilities of social media to target personalized marketing and advertising to key groups of voters in swing seats. The notion of data-driven campaigning attracted attention at a number of recent elections and during the EU referendum campaign (*Economist*, 2017). However, the use of data and marketing in itself is not, of course, new, but the Internet's potential for information surveillance provides opportunities to drill down ever further into voter sentiment.

In the 2017 campaign, superficially at least, the Conservatives appeared to lean towards a more data-driven, top-down approach. Labour with its newly reinvigorated party membership appeared to incorporate more of the citizen-led aspect. This may simply be a reflection of the respective parties' current strengths and structures rather than any necessary strategic choice. Moreover, as noted below, Labour appeared to combine elements of both data-driven and supporter-enabled digital campaigning. Interestingly, this seems to have been reflected in Labour's formal campaign organization. Andrew Gwynne, the campaign co-ordinator revealed that

> we placed digital at the heart of our activities, with HQ teams organised into separate campaign and organisational arms. The former led on delivering the right message to the right voters, the latter on engagement and mobilization. (*Guardian*, 2017).

In the aftermath of the election, there has been considerable criticism both internally and externally of the Conservatives (digital) campaign. Critics have argued that it was too-controlled, too-negative, too-top-down (leader focused), inflexible and appeared to want simply replicate some of the 2015 campaign tactics. In short, the party forgot the social element to social media (Morgan, 2017; Mason, 2017). The Conservatives had, indeed, rehired many of same digital advisors from 2015 and much emphasis again was placed on micro-targeted ads via Facebook (Ruddick, 2017). However, the messages failed to resonate and were much less likely to be shared. Social media analysts noted that whilst the approach was not necessarily wrong, the messages did not always match the targets (Booth and Hern, 2017). The over-confidence of the early part of the Conservative campaign meant that advertisements were often targeted towards soft Labour voters in marginal or even relatively safe Labour seats. Little emphasis was apparently placed on digital marketing in their own marginals. The 'strong and stable' mantra seemed to find little traction with the targeted swing voters, but might have had more impact on core Conservative supporters (Booth and Hern, 2017). Furthermore, the campaign did not appear very responsive even though the data reportedly coming into Conservative Headquarters in the latter part of the campaign suggested the strategy wasn't working. The Conservative social media campaign could arguably be encapsulated in MP Greg Knight's much-ridiculed online video. His Alan Partridge-style performance saw him walk awkwardly into a bland office and woodenly deliver a banal message, rounded-off with a 1970s style musical jingle (www.LBC.co.uk, 2017). Although, to be fair to Knight, this garnered over half a million views more than some of the messages put out by his party.

Labour, by contrast, was viewed as having a more slick, flexible, and positive online campaign with sharing and mobilization at its heart (Walsh, 2017). This could be seen not just in the public metrics of followers, likes and shares, but also in their below-the-radar social media marketing. The party appeared to have learnt the lessons from 2015 where they had been massively outspent by Conservatives who successfully targeted negative attack adverts. This time Labour married both data targeting and marketing ads while also extensively encouraging grassroots engagement. They reportedly spent over £1m aiming to match the Conservatives in Facebook advertising assisted by a new digital tool 'Promote' to produce targeted hyper-localized social media marketing (Wendling, 2017).

Labour also allied themselves to so-called 'influencers' with large existing social media audiences (Pringle, 2017). A range of celebrities from music, sport and television were used to endorse Labour's message through videos and at campaign rallies which were then shared virally on social media. According to Buzzfeed analysis, these celebrity endorsements were amongst the most shared election related articles on Facebook. The support of specific types of celebrity such as Stormzy and rapper Akala were seen as boosting Corbyn's anti-establishment image and reaching out to a younger audience. Crucially, however, the content and messages aimed to gain both clicks and encourage sharing. Labour placed considerable emphasis in this campaign on video content that was likely to be shared by friends (Segesten and Bossetta, 2017; Fletcher, 2017).

Labour's other main advantage in spreading its message was what Chadwick (2017) has referred to as the party-as-movement mentality. The surge in Labour membership post-2015 meant there was a ready army of digitally-skilled supporters. Yet, in the run up to election, doubts had been raised about how valuable an asset the newer members might be. Initial research on new Labour members suggested that they were Internet engaged, but were largely clicktivists distant from the party as whole (Poletti *et al.*, 2016). There were grumbles from some local parties that the new Corbynite supporters were not interested in the hard work of the traditional doorstep campaign (Chakelian, 2017). Ultimately, though, such fears seem to have been misplaced. Labour's official campaign, assisted by advisors from the Bernie Sanders grassroots US presidential bid, was heavily supported by new Corbyn-inspired activist networks, most notably Momentum. Formed initially to bolster Corbyn's leadership position and battle-hardened from his recent leadership re-election campaign, Momentum provided both online resources and ground-level co-ordination that other parties lacked. They helped launch online tools such as My Nearest Marginal, allowing supporters to find their nearest swing seat and join with other activists (Shabi, 2017). Phone canvassing apps were also deployed along with the traditional door-knocking days. Momentum claimed that a quarter of all UK Facebook users saw Momentum videos in the last week of the campaign. Much of this was done at low cost with Momentum capitalising on volunteer skills and allowing individual supporters to create DIY campaign material.

Additionally, Labour also benefited from having its message amplified through the growth of leftist social media news sites such as The Canary, Evolve Politics and Paul Mason News, who were also able to gain considerable shares online and motivate left-leaning activists. To some extent, supporter networks and social media sites enabled Labour to bypass and to counter negativity of mainstream ('MSM') outlets (Al-Kadhi, 2017; Littunen, 2017).

6.   The impact of the social media campaign

Previous UK election campaigns have usually begun with an overhyping of technology and ended with disappointment about its limited impact. The 2017 campaign followed a somewhat different pattern with less initial hype followed by an assumption that social media made a significant impact in two ways: the mobilization of additional younger voters especially for Labour and the challenging of the mainstream media agenda and more specifically newspaper attacks on Labour and Corbyn. Reflecting on the outcome of the election, Corbyn himself expressed little doubt about the importance of social media:

> [W]hilst a number of the print media were incredibly hostile to Labour ... in reality social media has far greater reach ... Those who follow Twitter, Facebook, Snapchat and so on really helped to get the message across and it certainly resulted in the voter registration that was so important[.] (Daly, 2017)

There is plenty of circumstantial evidence that social media driven campaigning facilitated the turnout of younger voters and helped with some surprise results. In the case of voter registration, certainly social media played a role in targeting harder to reach younger people. The formal registration drive conducted by the Electoral Commission used social media extensively, even joining forces with

Snapchat to launch a geofilter entitled 'Find Your Voice'. However, importantly, it was not only the usual formal political channels promoting voter registration but a host of sources, including: celebrity videos; citizen initiatives such as Rize-up.org; a crowd-funded registration project from online campaign group 38 Degrees; as well as numerous local reminders from universities and colleges. Labour underpinned this by consistently urging people to register to vote—mentioned at all Corbyn's rallies. In contrast, strikingly, the Conservatives only sent a single social media appeal to vote.

In addition to a registration boost, one prominent argument that surfaced after the campaign was how social media was becoming an increasingly influential alternative to mainstream media. A YouGov survey sheds some perspective on the supposed social media/mainstream media divide. It provided evidence of generational shifts in media consumption and of the increasing influence of social media amongst 18-24 year olds. A range of social media outlets have now become popular with young adults as regular news sources (notably, Facebook, Twitter and Buzzfeed). These are already more important than magazines and newspapers (with the exception of the *Guardian*). Startlingly, not a single 18-24 year old in the survey saw local papers as regular news sources. Nevertheless, mainstream BBC News remains by far and away the most dominant source for all age groups. Similarly, television is seen as the most influential media on vote choice—although for 18-24 year olds, it is closely followed by social media. All age groups believe that the digital age has diminished the influence of newspapers, but the press remains important for those over 40 (Mayhew, 2017c).

7. Conclusion

Despite the growth in popularity of social media, mainstream media is not yet politically redundant. Television, particularly BBC News, remains hugely important for all ages. The divide between MSM (especially TV) and social media is somewhat of an artificial one. Mainstream media events such as the set-piece interviews (like Neil on the BBC and Ridge on Sky), leaders' television appearances (*The One Show*) and the formal leadership debates were all important in shaping social media discussion. Rather than being parallel universes, the digital sphere and mainstream media increasingly overlapped and fed off one another in this campaign. Nevertheless, there is little doubt that Labour capitalised on the reach of social media into their target audience of young and new voters. It marks the first time in the UK that social media was properly at the heart of a party election campaign. It has been noted for some time that the Internet works best for the swift mobilisation of oppositionist movements that fitted well with the reinvigorated grassroots networks of Corbyn's Labour Party.

The Conservatives lacked both the leader and the messages to engage and enthuse audiences online or offline. Perhaps even more crucially, they lacked the energized digital networks to share and spread their message. The continued decline of the party's membership base and its ageing nature suggest that this structural disadvantage is unlikely to disappear soon (Chadwick, 2017). However, Labour's success in both overcoming press hostility and dominating social media platforms still didn't deliver victory. Moreover, in an era where support and partisanship need to be constantly maintained and rebuilt, Labour cannot automatically expect to maintain this advantage nor would the oppositional movement-type approach necessarily work if they were to gain office in the near future. As Charles (2017) noted, the rise of social media means the only certainty is to expect the unexpected.

References

Al-Kadhi, A. (2017, 9 June) 'Forget the Social Media Bubble—We Made Sure that Our Voices Were Heard at this Election', *Independent*.

Anstead, N. (2017) 'Data-driven Campaigning in the 2015 UK General Election', *The International Journal of Press/Politics*, **22**, 294–313.

Bauchowitz, S. and Hanska, M. (2017, 5 June) 'How the General Election is Shaping up on Twitter', Blogs LSE, accessed at http://blogs.lse.ac.uk/politicsandpolicy/how-the-ge2017-campaign-is-shaping-up-on-twitter/on-twitter on 6 December 2017.

Booth, R and Hern, A. (2017, 9 June) 'Labour Won Social Media Election, Digital Strategists Say', *Guardian*.

BBC (2017, 19 April) 'Theresa May Says No to General Election Debates', BBC News, accessed at http://www.bbc.co.uk/news/uk-politics-39633696 on 6 December 2017.

Blackledge, S. (2017, 31 May) '"Three Minutes of Nothing": *Herald* Reporter Reflects on PM Encounter', *The Herald*, accessed at http://www.plymouthherald.co.uk/three-minutes-of-nothing-herald-reporter-reflects-on-pm-encounter/story-30363961-detail/story.html on 6 December 2017.

Cecil, N. (2017, 14 June) 'How Jeremy Corbyn Beat Theresa May in the Social Media Election War', *Evening Standard*, accessed at https://www.standard.co.uk/news/politics/how-jeremy-corbyn-beat-theresa-may-in-the-social-media-election-war-a3564746.html on 6 December 2017.

Chadwick, A. (2017) 'Corbyn, Labour, Digital Media and the 2017 UK Election'. In Thorsen, E., Jackson, D. and Lilleker, D. (eds) *UK Election Analysis 2017*, p. 89, accessed at http://eprints.bournemouth.ac.uk/29374/10/UKElectionAnalysis2017_Thorsen-Jackson-and-Lilleker_v1.pdf on 6 December 2017.

Chakelian, A. (2017, 16 May) 'Armchair Activists or Mass Mobilisers? How Momentum is Shaping Labour's Campaign', *New Statesman*.

Charles, A. (2017) 'All Lols and Trolls'. In Thorsen, E., Jackson, D. and Lilleker, D. (eds) *UK Election Analysis 2017*, p. 102, accessed at http://eprints.bournemouth.ac.uk/29374/ 10/UKElectionAnalysis2017_Thorsen-Jackson-and-Lilleker_v1.pdf on 6 December 2017.

Coleman, S. (2017) 'Ducking the Debate'. In Thorsen, E., Jackson, D. and Lilleker, D. (eds) *UK Election Analysis 2017*, p. 43, accessed at http://eprints.bournemouth.ac.uk/ 29374/10/UKElectionAnalysis2017_Thorsen-Jackson-and-Lilleker_v1.pdf on 6 December 2017.

Crace, J. (2017, 10 July) 'The Making of the Maybot: A Year of Mindless Slogans, U-turn and Denials', *Guardian*, accessed at https://www.theguardian.com/politics/2017/jul/10/ making-maybot-theresa-may-rise-and-fall on 6 December 2017.

Cram, L., Llewellyn, C., Hill, R. and Magdy, W. (2017) 'General Election 2017: A Twitter Analysis', Neuropolitics Research Lab, School of Political and Social Science University of Edinburgh, accessed at http://blogs.sps.ed.ac.uk/neuropolitics/2017/06/ on 6 December 2017.

Daily Mail (2017a, 19 April) 'Crush the Saboteurs'.

Daily Mail (2017a, 7 June) 'Apologists for Terror'.

Daly, R. (2017, 25 June) 'Jeremy Corbyn Says Social Media was a Big Part in Labour's Election Support', *New Musical Express*, accessed at http://www.nme.com/news/ jeremy-corbyn-says-social-media-big-part-labours-election-support-2093864 on 6 December 2017.

Deacon, D., Downey, J., Stanyer, J. and Wring, D. (2015) 'Media Coverage of the UK General Election 2015', Report 5, May, Loughborough University Centre for Research in Communication and Culture, accessed at http://blog.lboro.ac.uk/crcc/general-elec tion/media-coverage-of-the-2015-campaign-report-5/ on 6 December 2017.

Deacon, D., Downey, J., Smith, D., Stanyer, J. and Wring, D. (2017*a*) 'Media Coverage of the 2017 General Election', Report 4, June, Loughborough University Centre for Research in Communication and Culture, accessed at http://blog.lboro.ac.uk/crcc/gen eral-election/media-coverage-of-the-2017-general-election-campaign-report-4/ on 6 December 2017.

Deacon, D., Downey, J., Smith, D., Stanyer, J. and Wring, D. (2017*b*) 'Two Parts Policy, One Part Process: News Media Coverage of the 2017 Election'. In Mair, J. et al. (eds) *Brexit, Trump and the Media*, London, Abramis, pp. 367–371.

Fletcher, R. (2017) 'Labour's Social Media Campaign: More Post, More Video, and More Interaction'. In Thorsen, E., Jackson, D. and Lilleker, D. (eds) *UK Election Analysis 2017*, accessed at http://eprints.bournemouth.ac.uk/29374/10/UKElectionAnalysis2017 _Thorsen-Jackson-and-Lilleker_v1.pdf, p. 92 on 6 December 2017.

Gibson, R. (2013). 'Party Change, Social Media and the Rise of 'Citizen-initiated' Campaigning', *Party Politics*, 21, 183–197.

Gwynne, A. (2017, 15 June) 'Theresa May Called a Snap Election, But We in Labour had Snapchat. No Contest', *Guardian*, accessed at https://www.theguardian.com/commen

tisfree/2017/jun/15/theresa-may-snap-election-labour-snapchat-campaigning on 6 December 2017.

Kaminska, M., Gallacher, J. D., Yasseri, T. and Howard, P. N. (2017) 'Social Media and News Sources During the 2017 UK General Election', Data Memo, 5 June, Oxford Internet Institute, accessed at http://comprop.oii.ox.ac.uk/wp-content/uploads/sites/89/2017/06/Social-Media-and-News-Sources-during-the-2017-UK-General-Election.pdf on 6 December 2017.

LBC (2017, 6 June) 'Tory Candidate Creates Worst Political Video Ever', LBC.co.uk, accessed at http://www.lbc.co.uk/politics/elections/general-election-2017/tory-candidate-creates-worst-political-video-ever/ on 6 December 2017.

Littunen, M. (2017, 7 June) 'An Analysis of News and Advertising in the UK General Election', Open Democracy UK, accessed at https://www.opendemocracy.net/uk/analysis-of-news-and-advertising-in-uk-general-election on 6 December 2017.

Mason, A. (2017, 2 July) 'Election Reflections: We Must Embrace New Technologies or We Will Be Left Behind', *Conservative Home*, accessed at https://www.conservativehome.com/platform/2017/07/adrian-mason-election-reflections-we-must-embrace-new-technology-or-we-will-be-left-behind.html on 6 December 2017.

Mayhew, F. (2017*a*, 15 June) 'Print ABCs', *Press Gazette*, http://www.pressgazette.co.uk/print-abc-metro-overtakes-sun-in-uk-weekday-distribution-but-murdoch-title-still-britains-best-selling-paper/ on 6 December 2017.

Mayhew, F. (2017*b*, 15 June) 'Website ABCs', *Press Gazette*, accessed at http://www.pressgazette.co.uk/website-abcs-general-election-campaign-boost-sees-independent-sun-and-birmingham-mail-double-daily-browsers/ on 6 December 2017.

Mayhew, F. (2017*c*, 31 July) 'Survey Reveal the Extent to Which Newspapers and Social Media Influenced Voting Decisions at the 2017 General Election', *Press Gazette*, accessed at http://www.pressgazette.co.uk/survey-reveals-extent-to-which-newspapers-and-social-media-influenced-voting-decisions-at-2017-general-election/ on 6 December 2017.

Morgan, R. (2017, 14 July) 'CCHQ Must Rebuild its Digital Strategy from the Ground Up'. *Conservative Home*, accessed at https://www.conservativehome.com/platform/2017/07/richard-morgan-cchq-must-rebuild-its-digital-strategy-from-the-ground-up.html on 6 December 2017.

Mortimer, C. (2017, 31 May) 'Theresa May Savaged by Party Leaders for Debate No-Show: "Good Leaders Don't Run Away"', *Independent*, accessed at http://www.independent.co.uk/news/uk/politics/theresa-may-election-debate-attacked-corbyn-tim-farron-caroline-lucas-good-leaders-dont-run-away-a7766121.html on 6 December 2017.

Oborne, P. (2005, 25 April) 'Election Unspun: Why Politicians Can't Tell the Truth', Channel 4.

Order-Order (2017, 20 March) 'UKIP Order Candidates to Close Down Social Media Sites', accessed at https://order-order.com/2017/03/20/ukip-order-candidates-to-close-social-media-accounts/ on 6 December 2017.

Parry, K. (2017) 'Seeing Jeremy Corbyn and Not Seeing Theresa May: The Promise of Civic Leadership'. In Thorsen, E., Jackson, D. and Lilleker, D. (eds) *UK Election Analysis 2017*, accessed at http://eprints.bournemouth.ac.uk/29374/10/UKElection Analysis2017_Thorsen-Jackson-and-Lilleker_v1.pdf, p. 124 on 6 December 2017.

Payne, S. (2017, 18 April) 'General Election: Theresa May Seizes the Moment to Bank Poll Lead', FT.com, accessed at https://www.ft.com/content/7ef72c62-2425-11e7-a34a-538b4cb30025 on 6 December 2017.

Poletti, M., Bale, T and Webb P. (2016, 16 November) 'Explaining the Pro-Corbyn Surge in Labour Membership', accessed at http://blogs.lse.ac.uk/politicsandpolicy/explaining-the-pro-corbyn-surge-in-labours-membership/ on 6 December 2017.

Ponsford, D. (2017, 18 May) 'UK Newspaper Website ABCs for April 2017', *Press Gazette*, accessed at http://www.pressgazette.co.uk/uk-newspaper-website-abcs-for-april-2017-no-sign-of-snap-general-election-traffic-boost/ on 6 December 2017.

Pringle, B. (2017, 31 May) 'Why Labour's Social Media Influencer Strategy is Working', *The Drum* on 6 December 2017.

Savage, M. and Hucillo, A. (2017, 10 June) 'How Jeremy Corbyn Turned a Youth Surge into Votes', *Guardian*, accessed at https://www.theguardian.com/politics/2017/jun/10/jeremy-corbyn-youth-surge-votes-digital-activists on 6 December 2017.

Scammell, M. (2017) ''Theresa May for Britain': A Personal Brand in Search of Personality'. In Thorsen, E., Jackson, D. and Lilleker, D. (eds) *UK Election Analysis 2017*, accessed at http://eprints.bournemouth.ac.uk/29374/10/UKElectionAnalysis2017_Thorsen-Jackson-and-Lilleker_v1.pdf, p. 130 on 6 December 2017.

Segesten, A. D. and Bossetta, M. (2017) 'Sharing is Caring: Labour Supporters Use of Social Media'. In Thorsen, E., Jackson, D. and Lilleker, D. (eds) *UK Election Analysis 2017*, accessed at http://eprints.bournemouth.ac.uk/29374/10/UKElectionAnalysis2017_Thorsen-Jackson-and-Lilleker_v1.pdf, p. 91 on 6 December 2017.

Shabi, R. (2017, 1 June) 'What Use is a Group of Cultish, Corbynista Clicktivists? Quite a Lot, Actually', *Guardian*.

Shaw, S. (2017) 'Meeting the Public: The Perils and Pitfalls of "Walkabout" Questions to Theresa May in GE2017'. In Thorsen, E., Jackson, D. and Lilleker, D. (eds) *UK Election Analysis 2017*, accessed at http://eprints.bournemouth.ac.uk/29374/10/UKElection Analysis2017_Thorsen-Jackson-and-Lilleker_v1.pdf, p. 32 on 6 December 2017.

Sun (2017, 23 May) 'The Sun Says: Deadly Disgrace'.

The Economist, (2017, 27 May) 'How Online Campaigning is Influencing Britain's Election', accessed at www.economist.com/news/britain/21722690-social-media-allow-parties-target-voters-tailored-messagesand-cat-videos-how-online on 6 December 2017.

Thorsen, E., Jackson D. and Lilleker D (eds) *UK Election Analysis 2017: Media, Voters and the Campaign*, Bournemouth, Centre for the Study of Journalism, Culture and Community, Bournemouth University.

Turner, G. and Kahn, J. (2017, 11 June) 'UK Labour's Savvy Use of Social Media Helped Win Young Voters', *Bloomberg*, accessed at https://www.bloomberg.com/news/articles/2017-06-11/u-k-labour-s-savvy-use-of-social-media-helped-win-young-voters on 6 December 2017.

Walsh, M. (2017) 'The Alternate and Influential World of the Political Parties' Facebook Feeds'. In Thorsen, E., Jackson, D. and Lilleker, D. (eds) *UK Election Analysis 2017*, accessed at http://eprints.bournemouth.ac.uk/29374/10/UKElectionAnalysis2017_Thorsen-Jackson-and-Lilleker_v1.pdf, pp. 96–97 on 6 December 2017.

Ward, S. J., Gibson, R. K. and Cantijoch, M. (2018). 'Digital Campaigning'. In Fisher, J., Fieldhouse, E., Franklin, M. N., Gibson, R. K., Wlezien, C. and Cantijoch, M. (eds) *The Routledge Handbook of Public Opinion and Voting Behaviour*, Routledge, London.

Waterson, J. (2017, 4 May) 'Corbyn's Media Gamble: The Labour Leader Has Ditched Newspaper Journalists in the Campaign Trail', *Buzzfeed*, accessed at https://www.buzzfeed.com/jimwaterson/jeremy-corbyn-has-ditched-newspaper-journalists-on-the?utm_term=.mx4lkXrro#.uqGzN0JJ8 on 6 December 2017.

Wendling, M. (2017, 10 June) 'Was It Facebook Wot Swung It?', BBC Trending.

Wring, D. and Ward, S.J. (2015) 'Exit Velocity: The Media Election', *Parliamentary Affairs*, **68 (suppl.)**, 224–240.

Britain Votes (2017) 222–236

MATTHEW FLINDERS*

The (*Anti-*)Politics of the General Election: Funnelling Frustration in a Divided Democracy

'All general elections are interesting; some are surprising; only a few can be described as astonishing,' David Denver notes in his contribution to this volume, 'The latter certainly applies to 2017.' This is certainly true but what also made the election remarkable was the emergence of anti-political sentiment as a key resource for a mainstream party, channelled through a particular blend of hybrid populism. To develop this argument and dissect what might be termed the (*anti-*) politics of the General Election this chapter is divided into three sections. The first section seeks to place the General Election within its broader historical and comparative context and places particular emphasis on the post-Brexit collapse of UKIP and how this changed the political landscape in ways that Labour would later exploit. The second section develops this argument by arguing that 'the Corbyn effect' was essentially synonymous with the adoption of a populist strategy that sought to re-frame the Labour Party as a fresh, new, anti-political, anti-establishment 'outsider' party. This re-positioning of the Labour Party under Jeremy Corbyn represents arguably the most 'astonishing' element of the 2017 General Election and helps explain how the party exceeded expectations to secure 'a glorious defeat'. The final section reflects on the long-terms risks of this strategy in terms of the perils of playing with populism.

1. The anti-political context of the General Election

The aim of this section is to provide the historical foundations and social context that framed the (*anti-*)politics of the General Election, in general, and the strategic positioning of the Labour Party, in particular. It therefore begins with a broad focus on anti-politics and narrows to a focus on British politics in the run up to

---

*Matthew Flinders, Department of Politics, University of Sheffield, m.flinders@sheffield.ac.uk

© *The Author 2018. Published by Oxford University Press on behalf of the Hansard Society; all rights reserved.*
For Permissions, please e-mail: journals.permissions@oup.com
doi:10.1093/pa/gsx058

the General Election. The core argument is that the political opportunity structure within the British party system altered significantly in the wake of Brexit and that this allowed the Labour Party to adopt an explicitly anti-political 'outsider' status under the leadership of Jeremy Corbyn. It was the replacement of one anti-political lightning rod (i.e. UKIP) with another (i.e. 'New *Old* Labour). But in terms of understanding this transition it is necessary to take five steps. The first step simply acknowledges the existence of a burgeoning and international seam of scholarship on democratic decline and political disaffection within which the words 'death', 'end', 'suicide', 'crisis' and 'hatred' loom large (see, for example, Tormey, 2015; Roberts, 2017). This literature reveals not only the rise of anti-political sentiment in advanced liberal democracies but also the rise of populist politicians and 'insurgent parties' in light of the widespread perception amongst large sections of the public that democratic politics is somehow failing. The existence of anti-political sentiment in the UK is therefore by no means exceptional but what might be more unusual from a comparative perspective is the manner in which the General Election involved a mainstream party stepping into the anti-political space created by the implosion of an insurgent party.

Our second step is therefore concerned with understanding the social and economic drivers of anti-political sentiment and how they might relate to the British context. Two drivers or explanations deserve brief comment. The first is the *economic inequality perspective* that highlights 'overwhelming evidence of powerful trends toward greater income and wealth inequality in the West, based on the rise of the knowledge economy, technological automation, and the collapse of manufacturing industry, global flows of labour, goods, peoples, and capital (especially the inflow of migrants and refugees), the erosion of organized labor, shrinking welfare safety-nets, and neo-liberal austerity policies' (Inglehart and Norris, 2016). It is not just that economic inequality is increasing but also that levels of economic insecurity are increasing. The 'gig economy' demands workers that are hyper-mobile and exist in a precarious economic position where security and social protections are scarce commodities. In a manner that offers the first hint of a new axis or bifurcation within British politics (discussed below), the critical element of the *economic inequality perspective* is that the nature of work and employment is changing rapidly. If you are older, less educated or live beyond thriving cities then securing well-paid or long-term employment is increasingly difficult. However, even if you are young, educated and live in the sunlit cosmopolitan uplands of Cambridge, Oxford, Bristol or Exeter then work is still likely to be a fairly precarious endeavour.

This argument flows into a focus on the second and related explanation for increasing 'anti-politics': the *cultural backlash theory*. Democratic disaffection from this perspective is not a purely economic phenomenon but is in large part a reaction *against* progressive cultural change. Public support for progressive values such as cosmopolitanism, feminism, environmentalism, etc., were to some extent based on the security delivered through post-war economic growth. In a period of global economic austerity, the 'cultural escalator' appears to have stopped or even to have gone into reverse in some countries as public commitment to progressive values has waned. 'The silent revolution of the 1970s', Ronald Inglehart and Pippa Norris conclude, 'appears to have spawned an angry and resentful counter-revolutionary backlash today' (2016, p. 5).

The third step involves a shift from these broad international explanations of social and political change to a consideration of their relevance in the British context. In this regard the rise and role of UKIP is critical. Put very simply, as the work of Goodwin and Milazzo (2015) illustrates, UKIP rose to become the most significant new independent party in post-war British politics by recognising and to some extent cultivating anti-political sentiment as a political resource (i.e. as a commodity to be tapped into and exploited). Under Nigel Farage, UKIP presented a populist and simple critique of mainstream politics' 'establishment elites' that focused on their perceived failure to control immigration. The party therefore cultivated a reputation as an 'outsider' or 'insurgent' party that was willing to challenge the mainstream on behalf of 'the common people' or 'great British public'. In so doing, UKIP emphasised the growth of economic inequality and insecurity while highlighting perceived threats to British culture and tradition. Moreover, the UKIP 'offer' transcended traditional partisan and class divides in the sense that it appealed to those on the right who were concerned about traditional British values and European encroachment, and those on the left who felt the Labour Party now looked down upon traditional working-class sentiments and values, such as patriotism and flying the flag of St George. Carried on a wave of anti-political sentiment, UKIP enjoyed successes in 2014 and 2015 that included gaining 163 seats in the 2014 local elections, securing the greatest number of votes (27.5%) of any British party in the 2014 European Parliament elections (producing 24 MEPs), winning two by-elections in late 2014 and then securing over 3.8 million votes (12.6%) at the 2015 General Election. UKIP had fractured the traditional party system and exerted a strong blackmail effect on the mainstream parties (see Ford and Goodwin, 2014; Goodwin and Heath, 2016a, b).

The influence of UKIP was evident in David Cameron's Bloomberg speech in January 2013 that contained a commitment to hold a referendum on the UK's membership of the EU should the Conservatives win the 2015 General Election—a commitment intended to allow Conservative MPs to fight off the UKIP threat in many constituencies. The disproportionality embedded within the simple-plurality electoral system prevented the 2015 UKIP surge being translated into seats in Parliament but the result did reveal the manner in which anti-political sentiment could be almost sown, cultivated and harvested as a political fuel or resource. The subsequent Brexit referendum demonstrated the existence of an increasingly 'divided democracy' in which anti-elite, anti-establishment, anti-

European, anti-mainstream variants of anti-political sentiment could coalesce around one issue: membership of the EU. With the benefit of hindsight what was particularly noteworthy about the 'Leave' campaign was the manner in which relatively simplistic and emotionally charged statements could forge a powerful and ultimately successful connection with both longstanding British cultural idiosyncrasies *vis-à-vis* the EU and also more recent economic and cultural social anxieties, notably concerning immigration.

The shared and arguably most critical, but under-acknowledged, element of the UKIP surge in 2015, the Brexit referendum in 2016 and the 2017 General Election was the role of emotional resonance (or lack thereof). As Alan Finlayson (2017) has noted, Brexit became a campaign of anti-political politics harbouring resentment at losses and scepticism about promises. The sense of a loss of tradition, a mythical integrity, an eviscerated global status, a romanticised past plus a nativist and nationalist anxiety were all set against the perceived excesses of a distant European elite. The weakness in the response of the mainstream parties, politicians and 'Remainers' was arguably their failure to grasp *why emotions matter*. Against a backdrop of economic austerity and cultural anxiety the political appeal of the rhetorical emphasis placed by both UKIP and the 'Leave' campaign on 'putting Britain first', 'taking back control', 'strengthening borders' and 'saving money' tapped into a powerful source of emotive desire. This desire may not have been 'rational' from the point of view of a scientific evidence-based analysis but the emergence of 'expert rejection' underlined how emotions trump rationality. If you feel scared, threatened, alienated, pessimistic, trapped or unloved, then no matter how many times you are told such feelings are irrational the feelings remain true. As J. D. Taylor argues in his wonderful book, *Island Story* (2016), politics is a matter more of feeling than reason and it is possible to suggest that UKIP possessed a more sensitive emotional antennae than the mainstream parties.

Table 14.1 The 'old' and 'new' bifurcations of British politics

Traditional Post-War Bifurcation	
Tory	Labour
Urban and rural, educated middle and upper classes working largely within the private sector, or with family money. Plus some working-class supporters.	Traditional working class and public sector employees, largely in densely populated industrial areas.
Post-Millennium Emergent Axis	
Tory	Labour
Backwater (but needing to expand their bandwidth into the cosmopolitan sphere).	Cosmopolitan (with elements of the backwater constituencies).

Table 14.2 The new tribes

	Cosmopolitan	Backwater
Exemplar	Cambridge	Clacton
Outlook	External/Global	Internal/National
View on European Union	Relatively Positive	Generally Negative
View on immigration	Relatively Positive	Generally Negative
Ethnicity	Diverse/Integrated	Generally White/Polarised
Dominant spatial features	Integrated transport, bright, fast-paced, 24/7	Limited public transport, dilapidated public infrastructure, etc.
Urban Geography	Apple stores, juice bars, out of town mega-malls, university buildings, etc.	Pit villages without pits, fishing ports without fish, steel cities without steel, railway towns without railways, seaside piers without tourists.[1]
Employment sectors	Knowledge economy, entertainment, financial services, service sector, etc.	Food production, agriculture, call centres, etc.
Employment status	Precarious-gig economy, fluid, flexible, 'portfolio careers'	Precarious-seasonal, minimum wage, zero hour contracts
Progressive values	Likely	Unlikely
Orientation	Future-focused	Backward-looking
Age/Education	Young/Educated	Older/Less Educated
Anti-Political	Yes	Yes
Psycho-geography	Anywheres	Somewheres
Identity profile	Achieved identity (via success)	Ascribed identity (via place or group)
Epithet	'Looking Forward'	'Left Behind'

Source: Created through synthesising the complementary social profiles offered by Jennings and Stoker (2016), Jennings *et al.* (2017) and Goodhart (2017).

This leads to a fourth step that connects anti-political momentum with the shifting political terrain on which the General Election was fought: the emergence of a new bifurcation or axis within British, or more specifically *English*, politics (see Tables 14.1 and 14.2 above).

Such simplistic binary models are clearly problematic in terms of providing a refined and sophisticated grasp on an increasingly complex social reality but they point to what might be termed an increasing 'social stretch' within British society and in many other liberal democracies. What Table 14.1 and Table 14.2 illustrate is evidence of a shift from a relatively simple and class-based divide between traditional Tory and Labour voters (i.e. the traditional post-war bifurcation) towards a more diagonal, fluid and opaque political axis in which traditional

---

[1]Developed from the related arguments made by Ruth Davidson in http://unherd.com/2017/07/ctrl-alt-del-conservatives-must-reboot-capitalism/

voting groups have been splintered (see Jennings and Stoker, 2016). The aim of Table 14.1 and Table 14.2 is not to suggest that the traditional 'left'/'right' spectrum no longer matters but simply that socio-political linkages are becoming more complex. The traditional post-war bifurcation, with its layer-cake type qualities, is to some extent now overlaid with a more multifaceted post-millennium axis. At the heart of this new axis is a contrast between growing cosmopolitan (southern) cities and shrinking provincial settings or 'backwaters'. The latter are home to those who generally lose out from the forces of globalisation and are therefore loci of economic deprivation and significant cultural tensions. The Brexit surge was therefore largely focused within backwater coastal resorts of the East of England and large post-industrial areas of Northern England. The emergence of this new axis matters because the political demands placed upon political parties by citizens in cosmopolitan as opposed to backwater (or 'non-cosmopolitan') areas are likely to be very different, almost to the extent of being diametrically opposed. The demand-side expectations placed upon democratic politics are therefore arguably increasing in terms of complexity. Subsequently political parties seeking to secure a governing majority will somehow have to bridge both worlds, both 'Englands' to paraphrase Jennings and Stoker. The implication being that parties will have to offer a broad political 'bandwidth' in order to straddle these increasingly divided polarities; this, in turn, heightens the risk of political instability, rupture, failure and therefore *increased* anti-political sentiment.

This is a critical point. The traditional post-war bifurcation (Table 14.1) demanded that the two main political parties adopted a 'big tent', 'catch-all', 'wide-net'—call it what you will—approach to have any chance of securing a parliamentary majority. This was captured in Anthony Downs' (1957) left-right bell-curve and its emphasis on the centre or median voter. What the initial analysis of data from the General Election seems to be suggesting is that voter distribution may have shifted in a centrifugal manner. This shift towards 'two Englands' or 'two tribes' is crucial in making it more difficult to find the political bandwidth necessary to form a stable parliamentary government. A critique of 'mainstream' or 'established' politics has been a key element of this dynamic.

This emphasis on bandwidth bring us to a fifth and final step that focuses upon the collapse of UKIP as the main 'outsider' anti-political party in the UK in the wake of the Brexit decision. UKIP's narrow policy focus—immigration and membership of the European Union—couched within an aggressively anti-elite, anti-establishment, anti-mainstream, anti-political posture, allowed it to attract disaffected voters from both the left and the right of the political spectrum. But the Brexit vote undermined its basic *raison d'être* and surveys quickly revealed a hemorrhaging of support; and in the May 2017 local elections UKIP lost all of its 145 town and district councillors. The party's dismal performance in the General

Election was therefore not unexpected. But what was not expected was that the UKIP surge of 2015 would be replaced by a Labour surge in 2017. The argument developed in the next section is that this occurred because Jeremy Corbyn adopted an explicitly anti-political 'outsider' platform that to some extent occupied the political space created by the demise of UKIP.

2. The anti-political content of the General Election

The argument is not that Labour adopted a stance of raw or aggressive populism. But it is that Labour flirted with populist tendencies and inflamed anti-political sentiment by expressing outrage against the status quo, adopting a language of 'us' (i.e. *for the people*) as against 'them' (i.e. *for themselves*), offering simplistic solutions to complex problems and arguably over-inflating the public's expectations as to what any party could realistically deliver should it be elected. Under Jeremy Corbyn the 'New 'Old' Labour Party' offered a mutant or hybrid form of left-wing populism and in order to explain this argument a five-part framework is developed that focuses upon: (i) the 'Corbyn effect'; (ii) the 'May-(bot) effect'; (iii) the 'UKIP effect'; (iv) the 'Youth-effect'; and (v) the 'divided democracy'.

In many ways it is not just the General Election that was astonishing but that Jeremy Corbyn led the Labour Party into the election in the first place. Yet Corbyn was elected leader by a landslide, helped by the support of new 'registered supporters' who had been able to pay just £3 in order to vote in his election. In many ways Corbyn was already adopting the role as a left-wing 'outsider' candidate offering a distinctive shift that recognized the impact of both the economic and cultural drivers of anti-political sentiment. The challenge, however, was for him to broaden his appeal within and beyond parliament and in the wake of his leadership victory this appeared a major challenge. In June 2016, Labour MPs passed a vote of no confidence in their leader by 172-40 and the party's vote share then declined in each of the five by-elections held from October 2016 to February 2017 (excluding Batley and Spen).

Yet during the actual election campaign, a positive 'Corbyn effect' began to emerge, on the basis of cultivating, attracting and channelling anti-political sentiment. Although strangely counter-intuitive given his three decades as a full-time Westminster figure, Corbyn came across to large sections of the public as something of an anti-political cult hero. 'Corbynmania' exploited a rich vein of social feeling by offering a candidate who appeared principled, straight talking and 'different' to the mainstream. The unkempt appearance, the scruffy beard, the cycle-clips, penchant for taking days off and sometimes shambolic interview appearances reinforced a view that Corbyn represented something very different to the smooth talking, media managed 'professional' politicians that he explicitly set himself against. More importantly, Corbyn understood the role of emotions and personal contact. Whereas Theresa May adopted something of a bunker mentality, Corbyn embarked upon a remarkable number of speaking engagements across the UK, 122 within 33 days, which proved critical in terms of allowing him to cut through his generally negative portrayal in the media. Even his fiercest critics conceded that his rhetoric and criticism of mainstream politics was injecting new energy and dynamism into politics and the more he travelled the country 'pressing the flesh' the more the polls narrowed. Indeed, political apathy amongst many social groups suddenly turned into political hope and excitement as the once 'no hoper' Corbyn suddenly became 'a crowd puller'.

Unvarnished he was and Obama-like he certainly was not but Corbyn clearly connected amongst some sections of British society in a manner that had been completely unexpected. The Labour Party, in general, and Corbyn, in particular, had undertaken a populist makeover in order to capitalise on the anti-political mood that existed. This strategy was first glimpsed in December 2016 when John Trickett, then the Labour elections co-ordinator, stated that 'We [the Labour Party] need to frame an argument about Britain, its past, present and future—but we will be doing that in a carefully modulated way'. That carefully 'modulated way' translated into a strategy that exploited the existence of anti-establishment, anti-elitist, anti-political populist sentiments. To some extent this strategy seemed to 'work' and what was clear with the issue of emotional intelligence and resonance in mind (discussed above) is that Jeremy Corbyn seemed to pass the 'cup of coffee test' with more people as the campaign progressed.[2] Mrs May, however, did not pass this test, which brings the discussion to this section's second theme and the manner in which the Conservative Party *did* appear to connect with anti-political sentiment, but in a very negative manner.

There are at least two ways in which the Conservative campaign managed to fuse with anti-political sentiment—one political, one personal—and the two are related. The first issue reintroduces the role of UKIP and its blackmail effect on other parties. Theresa May's 'hard' Brexit stance, combined with her promise to be a 'bloody difficult women' in negotiations, and in her attack upon the 'bureaucrats of Brussels' were all intended to reassure UKIP supporters that they could now enter the Tory fold. And yet, in making this shift to appease voters on the right, May arguably alienated an increasing number of more moderate supporters. As the campaign moved on, the Tories' stance seemed to harden, to the extent that May increasingly emphasized that 'no deal was better than a bad deal' and seemed to be threatening to simply walk away from the EU.

---

[2] The 'cup of coffee test' simply relates to whether an individual thinks they would enjoy sitting down and having a coffee or a beer with a candidate. It therefore emphasises subjective interpretations of whether a candidate is a 'good guy' or a 'good woman' over their party affiliation or policy portfolio.

Put slightly differently, the more the Conservative campaign progressed the more it almost seemed to prove and sustain a number of negative public beliefs about politicians. 'May-*hem*' was created by numerous policy reversals—a 'Remainer' who would now lead the UK to Brexit, an opponent of an early election who 'reluctantly' decided to hold one, and—critically—the U-turn on a key element of the Conservative Party's manifesto in relation to social care and the alleged 'dementia tax'. The mantra of 'strong and stable', repeated robotically in every interview irrespective of the question, quickly emerged as an electoral liability that fuelled public concerns about machine politics and the 'on-message' politicians who could not think for themselves. Indeed, in a climate when politicians are widely perceived by the public to be detached and generally disinterested in the lives of ordinary people, Theresa May's approach to the campaign seemed almost designed to fit with such beliefs. A preference for carefully scripted media engagements and an almost complete lack of spontaneous public interaction increasingly made Theresa May look aloof, cold, distant and almost arrogant. Hubris rapidly descended into concerns about nemesis but by that point the phrase 'May-*bot*' had entered the political lexicon and would forever be linked to Theresa May.

Jeremy Corbyn ran a good campaign because he cultivated his reputation as a radical anti-austerity 'outsider' candidate who was vociferous in his attack on elites and mainstream politics. He promised a 'new politics' that explicitly reached out to different communities *across* the emergent axis in British politics. Theresa May, by contrast, ran a bad campaign which appeared to confirm pre-existing prejudices about the political class and then risked alienating her core voting constituencies with the publication of a misfiring manifesto. Rephrased, the political bandwidth of the Labour campaign widened as the Conservative Party's bandwidth seemed to narrow and this was arguably evident from the moment their respective manifestos were published. Labour's was distinctive in making a broad range of bold promises—abolishing tuition fees, renationalising the railways, post office and utilities, free childcare, guaranteeing the 'triple lock' on pensions, maintaining universal benefits, etc.—which really did attempt to offer a wide bandwidth: it really was *For the Many, Not the Few* (the manifesto's title). The Conservative manifesto—*Forward Together*—was unusual for the opposite reason, containing almost no 'retail' policies. This focus on bandwidth leads into a discussion of 'the UKIP-effect' (our third issue).

Often framed in terms of 'a revolt on the right' the rise of UKIP had also been 'a problem for the left', as the party sought to attract large sections of the public who felt 'left behind'. It therefore cut into the Labour Party's traditional working-class vote and this is reflected in the electoral geography of its strongest results (economically deprived, low income, low education, low skills and largely white parts of the country). In the wake of the Brexit referendum and their disastrous performance in the 2017 local elections the dominant assumption had been that most of the 3.9 million people who had voted for UKIP in the 2015 General Election would now vote for the Tories, thereby helping to ensure the widely expected landslide. The 'outsider' status of Jeremy Corbyn with his vociferous criticism of mainstream politics and anti-austerity redistributive agenda proved attractive to many who had previously felt 'left behind' and this was particularly true for younger voters.

A fourth feature of the (*anti-*)politics of the General Election was therefore the role and behaviour of the youth vote. Surveys, opinion data and election results have repeatedly revealed that: younger people tend to be more disillusioned, disengaged and frustrated with 'mainstream' politics than any other demographic group; younger people tend to be far more left-leaning and cosmopolitan in outlook; but they are also the cohort least likely to actually turn out to vote (Sloam, 2017). The challenge for the Labour Party was therefore how to energise the youth vote in order to translate anti-political sentiment into support for a 'new politics' platform. According to the analysis of IpsosMORI this is exactly what occurred as the General Election witnessed the highest young voter (18 to 24 years) turnout in a quarter of a century and this may explain a large amount of the unexpected Labour surge. Younger voters appear to have been energised by Jeremy Corbyn's campaign and put off by May's 'hard' Brexit stance. More importantly what the General Election revealed was the existence of an increasingly divided democracy involving major inter-generational tensions. Younger people expressed themselves as left-of-centre cosmopolitans, Sloam (2017) argues, reacting against austerity politics and the cultural conservatism of elders, whilst some also felt resentment over the support for the Leave campaign in the EU referendum being strongest among older voters.

The (*anti-*)politics of the 2017 General Election therefore revolves around the funnelling of frustrations within mainstream politics into a unique alliance in favour of a 'new politics'. It was therefore less 'anti-politics' and more 'pro-politics-but-a-different-way-of-doing-politics' that managed to offer a wide political bandwidth that could reach *across* the new bifurcation that increasingly exists between cosmopolitan and backwater areas. Labour managed to win over a majority of 2016 Remain voters and about quarter of 2016 Leave voters which, in turn, raises the question of how it managed to straddle that divide. One response is that the party channelled anti-political sentiment through careful strategic framing, offering a very positive narrative of social change (i.e. pro-a-different-politics) and—critically—the Labour Party focused on a far wider range of issues and policy areas other than Brexit. With reference to the final row of Table 14.1, Labour did succeed in terms of achieving strong support in cosmopolitan areas. The Conservatives, by contrast, largely failed to reach beyond their core constituencies and this explains the unexpected narrowness of the result. But what it also reveals is the existence of an increasingly polarized society or 'divided democracy' in England and to some extent the critical element of the General Election was the manner in which Jeremy Corbyn was able to build a broad alliance—almost a social movement—through the utilization of anti-political sentiment. And while widely interpreted as a dazzling success for the Labour Party, playing with populism in such an explicit manner could also be seen as an incredibly dangerous game to play, especially in the context of an increasingly polarized society.

3. Conclusion: The perils of playing with populism

The astonishing element of the General Election was the manner in which the Labour Party adopted an explicitly anti-political, anti-mainstream, 'outsider' status (almost to the extent that it existed outside and beyond its own parliamentary party). It was a strategy that delivered 'a glorious defeat' and bestowed 'an inglorious victory' on Theresa May's Conservative Party. Labour succeeded in cultivating and funnelling frustration, with Corbyn acting as a lightning rod for anti-austerity, anti-establishment and anti-mainstream politics. He also forged a particular connection with the young, ethnic minorities and significant sections of the white working class who had previously been seduced by the promises of UKIP.

Yet the extent or nature of this (re)connection should not be misrepresented. As Tables 14.1 and 14.2 suggest they might, the Labour Party gained most ground in seats with the largest concentrations of middle class professionals and rich people, while the Tories made their biggest gains in some of the poorest seats in England and Wales. This exemplifies the bandwidth 'stretch' that any party must now somehow grapple with to secure office. The critical issue is *how* Jeremy Corbyn and the Labour Party made such electoral strides and what it might have *cost* in terms of playing with populism. Put slightly differently, the dilemma for any politician or political party is that success demands a certain level of broad popularity but it also involves being able to resist the temptations of populism (i.e. *to be popular but not populist*). Highlighting this dilemma is valuable as it allows us (i) to reflect upon where the boundary might lie between political popularity and political populism; (ii) to explore why evidence of an increasing social bifurcation might create challenges that make the temptations of populism even more attractive to all parties; and (iii) why this temptation must be avoided given evidence of democratic deconsolidation in many countries.

The first question forces us to reflect upon whether it is fair to equate Corbynism with populism. Although some have rejected this interpretation, it is difficult not to see Corbyn's success as synonymous with anything other than a distinctive brand of populism. There was an underlying and faintly sinister streak of intolerance towards anyone who criticised the Labour leadership. This led to accusations of bullying and harassment by numerous MPs who were unhappy with the direction of the party. The campaign utilised divisive rhetorical language based upon allusions to (corrupt) 'them' (i.e. 'professional' mainstream politicians, 'the elite', 'the establishment') and idealised notions of (pure) 'us' (i.e. the public, 'the people' or 'normal' people). The opening lines of Corbyn's first speech of the 2017 campaign made this clear,

> The dividing lines in this election could not be clearer from the outset
> ... It is the establishment versus the people and it is our historic duty to
> make sure that the people prevail ... We don't fit in their cosy club.
> We're not obsessed with the tittle-tattle of Westminster or Brussels. We
> don't accept that it is natural for Britain to be governed by a ruling elite,
> the City and the tax-dodgers, and we don't accept that the British people
> just have to take what they're given, that they don't deserve better.

It was a left-wing strain of populism that was as monist as it was moralist. It offered simple solutions to complex problems (usually a combination of nationalisation and increased public spending) and was particularly attuned to the plucking of popular emotions. It was populism aimed carefully at the middle-classes, working classes, the precariat and the unemployed; it was a patchwork quilt of promises designed to stretch over a broad bandwidth by allowing voters to focus on the part of the quilt that was specifically designed to appeal to them. 'Our job is to make Jeremy Corbyn the Left's Donald Trump,' whispered a political adviser at Labour's 2016 Christmas party: 'Trump shows if we take the anti-establishment message and run with it, anything is possible' (see Evans, 2017).

And run with it they certainly did. The problem, however, is that playing with populism is the political equivalent of playing with fire. Populism is a dangerous political virus. At times, Corbyn and the Labour Party strayed beyond that admittedly muddy boundary between courting popularity and invoking populism. This risk or danger with populism is that it over-inflates the public's expectations about what democratic politics can deliver and therefore makes failure to some extent inevitable. This takes us back to Bernard Crick's classic *In Defence of Politics* (1965) and his argument about 'the disillusionment of unreal ideals' that may be created by politicians who claim to be able to make 'all sad hearts glad'. This is not to suggest that, if elected, Labour could not have achieved a large amount, but it is to suggest that at times the social momentum that the anti-political rhetoric of Corbyn-ism managed to create might have overlooked both the innate, and inevitably dysfunctional, aspects of democracy while also almost denying the constrained capabilities of national politicians in the twenty-first century. Populist anti-political waves, like forest fires, can be easy to ignite if the right economic and cultural conditions exist in the sense of widespread frustration, fear and anxiety. But populist waves, again like forest fires, can be very hard to control or contain once a degree of momentum has been established; their destructive democratic power might be misunderstood until a dark and sometimes authoritarian situation has developed.

Let me just underline and reiterate that I am not suggesting that if Jeremy Corbyn had been (or ever were) elected as Prime Minister that this would have inevitably led to a situation of authoritarian rule. I'm simply highlighting the manner in which his campaign adopted a risky strategy by playing with populism and that there was something both distinctive and worrying about the ease with which this occurred and its potential implications. From a democratic perspective UKIP's rise was arguably disconcerting but such concerns were to some extent allayed by the fact that it was so clearly a populist insurgency by an outsider party *against* the mainstream. A Corbyn-fuelled Labour victory in the General Election might have given more cause for concern due to the manner in which populism would have infiltrated the mainstream. Anyone wanting to understand this argument in more detail would be well served by reading John Lukacs' *Democracy and Populism* (2005) as it underlines how populism is fuelled by the cultivation of fear and hatred that inevitably tends to eviscerate public confidence in democratic politics and is therefore ultimately destructive. And yet this chapter's focus on British politics allows us to reflect upon and understand why the prevalence of populism appears to be increasing—advanced liberal democracies are possibly becoming harder to govern.

The crucial issue here relates to this chapter's repeated focus on the issue of party political 'bandwidth'. The established political parties are largely creatures of the late nineteenth and twentieth centuries that solidified after the Second World War around relatively clear and stable electoral blocs—the structures Lipset and Rokkan (1967) famously observed were 'frozen' to an unprecedented degree. The evolution of society combined with technological developments and the impact of globalization has 'melted' those blocs which is captured, albeit imperfectly, in the contrast between the 'cosmopolitan' and 'backwater' voters, or between the 'somewheres' and the 'anywheres'. The democratic paradox or challenge of governing is therefore made greater by the need to offer a coherent political 'offer' to a broader range of social groupings. The basic problem is that the more a party or candidate ties itself down to a specific policy position or decision the more likely it is to alienate a section of society whose support it needs to secure office. Put slightly differently, the challenge for democratic politics, especially in majoritarian polities, is therefore to build an electoral coalition that somehow straddles the divides created by the emergence of these new tribes while at the same time being honest about the limits of democratic politics.

In this context populism represents an easy option due to the manner in which it offers great political 'bandwidth' that can exacerbate socio-cultural or economic divisions in a manner that unites tribes against 'them'. It can be thrown like a net over the anxious or fearful, and it manipulates emotional triggers through the demonization of foreigners, bankers, immigrants, experts, elites, mainstream politicians, etc. Populism is not an ideology. It is a thin and dangerous political strategy to obtain and retain power. The paradox, however, is that in adopting explicitly negative, cynical and populist anti-political platforms in order to secure power politicians may themselves unwittingly serve to advance the *de*consolidation of democracy (see, for example, Foa and Mounk, 2016, 2017; Jennings *et al.*, 2017). The challenge for democratic politics is to resist the temptations of shallow populism and instead to take the more difficult path that seeks to redefine, reinvigorate and most of all reimagine the theory and practice of democratic politics in order to close the worrying gap that appears to be growing between the governors and the governed. This may be the core message arising from the (*anti-*)politics of the General Election.

References

Ashcroft, M. (2017) 'How Did this Result Happen?', accessed at http://lordashcroftpolls.com/2017/06/result-happen-post-vote-survey/ on 9 June 2017.

Chu, B. (2017, 18 June) 'We All Need to Stop Calling Jeremy Corbyn a Populist Because Populism is a Dangerous Political Virus', *Independent*, accessed at http://www.independent.co.uk/voices/jeremy-corbyn-populist-labour-donald-trump-boris-johnson-theresa-may-dangerous-a7795676.html on 19 June 2017.

Corbyn, J. (2017) Opening General Election Speech, 20 April, accessed at http://press.labour.org.uk/post/159785074074/jeremy-corbyn-first-speech-of-the-2017-general on 22 April 2017.

Crick, B. (1962) *In Defence of Politics*, London, Weidenfeld & Nicolson.

Downs, A. (1957) *An Economic Theory of Democracy*, New York, NY, Harper.

Evans, J. (2017) 'Labour in 2017. Can Corbyn Ride Anti-elitism Wave?', accessed at http://www.bbc.co.uk/news/uk-politics-38408198 on 2 January 2017.

Finlayson, A. (2017) 'Brexitism', *London Review of Books*, **39**, pp. 22–23.

Flinders, M. (2018) 'Anti-Politics and Brexit'. In Diamond, P., Nedergaard, P. and Rosamond, B. (eds) *Routledge Handbook on Brexit*, London, Routledge.

Ford, R. and Goodwin, M. (2014) *Revolt on the Right*, London, Routledge.

Foa, R. and Mounk, Y. (2016) 'The Democratic Disconnect', *Journal of Democracy*, **27**, 5–17.

Foa, R. and Mounk, Y. (2017) 'The Signs of Deconsolidation', *Journal of Democracy*, **28**, 5–16.

Goodhart, D. (2017) *The Road to Somewhere*, London, Hurst.

Goodwin, M. and Heath, O. (2016a) *Brexit Vote Explained*, York, Joseph Rowntree Foundation.

Goodwin, M. and Heath, O. (2016b) 'The 2016 Referendum, Brexit and the Left Behind', *Political Quarterly*, **87**, 323–332.

Goodwin, M. and Milazzo, C. (2015) *UKIP: Inside the Campaign to Redraw the Map of British Politics*, Oxford, Oxford University Press.

Inglehart, R. and Norris, P. (2016) 'Trump, Brexit and the Rise of Populism', Harvard Kennedy School, Faculty Research Working Paper Series.

Institute for Global Change (2017) *The Centre in the UK, France and Germany*, London, IGC.

IpsosMORI (2017) *Understanding Society: Beyond Populism*, London, IpsosMORI.

Jennings, W. and Stoker, G. (2016) 'The Bifurcation of Politics: Two Englands', *Political Quarterly*, **87**, 372–382.

Jennings, W., Clarke, N., Moss, J. and Stoker, G. (2017) 'The Decline in Diffuse Support for National Politics', *Political Opinion Quarterly*, **81**, 748–758.

Lipset, S. M. and Rokkan, S. (1967) 'Cleavage Structures, Party Systems, and Voter Alignments: An Introduction'. In Lipset S. M. and Rokkan, S. (eds), *Party Systems and Voter Alignments*, New York, NY, The Free Press, pp. 1–64.

Lukacs, J. (2005) *Democracy and Populism: Fear & Hatred*, New Haven, CT, Yale University Press.

Piketty, T. (2014) *Capital in the Twenty-First Century*, Harvard, Harvard University Press.

Roberts, R. (2017) *Four Crises of American Democracy*, Oxford, Oxford University Press.

Sloam, J. (2017) 'Younger Voters Politically Energised'. In Thorsen, E., Jackson, D. and Lilleker, D. (eds) *UK Election Analysis, 2017*, London, PSA.

Tormey, S. (2015) *The End of Representative Politics*, London, Wiley.

Whiteley, P. Clarke, H. and Goodwin, M. (2017) 'Was this a Brexit Election After All? Tracking Party Support Among Leave and Remain voters', LSE Blog, accessed at http://blogs.lse.ac.uk/brexit/2017/06/15/was-this-a-brexit-election-after-all-tracking-party-support-among-leave-and-remain-voters/ on 15 June 2017.

Britain Votes (2017) 237–254

EMILY HARMER AND ROSALYND SOUTHERN*

More Stable than Strong: Women's Representation, Voters and Issues

Theresa May's unexpected accession to the Tory leadership after the historic EU Referendum meant that for the first time since 1987, the General Election was called and contested by a female Prime Minister. The election was notable therefore for an abundance of leading female figures, more so than any previous election. May and Nicola Sturgeon, the Scottish National Party (SNP) leader, dominated the post-Brexit narrative for some months (their meeting on the subject leading to the controversial 'Legs-it' front page in the *Daily Mail*) whilst female leaders such as Leanne Wood (Plaid Cymru), Arlene Foster (Democratic Unionist Party) and Caroline Lucas (co-leader of The Green Party) also formed part of the campaign. Despite repeated assurances to the contrary, May called the election after formally triggering Article 50 and just eight weeks prior to the opening of negotiations to establish a deal to leave the EU. May sought to present herself as a strong and competent leader who would make use of her reputation as a 'bloody difficult woman' to negotiate the best deal possible. Our analysis assesses the importance placed on women during the campaign by firstly discussing how women were portrayed. We then go on to discuss the parties' attempts to appeal to women voters through an analysis of their manifesto offerings, before discussing how women actually voted. Finally, we analyse the extent to which the representation of women in parliament was altered as a result of the election.

1.   The campaign

Theresa May had been receiving high favourability ratings for months, especially compared to Labour's Jeremy Corbyn, and it seemed to many that the election would be impossible for her to lose. The Conservatives' campaign strategy foregrounded May and presented her as a competent and secure (or 'strong and

*Emily Harmer, Department of Communication and Media, University of Liverpool, e.harmer@liverpool.ac.uk; Rosalynd Southern, Department of Communication and Media, University of Liverpool, r.southern@liverpool.ac.uk

doi:10.1093/pa/gsx072

stable') choice for Prime Minister, in contrast to her main opponent. The campaign was widely criticised for being highly stage-managed and May was accused of being robotic and socially awkward. Commentators singled her out for criticism for refusing to engage with non-party supporters, whereas Corbyn appeared frequently at public events. Presidentialized campaigns can be fraught with danger for women leaders. The main risk is reinforcing stereotypical assumptions about the incompatibility between traditional understandings of femininity and conventional ideals of political leadership. Female politicians are generally viewed as more compassionate, honest and warmer than men, whilst men are viewed as more competent, decisive and stronger leaders (Dolan and Lynch, 2014; Kahn, 1996; King and Matland, 2003; Lawless 2004). These differences are problematic because stereotypically masculine traits are more highly valued by the electorate (Huddy and Terkildsen, 1993) which goes some way to explain the continued over-representation of men in politics. Women therefore risk being seen as 'compassionate' but lacking the necessary 'aggression' expected of leaders. Even when portrayed as aggressive, this becomes a problematic transgression of gender norms (Murray, 2010). Jamieson (1995) describes this as a 'competence/femininity' double bind in which masculinity is associated with leadership, but negative consequences may await women who display masculine leadership qualities. Jamieson argues that because women's emotions are deemed to hinder their intellectual and leadership abilities, the bind reinforces that: women are emotional, so being emotional means failing as a leader, and conversely successful leadership is unemotional, but being unemotional means failing as a woman. Arguably, May was negatively impacted by these unspoken assumptions due to her socially awkward and unemotional behaviour on the campaign trail and her inability to empathise with various voters who expressed concerns about cuts to social security and the NHS, such as when she justified the continuation of the public sector pay freeze to a nurse who was struggling financially on the *Question Time Leaders' Special*.

There is little evidence that the Conservatives were concerned about these risks. May even appeared alongside her husband on *The One Show* on BBC1 in an interview that avoided substantive discussion altogether and focused primarily on aspects of their personal lives and relationship. The purpose of the interview may have been for her to show a softer, more human, side, but the exploration of the Mays' division of domestic chores into 'boy and girl jobs' seemed at odds with a woman seeking to convince voters of her public sphere leadership credentials. This contrasts markedly with May's reluctance to participate in the televised leaders' debates. Although such debates are often seen as highly masculinised competitions, where leaders pit their intellectual strength and wit against one another—much like Prime Minister's Questions—the 2015 debates featured an array of women leaders, and many performed well in this environment. It is therefore surprising that May would emphasise her personal life over her debating prowess given that she wanted voters to evaluate her experience and competence.

The Conservatives' manifesto probably added to these negative perceptions. Proposals to scrap free school dinners for all but the poorest children, and changes to social care policy which was quickly dubbed the 'dementia tax' were portrayed as evidence that May is cold and out-of-touch with ordinary voters. Such a charge would be difficult for any prime ministerial candidate to mitigate but such perceptions are particularly difficult for women, given traditional gendered expectations about women being compassionate and caring. The *Daily Mirror* even featured criticism from a finalist of cooking programme *Masterchef* who argued (unfairly) that May would not have introduced this policy if she had children. References to May as the school 'lunch snatcher' (*Daily Mirror*, 19 May 2017) that proliferated amongst Labour supporting media outlets were particularly gendered, and moreover demonstrated the extent to which Margaret Thatcher still looms large in the public imagination. May was also criticised for sending Home Secretary Amber Rudd as her stand-in for the televised leaders' debate despite Rudd's recent bereavement. Framing female politicians in this way reinforces the sexist (and sometimes misogynistic) representations that have long been employed in media discourses (Ross, 2010), although it is clear that May and her party did nothing to foresee the potential pitfalls of campaigning on a presidentialized platform as a woman. Even the much-repeated Tory campaign slogan 'strong and stable' was arguably risky in this context, with 'strong' only serving to reinforce the idea of transgressing gender norms and 'stable' underlining her mechanical approach to the campaign.

Other women politicians received similarly difficult media coverage. Labour's Diane Abbott was singled out for harsh criticism by news media and the Conservative Party alike for performing poorly in a couple of broadcast interviews. Her interview with *LBC* where she got her figures wrong on the cost of increased police recruitment was described as 'the most embarrassing political interview' and as a 'car-crash performance' (*Daily Telegraph*, 2 May 2017), but less attention was given to Chancellor Phillip Hammond's mistake about the cost of HS2 two weeks later (*Independent*, 18 May 2017). Clearly this was motivated by the political partisanship of much of the British press, but it is also important to recognise the extent to which intense criticism of Abbott has been a familiar feature of news coverage throughout her political career which has been attributed to her being the most prominent black woman in British public life (Gabriel, 2017). Black, Asian and Minority Ethnic female candidates have been historically underrepresented in British politics, but also tend to receive exceptionally negative coverage due to their intersectional differences (Ward, 2016).

Whilst women politicians were prominent in the campaign, much like the 2015 election women voters were not particularly prominent (Campbell and Childs, 2015; Harmer, 2017a). In previous elections women voters have featured in marginal but distinct ways. A common trope since 1997 was to speculate about the voting intensions of target voters like Worcester Woman and 'mumsnetters' (Harmer and Wring, 2013). No female target group received attention although a few individual women gained some coverage as a result of encounters with politicians or the press. One vox pop with 'Brenda from Bristol' just after the election was announced seemingly summed up many voters' thoughts when she declared, 'Not another one!' (*New Statesman*, 19 April 2017). Cathy Mohan, who tackled Theresa May about cuts to disability benefits in Abingdon, also received much coverage (*Guardian*, 16 May 2017).

Women voters may have been marginal within the mainstream campaign, but there was one political party which sought to put women voters and their perceived interests at the forefront. The Women's Equality Party (WEP) was formed in 2015 and this was the first election that they had parliamentary candidates (Evans and Kenny, 2017). The most high-profile candidate (and party leader) Sophie Walker stood against controversial Conservative MP Philip Davies in his Shipley constituency. Davies had attracted their attention due to his filibustering to block legislation aimed at implementing better support for victims of domestic violence (*Guardian*, 16 December 2017) and his frequent comments about women, LGBT people and those with disabilities (*Daily Telegraph*, 17 June 2011). Targeting Davies was controversial due to fears over potential vote-splitting and the fact that the WEP failed to engage with local feminist groups (Evans and Kenny, 2017). Walker received just 1.9% of the vote in Shipley and the other six candidates also received very small vote shares (WEP, 2017).

Mainstream broadcast and print media coverage of the campaign was a largely male-dominated affair, despite the presence of high profile women party leaders, including the Prime Minister. Deacon *et al.* (2017) reported that 63% of all individuals who appeared in the news were male compared to 37% female. Amongst politicians, women accounted for 40% but amongst other kinds of source, male voices were preferred. Online news was equally male dominated. Our own analysis of five news websites[1] demonstrated that women who were not politicians received very little news coverage at all. This is surprising given that the most prominent politician in our study was the Prime Minister, who appeared in 37.3% of all items in our study (Harmer and Southern, 2017). Figure 15.1 shows that of all the sources referred to online coverage just 36.8% were women.

---

[1]We conducted a detailed content analysis of weekday news coverage of the UK General Election (i.e. Monday to Friday inclusive) between 4 May and 6 June 2017 from the following news outlets: BBC News, *Mail Online*, *Guardian*, *The Huffington Post* and Buzzfeed. The first four outlets were chosen because they represent the four most used online brands in the UK (Newman, 2017). Buzzfeed was also included because it is the second most read only-online outlet after the Huffington Post. We analysed the ten most prominent election related news stories on the main news page at 9am each morning. We recorded up to three themes per story, the main people featured and their sex.

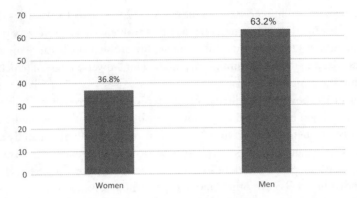

Figure 15.1. Percentage of women and men in online election news (4 May-7 June)
Source: Harmer and Southern, 2017.

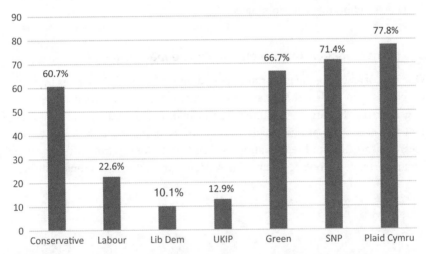

Figure 15.2. Percentage of women by party in online election news (4 May-7 June)
Source: Harmer and Southern, 2017.

Some parties were better than others at foregrounding women speakers though (Figure 15.2). For the Conservatives, 60.7% of all online news individual appearances were by a female politician—the vast majority of these were the Prime Minister herself. Other political parties whose female leaders dominated their parties' appearances were the SNP (with 71.4% of their appearances being made by women representatives), Plaid Cymru (77.8%) and the Green Party (66.7%). The Labour Party sources instead tended to be dominated by men (mainly Corbyn) as Labour women only accounted for 22.6% of all appearances by Labour sources. UKIP and the Liberal Democrats managed the fewest women campaigners in online news, accounting for 12.9% and 10.1% respectively (Harmer, 2017b). The data reflects the fact that women leaders were very prominent throughout the campaign. This is potentially problematic because the media attention given to the leaders limits the potential for a diverse range of female voices within the campaign.

Figure 15.3 shows that ordinary women received lower representation in the media than might be expected given how accessible members of the public are to journalists. Women accounted for 39% of all citizens featured in our study of online news. Women in non-political roles were very marginal in the coverage (Harmer, 2017b). For other kinds of sources women were completely absent. Every individual pollster or other kind of expert who received any mention or reference in the news was male, reinforcing the extent to which the public discussion of politics continues to be dominated by male voices and concerns. Despite the presence of so many women leaders in the campaign, the media coverage of it still remained stubbornly male dominated.

2. Parties' appeals to women voters: The manifestos

One way of assessing the importance placed on women and their votes by political parties is to analyse their manifesto pledges for explicit or implicit references to gendered policy areas. As Campbell and Childs (2015) make clear, it is important to analyse the pledges made in manifestos as these are the most explicit means of targeting and representing women voters. Some parties offered a more extensive range of policies than others. Here, we present a summary of eight

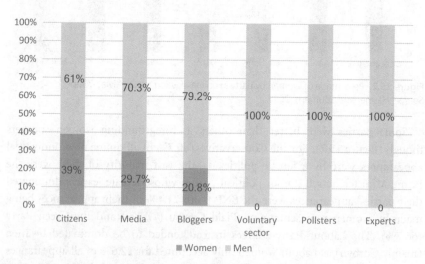

Figure 15.3. Percentage of women by social category in online election news (4 May-7 June)
Source: Harmer and Southern, 2017.

political parties, the seven represented at Westminster (Sinn Féin's MPs do not take their seats) plus UKIP.

All of the parties made some mention of specific gendered policy areas (although the DUP and Plaid Cymru had fewer mentions than most, with the DUP only highlighting one pledge to pursue pension equality). Plaid Cymru argued that their policy pledges from the 2015 General and 2016 Welsh Assembly elections were still valid, meaning that more detail was possibly omitted from their 'Action Plan for 2017' that was published for this election. By contrast, the Green Party and SNP produced specific mini-manifestos aimed at women. The policy areas which directly referred to women followed a similar pattern to recent elections, with key policy areas revolving around women's caring responsibilities and work-life balance (Campbell and Childs, 2015). We have divided the policies offered into the following areas:

(1) Violence against women

(2) International development

(3) Legal/judicial matters

(4) Employment

(5) Social Security

(6) LGBT+ issues

(7) Education

(8) Issues affecting minority women

(9) Public Life

For three of the main parties discussed, many policy areas affecting women are devolved to the respective national government or executive, therefore complicating the messages of the SNP, Plaid Cymru and DUP who are only appealing to small subsections of the electorate, and yet including them in their manifestos for the general election signals a set of clear priorities as far as women are concerned. Table 15.1 shows which issues were foregrounded by each party. The following discussion will attempt to contextualise the policy positions of each party, since although there is a consensus on the range of issues associated with women, the approaches of each party can be very different.

The Conservative manifesto was fairly light on gender-specific policy details, particularly with issues surrounding social security. No pledges were made to reconsider controversial policy areas such as pension inequalities highlighted by the WASPI campaign or to address criticism of the so-called 'rape clause' whereby women can only claim child benefit for a third child if they are willing to complete a form explaining that the child resulted from rape. This policy has been widely criticised for being indifferent to circumstances where women would not

Table 15.1 Summary of Manifesto Commitments of Main Political Parties

		Con	Lab	LD	SNP	PC	GREEN	UKIP	DUP
VAWG	Domestic violence	X	X		X		X		
	Sexual violence	X			X		X		
INTERNATIONAL DEVELOPMENT	Forced marriage/ 'Honour-based violence'		X				X	X	
	Trafficking	X					X		
	Girl's education	X					X		
	Sexual health								
LEGAL/JUDICIAL	VAWG	X	X		X				
	Women offenders		X	X	X	X			
	Family courts	X	X	X	X		X	X	
	Sexual violence legal process	X	X	X	X	X	X		
	Sex work			X			X		
	Abortion		X		X		X		
EMPLOYMENT	Pay gap	X	X		X	X	X		
	Parental leave	X	X		X		X		
	Maternity discrimination		X	X					
	Maternity pay		X	X					
	Discrimination	X	X		X		X		
SOCIAL SECURITY	Pensions		X	X	X	X	X	X	X
	Rape clause		X	X	X	X	X		
	Maternity services		X	X	X		X		
	Child care		X	X	X	X		X	
	'Tampon tax'/Sexual health		X		X				
LGBT+	Hate crime	X	X		X		X	X	
	Rights		X	X	X	X	X		
EDUCATION	Sex and relationships		X				X	X	
	Gender/sexuality based bullying		X	X			X		
	English language provision								
MINORITY WOMEN	FGM	X	X				X		
	Breast-ironing								
	Face-coverings							X	
PUBLIC LIFE	Gender quotas		X	X	X			X	
	Gender audits		X	X	X			X	
	Media representations							X	

wish to reveal such information as well as ignoring the personal impact of disclosure. Instead the Conservatives confined their gendered policy pledges to reasonably uncontroversial areas such as tackling violence against women at home and abroad, tackling workplace discrimination and supporting shared parental leave. They were the only party which did not make any specific pledges on social security aimed at women.

In contrast, the Labour manifesto offered the most extensive range of gendered policy pledges. Labour's priorities focused heavily on social security, promising to address pension inequality, the so-called 'Tampon Tax' and child care provision by funding it directly rather than passing subsidy to parents. Labour also made a range of pledges to support women in the workplace such as increased support to tackle employment and maternity discrimination in particular, as well as increasing paid paternity leave. Labour's offer to women voters focused on policy areas most associated with the left, unsurprisingly, but despite this, women voters continue to be most explicitly invoked in traditionally gendered policy areas rather than in a range of policies across the board.

The Green Party published a range of separate manifestos aimed at specific sectors of the electorate. Although they were careful not to label their 'Manifesto for Gender Equality' as being explicitly for women, many of the policy areas discussed were similar to those focused on by other parties. The document offers an extensive range of gendered policy pledges, including a raft of measures to tackle violence against women, domestic and sexual violence, calls to decriminalise sex work and pledges to end pensions inequality and the 'Rape Clause'. In many ways the Greens offered the most radical range of policies to tackle gender equality. The SNP similarly offered a specific mini-manifesto aimed at women which focused most prominently on social security like pensions inequality, improving maternity services and ending the 'rape clause'.

Where the UKIP manifesto did discuss policies targeted at women, they tended to be policies about women rather than for them. Most policies focus on measures aimed at minority women, most of which could be seen as deeply problematic—for example, pledging to institute a screening process for girls deemed as most risk of FGM. Their most high-profile policy proposal affecting women was the proposed ban on face coverings in public. They argued that full-veils were oppressive, a security risk, and perhaps most controversially, bad for women's health as they could lead to vitamin D deficiency (UKIP 2017). These proposals were couched in the language of protecting women from their own culture, reinforcing problematic stereotypes about women and non-white women in particular. The inclusion of these policy proposals not only reflects UKIP's wider political agenda, but also reminds us of the importance of holding political parties to account for the way they portray women in their campaign communications and the implications of such policies.

Plaid Cymru's and the DUP's manifestos offered the fewest policies designed to appeal to women. Plaid Cymru focused on legal or judicial matters, such as improving the way courts treat victims of sexual violence, and social security issues. There was no mention in the manifesto of policies designed to tackle gender-based violence or improving the position of women in employment or public life. The DUP only explicitly mentioned women once in their manifesto in relation to tackling pension inequality. This lack of engagement with women voters has caused some concern since the political views of the DUP have received greater scrutiny outside of Northern Ireland as a result of their agreement to support the Conservative government. Their socially conservative stance on marriage equality and abortion (the latter shared with many nationalists) has been highlighted and has contributed to same-sex marriage remaining prohibited in Northern Ireland and women having far fewer abortion rights than their counterparts in the rest of the UK (Thomson, 2016).

As Table 15.1 makes clear, women were explicitly mentioned in all of the manifestos under discussion and although there was a good deal of variation between the parties in terms of their priorities and approaches, there was a high degree of consensus about the policy issues which are seen as important to women voters. This appears to have changed very little from previous elections (Campbell and Childs, 2015). This shows the extent to which parties remain committed to only incorporating relatively safe, liberal feminist ideas within their policy platforms. Only the Green Party manifesto represented much of an attempt to go beyond this consensus, with its commitment to decriminalising sex work and the detention of women asylum seekers.

3. Candidates

Due to this being a snap election, the selection process for most parties was a hurried one. The approach taken by the Labour Party was indicative of many of the other parties' processes. They invoked an 'emergency' selection process, bypassing the input of local party members who would usually have a vote under ordinary circumstances. Advertisements for vacant seats were posted with closing dates just two days later and the National Executive Committee (NEC) made the final decision. Planned all-women shortlists in many of these seats were suspended due to the urgent nature of the selection, although they were kept in seats where female MPs were retiring. In response to some criticism of this, the Labour NEC later announced their commitment to 50% female candidates at the next general election (Edwards, 2017).

In contrast, the Liberal Democrats did follow through with their recently-adopted commitment to all-women shortlists where male MPs were stepping down, which they adopted after their near wipe-out in 2015 left them with no

Table 15.2 Candidate gender by party, 2015 and 2017 elections

	2015 (Female*)	% Female	2017* (Female*)	% Female
Con	648 (169)	26	638 (184)	29
Lab	631 (214[i])	34	631 (256[ii])	41
Lib Dem	631 (166)	26	630[iii] (184[iv])	29
UKIP	625 (78)	13	378 (49)	13
Green	573 (216)	38	476[v] (164[vi])	35
SNP	59 (21)	36	59 (20)	34
PC	40 (10)	25	40 (11)	28
Sinn Féin	18 (6)	33	18 (7)	39
SDLP	18 (5)	28	18 (6)	33
DUP	16 (0)	0	17 (2)	12
WEP	~	~	7 (7)	100
Total		26		29

[i]Including one trans woman;
[ii]Including two trans women;
[iii]Including one non-binary transgender candidate;
[iv]Including two trans women;
[v]Including two non-binary candidates and a trans man;
[vi] Including one trans woman
*Transgender and non-binary candidates are highlighted here simply to give visibility to them as representatives.
Sources: 'General Election 2015: Results and Analysis', House of Commons Library Briefing Paper, 2015, p. 58 and 'General Election 2017: Results and Analysis', House of Commons Library Briefing Paper, 2017, p. 47.

female MPs. This and other measures to promote diversity in the parliamentary party, including ensuring at least two candidates for every selection were from under-represented group, led to 19 out of their top 20 target seats having female candidates (*New Statesman*, 25 April 2017). Table 15.2 shows the overall percentage of female candidates for these and other parties.

As Table 15.2 shows, apart from the Women's Equality Party, Labour fielded the largest percentage of female candidates at 41%. This was higher than their percentage of female candidates at the last general election (34%), but lower than the percentage of female MPs Labour held at the time of the dissolution of Parliament (44%). Still, they were ahead of their main rival, the Conservatives who, despite a female leader, fielded female candidates in only 29% of seats, although this was up slightly from 2015 when they stood female candidates in 26% of cases. The Liberal Democrats also stood female candidates in 29% of cases, up only slightly from the 26% in 2015, despite the efforts described above to boost female selection. The Greens stood female candidates in 35% of the seats they contested, a fall from 2015, where the figure was 38%. UKIP stood female candidates in only 13% of the seats they contested, by far the lowest of the UK-wide parties. The SNP stood female candidates in 34% of seats, above the average for parties overall but lower than the proportion they stood in 2015 (36%). Plaid

Table 15.3 Female MPs by party after the 2017 General Election

	N	%	Female Representation on Dissolution
Conservatives	67	21	21% (70)
Labour	119	45	44% (101)
Lib Dems	4	33	11% (1)
SNP	12	34	32% (18)
Green	1	100	100% (1)
Other	5	22	23% (5)
All	208	32	30% (196)

Source: 'Women in the House of Commons', Commons Library Briefing Paper, 2017, p. 4.

Cymru stood female candidates in 28% of the seats they contested, higher than last time (25%) but still some way behind some of the other parties. The Northern Irish parties showed much variation. Sinn Féin selected female candidates in 39% of cases. This contrasts with the DUP who stood female candidates in only 12% of cases, the lowest of any party included here, although it was an improvement from the last general election where they stood no female candidates at all.

We now turn to the number of female MPs actually elected, as shown in Table 15.3. Overall there was an incremental increase in female representation, from 30% to 32%. In the lead-up to the election there had been concerns that for the first time since 1979 the proportion of female MPs would fall due to the expected Conservative landslide. A forecast conducted by Hudson (2017) predicted 194 female MPs following the election, meaning a slight drop from the 196 female MPs there were going into the election.

In the event the feared decrease did not happen, but the small increase in female members is still far from the 50% representation needed to achieve parity. A few months before the election was called, the House of Commons Women and Equalities Committee (2016) recommended that the government should seek to introduce legislation to compel political parties to ensure at least 45% of their candidates were women, enforced by fines, among other sanctions, for non-compliance. Observing the sluggish progress seemingly being made on this front, and the very real possibility that female representation could have stalled or reversed, this does not seem unreasonable. Despite the percentage of female candidates overall increasing since the last election (from 26% to 29%), many of the parties, including the more progressive ones such at the Green Party and the SNP, stood a lower proportion of female candidates than at the last general election. This suggests that even progressive parties can slip back on female representation and a legislative mechanism which demanded more from parties on this front may be the only way to prevent this altogether. Despite this, there were some success stories in terms of underrepresented groups. The number of black and minority ethnic women increased by six. These included Preet Gill, the first Sikh female MP, Layla Moran, the Liberal Democrats first BAME woman MP and Marsha de Cordova who was one of two new disabled MPs joining parliament for the first time.

4. Women voters

Historically, there has been little in the way of a gender gap in UK general election voting. (Campbell, 2006). However, a generational gender gap has been identified in previous elections (Norris, 1999) and there was much talk in the run up to the 2017 election about Jeremy Corbyn enthusing and mobilising younger voters. A surge in the youth vote could potentially lead to a gender gap in voting overall, as younger women have recently tended to vote for Labour at much higher rates than they voted Conservative (Campbell and Childs, 2015).

In order to assess the gender differences in vote, we analysed wave 13 of the British Election Study (BES) online survey. The survey was conducted just after the election in June 2017 and respondents were asked to recall how they voted. Figure 15.4 shows the overall gender differences in votes for each party. The data show that women were slightly more likely to have voted for Labour with 42% of women having supported Labour compared to 39% of men. There were only very small gender differences in vote for other parties. This gap is broadly in line with the 2015 post-election data where 36% of women voted for Labour compared to 33% of men (BES wave 6).

Figure 15.5 breaks down the results by age also. Here a notable pattern emerges. Younger women voted overwhelmingly for Labour with 66% of those in the 18-24 age group supporting Labour compared to 15% supporting the Conservatives. For the 26-34 year old age group, 54% of women voted for Labour compared to 28% for the Conservatives. In 2015 a gap of this nature was present but to a lesser degree, with 40% and 29% of 18-24 year-old women voting for Labour and the Conservatives respectively, with similar figures for the 24-34 year-old group (BES wave 6).

In terms of a gender gap between male and female voters within age groups, there is a gender gap in Labour support of over 8% among 18-25 year-olds and almost 6% among 26-34 year-olds. This is similar to the gender gap in 2015 where women in the 18-24 age group voted for Labour at around 9% higher than men and women in the 25-34 age group voted for Labour at 4% higher than men (BES wave 6). These data support the gender generation gap theory put forward by Norris (1999) and indicates seemingly an ongoing pattern.

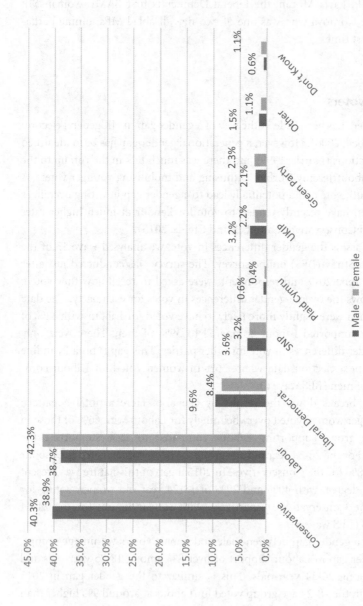

Figure 15.4. General Election 2017 recalled vote by gender
Source: BES Wave 13 (9 June–23 June 2017). N = 26,383, weighted.

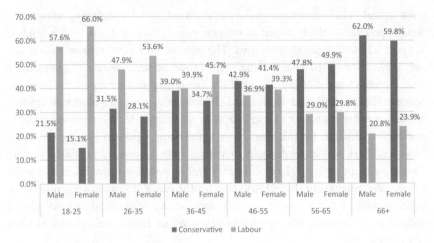

Figure 15.5. General Election 2017 recalled vote by gender and age
Source: BES wave 13 (June 9-23 June 2017). N = 22, 379, weighted.

In contrast to 2015 however, where women in the 46-55 age group and above voted Conservative at a higher rate than men (BES wave 6), in 2017 women from all age groups voted for Labour at slightly higher rates than men. This suggests that women across the board were sceptical of the Conservatives' proposed programme. In terms of the salient issues, many of them were gendered. The 'dementia tax' may have resonated more negatively with women as they tend to live longer than men and more of them may have felt they would be affected. Labour's stronger offers on women's pensions and childcare may well have cut through on the evidence here. More broadly, there is evidence that women have long borne the brunt of the government's public spending cuts programme disproportionately (Women's Budget Group, 2017) and it may be that this has affected women's vote choice.

5. Conclusions

Although in some ways women did clearly play a significant part in the election campaign, in others there was little change from previous elections. Familiarly gendered tropes were in abundance throughout the campaign with the emphasis on May's 'coldness' and the disproportionate criticism of Diane Abbott being two prominent examples. In terms of the extent of representation of female politicians in the media, women fared reasonably well due to the high number of female leaders, and the media's emphasis on leaders. In contrast they fared very poorly in terms of the use of female experts, pollsters and even citizens.

The range of policies aimed at women in most parties' manifestos suggests that parties are keen to compete for female electoral support, but there were few truly radical policies from any of the parties, most of them preferring to replicate similar policies to those aimed at women in previous elections, which tend to support a liberal feminist consensus. The increase in female representation was very slight. From 2010 to 2015 female representation increased by 7%, in contrast with a mere increase of just 2% in 2017. The emergency nature of the selection process likely contributed to this and the reluctance of most parties to impose quotas or other measures to increase their number of female representatives is another explanation for this stagnation. Continuing a pattern observed in 2015, however, there was a gender gap in voting, with women more likely to vote Labour, with an especially large difference among young women. From a feminist perspective, progress in the 2017 election for the cause of women's equality in the political realm was very modest. It was more a case of business as usual than a radical improvement, despite the presence of so many high-profile women representatives.

References

Apostolova, V., Audickas, L., Baker, C., Bate, A., Cracknell, R., Dempsey, N., Hawkins, O., McInnes, R., Rutherford, T. and Uberoi, E. (2017) 'General Election 2017: Results and Analysis', London, House of Commons Library.

Bloom, D. (2017, 21 April). *How Labour is Selecting its Candidates at the 2017 Election*, accessed at http://www.mirror.co.uk/news/politics/how-labour-selecting-candidates-2017-10265227 on 15 June 2017.

Campbell, R. and Childs, S. (2015) 'All Aboard the Pink Battle Bus? Women Voters, Issues, Candidates and Party Leaders', *Parliamentary Affairs*, **68**, 206–223.

Campbell, R. (2006) *Gender and the Vote in Britain*. Colchester, ECPR Press.

Deacon, D., Downey, J., Smith, D., Stanyer, J. and Wring, D. (2017) *Media Coverage of the 2017 General Election Campaign Report 4*. Loughborough, Loughborough University Centre for Research in Communication and Culture.

Dolan, K. and Lynch, T. (2014) 'It Takes a Survey: Understanding Gender Stereotypes, Abstract Attitudes, and Voting for Women Candidates', *American Politics Research* **42**, 656–676.

Edwards, P. (2017) 'It's Official: Local Parties Will Select Their Own Candidates for the Next Election NEC says', accessed at https://labourlist.org/2017/07/its-official-local-par ties-will-select-their-own-candidates-for-next-election-says-nec/ in July 2017.

Evans, E. and Kenny, M. (2017) 'The Women's Equality Party and the 2017 General Election'. In Thorsen E., Jackson, D. and Lilleker, D. (eds) *UK Election Analysis 2017: Media, Voters and the Campaign*, Bournemouth, Centre for the Study of Journalism, Culture and Community Bournemouth University.

Gabriel, D. (2017) 'The othering and objectification of Diane Abbott MP'. In Thorsen E., Jackson, D. and Lilleker, D. (eds) *UK Election Analysis 2017: Media, Voters and the*

Campaign, Bournemouth, Centre for the Study of Journalism, Culture and Community Bournemouth University.

Harmer, E. and Wring, D. (2013) 'Julie and the Cybermums: Marketing and Women Voters in the UK 2010 General Election', *Journal of Political Marketing*, **12**, 262–273.

Harmer, E. (2017a) 'Pink Buses, Leaders' Wives and "The Most Dangerous Woman in Britain": Women, the Press and Politics in the 2015 Election'. In Wring D., Mortimore, R. and Atkinson, S. (eds) *Political Communication in Britain: Polling, Campaigning and Media in the 2015 General Election*, London, Palgrave Macmillan.

Harmer, E. (2017b) 'Online Election News Can be Bloody Difficult (for a) Woman'. In Thorsen, E., Jackson, D. and Lilleker, D. (eds) *UK Election Analysis 2017: Media, Voters and the Campaign*, Bournemouth, Centre for the Study of Journalism, Culture and Community Bournemouth University.

Harmer, E. and Southern, R. (2017) 'Process, personalities and polls: Online News Coverage of the UK General Election 2017'. In Thorsen, E., Jackson, D. and Lilleker, D. (eds) *UK Election Analysis 2017: Media, Voters and the Campaign*. Bournemouth: Centre for the Study of Journalism, Culture and Community Bournemouth University.

Hawkins O., Keen R. and Nakatuude N. (2015) '*General Election 2015: Results and Analysis, House of Commons Library Briefing Paper*', London, House of Commons Library.

Huddy, L. and Terkildsen, N. (1993) 'Gender Stereotypes and the Perception of Male and Female Candidates', *American Journal of Political Science*, **37**, 119–147.

Hudson J. (2017) in 'Political Studies Association Media Briefing Pack', The Political Studies Association, accessed at https://www.psa.ac.uk/sites/default/files/PSA%20GE2017%20Briefing%20Pack.pdf in May 2017.

Jamieson, K. (1995) *Beyond the Double Bind: Women and Leadership*, New York, NY, Oxford University Press.

Kahn, K. (1996) *The Political Consequences of Being a Woman: How Stereotypes Influence the Conduct and Consequences of Political Campaigns*, New York, NY, Colombia University Press.

Kelly, R. and Everett, M. (2017) '*Women in the House of Commons. Background Paper*', London, House of Commons Library.

King D. and Matland R. (2003) 'Sex and the Grand Old Party: An Experimental Investigation of the Effect of Candidate Sex on Support for *a Republican Candidate*', *American Politics Research*, **31**, 595–612.

Lawless, J. (2004) 'Women, War, and Winning Elections: Gender Stereotyping in the Post-September 11th era', *Political Research Quarterly*, **57**, 479–490.

Murray, R. (2010) *Cracking the Highest Glass Ceiling: A Global Comparison of Women's Campaigns for Executive Office*, Santa Barbara, CA, Praeger.

Morris, R. (2017, 25 April) *How the Lib Dems Learned to Love All-women Shortlists*, accessed at http://www.newstatesman.com/politics/staggers/2017/04/how-lib-dems-learned-love-all-women-shortlists on 20 June 2017.

Newman, N. (2017) *Reuters Institute Digital News Report 2017*, Oxford, Reuters Institute for the Study of Journalism Oxford University.

New Statesman (2017, 19 April) 'Brenda from Bristol's Reaction to the Snap General Election Speaks for Us All', accessed at http://www.newstatesman.com/politics/june2017/2017/04/brenda-bristol-s-reaction-snap-general-election-speaks-us-all on 18 June 2017.

Norris, P. (1999) 'Gender: A Gender Generation Gap?' In Evans, G. and Norris, P. (eds) *Critical Elections: British Parties and Voters in Long Term Perspective*, London, Sage.

Ross, K. (2010) *Gendered Media: Women, Men and Identity Politics*, Landham, Rowman and Littlefield.

Thomson, J. (2016) 'Abortion and Same-sex Marriage: How Are Non-sectarian Controversial Issues Discussed in Northern Irish politics?' *Irish Political Studies*, **31**, 483–501.

UKIP (2017) *Britain Together: UKIP 2017 Election Manifesto*, London, UKIP.

Ward, O. (2016) 'Intersectionality and Press Coverage of Political Campaign: Representations of Black, Asian, and Minority Ethnic Female Candidates at the UK 2010 General Election', *International Journal of Press/Politics*, **22**, 43–66.

Women's Budget Group (2017) 'Gender Impact Assessment of the Spring Budget', accessed at https://wbg.org.uk/news/rethinking-austerity-overdue-hit-women-ethnic-minorities-hardest/ on16 June 2017.

Women's Equality Party (2017) 'Our General Election Results', accessed at http://www.womensequality.org.uk/ge_results on 11 July 2017.

Women and Equalities Committee (2016) *Women in the House of Commons After the 2020 Election*, accessed at https://publications.parliament.uk/pa/cm201617/cmselect/cmwomeq/630/630.pdf on June 2017.

Britain Votes (2017) 255–266

SARAH HARRISON*

Young Voters

The non-participatory and participatory aspects of the electoral behaviour of young British people have attracted considerable attention. The discussion of young citizens in elections has mostly focused on their chronically low levels of mobilisation. However, in the context of the General Election 2017, young people were under the spotlight for different reasons, including the party preference gap between young and other voters. Differences in youth voting compared to older voters were also evident in the 2016 Brexit Referendum. The Scottish Independence Referendum of 2014 brought new salience to the debate on giving 16 year olds the right to vote—they were allowed to in the UK for the first time —as most exercised their newly-awarded franchise in that campaign and many appeared to be politically engaged. The estimated turnout of 75% for 16 and 17 year olds compared to 54% of 18-24 year olds. It was unsurprising that, in the weeks leading up to the unanticipated General Election of 2017, the intentions and expected turnout of young people were closely scrutinised. Indeed, discrepancies between pollsters' forecasts were even largely attributed to the question of whether young people would vote in as high numbers as they were promising.

This chapter examines the role of young people in the 2017 General Election. In order to provide an insight into their perceptions and motivations, I look at the specific context of this election for young people, and notably the implications of the Brexit result on the attitudes of young people leading up to the 8 June Election. Using new survey data[1] drawn from the responses of thousands of voters (young and old) I then explore the important role played by young voters in the General Election, from the first indications regarding their registration and turnout to the motivations behind their electoral choice, and the analysis of a

---

*Sarah Harrison, Department of Government, London School of Economics and Political Science, s.l.harrison@lse.ac.uk

[1] Survey data fielded by ECREP-Opinium. Data are used from two separate panels: (i) Panel study survey conducted during the 2016 EU Referendum was fielded in 3 waves: wave 1: 22-28 April 2016 (3008 respondents), wave 2: 17-19 May 2016 (2111 respondents), wave 3: 24-30 June (2113 respondents) and was weighted to reflect a national representative audience; (ii) Survey conducted after the 8 June General Election 2017. The sample consisted of 2004 British respondents between 13 and 16 June 2017. The data were weighted for demographic and social variables but also to match the actual turnout and vote choice of the population.

doi:10.1093/pa/gsx068

number of cases where their mobilisation seemed to change the outcome of a constituency vote. I assess the extent to which young people used their vote to claim their electoral weight within the polity, their ability to shape their future, but also to express a clear desire for change and significant levels of democratic frustration.

The challenge of engaging young people in politics has exercised all democracies. Young citizens report particularly high levels of distrust of political systems, institutions, and social elites, leading to claims of a contemporary 'crisis of democracy' (see for example Newton, 2001; Mishler and Rose, 1997). A growing sense of dissatisfaction towards political systems has been associated with young people (Torcal and Montero, 2006). This has been accompanied by a distinct shift away from many traditional modes of political participation, often evidenced by low turnout in elections (LeDuc *et al.*, 1996, 2002; Franklin, 2004) and the collapse of membership levels of political parties and unions (Scarrow, 1996; Katz and Mair, 1994; Pharr and Putnam, 2000). Whilst such trends are not confined to young people, for this age group, the evidence is most acute. Specifically, Norris *et al.* (2002) found that the participation of young voters has declined across many democracies, and Henn *et al.* (2002) refer to a general trend of youth disengagement from all forms of traditional political activity. Nonetheless, there is ample debate concerning the interpretation of this decline in youth participation. Cammaerts *et al.* (2014, 2016), for instance, question the existence of widespread youth apathy. They suggest instead that there is a genuine appetite for involvement, underlining that young people insist that elections remain the key to democratic participation but often feel the political offer fails to address their concerns.

1.   An unusual focus on the youth electorate: From the Brexit Referendum to the General Election 2017

In the aftermath of the result of the Brexit Referendum, much debate ensued concerning the participation and preferences of the youth electorate. Young people were criticised initially for their low turnout in the Referendum. Participation was reported to be only 46% for the 18-24-year-old electorate (Sky Data, 2016). However, on closer inspection this figure of 46% was in fact an estimate based on previous data concerning voting regularity in the 2015 election. Yet, we know that young people are much less likely to be registered to vote. In July 2014, the Electoral Commission confirmed that 'younger people (under 35) are considerably less likely to be registered' with only 70.2% of 20-24 year olds present on electoral registers, against 95.5% of 65+ year olds (UK Electoral Commission, 2014). Therefore, an estimation of turnout based on an overall proportion of the total population can be misleading particularly in the case of young people.

Allowing for low registration which has to be taken into account, turnout for the younger population was in fact substantially higher than previously reported. It was 64% for the 18-24 age group, only eight points below the national average. Whilst still below that of older voters, turnout for young people was probably closer to the national average than in any other national election in recent memory.

Traditionally, when thinking of the fracture lines that have split the vote of the British electorate over the years, the impact of social class (Butler and Stokes, 1974; Butler and Kavanagh, 2002), the North South divide (McMahon *et al.*, 1992) or the differences between cities and the country (Jennings and Stoker, 2017) have been considered as the most important cleavages in explaining voter behaviour. However, the youth vote drew exceptional attention in the aftermath of the 2016 Brexit Referendum. The result reflected a substantial generational divide with an overwhelming majority of young people voting for the UK to remain in the European Union (Skinner and Gottfried, 2017). The exposition of a stark divergence between the preferences of young and older voters in relation to Britain's place within and relationship with the European Union is not a particularly new phenomenon. Indeed, it was previously highlighted by a series of questions that we included in a survey which probed implicit and explicit associations with the EU (Bruter and Harrison, 2016). When asked to compare the EU to an animal, older Brits chose a representation of an elephant, whilst younger respondents preferred to associate the EU with a lion. When asked to compare the EU to a painting, older Brits chose Guernica and the young a Dance by Matisse. Similarly, when we asked for a human trait, the top answer amongst the old was stupidity and amongst the young intelligence. The symbolism of these contrasted visions should not be dismissed as they offer a real insight into the juxtaposed visions that British citizens hold. These perceptions of the EU shed light upon the divisions within British society and how differently the younger and older generations perceive the EU. In line with this stronger sense of identity association with Europe and a stronger attachment to the cultural aspects of the shared community, young people also showed higher levels of emotion in the wake of the Referendum result. 46% of those aged 18-24 admitted to having tears in their eyes when they discovered the result of the Referendum, and 51% felt anger and 46% disgust at those who had voted differently from them (Bruter and Harrison, 2017).

2.   Registration and voting at the General Election

Efforts to increase voter registration were again prioritised during the run up to the election in June 2017. An enthusiastic registration drive from social networks including Facebook and Snapchat that encouraged their users to register to vote contributed to the efforts of getting more young people engaged. Similarly, campaigns led by 'Bite the Ballot' and #TurnUp encouraged young voters to register and to turnout on Election Day, echoed by contemporary musicians ranging from Pink Floyd frontman David Gilmour to Grime artist JME. A website 'mynearestmarginal.com' also encouraged tactical voting from students suggesting that they register at the address where their vote would count the most. Furthermore, the Labour Party made explicit efforts to mobilise young voters by implementing digital technology and media communication tools that targeted specific messages to local electorates, and more notably by promising to abolish university tuition fees should they form the next government.

The Cabinet Office reported that 246,000 young people under the age of 25 (compared to just 10,000 people over the age of 65) registered on the last possible day before the general election. This was the first tangible indication that young people's stated intention to mobilise should be taken seriously by all involved in the election. In addition, the question of whether the young would seek their 'revenge' after being marginalised in the Referendum was one of the most anticipated issues concerning the election. In this context, it is not surprising that young people were seen as a potential target by some political parties and a threat by others. Most parties from the so-called 'progressive camp' (Labour, Liberal-Democrats, Greens, SNP) tried to address young people and the resentment that many expressed over the Brexit result.

On election night, it soon became clear that young people's promised mobilisation and coordinated effort to oppose the incumbent Government had gone beyond everyone's expectations in shaping the outcome of a hung parliament. According to Figure 16.1, turnout of 18-24 year olds was a remarkably high 71%, although this is contested by the British Election Study. This reports 18-24 year old turnout as little different from 2015, but notes increased turnout among 30-40 year olds and a bigger Labour vote share among all age categories up to 40.

As the 2014, 2016 and 2017 contests illustrated, some young people can be motivated to participate when the stakes are perceived to be high. The emphasis on optimistic plans and prognoses for the future seem to echo particularly well for young people. In light of these various motivations that often underpin young people's choice of vote, we now turn to the specific details of the election result.

In terms of party choice, young voters aged 18-24 voted in especially higher numbers for the Labour party (63% compared to 40% for the overall population) and much less for the Conservative party (24% as opposed to 42% for the overall population). Support for the Liberal Democrats amongst young people was higher in some constituencies with large student populations, and in particular where the Liberal Democrats were the main adversaries of the Conservatives.

REGISTERED VOTER TURNOUT

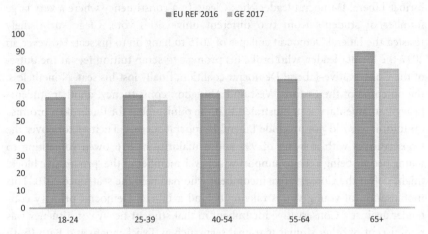

Figure 16.1. Turnout by age amongst registered voters in the 2016 EU referendum and the 2017 General Election
Sources: Please see Note 1

These results raise some critical questions. Was the youth vote predominantly a vote 'for Labour' or 'against the Tories'? Did it vary according to local context and battles? And what were the key motivations behind it? Before turning our attention to the electoral motivations of young voters and how they differed from those expressed by the rest of the British population, we will now briefly examine a few key constituencies where young voters—and notably students—represent a prominent segment of the electorate to identify their effect at the local level.

3. Three key constituencies: Cardiff North, Sheffield Hallam, and Oxford West

An interesting picture emerges when we look at the results from these three constituencies with traditionally large populations of young people. At the local level, large young and student populations typically benefited Labour, including against the Liberal Democrats in Sheffield Hallam, but could also benefit other anti-Conservative candidates, including the Liberal Democrats in constituencies such as Oxford West, Eastbourne, Twickenham and Bath.

In 2015, Cardiff North was identified as one of the top ten constituencies with the largest proportions of student population in the country, and one which Labour critically needed to win. They failed to do so and the Conservatives increased their majority to over 2,000. But in 2017 the fortunes of the two parties were reversed and, with a 6% swing, Labour won by over 4,000 votes. Sheffield

Hallam has been in the spotlight for several consecutive elections as the seat of former Liberal Democrat leader Nick Clegg. In a constituency where a very large number of students from two different universities vote, Clegg surprisingly resisted the Liberal Democrat collapse of 2015 to hang on to his seat. However, in 2017 the former leader, who broke his promise to scrap tuition fees at the outset of the Conservative-Liberal Democrat coalition, finally lost his seat. Nonetheless, the outcome of the Oxford West and Abingdon constituency, another student-heavy Parliamentary seat, illustrated that the punishment for the broken promise on tuition fees did not preclude Liberal Democrat success. Their victory over the Conservatives with a swing of 9% and a majority of 816 owed something to young people being keen to support whichever member of the 'progressive block' might defeat the Conservative incumbent who had held the seat since 2010. This mobilisation of young voters rallying behind a Liberal Democrat primary contender against a Conservative incumbent in that student-heavy constituency was reminiscent of other similar marginal seats such as Twickenham and Bath (both seats were taken from the Conservatives).

The electoral results of these three constituencies (where the weight of the youth vote was substantial) raise important questions regarding the motivations underpinning the preferences of young citizens who voted. Why did young people choose to mobilise so much more than usual and why did they vote the way they did and what did they try to achieve? The next section explores the motivations behind the youth vote by examining the responses to a selection of questions from our survey conducted in the aftermath of the election.

4. Motivations of the youth vote: Desire for change and a rejection of 'hard Brexit'

Whilst the youth vote was clearly far more important than most commentators had expected, and whilst it clearly benefited Labour and in some specific cases the Liberal Democrats, a number of possible hypotheses can be offered to understand what motivated the electoral choice of the young. A first possibility is that the young were seduced by specific policies proposed by the Labour Party, notably the abolition of tuition fees directly targeted towards the young electorate. This is particularly relevant as the Conservative Party failed to address the preferences of the young electorate and largely underestimated their weight in the result. Whilst the Conservative Party failed to address young people in their manifesto, in contrast, young voters may have been indeed seduced by the personality and direct appeals of the Labour leader, Jeremy Corbyn. Yet the Labour Party had accepted the result of Brexit and pledged to implement the democratic decision of the voters, an acquiescence regarding the result which perhaps ought to have disappointed most young people. The election was perceived as an opportunity for young people to express their discontent about the Brexit result and their frustration towards the way politics is conducted.

To arbitrate between those conflicting explanations, we asked respondents about the specific motivations underpinning their choice of vote. These motivations included all of the following: the wish to express their frustration at the current political situation; the desire to express their enthusiasm for the programme of the party that they chose; the desire to position themselves against a version of Brexit that would be unacceptable to them; the wish to express their enthusiasm at the leader of the party they voted for; a vote for change; a vote for stability; or a desire to be better represented even if it did not influence who governed the country. On the whole, all of those motivations proved highly relevant to young citizens and the population in general alike. However, the most interesting finding concerns the nature of the differences between the prominence of given motivations for 18-24 year olds as compared to the rest of the sample.

Four key reasons provided the main motivations uniquely characteristic of the youth vote: (i) the expression of democratic frustration; (ii) the positioning against Brexit; (iii) the desire for change; (iv) and the support for the party programme. By contrast, enthusiasm for the party leader, stability, and representation were not significantly higher amongst young people compared to their older counterparts. These findings and the comparison with other voters are summarised in Table 16.1.

Specifically, young voters were found to be 16% more likely to be motivated by a desire for change than the average voter; 12% more likely to use their vote to express their opposition to a certain vision of Brexit; 11% more likely to express frustration at the current political situation; and 11% more likely than the average voter to express their support for the programme of the party that they voted for. All four of those motivations were mentioned by over 80% of young people aged

Table 16.1 Differentials in voting motivations of 18-24 year olds compared to other voters, 2017 General Election

Electoral Choice Motivation	Differential (young–average)
Desire for change	+16
Opposition to form of Brexit	+12
Frustration	+11
Support for party programme	+11
Support for party leader	+6
Representation	+1
Stability	0

Source: ECREP-Opinium. See Note 1.

18-24. By contrast, there was no major difference between respondents aged 18-24 and the rest of the population when expressing the desire for stability, better representation, or expressing enthusiasm for the leader of the party they voted for, all of which were largely in line with the answers of the rest of the population. It is noteworthy that in contrast to the prominent narrative in the media in the aftermath of the election, the personality of the party leader does not seem to be a notably higher motivation for young people compared to the rest of the population.

The most striking aspect of these findings is that they highlight the specificity of motivations amongst young people, in particular those with a negative connotation. Indeed, the first three motivations for vote choice were: (i) desire for change, including a rejection and negation of the status quo expressed as a direct desire to depart from the existing politics; (ii) strong opposition to the Brexit process and the necessary changes that it would bring in terms of the reformulation of vision and identity of the UK; and (iii) a sense of frustration with the current political situation. Insights gained from additional qualitative details provided by young voters themselves highlighted that the desire for change also included negativity towards the introduction of widespread austerity measures (of which young people were often seen as the victims), and the desire to express support for party programmes and policies with prominent references to youth-specific measures such as the promised abolition of tuition fees, which became a central part of the Labour manifesto during the campaign.

In summary, the motivations expressed by young voters seem to encapsulate their desire to oppose a certain direction and vision for the future of the UK. This sense of negativity expressed towards the political system is also illustrated by findings that confirm differences in levels of frustration between younger and older age groups, as Table 16.2 shows although high standard deviations suggest the need for cautious interpretation. Overall, 18-24 year olds claim to experience higher levels of frustration with the democratic system than people aged 25 and over. The largest differences between younger and older citizens concern frustration towards the political system. Within the indices, items that were particularly salient within the dominant political dimension were, for example, the perception that politicians do not fight for the socio-tropic interest but only for their own, the feeling of not being listened to, and the lack of long-term vision from politicians. These three items featured in the highest difference of means between the young and older age groups. Lower differences existed between younger and older voters for frustration expressed towards the institutional framework, such as the criticism concerning the absence of democratic involvement for all citizens. In terms of ideological frustration, young people reported that the existing offer does meet their preferences.

Table 16.2 Frustration indices amongst young and older voters in the 2017 General Election

Frustration Indices	18-24	25 and over	Difference
Political	53.9 (27.9)	50.1 (28.1)	+3.8
Absence of socio-tropic interest	*59.2 (31.6)*	*52.5 (31.8)*	*+6.7*
Not listened to	*53.0 (28.7)*	*49.1 (30.2)*	*+3.9*
Lack of long-term vision	*52.2 (29.9)*	*48.5 (30.1)*	*+3.7*
Institutional	45.4 (26.1)	43.2 (26.6)	+2.2
Lack of inclusive democracy	*43.7 (27.6)*	*40.2 (27.5)*	*+3.5*
Ideological	44.2 (26.6)	41.8 (24.9)	+2.4
Lack of political offer	*46.4 (28.4)*	*42.5 (28.0)*	*+3.9*
Overall	48.9 (25.5)	45.9 (25.2)	+3.0

Source: ECREP-Opinium. See Note 1. Standard deviations in brackets.

This insidious feeling of frustration also tainted young people's perceptions of the atmosphere of the General Election. When asked to characterise the atmosphere of the campaign election, the main adjectives mentioned by young people aged 18-24 were tense (38%), democratic (31%), aggressive (28%) and fractious (27%). By contrast, only 9% of young citizens described the atmosphere of the election as constructive and only 8% as respectful. Even more importantly, however, when asked how they felt towards people who voted differently from them, young people felt more hostility than the rest of the population. While 71% expressed anger at people who voted for the party they liked least (in contrast to 45% for the national average), 75% expressed frustration (versus 62%), 66% expressed distrust (versus 57%), and 57% even described feeling some disgust towards those people who voted for the party that they liked least (versus 44%). This persistence of negative feelings towards what is perceived as an opposing part of the electorate is critical, not only because it emphases how politically isolated many of the young feel in British society, but also because it is, in all likelihood, one of the main factors that led to a much higher mobilisation of the young than originally expected: to ensure their voice would no longer be unheard. Such inter-generational hostility may not necessarily be seen as healthy for the polity.

5. Conclusion: A 'youthquake'?

When the 2017 General Election was announced, many observers expected that young voters would be largely irrelevant to the final outcome of the election due to their lack of enthusiasm for politics, accompanied by poor mobilisation and perennial low levels of turnout in elections. Instead, young people became possibly the most featured demographic group of the election. The youth vote contributed to the denial of a Conservative overall majority. Young voters were keen to express their desire for change, demonstrate opposition to Brexit a year after the Referendum, and indicate frustration at the perceived current political situation. Yet the extent of youth support for Labour, a party committed to Brexit, indicated disjuncture between the ambitions of many and the willingness of their electoral choice to articulate their political position.

The General Election showed that young people are not disengaged from political debate. Young people, perhaps more so than any than other age category, have ideals and aspirations about what democracy should be and how their political system should deliver those expectations. It is clear from their discourse that they are eager to hear messages of positive transformation and are willing to support ambitions that will help create solidarity and social cohesion. Many young people tend to be suspicious of elites and politicians, yet they find it easier to get passionate about an issue than they do about a party. In this context, we witnessed high turnout among 18-24 year olds in the Brexit Referendum.

Our findings reveal that young voters—those between the ages of 18 and 24 years old—were significantly more motivated by a desire for change, a rejection of the vision of Brexit promoted by the Government and frustration with the current political climate than the rest of the voting population. It is clear that Brexit has left many young people feeling marginalised and that their identity has been redefined by older generations. They decided to embrace the next available opportunity to have their voice heard and try to correct the trajectory of a future which the Brexit vote had made so divergent from their own overwhelming preference—whatever the illogicality of supporting Labour in this context. The perception that Labour might offer a softer Brexit or even reverse the exit policy may have prevailed. The question begged is whether the referendum-based engagement, sustained in a Brexit-dominated election, will be maintained in future elections. The current level of political turmoil suggests the answer is probably yes.

References

Bruter, M. and Harrison, S. (2012) How European Do You Feel? The Psychology of European Identity. Report published in collaboration with Opinium Research and Lansons Communications, accessed at http://opinium.co.uk/how-european-do-you-feel/ on 19 July 2017.

Bruter, M. and Harrison, S. (2016) *Impact of Brexit on Consumer Behaviour*, accessed at http://opinium.co.uk/wp-content/uploads/2016/08/the_impact_of_brexit_on_con sumer_behaviour_0.pdf on 23 September 2017.

Bruter, M. and Harrison, S. (2017) 'Understanding the Emotional Act of Voting', *Nature: Human Behaviour*, **1**, 1–3.

Butler, D. and Stokes, D. (1974) *Electoral Change in Britain*, London, Macmillan.

Butler, D. and Kavanagh, D. (2002) *The British General Election of 2001*, Basingstoke, Palgrave.

Cammaerts, B., Bruter, M., Banaji, S., Harrison, S. and Anstead, N. (2016) *Youth Participation in Europe: In Between Hope and Disillusion*, Basingstoke, Palgrave.

Cammaerts, B., Bruter, M., Banaji, S., Harrison, S. and Anstead, N. (2014) 'The Myth of Youth Apathy: Young Europeans' Critical Attitudes Toward Democratic Life, *American Behavioral Scientist*, **58**, 645–664.

Electoral Commission (2014) *The Quality of the 2014 Electoral Register*, accessed at http://www.electoralcommission.org.uk/__data/assets/pdf_file/0005/169889/Completeness-and-accuracy-of-the-2014-electoral-registers-in-Great-Britain.pdf on 29 September 2017.

Franklin, M. N. (2004) *Voter Turnout and the Dynamics of Electoral Competition in Established Democracies since 1945*, Cambridge, Cambridge University Press.

Henn, M., Weinstein, M. and Wring, D. (2002) 'A Generation Apart? Youth and Political Participation in Britain', *British Journal of Politics and International Relations*, **4**, 167–192.

Jennings, W. and Stoker, G. (2017) 'Tilting Towards the Cosmopolitan Axis? Political Change in England and the 2017 General Election', *The Political Quarterly*, **88**, 359–369.

Katz, P. and Mair, P. (1994) *How Parties Organise*, London, Sage.

LeDuc, L., Niemi, R. and Norris, P. (eds) (1996) *Comparing Democracies: Elections and Voting in Global Perspective*, London, Sage.

McMahon, D., Heath, A., Harrop, M. and Curtice, J. (1992) 'The Electoral Consequences of North-South Migration', *British Journal of Political Science*, **22**, 419–443.

Mishler, W. and Rose, R. (1997) 'Trust, Distrust and Skepticism: Population Evaluations of Civil and Political Institutions in Post-communist Societies, *The Journal of Politics*, **59**, 418–451.

Newton, K. (2001) 'Trust, Social Capital, Civil Society, and Democracy', *International Political Science Review*, **22**, 201–214.

Norris, P., Niemi, R. G. and LeDuc, L. (eds) (2002) *Comparing Democracies 2: New Challenges in the Study of Slections and Voting*, London, Sage.

Pharr S. and Putnam, R. (eds) (2000) *Disaffected Democracies? What's Troubling the Trilateral Countries?*, Princeton, NJ, Princeton University Press.

Scarrow, S. (1996) *Parties and Their Members*, Oxford, Oxford University Press.

Skinner, G. (2015) *How Britain Voted in 2015*, IPSOSMori, accessed at https://www.ipsos.com/ipsos-mori/en-uk/how-britain-voted-2015 on 23 September 2017.

Skinner, G. and Gottfried, G. (2017) *How Britain Voted in the 2016 EU Referendum*, accessed at https://www.ipsos.com/ipsos-mori/en-uk/how-britain-voted-2016-eu-refer endum on 23 September 2017.

Sky Data (2016) accessed at https://twitter.com/SkyData/status/746700869656256512 on 23 September 2017.

Torcal, M. (2006) 'Political Disaffection and Democratization History in New Democracies'. In Torcal, M. and Montero, J. M. (eds) *Political Disaffection in Contemporary Democracies: Social Capital, Institutions, and Politics*, London, Routledge, pp. 157–189.

Van der Eijk, C. and Franklin, M. (2009) *Elections and Voters*, Basingstoke, Palgrave Macmillan

Van der Eijk, C. and Franklin, M. N. (1996) *Choosing Europe? The European Electorate and National Politics in the Face of Union*, Ann Arbor, MI, University of Michigan Press.

Britain Votes (2017) 267–276

JONATHAN TONGE, CRISTINA LESTON-BANDEIRA AND STUART WILKS-HEEG*

Conclusion: An Election that Satisfied Few and Solved Little

Rarely can a partial election victory have felt so akin to a defeat for a party. As the Conservatives scrambled in the aftermath to clinch an expensive deal with their only friends at Westminster, the Democratic Unionist Party, they ruefully reflected on how their majority had been mislaid. A Prime Minister who had called an unnecessary election had witnessed her Party's apparently unassailable position at the outset of the contest eroded. The Conservatives' lead over Labour diminished almost daily; ditto her lead over Jeremy Corbyn. An election without reason, an awful campaign and an uninspiring manifesto combined to provide the hollowest of partial victories.

Britain Votes 2015 concluded by arguing that the sunlit uplands apparently offered by the surprise Conservative overall majority were cloudier than might be immediately apparent. It highlighted the dangers of the Brexit referendum as an exercise in internal party management and the continuing problems for the Conservative Party—short on members, young votes and ideas. The 2015 election was won primarily on economic competence; an election which strayed beyond that territory could be more problematic. The 2017 election was not a contest in which fiscal prudence and responsibility dominated to the extent of 2015. By 2017, the Conservatives had abandoned the deficit elimination targets trumpeted in 2015 and the Labour Party could reasonably gamble that another election fought on austerity terms might bore the voters. The 2017 outcome demonstrated that a cautious take on the Conservatives' 2015 victory was justified. That said, a remotely competent Conservative campaign in 2017 would surely have delivered a reasonable parliamentary majority, given the evidence of council election results only one month earlier. Instead, May's campaign was beset by difficulties. As Bale and Webb have charted, disagreements over the wisdom of calling the election, a lack of trust between Conservative HQ and grassroots activists, an overly presidential campaign (only a good idea if the leader has something to say), an

*Jonathan Tonge, Department of Politics, University of Liverpool, j.tonge@liverpool.ac.uk;
Cristina Leston-Bandeira, School of Politics and International Studies, University of Leeds,
c.leston-bandeira@leeds.ac.uk; Stuart Wilks-Heeg, Department of Politics, University of Liverpool,
swilks@liverpool.ac.uk

doi:10.1093/pa/gsx069

underestimation of Corbyn the campaigner (perhaps his main asset) and a sharp drop in levels of activism were all evident.

Whatever the campaigning inadequacies, the Brexit context of the election ought to have helped deliver a Conservative victory. The British Election Study shows that the Conservatives netted 60% of the Leave vote and indicates that more than half of UKIP's 2015 voters who voted again in 2017 switched to the Conservatives, with only 18% supporting Labour. That this did not get the Conservatives over the line owed much to Labour's solid position as the party of Remain, irrespective of party policy. Labour won the majority of the Remain vote, compared to only one-quarter backing the Conservatives and a mere 15% for the party of Remain, the Liberal Democrats (Fieldhouse and Prosser, 2017). According to the Ashcroft polls, nearly half of the under-50 Conservative supporters in 2015 who had backed Remain in 2016 did not back the Conservatives in 2017 (Ashcroft, 2017, p. xi). There were other pluses for Labour, illuminated in the British Election Study. The Party won a majority of vote switchers from 2015 and a majority of those undecided who to vote for at the start of the campaign, contributing to the rapid erosion of a 14% Conservative lead at the commencement of the contest (Fieldhouse and Prosser, 2017). Labour's increase in vote share was above 12% in three types of constituencies: where turnout rose by more than 5%; where 18-24 year olds comprised over 10% of electors; and where the proportion of students was above 9% (*Observer*, 2017).

As Eunice Goes has shown, Labour provided grassroots mobilisation while the leadership provided generous retail offers. Some were outright giveaways, the free university education pledge being one example. A more energetic and focused Conservative campaign might have concentrated more forensically upon affordability and whether Labour's 'fully costed' manifesto was a 'properly costed' one. Huge increases in NHS funding were likely to be universally popular (the Conservatives were also pledging significant extra cash) but other pledges were more targeted. The university tuition fee pledge attracted considerable interest, while costing £10 billion annually. There would also be a 'National Transformation Fund' that would 'invest £250 billion over ten years in upgrading our economy' (Labour Party, 2017, p. 11). Yet Labour's insistence that only the top 5% of earners, those with incomes of more than £80,000 per year, would pay more in tax was not seriously challenged. Nor was Labour's absence of a figure for the proposed rise in corporation tax in an extensive, 128-page manifesto.

The Conservatives were obliged to defend (or even adjust, mid-campaign) their own policies such as the so-called 'dementia tax'. The retention of the Party's huge lead among older voters suggests perhaps that little damage was wrought by that policy. Moreover, the manifesto listing of an 'ageing society' as one of the Conservatives' five great challenges and the determination to tackle some of its financial implications was reasonable (Conservative Party, 2017, p. 6). The plan to raise the means-test threshold to £100,000 would provide some protection for those with modest assets. However, the Conservative leadership appeared nervous and uncertain when challenged on the details. The inclusion of a person's property as an asset meant that many in need of social care might have to sell their home to pay for prolonged care, yet the Conservatives struggled to admit that this was indeed the case.

The problems afflicting the Conservatives should not be exaggerated. This was the fifth consecutive election at which the Party increased its vote share, reaching its highest proportion since 1983. An important point made by David Denver is that the change in vote share coefficient for the Conservative and Labour parties is modest. Changes in vote shares at a constituency level for the 'big two' were not closely related. Both increased their vote shares and this was not an election of large-scale switching between either party (the level was akin to the two previous elections), but more about the bolstering of two-party politics. Conservatives were never going to desert their party for a Corbyn-led Labour Party. Moreover, this was something of a patchwork quilt of an election result, with swings to the Conservatives in north-east England and Scotland, hardly any swing at all in the Midlands and a huge swing to Labour in pro-EU London.

Perhaps the primary issue for the Conservative Party is its life-cycle reliance upon voters becoming conservative—small and large c—as they grow older. If this does not happen, the Conservatives need the turnout of younger voters to be low. Based on the 2017 result, life-cycle effects in terms of producing majority Conservative support are not occurring until voters are reaching their late forties. The Conservatives have not won a handsome majority at an election for three decades. The Party strengthened its position among the working-class but lost ground in the larger middle-class. The traditional class model of voting is now perhaps mere embellishment and detail, 'turned completely upside down in 2017' (Ford, 2017, p. 28), as the Conservatives saw big gains (13%) among the skilled working class but lost middle-class voters to Labour. Worryingly for the Conservatives, there was (unusually for British politics) evidence of a gender voting gap, as discussed earlier by Emily Harmer and Rosalynd Southern, with a modest lead for Labour of 3.6% among women. A woman leader did not hide another gender gap—that of few women Conservative MPs, at 21% comfortably the lowest percentage of the sizeable British parties at Westminster.

This inability to reach sufficient groups of voters has led the Conservatives to rely upon two very different parliamentary partners—the Liberal Democrats and the DUP—to nudge them over the finishing line in recent years. The price for the DUP's support was predictably high, no doubt ongoing and undermining of a Conservative case based upon fiscal prudence, regardless of whether the term inducement or bribe is deployed. These criticisms cannot be fully allayed by the Prime Minister's restatement of her party as Conservative and Unionist, portraying the hitherto largely ignored DUP as natural allies (although they clearly are on Brexit). It was, palpably, a case of needs must and, for all the understandable hostility and sanctimony, any other governing party would have acted similarly to remain in office.

Labour's buoyancy as a rejuvenated party is juxtaposed with the reality of a third consecutive substantial election defeat, a lack of clarity on what its leadership requires from Brexit, continuing scepticism from many electors over its economic competence and a parliamentary party still sufficiently far from convinced by the leader; at best, Corbyn-lite rather than Corbynite. The party's unexpected headway in June 2017, however, bolstered confidence to the point where the party leader could claim, less than four months later at Labour's annual conference, that the party's ideas, such as free university education and the nationalisation of energy, rail and mail, were mainstream, part of a new political centre ground. Moreover, Labour does not have to take the hard decisions on Brexit; as such the party can position itself around whatever ideas offered the greatest immediate electoral advantage until Brexit is enacted. The next election will be fought on Labour's manifesto policies rather than Corbyn's past. As such, coherence and competence will be required to an extent beyond that demanded in 2017.

So where can Labour progress to make the seat gains necessary to enter government? Scotland potentially offers fertile ground, notwithstanding the disarray of Scottish Labour over the last decade. Setting aside the effectiveness of Ruth Davidson as Scottish Conservative leader, Ailsa Henderson and James Mitchell have shown that it is Labour which is best placed, electorally, with lots of close constituency second places, and politically, if Scotland's national conversation does move away from nationalism versus unionism. The SNP's electoral fortunes may now rest more upon the quality of its governance rather than its referendum pledges on the national question. Meanwhile, Wales remains solidly Labour and modest further gains are possible.

The one UK-wide party of opposition to Brexit, the Liberal Democrats, flopped. As Cutts and Russell have demonstrated, the Liberal Democrats still rely on votes that are lent rather than owned, bereft of a clear political identity and programme to enthuse support. 2017 represented a clear opportunity for the Party to attract a substantial proportion of the 48% Remain vote in the previous year's referendum, yet a combination of a lack of a distinctive programme beyond Brexit opposition, the legacy of coalition with the Conservatives deterring potential Labour deserters and the inability of Tim Farron as party leader to shape the campaign, all contributed to a very modest performance in potentially favourable circumstances.

What of UKIP and the Greens? While they are very different parties, James Dennison has shown that there are several parallel explanations for the decline of UKIP and the Greens between 2015 and 2017. In both cases, these parties lost their respective places in the UK party system, media interest in them declined, while membership levels and financial donations also fell. The root causes were different, although they were in many ways mirror images. UKIP's position was undermined by Theresa May's decision to position the Conservatives as the party of Brexit after the 2016 referendum vote. The Greens, by contrast, faced the challenge of Jeremy Corbyn repositioning the Labour Party on the same part of the political spectrum which the Greens had been almost the sole occupants of since the early 2000s. As the title of Dennison's chapter aptly puts it, UKIP and the Greens found that the rug had been pulled from under them. A continuation of the current political circumstances could challenge their very survival. While the existential threat facing UKIP is arguably much greater, the uncertainties and controversies surrounding the nature of the UK's withdrawal from the EU may yet create the conditions for UKIP's revival, particularly if Nigel Farage returns to lead the party.

Faced with a dual squeeze on their respective positions in the party system and on their respective resource bases, both parties fielded fewer candidates in 2017 than 2015. The Greens attempted to forge a 'progressive alliance' with Labour and the Liberal Democrats, involving electoral pacts in key constituencies, but the Party was ultimately reduced to standing its own candidates down to help Labour or the Liberal Democrats without reciprocal arrangements. Only 11% of the electorate reported having been contacted in the last few weeks of the campaign by UKIP and 12% by the Greens, compared to 40% and 22% respectively in 2015. With voters realigning around the main two parties in 2017, the fate of UKIP and the Greens was sealed.

Despite these commonalities, Dennison underlines that UKIP and the Greens experienced very different patterns of change in their respective voter bases from 2015 to 2017. The 594,000 voters who opted for UKIP in 2017 were, by and large, UKIP loyalists. Moreover, 2017 UKIP voters were virtually identical to their 2015 counterparts in their socio-demographic profiles and political attitudes. By contrast, the Greens experienced a remarkable turnover in their electoral base. Only 25% of Green voters in 2017 had also cast ballots for the party in 2015. Any change in the Green Party's fortunes is therefore likely to depend on Labour moving back towards the centre ground—a scenario which would appear unlikely in the coming years.

For all parties, the 2017 election campaign might be considered exceptional, its calling a surprise (not least to most of the Government's own MPs), its punctuations, due to terrorism, stark and its conduct often novel, in terms of the tactics used. In terms of the usual financial asymmetry of resources, Justin Fisher has shown how Labour enjoyed healthy finances prior to the election, thanks to its massive increase in party membership. Whilst the Conservatives proved as adept as ever in raising finance quickly during the campaign, their financial advantage was somewhat offset to a degree by the sudden calling of the election. Given some controversial claims and cases following the 2015 contest, parties were careful to dissociate national from local/constituency campaign spending.

As the contributions from Wring and Ward and Dommett and Temple indicate, 2017 saw an increase in digital campaigning, partly to offset the lack of time to prepare more long-term campaigning. Digital campaigning is changing the way parties engage with the public. Facebook campaigns were of considerable utility to the Conservatives in 2015. In 2017, Labour upped its social media game. Labour may benefit particularly (but far from exclusively) from 'satellite campaigns', which are not led by the actual parties but by other groups. These may not be under the same restrictions and rules (particularly financial stringencies) that shape traditional party campaigning. This raises important questions about the future of campaigning, namely in terms of party control and activist organisation.

In terms of modern campaigning activity, the 2017 election showed levels of mobilisation by young people not seen before. A slight increase in turnout among 18-24 year olds, a category still considerably voting-averse as in the previous quarter-of-a century, contributed to Labour's advance, but more important was Labour's much-improved share of the youth vote. In the six weeks following the calling of the election, three million people applied to join the electoral registers, with more than a third of those applying aged under 25. On the final day of registration, more than two-thirds of the 622,000 who applied to join the registers were aged under 35. Even allowing for the probability that a sizeable portion of these were 'duplicate' applications from electors already registered and not net additions to the register, the surge in younger voters joining the registers was evident. Social media provided an ideal forum for oppositional campaigning and protest against the status quo, although Eunice Goes' analysis of Labour's effort also highlighted the Party's capacity, with its high membership, to deploy activists on more traditional doorstep campaigns and to provide favourable media visual coverage for Labour via the large public election rallies for the leader. Momentum's website, My Nearest Marginal, helped facilitate the arrival of thousands of activists to key Labour targets, defensive or offensive. More than 70,000 activists used the site to help organise rallies, street canvassing, and text messaging. With a high rate of opening, texting is more effective in conveying messages than easily deleted emails.

New techniques were accompanied by new voters. As Sarah Harrison's contribution has illuminated, young people used their vote to claim their electoral weight within the polity, their ability to shape their future restated after many were affronted by the Brexit referendum result. The 2017 election allowed expression of a desire for change amid significant levels of democratic frustration. Despite the importance of new campaigning techniques and new voters, however, the 2017 election saw an interplay of old and new campaign features. As has been demonstrated in Wring and Ward's consideration of the media's coverage of the contest, traditional broadcast media, especially television, remains very important as an information source, notwithstanding the growth of social media, which can still act as an echo chamber rather than a game-changer. And contrary to expectations and to the role played by social media, this was in many ways a traditional type of election, being highly presidentialised and focused on the two main parties.

The increased participation of young voters has been welcomed and may feed into the continuing debate over whether the voting age should be lowered. Of the Westminster parties, only the Conservatives and the DUP are opposed, although there is no evidence of a groundswell of support for change among the broader adult population. The context of the election, held so soon after the EU referendum, was clearly important. A young person's narrative could emphasise the generation gap, a feeling of 18-24 year olds being marginalised from national policy priorities. Although not opposed to Brexit, Labour's own EU withdrawal policy was ambiguous or contradictory. Labour could, however, entice young voters in other areas, particularly housing, where the party promised to restore housing benefit for young people, in addition to the abolition of university fees. Youth mobilisation created a new pool of voters for a Labour Party unlikely to win many converts directly from its main rival.

Since Labour did not win the election, the viability of its 2017 manifesto will not be tested. While opinion polling underlined the popularity of its signature policies, serious questions remain about whether a Labour-led government would have been able to deliver them. Importantly, Matthew Flinders has demonstrated that there are risks associated with populist policies, regardless of their party origin. While populism offers mainstream political parties a means to achieve greater political 'bandwidth', it offers few, if any, viable solutions to the complex problems that are giving rise to anti-political sentiment. As Flinders stresses, there is mounting evidence of a growing gap between those who govern and those who are governed, of which the rise of populism is a direct symptom. Yet, as he also underlines, the challenge which populism fails to address, for a party seeking to govern, is that of offering a political programme that can command an electoral majority by bridging the new social divides, while also recognising the constraints under which contemporary governments operate.

Of course, the main current challenge of populism may lie in anti-EU sentiment to which many young people remain impervious. Overwhelmingly Brexit provided the context of the election, impacting upon main party choice even though the apparent 'choice' was Brexit (Conservative) or Brexit (Labour). For hardcore Brexiteers, the UK's decision to leave the EU would hopefully precipitate a domino effect in other EU countries. Yet rather than the emergence of populist anti-EU contagion, Sara Hagemann has demonstrated that the more significant effect of Brexit for the EU will be that it changes the internal dynamics of EU institutions at a time when the EU faces a series of challenges that go far beyond Brexit. Her analysis of patterns of voting and decision-making within the Council of the EU and the European Parliament underlines the extent to which some other member states have seen the UK as a counter-weight to France and Germany. In particular, the UK's departure will weaken the position of those countries outside the Eurozone and those which have tended to follow the UK's lead in resisting greater social regulation and intervention. The spread of populist, anti-EU sentiment appears to have been contained. The clear defeat in the French presidential election of the anti-EU Front National presidential candidate Marine Le Pen by the pro-EU centrist Emmanuel Macron, and the success of Macron's new party, En Marche!, in the legislative elections was of particular significance. Indeed, despite an unexpectedly strong showing for the radical right AfD (Alternative für Deutschland) in Germany, Hagemann argues that the events of 2017 have, on balance, strengthened unity between member states and created the context for further integration. As such, the UK Government has not only been weakened by the UK election result, but now faces negotiations with a more united and more confident EU which has largely seen off the populist threat. While the UK general election will not strengthen the UK's negotiating position in the way that Theresa May had intended, the longer-term consequences of Brexit for the EU remain far from clear.

Finally, how well did our electoral system perform? As John Curtice has indicated, narrow or non-existent parliamentary majorities might become the norm not the exception. The current system should operate to strongly discourage votes or seats going to third or other parties (a tendency captured by Duverger's Law) and, relatedly, function so that it rewards the largest party with a 'winner's bonus' (a pattern consistent with the so-called Cube Law). In turn, such outcomes depend on there being sufficient numbers of marginal seats so that a clear swing of the pendulum in electoral support causes a majority for one of the two major parties to be replaced by a majority for the other. Yet, despite an unexpected resurgence in the two-party vote and the Conservatives securing the largest share of the vote achieved by any party since Labour's 1997 landslide victory, Duverger's Law and the Cube Law did not apply in 2017. A total of 70 MPs were elected from parties other than the Conservatives or Labour, ten times the number in 1959. And despite an increase in vote share from 36.8% to 42.4% as the winning party, the Conservatives lost their majority.

Curtice has highlighted the significance of long-term shifts in the geography of party support in explaining the growing apparent failure of the electoral system to produce majority governments. In Northern Ireland, Scotland and Wales, the electoral system readily converts geographical concentrations of electoral support for parties other than the Conservative and Labour into parliamentary seats. Of the 70 seats won by third parties in 2017, 35 went to the SNP, ten to the DUP, seven to Sinn Féin and four to Plaid Cymru. At the same time, there has been a long-term trend towards the geographical concentration of support for the two main parties, with Labour becoming increasingly dominant in densely-populated metropolitan areas and the Conservatives almost equally so in smaller towns and rural areas, particularly in the south. As a consequence of both trends, there are now about half the number of Conservative-Labour marginals than there were in the 1950s or 1960s, making it increasingly difficult for either party to secure an overall majority.

Changes to constituency boundaries will not alter this position. Since the 1950s, there has been a tendency for the electoral system to exhibit greater bias against the Conservatives as time elapses since the last set of revisions to constituency boundaries. However, despite ongoing delays to current boundary change proposals, the disadvantage experienced by the Conservatives on the existing boundaries all but disappeared in 2017. Indeed, on some measures, the electoral system operated in the Conservatives' favour. Noting this 'dramatic and unprecedented change' in electoral bias, Curtice locates the reasons in the higher than average increase in turnout in Labour-held seats and the related tendency for the Conservatives' vote share to increase more sharply in constituencies with smaller electorates.

Ironically, for an election at which the electoral system clearly failed to operate as intended, the 2017 result was the most proportional outcome since 1970. Clearly, proponents of the existing system make no claims for its capacity to deliver relatively proportional outcomes. Yet, during its 'golden age' in the 1950s and 1960s, elections tended to deliver single-party majority governments without producing substantial deviations from proportionality. There are therefore strong grounds to revisit the debate about the merits of the electoral system—but of course this will not happen. The post-2017 Parliament will be busy enough.

The 2017 election left no Westminster party, except the DUP, satisfied. The Conservatives foolishly mislaid a majority; Labour completed a hat-trick of defeats; the Liberal Democrats flopped; the SNP lost ground; UKIP collapsed; and the Greens and Plaid Cymru stayed static. The taut parliamentary arithmetic at least ensures that all parties remain very much in the game.

References

Ashcroft, M. (2017) *The Lost Majority: The 2017 Election, the Conservative Party, the Voters and the Future*, London, Biteback.

Conservative Party (2017) *Forward, Together: Our Plan for a Stronger Britain and a Prosperous Future. The Conservative and Unionist Party manifesto 2017*, London, Conservative Party.

Fieldhouse, E. and Prosser, C. (2017) 'The Brexit election? The 2017 General Election in Ten Charts', accessed at http://www.britishelectionstudy.com/bes-impact/the-brexit-election-the-2017-general-election-in-ten-charts/#.Wdu4E1RSxkA on 9 October 2017.

Ford, R. (2017, 11 June) 'The New Electoral Map of Britain: From the Revenge of Remainers to the Upending of Class Politics', *Observer*, p. 16.

Labour Party (2017) *For the Many not the Few. The Labour Party Manifesto 2017*, London, Labour Party.

Observer (2017, 11 June) 'Analysis: How the Vote Changed from 2015', p. 15.

INDEX

doi:10.1093/pa/gsy007